Caste and Race in India

Caste and Race in India

G. S. Ghurye

Published by
Asmita Mohite for
POPULAR PRAKASHAN PVT. LTD.
301, Mahalaxmi Chambers
22, Bhulabhai Desai Road
Mumbai - 400 026
info@popularprakashan.com

First published by Routledge and Kegan Paul, London in
the History of Civilization Series in 1932
Second Edition, 1950
Third Edition, 1956
Fourth Edition, 1961
Fifth Edition, 1969
Reprinted, 1979
Reprinted, 1986
Reprinted, 1988
Reprinted, 1990
Reprinted, 1993
Reprinted, 1994
Reprinted, 1996
Reprinted, 1999
Reprinted, 2004
Reprinted, 2008
Reprinted, 2011
Reprinted, 2014
Reprinted, 2016
Reprinted, 2019
Reprinted, 2020
Reprinted, 2022
Reprinted, 2023

(3247)
ISBN: 978-81-7154-205-5

PRINTED IN INDIA
by Saurabh Printers (P) Ltd.
Plot No. 67 A-68, Ecotech, Ext. I
Kasna, Greater Noida-201306 (U.P)

Contents

Preface vii

1 Features of the Caste System 1
2 Nature of Caste-Groups 17
3 Caste Through the Ages—I 23
4 Caste Through the Ages—II 40
5 Race and Caste 60
6 Elements of Caste Outside India 74
7 Origins of the Caste System 85
8 Caste, Sub-caste: Fusion or Fission? 95
9 Caste, Sub-caste and Kin 111
10 Caste During the British Rule 142
11 The Scheduled Castes 161
12 Caste and Politics: General 177
13 Caste and Politics in Tamil Nadu 187
14 A Casteless Society or a Plural Society? 212

Appendices A to G A-1
Bibliography B-1
Index I-1

Preface

This is the fifth edition of the book *Caste and Race in India* published in 1932 in C. K. Ogden's *History of Civilization* series. It has been possible for me, while engaged on this edition, to measure up an amount of material made available during the past thirty years and more touching on three aspects of the institution. Two of them were left untouched then for lack of data which could enable one to pronounce an opinion with some degree of confidence and fair amount of logic. They are now dealt with for the first time in Chapters eight and nine.

The third aspect, that of political development of the institution was touched upon thirty-six years ago for the first time in this book but was positively ignored by the critical public of the day. Slowly but surely during the last two decades, however, students of caste have been forced into the study of this aspect. This development and the political aspect of caste in Tamil Nadu, which has clamoured for special notice during the last two decades, are laid out in Chapters twelve and thirteen. As they were more or less ready in September-October 1967, they came in handy for me when on 14th October, 1967 I had to inaugurate the Conference of Indian Sociologists in Bombay. Their substance was made known then through the observations I made by way of inaugurating the Conference.

"History has to be rewritten because History is the selection of those threads of causes or antecedents that we are interested in—and the interest changes in fifty years," observed the great American Jurist, Oliver Wendell Holmes (*Holmes-Laski Correspondence*). I have endeavoured to recast the book with that end in view. Successful performance of the task imposes the duty of projecting into the future, which I have attempted to accomplish in the last Chapter. Questioning its appropriate heading I have invited the reader to decide whether the trend is not towards a 'Plural Society' whose central operative will is distracted by sectional selfish appropriations and raucous demands!

1-5-1969 **G. S. Ghurye**

1

Features of the Caste System

A foreign visitor to India is struck by the phenomenon known as the caste system. He may not understand the full working of the system, but he is aware of the fact that Hindu society is divided into groups, known as castes, with varying degrees of respectability and circles of social intercourse. Baines observes: "It needs but a very short time in the country to bring home to the most casual observer the ubiquity of the institution, and to make him acquainted with some of the principal exoteric features."[1] This is due not only to the fact that caste is the most general form of social organization in India but also because it presents such a marked contrast to the social grouping prevalent in Europe or America. Owing to these two features—ubiquity and strangeness—the institution has found many able scholars devoted to its study. With all the labours of these students, however, we do not possess a real general definition of caste. It appears to me that any attempt at definition is bound to fail because of the complexity of the phenomenon. On the other hand, much literature on the subject is marred by lack of precision about the use of the term. Hence I propose to give a description of the factors underlying this system of castes.

The earliest account of this institution, given by a foreigner of the third century B.C., mentions two of the features characterizing it before it was modified by close cultural contact with Western Europe during the last century. "It is not permitted to contract marriage with a person of another caste, nor to change from one profession or trade to another, nor for the same person to undertake more than one, except he is of the caste of philosophers, when permission is given on account of his dignity."[2] Though this statement of Megasthenes brings two of the most salient features of the institution to the forefront, yet it fails to give a complete idea of the system.

The outstanding features of Hindu society when it was ruled by the social philosophy of caste, unaffected by the modern ideas of rights and duties, may be discerned to be six.

(1) *Segmental division of society*: This caste-society was not a more-or-less homogeneous community in which, whatever distinctions of social status may exist, they are so much in the background that a special inquiry has to be made in order to realize their presence, but a society in which various groups with distinct appellations were prominent. Castes were groups with a well-developed life of their own, the membership whereof, unlike that of voluntary associations and of classes, was determined not by selection but by birth. The status of a person depended not on his wealth as in the classes of modern Europe, but on the traditional importance of the caste in which he had the luck of being born. On the distinction between caste and class, as far only as cleavage into well-marked groups is concerned, MacIver observes: "Whereas in eastern civilizations the chief determinant of a class and status was birth, in the western civilization of today wealth is a class-determinant of equal

or perhaps greater importance, and wealth is a less rigid determinant than birth: it is more concrete, and thus its claims are more easily challenged; itself a matter of degree, it is less apt to create distinctions of kind, alienable, acquirable, and transferable, it draws no such permanent lines of cleavage as does birth."[3] To restrict myself to the Marathi region, a person is born either a Brahmin, Prabhu, Marāthā, Vāni, Sonār, Sutār, Bhandāri, Chāmbhār, or a Mahār, etc. If he chances to take a vocation which is not earmarked for a particular caste—say the military—he remains a casteman all the same. A Brahmin general and a Marāthā general, though of equal status in the army, belong to two different status-groups in their private life and there could not be any social intercourse between them on equal terms. But this is not the case in a class-society where status is determined by vocation and consequent income. A class has no council, standing or occasional, to regulate the conduct and guide the morals of its members, apart from the laws of the community as a whole. Members of one class follow different vocations, which, when organized, possess standing executive committees, which govern the members of their profession according to their rules. These rules generally exclude the legitimate province of the wider community, and refer only to professional etiquette or economic gain. "In the case of the brain-working profession, these common rules and this authoritative direction seek to prescribe such matters as the qualifications for entry, the character of the training, the methods of remuneration, the conditions of employment, the rules of behaviour towards fellow professionals and the public, the qualifications and methods of selection for public appointments, and the terms of service, the maintenance of the status of the profession, and the power of expulsion."[4] Most of the castes on the other hand, excepting the high ones like the Brahmin[5] and the Rajput, have regular standing councils deciding on many more matters than those taken cognizance of by the committees of the trade unions, associations, or guilds, and thus encroaching on the province of the whole community. How the Brahmin and other castes managed their affairs is not quite clear, but in the case of the Brahmins of Southern India at least, it seems from an epigraphic record that as occasion arose they used to call a special meeting of the members of the caste.[6] The assembly could get its decree executed by the king's officials. The governing body of a caste is called the Panchāyat. Some of the offences dealt with by it are: (a) eating, drinking, or having similar dealings with a caste or sub-caste, with which such social intercourse is held to be forbidden; (b) keeping as concubine a woman of another caste; (c) seduction of or adultery with a married woman; (d) fornication; (e) refusal to fulfil a promise of marriage; (f) refusing to send a wife to her husband when old enough; (g) refusing to maintain a wife; (h) non-payment of debt; (i) petty assaults; (j) breaches of the customs of the trade peculiar to the caste; (k) encroaching on another's clientele, and raising or lowering prices; (l) killing a cow or any other forbidden animal; (m) insulting a Brahmin; (n) defying the customs of the caste regarding feasts, etc., during marriage and other ceremonies.[7] It will be seen from this list that some of the offences tried by the governing bodies of castes were such as are usually dealt with by the State in its judicial capacity. Thus, a caste was a group with a separate arrangement for meting out justice to its members apart from that of the community as a whole, within which the caste was included as only one of the groups. Hence the members of a caste ceased to be members of the community as a whole, as far as that part of their morals which is regulated by law was concerned.[8] This quasi-sovereignty of the caste is particularly brought to notice by the fact that the caste council was prepared to re-try criminal offences decided by the courts of law.[9] This means that in this caste-bound society the amount of community-feeling must have been restricted, and that the citizens owed moral allegiance to their caste first, rather than to the community as a whole. By segmental division I wish to connote this aspect of the system. The punishments that these councils awarded were: (1) out-casting, either temporary or permanent; (2) fines; (3) feasts to be given to the castemen; (4) corporal punishment; and (5) sometimes religious expiation. The proceeds of the fines were generally spent on a common feast. Sometimes the perquisites of the Panchāyat were bought out of them and sometimes again they were devoted to charitable purposes.[10] This description of the activities of a caste-council will enable us to appreciate the remark, "The caste is its own ruler."[11] The diversity in the administration of law necessarily led to differences in moral standards of the various castes. There was thus created a cultural gulf between the castes. I may note some of the items of cultural differences among the castes to bring out clearly the implications of the segmentation. Many of the castes have their special deities. Among such castes the following may be noted from Southern India: Komati, Kamsala, Gamalla, Idiga, Māla and Madiga;[12] from the Central Provinces, Ahir;[13] from the Uttar Pradesh: Aheriyā, Baheliyā, Kharwār, Korwā, Chero, Bhuiyār, Dom, Musāhar, and Nāi;[14] and from Gujarat: Vaishyas.[15] About the differences in religious outlook of the Madras castes it has been said: "Amongst the Brahmin community this one fact stands off clear and distinct, that they do not indulge in the worship of Grāma Devatā, the village gods, to which the aboriginal population almost exclusively bows down."[16] The customs about marriage and death vary widely among the different castes. Brahmins did not permit widow-marriage nor tolerate concubinage as a caste-practice. This could not be said of many lower castes. Not only were there such differences in cultural matters among the different castes, but in theory also different standards of conduct were upheld. Thus the Brahmin Government of Poona, while passing some legislation prohibiting the manufacture and sale of liquors, excluded the Bhandāris, Kolis and similar other castes from the operation thereof, but strictly forbade the use of drink to 'Brahmins, Shenvis, Parbhus and Government officers'.[17] These differences of morals and customs were so manifest that the early British Courts in India not merely asked the opinion of their pundits, but took the evidence of the heads of the castes concerned as to their actual usages. The collection of laws and customs of Hindu castes, made by Steele under the orders of Government, was intended to help the courts to ascertain the diverse customs. The Hindus have no standing arrangements for the disposal of their dead. When any person dies it is the caste-fellows who are to be invited to carry the corpse to the cremation-ground and to dispose of it. At the time of marriage a feast has, by common consent, to be given to all the members of one's own caste resident in the village or the town. At the preparation of these feasts as well as in connection with other items of the marriage ceremony it is again the caste-people who run to one's help. These and similar affairs of day to day life require the co-operation of one's caste-people. Hence castes are small and complete social worlds in themselves, marked off definitely from one another, though subsisting within the larger society.

(2) *Hierarchy*: In my discussion of the subject so far I have used the comparative degree with reference to the status of different castes, thus assuming beforehand one of the principal characteristics of the caste society, viz., the hierarchy of the groups. Everywhere in India there is a definite scheme of social precedence amongst the castes, with the Brahmin at the head of the hierarchy. Only in Southern India the artisan castes "have always maintained a struggle for a higher place in the social scale than that allowed to them by Brahmanical authority. . . . There is no doubt as to the fact that the members of this great caste (Kammālan) dispute the supremacy of the Brahmins, and that they hold themselves to be equal in rank with them." John Fryer, who visited India in 1670, seems to refer to this attitude.[18] In any one of the linguistic divisions of India there are as many as two hundred castes which can be grouped in classes whose gradation is largely acknowledged by

all. But the order of social precedence amongst the individual castes of any class cannot be made definite, because not only is there no ungrudging acceptance of such rank but also the ideas of the people on this point are very nebulous and uncertain. The following observations vividly bring out this state of things. "As the society now stands . . . the place due to each community is not easily distinguishable, nor is any common principle of precedence recognized by the people themselves by which to grade the castes. Excepting the Brahmin at one end and the admittedly degraded castes like the Holeyās at the other, the members of a large proportion of the intermediate castes think or profess to think that their caste is better than their neighbours' and should be ranked accordingly."[19] Martin remarks about Bihar that the Shudras there were usually divided into four classes, but adds: "The people, who assisted me in making up this account, could not with certainty refer each caste to its class; for they never had bestowed pains to enquire concerning the various claims of such low persons."[20]

(3) *Restrictions on feeding and social intercourse*: There are minute rules as to what sort of food or drink can be accepted by a person and from what castes. But there is very great diversity in this matter. The practices in the matter of food and social intercourse divide India into two broad belts. In Hindustan proper, castes can be divided into five groups; first, the twice-born castes; second, those castes at whose hands the twice-born can take 'Pakkā' food; third, those castes at whose hands the twice-born cannot accept any kind of food but may take water; fourth, castes that are not untouchable yet are such that water from them cannot be used by the twice-born; last come all those castes whose touch defiles not only the twice-born but any orthodox Hindu.[21] All food is divided into two classes, 'Kachchā' and 'Pakkā', the former being any food in the cooking of which water has been used, and the latter all food cooked in 'ghee' without the addition of water. "As a rule a man will never eat 'Kachchā' food unless it is prepared by a fellow caste-man, which in actual practice means a member of his own endogamous group, whether it be caste or sub-caste, or else by his Brahmin 'Guru' or spiritual guide."[22] But in practice most castes seem to take no objection to 'Kachchā' food from a Brahmin.[23] A Brahmin can accept 'Kachchā' food at the hands of no other caste; nay, some of them, like the Kanaujiā Brahmins, are so punctilious about these restrictions that, as a proverb has it, three Kanaujiās require no less than thirteen hearths.[24] As for the 'Pakkā' food, it may be taken by a Brahmin at the hands of some of the castes only. On the whole, however, as E. A. Blunt has made out, there is "no relation between a caste's social position and the severity of its cooking taboo"; as many as thirty-six out of seventy-six castes of U.P. take 'Kachchā' cooked food from only their own members and none others.[25]

The ideas about the power of certain castes to convey pollution by touch are not so highly developed in Northern India as in the South. The idea that impurity can be transmitted by the mere shadow of an untouchable or by his approaching within a certain distance does not seem to prevail in Hindustan. No Hindu of decent caste would touch a Chamār, or a Dom; and some of the very low castes themselves are quite strict about contact. Thus "The Bansphor and Basor, themselves branches of the Dom caste, will touch neither a Dom, nor a Dhobi, whilst the Basor, with all the intolerance of the parvenu, extends his objections to the Musāhār, Chamār, Dhārkār and Bhangi."[26]

In Bengal the castes are divided into two main groups: (1) the Brahmins, and (2) the Shudras. The second class is further divided into four sub-classes, indicating their status as regards food and water: (a) the Sat-Shudra group includes such castes as the Kāyastha and Nabashākh; (b) then come the Jalācharaniya-Shudras, "being those castes, not technically belonging to the Nabashākh group, from whom Brahmins and members of the higher castes can take water"; (c) then follow the JalābyabahĀryas-Shudras, castes from whose hands a Brahmin cannot take water; (d) last stand the Asprishya-Shudras, castes whose touch is so impure as to pollute even the Ganges water, and hence their contact must be avoided. They are thus the untouchables.[27] In the matter of food Western Bengal resembles Hindustan except in this that in Bengal there are some people who will not accept any 'Kachchā' food even from the hands of a Brahmin. 'Pakkā' food can be ordinarily taken not only from one's own or any higher caste, but also from the confectioner class, the Myrās and Halwāis.[28] As regards the position of the untouchables the following observation will give a clear idea. "Even wells are polluted if a low caste man draws water from them, but a great deal depends on the character of the vessel used and of the well from which water is drawn. A masonry well is not so easily defiled as one constructed with clap pipes, and if it exceeds three and a half cubits in width so that a cow may turn round in it, it can be used even by the lowest castes without defilement. . . ." Certain low castes are looked down upon as so unclean that they may not enter the courtyard of the great temples. These castes are compelled to live by themselves on the outskirts of villages.[29]

In Eastern and Southern Bengal[30] and in Gujarat and the whole of Southern India there is no distinction of food as 'Kachchā' for the purposes of its acceptance or otherwise from anyone but a member of one's own caste. In Gujarat[31] and Southern India, generally speaking, a Brahmin never thinks of accepting water, much less any cooked food, from any caste but that of the Brahmins, and all the other castes or groups of castes more or less follow the principle of accepting no cooked food from any caste that stands lower than itself in the social scale. This rule does not apply with the same strictness to accepting water. Again as a rule, a lower caste has no scruples in accepting cooked food from any higher caste. Thus all the castes will take cooked food from the Brahmin.

The theory of pollution being communicated by some castes to members of the higher ones is also more developed in Gujarat. Theoretically, the touch of a member of any caste lower than one's own defiles a person of the higher caste; but in actual practice this rule is not strictly observed. In the Maratha country the shadow of an untouchable is sufficient, if it falls on a member of a higher caste, to pollute him. In Madras, and especially in Malabar, this doctrine is still further elaborated, so that certain castes have always to keep a stated distance between themselves and the Brahmin and other higher castes so as not to defile the latter. Thus the Shānār, toddy-tapper of Tamilnad, contaminates a Brahmin if he approaches the latter within twenty-four paces.[32] Among the people of Kerala, a Nāyar may approach a Nambudiri Brahmin but must not touch him; while a Tiyan must keep himself at the distance of thirty-six steps from the Brahmin, and a Pulayan may not approach him within ninety-six paces.* A Tiyan must keep away from a Nāyar at twelve paces, while some castes may approach the Tiyan, though they must not touch him. A Pulayan must not come near any of the Hindu castes. So rigid are the rules about defilement which is supposed to be carried with them by all except the Brahmins, that the latter will not perform even their ablutions within the precincts of a Shudra's habitation.[33] Generally the washerman and the barber that serve the general body of villagers, will not render their services to the unclean and untouchable castes. "Even a modern Brahmin doctor, when feeling the pulse of a Shudra, first wraps up the patient's wrist with a small piece of silk so that he may not be defiled by touching his skin."[34]

* For a slightly different scale of distances see M. S. A. *Rao's Social Change in Malabar*, 1957, p. 21.

(4) *Civil and religious disabilities and privileges of the different sections*: Segregation of individual castes or of groups of castes in a village is the most obvious mark of civil privileges and disabilities, and it has prevailed in a more or less definite form all over India. Southern India, as in the matter of ceremonial purity and untouchability, stands out distinct in the rigidity of these rules. In Northern India generally, in the Maratha country and, as it appears, sometimes in the Telugu and Kanarese regions, it is only the impure castes that are segregated and made to live on the outskirts of villages. It does not seem that other groups of castes have distinct quarters of the town or village allotted to them excepting in parts of Gujarat. In the Tamil and Malayalam regions very frequently different quarters are occupied by separate castes or sometimes the village is divided into three parts: that occupied by the dominant caste in the village or by the Brahmins, that allotted to the Shudras, and the one reserved for the Panchamas or untouchables. In a village of the Ramnad District, the main portion is occupied by the Nāyakars, shepherds, artisans, washermen, and barbers, forming a group living in the north-east corner of the village, while the untouchables ply their trades in the north-west and the south-east corners.[35] In Trichinopoly district the villages have the houses arranged in streets. "The Brahmin, Shudra and Panchama quarters are separate, and in the last of these the Pallans, Paraiyans and Chakkiliyans live in separate streets."[36] In Madras, Pallis or agriculturists live in separate quarters "distinctively known as the Palli teru."[37] Sometimes, as in the district of Bellary, it is only the untouchable, like the Mādiga, that is singled out for segregation, all other castes living in close proximity to one another.[38] In some parts of the Maratha country castes have been allotted distinct quarters of the village called by the name of the caste: Brahmin-āli, or wādā, Prabhu-āli, Sonār-āli, etc. The depressed classes, like the Māng, Mahār, etc., are forced to live on the outskirts of the village.[39]

In Southern India certain parts of the town or village are inaccessible to certain castes. The agitation by the impure castes to gain free access to certain streets in Vaikam in Travancore brings into clear relief some of the disabilities of these castes. It is recorded that under the rule of the Marathas and the Peshwas, the Mahārs and Māngs were not allowed within the gates of Poona after 3 p.m. and before 9 a.m. because before nine and after three their bodies cast too long a shadow, which falling on a member of the higher castes—especially Brahmin—defiles him.[40] However, in the Dravidian south,* the very land of the supreme dominance of the Brahmin, the Brahmin was restricted in his rights of access to any part of the village. It is well known that in a village which is a gift to the Brahmins, a Paraiyan is not allowed to enter the Brahmin quarter; but it is not known to many students that the Paraiyans will not permit a Brahmin to pass through their street; so much so that if one happens to enter their quarters they would greet him with cow-dung water. "Brahmins in Mysore consider that great luck will await them if they can manage to pass through the Holeya (untouchables) quarter of a village unmolested."[41] All over India the impure castes are debarred from drawing water from the village well, which is used by the members of other castes. In the Maratha country a Mahār—one of the untouchables—might not spit on the road lest a pure-caste Hindu should be polluted by touching it with his foot, but had to carry an earthen pot, hung from his neck, in which to spit. Further he had to drag a thorny branch with him to wipe out his footprints and to lie at a distance prostrate on the ground if a Brahmin passed by, so that his foul shadow might not defile the holy Brahmin.[42] In the Punjab, where restrictions regarding pollution by proximity have been far less stringent than in other parts of India, a sweeper, while

* Specifically speaking of Tamil Nadu.

walking through the streets of the larger towns, was supposed to carry a broom in his hand or under his armpit as a mark of his being a scavenger and had to shout out to the people warning them of his polluting presence.[43] The schools, maintained at public cost, are practically closed to such impure castes as the Chamars and Mahārs. "Both teachers and pupils in the schools make it most difficult for low-caste boys to sit in the class-rooms."[44] In Gujarat the depressed castes used to wear a horn as their distinguishing mark.[45] From certain decisions noted by the Peshwas in their diaries one can form some idea about the disabilities of some of the castes in the Maratha country. The rulers upheld the claim of the potters, opposed by the carpenters, that they could lead their bridal processions on horse-back, and that of the copper-smith, against the Lingāyats, to go in procession through public streets.[46]

In Dravidian India the disabilities of the lower castes went so far as to prescribe what sort of houses they should build and what material they might employ in the construction thereof. The Shānārs and Izhavās, toddy-tappers of the eastern and the western coasts, were not allowed to build houses above one storey in height.[47] In Malabar the house is called by different names according to the occupant's caste; and peoples of inferior castes dare not refer to their own homes in the presence of Nambudiri Brahmin in more flattering terms than as 'dung-heaps'.[48]

The toddy-tappers of Malabar and the east coast, Izhavās and Shānārs, were not allowed to carry umbrellas, to wear shoes or golden ornaments, to milk cows or even to use the ordinary language of the country.[49] In Malabar, Brahmins alone were permitted to sit on boards formed in the shape of a tortoise, and if a member of any other caste were to use such a seat he was liable to capital punishment.[50] Members of all castes, except the Brahmins, were expressly forbidden to cover the upper part of their body above the waist.[51] In the case of women also, until 1865 they were obliged by law to go with the upper part of their bodies quite bare, if they belonged to the Tiyan or other lower castes.[52] Under the Peshwas a greater distinction was made in the punishment on account of the caste of the criminal than of the nature of the crime itself. Hard labour and death were punishments mostly visited on criminals of the lower castes.[53]

In Tamilnad there has been for ages a faction among the non-Brahmin castes dividing most of them into two groups, the right-hand castes and the left-hand castes. The 'right-hand' castes claim certain privileges which they strongly refuse to those of the 'left-hand', viz. riding on horse-back in processions, carrying standards with certain devices, and supporting their marriage booths on twelve pillars. They insist that the 'left-hand' castes must not raise more than eleven pillars to the booth nor employ on their standards devices peculiar to the 'right-hand' castes.[54]

Brahmanic ceremonies are to be performed with the help of a ritual, and two types of rituals have been evolved; the Vedic and the Puranic. The Vedic ritual is based on the Vedic mantras and is regarded as of great sanctity, while the Puranic is based on formulae of less sanctity, and not on revealed knowledge. How great this feeling of sanctity about Vedic lore was can be gauged from the fact that in 1843 a Brahmin professor advised the Bombay Board of Education not to publish a certain book because it contained quotations from Panini's grammar which, if printed, would be desecrated.[55] The Shudras are asked to content themselves with the Puranic ritual, while for the impure castes, a Brahmin, unless he is a pseudo-Brahmin or an apostate, would not minister at all. During the career of Sawai Madhavrao, the Peshwa government had decreed that the Mahārs, being *atishudras*, 'beyond Shudras', could not have their marriage rites conducted by the regular Brahmin priests. They were asked to content themselves with the services of their castemen-priests, the Medhe-Mahārs.[56] It is only from the hands of the clean Shudras, again, that a Brahmin will accept any gifts which are meant to store up merit for the donor. Such an advanced caste as the Prabhus in the Maratha country had to establish its right of carrying on the sacred rites according to the Vedic formulae which was being questioned during the period of the later Peshwas.[57] Certain sacraments cannot be performed by any other caste than the Brahmins. The most sacred literature cannot be studied by the Shudras. No caste can employ any other priests than the Brahmins, with very few exceptions, in Southern India. The artisans of Madras seem to employ their own priests; and the goldsmith caste of the Maratha region established their right of employing their caste-fellows as priests during the last part of the Peshwa-rule.[58] The innermost recesses of temples can only be approached by the Brahmins, clean Shudras and other high castes having to keep outside the sacred precincts. The impure castes, and particularly the untouchables, cannot enter even the outer portions of a temple but must keep to the court-yards. In South Malabar, the high castes do not allow the Tiyans to cremate their dead.[59]

A Brahmin never bows to anyone who is not a Brahmin, but requires others to salute him; and when he is saluted by a member of a non-Brahmin caste he only pronounces a benediction. Some of the lower castes carry their reverence for the Brahmins, especially in Northern India, to such extremes that they will not cross the shadow of a Brahmin, and sometimes will not take their food without sipping water in which the big toe of a Brahmin is dipped. The Brahmin, on the other hand, is so conscious of his superiority that he does not condescend to bow even to the idols of gods in a Shudra's house.[60] The Brahmin has been regarded as the most important subject, needing protection from the king, so much so that the king is styled the protector of the Brahmins and the cows, other subjects being regarded as too insignificant to be mentioned.

In the Maratha country, at the beginning of the seventeenth century, the great preacher Ramdas tried to inculcate in the minds of the people the idea of unity based on the bond of common locality. During the latest period of the Peshwa-rule (latter half of the eighteenth century), however, this ideal dwindled into the orthodox one wherein Brahmins figure prominently, the State having no higher function than that of pampering them.[61] Under the Hindu rulers the Brahmins must have secured to themselves many pecuniary privileges, denied to others, on the strength of this orthodox theory of the proper function of the State, and perhaps more because they happened to occupy the posts of importance. Thus in the Maratha region during the period referred to above, the Konkanasth Brahmin clerks obtained the privilege of their goods being exempted from certain duties and their imported corn being carried to them without any ferry-charges. Brahmin landholders of a part of the country had their lands assessed at distinctly lower rates than those levied from other classes. Brahmins were exempted from capital punishment, and when confined in forts, they were more liberally treated than the other classes.[62] Forbes makes the following observation: "The Brahmins of Travancore, as in most other parts of India, have taken care to be exempted as much as possible from punishment; at least, their sentence is far more lenient than that passed on the other castes for the same crimes."[63] In Bengal the amount of rent for land frequently varied with the caste of the occupant.[64]

(5) *Lack of unrestricted choice of occupation*: Generally a caste or a group of allied castes considered some of the callings as its hereditary occupation, to abandon which in pursuit of another, though it might be more lucrative, was thought not to be right. Thus a Brahmin thought that it was correct for him to be a priest, while the Chāmbhār regarded it as his duty to cure hides and prepare shoes. This was only generally true, for there were groups of occupations like trading, agriculture, labouring in the field, and doing military service which were looked upon as anybody's, and most castes were

supposed to be eligible for any of them.[65] Among the artisans, occupations which were more or less of the same status were open to the members of these castes without incidental degradation. No caste would allow its members to take to any calling which was either degrading, like toddy-tapping and brewing, or impure, like scavenging or curing hides. It was not only the moral restraint and the social check of one's caste-fellows that acted as a restraint on the choice of one's occupation, but also the restriction put by other castes, which did not allow members other than those of their own castes to follow their callings. Of such restrictive regulations there were in operation only those concerning the profession of priests, no one not born a Brahmin being allowed to be a priest. The effect of these rules was that the priestly profession was entirely monopolized by the Brahmins, leaving aside the ministrants of the aboriginal deities, while they were seen plying any trade or calling which suited their tastes and which was not polluting. The majority of the Konkanasth and Deshasth Brahmins of the Maratha country were devoted to secular pursuits filling offices of every kind, including the village accountantship.[66] During the Maratha upheaval and after, the Brahmins entered the profession of arms in fairly large numbers. Before the Indian Mutiny the Kanaujiā Brahmins used to enter the Bengal army as sepoys in large numbers.[67] Some of the Rārhi Brahmins of Bengal accepted service under Mohammedan rulers.[68] Some of the Brahmins of Rajasthan served their Marwadi masters.[69] The majority of the Brahmins in the lower Karnatak, according to Buchanan, almost entirely filled the different offices in the collection of revenue and even acted as messengers.[70] Of the Hindustani Brahmins of Central India it is said that a considerable population of them are concerned in trade.[71] The Hāvig Brahmins of the Tulu country did all kinds of agricultural labour excepting holding the plough.[72] About the Kanaujiā Brahmins of Uttar Pradesh it is asserted that they even till the soil with their own hands, while shop-keeping and hawking form the main source of livelihood for the Sanadhya Brahmins of that region.[73] In Rajasthan the Brahmin is not only willing to do all the labour that his piece of land requires, but is also ready to sell his labour to other more fortunate occupants.[74] Brahmins in Madras appear as civil, public, and military servants, traders, cultivators, industrialists, and even labourers.[75] It seems that in the days of Akbar, too, the Brahmins were engaged in trade, cultivation, or any advantageous pursuit in general.[76]

More castes than one are engaged in agriculture. Thus we have the Vellālas, the Pallis, the Agamudaiyans, the Malaiyālis in Madras.[77] As regards the five artisan castes, grouped together as Pānchakalsi, it is observed that it is not impossible for individuals to pass from one occupation to another without any alteration of social status or loss of right of intermarriage.[78] Weaving is practised by many of the menial castes including even the impure castes of Mahārs and Chamārs. If one looks at the Census Reports, especially those for 1901, one finds groups, which are regarded as separate castes, following more callings than one. The following remark of Russell is very instructive from this point of view. He observes: "Several castes have same traditional occupation; about forty of the castes of the Central Provinces are classified as agriculturists, eleven as weavers, seven as fishermen and so on."[79] In 1798 Colebrooke wrote: "Daily observation shows even Brahmins exercising the menial profession of a Shudra. We are aware that every caste forms itself into clubs or lodges, consisting of the several individuals of that caste residing within a small distance, and that these clubs or lodges govern themselves by particular rules or customs or by-laws. But though some restrictions and limitations, not founded on religious prejudices, are found among their by-laws, it may be received as a general maxim that the occupation appointed for each tribe is entitled to a preference. Every profession, with few exceptions, is open to every description of person."[80] When Irving says,[81] "If we except the priesthood, caste has not necessarily any effect on the line of life in which a man embarks," he certainly overstates the position, and the following observation of Baines strikes the true note. "The occupation, again, which is common to the latter (the caste), is a traditional one, and is not by any means necessarily that by which all, or even most, of the group make their living in the present day."[82]

(6) *Restrictions on marriage*: Most of the groups, whose features I have attempted to characterize above, are further divided into a number of sub-groups every one of which forbids its members to marry persons from outside it. Each of these groups, popularly known as sub-castes, is thus endogamous. This principle of strict endogamy is such a dominant aspect of caste-society that an eminent sociologist is led to regard endogamy as "the essence of the caste system."[83] There are, however, a few exceptions to this general rule of marrying within one's own group which are due to the practice of hypergamy. In some parts of the Punjab, especially in the hills, a man of a higher caste can take to wife a girl from one of the lower castes, while, in Malabar, the younger sons of the Nambudiri and other Brahmins consort with the Kshatriya and Nāyar women, among whom mother-right prevails. Excepting for these cases of inter-caste hypergamy each group has to contract matrimonial alliances within its own limits. Outside of this practice the only other authentic case where inter-caste marriage is allowed is that of some of the artisan castes of Malabar.[84] Any man venturing to transgress this law will be put out of his own sub-caste and it is doubtful if he would be admitted into the folds of any other respectable caste. To illustrate from the Maratha region, a Konkanasth Brahmin must marry a girl born in a Konkanasth Brahmin family, while a Karhādā Brahmin must similarly seek his partner from amongst the Karhādā Brahmins and so on, the principle being that marriage must be arranged within the group which is most effectively considered to be one's own. If this rule is violated expulsion from the membership of the group is generally the penalty which the offending parties have to suffer. In Gujarat the unit within which all matrimonial alliances must be contracted is very often still smaller than the so-called sub-caste of the Marathi region. Among the Baniās, the trading caste, for example, there are not only the divisions of Shrimāli, Porwāl, Modh, etc., but there are further sub-divisions like Dasā Porwāl and Visā Porwāl.[85] This is not all. The Dasās are still further required to contract their marriages either from amongst the Dasās of Surat or of Bombay according as they belong to Surat or Bombay. When the groups are so much subdivided the penalty for transgressing the rule of endogamy in reference to the smallest unit is not expulsion of the offending parties but the gratification by them of the offended group.

To regard endogamy as the chief characteristic of a caste is to treat all so-called sub-castes as the real castes. Gait[86] advances two reasons against this procedure of raising sub-castes to the position of castes, viz. it would be "contrary to the native feeling on the subject," and would be "highly inconvenient in practice, as it would create a bewildering multiplicity of castes." As for the second objection, we may safely pass it over, as it concerns only an administrative difficulty. As regards the Indian sentiment against making a sub-caste into a caste, it must be pointed out that, at best, this is the representation of only one side of the problem; for if, to confine myself to the Marathi country, a Sāraswat Brahmin is known to the outsiders as a Sāraswat, to a Sāraswat he is better known either as a Shenvi or as a Sāshtikar or Pednekar. Stated generally, though it is the caste that is recognized by the society at large it is the sub-caste that is regarded by the particular caste and the individual. It is mainly indifference towards others, so characteristic of the Indian system, that is responsible for this attitude. For a Brahmin most others are Shudras, irrespective of high or low status; and for two or three higher castes that are allied to the Brahmins in culture, the rest of the population, excepting the impure castes and some other specific groups, is Kulwādi or Shudra—a generic term for manual workers. The higher castes are grouped together as either Ashrafin in Bihar,[87] Bhadralok in Bengal, or Pāndhar-peshe in Maharashtra. Further, if we are to take some kind of Indian sentiment as our guide in our analysis, then, as according to the orthodox theory on this matter there are only two, or at the most three castes in the present age, we shall have to divide the whole population of any major linguistic province into two castes, Brahmin and Shudra, or at the most three, where the existence of the Kshatriya is grudgingly granted. Evidently no scientific student of caste, not even Gait himself, has proposed to follow Indian opinion on this matter. There is ample reason why, to get a sociologically correct idea of the institution, we should recognize sub-castes as real castes.

Of the features of caste society dealt with so far three pertain to the caste as a whole; for the status in the hierarchy of any sub-caste depends upon the status of the caste, from which follow the various civil and religious rights and disabilities, and the traditional occupation is determined by the nature of the caste. The other three features, which are very material in the consideration of a group from the point of view of an effective social life, viz. those that regulate communal life and prescribe rules as regards feeding, social intercourse and endogamy, belong to the sub-caste. In the matter of the Panchāyat or the caste-council, which is the tribunal for enforcing the moral and economic rules of the group, the sub-caste generally possesses its own council. In the Punjab this is the case in all castes, except the artisans and menials. "Where the sub-divisions are not very clearly defined, or where the numerical strength of the whole caste is small, there is one governing body for the whole caste."[88] The following description of the sub-caste in Bengal clearly brings out the function I have mentioned as peculiar to it. "Almost every caste is divided into a number of smaller groups which will only marry amongst themselves. Usually these groups will not eat together and often they will not even take water from each other or smoke from the same 'hukkā'. . . . These endogamous groups are generally known as sub-castes. Each sub-caste manages its own affairs quite independently of the others, and in the case of the lower castes each has its own separate *Panchāyat* or standing committee, by which all social questions are decided."[89] In Uttar Pradesh it is the sub-caste that forms the unit of social organization, and as such has its own council to look after its affairs quite independently of the similar councils of the other sub-castes.[90] Further, inter-dining and inter-drinking are restricted to the group which is endogamous.[91] About the Central Provinces Russell observes[92]: "The real unit of the system and the basis of the fabric of Indian society is this endogamous group or sub-caste." Though this group is usually little known outside a man's own caste, yet it is the members of the sub-caste that attend "the communal feasts held on the occasions of marriages, funerals and meetings of the caste (sub-caste) Panchāyat." The remark of the Census Operator for Madras that it is the small endogamous sub-divisions "which are for all social purposes the real castes"[93] is corroborated by F. J. Richards in the case of Salem District when he observes: "The Unit of Hindu society is the endogamous group or sub-caste."[94] The description of the sub-caste of a Hindustani caste given by Sherring will illustrate this. He observes about the Bārhai or carpenter caste of Hindustan that its seven sub-castes "are so distinct from one another that they hold no direct social intercourse with each other, either by marriages, or by eating or smoking together."[95] Further, some of the sub-castes have such a distinctness about their cultural items, as for example among the Vellālas, that it is not possible to give a general account of the marriage and other customs applicable to all the sub-divisions. While some of them recognize freedom of divorce and re-marriage and even polyandry, others follow strictly the Brahmanic rules.[96] The remark of Gait that "as a rule the prohibition of intermarriage between members of the different sub-castes is far less rigid than it is between members of different castes, and when the rule is broken, the penalty is usually not expulsion, but merely some form of atonement, after which the member of the higher of the two sub-castes concerned, and possibly his or her parents, take rank in the lower,"[97] may be urged as a potent reason why sub-castes should be treated as strictly subordinate to a caste. Here it must be pointed out that in Uttar Pradesh at least "the penalty for breaches of sub-caste endogamy appears to be as severe as the penalty for similar breaches of caste-endogamy", and that, though the penalty for the transgression of rules about sub-caste commensality varies in different castes, it seems that generally caste and sub-caste commensality are much on a par in this respect.[98] Hence it is but proper to treat endogamy within each of the groups constituting caste-society as one of its principal features.

So far I have treated of the distinctions between groups in the caste-society, which were held together in a chain by the fact that they were arranged in a system, the apex of which was formed by the group designated Brahmin. Each of these groups, major as well as minor, generally known as castes and sub-castes, has a name. When any group of the same name happens to have a wide distribution, language delimits effective social intercourse, which obtains only amongst members of the same group speaking the same language. Whatever might have been the situation in the past, when the jurisdictional factor, as Jackson terms it,[99] was a force affecting such social intercourse, in the beginning of the nineteenth century linguistic boundaries fixed the caste-limits. In any linguistic area there were from fifty to two hundred of these major groups divided into five hundred to two thousand minor groups. An individual's circle of community-feeling was any of these minor groups, in which he or she was born; but as far as civic life was concerned it was the major group that decided the status of an individual.

Of the major groups about half a dozen in each linguistic region were formed by primitive tribes, which were slowly absorbing whatever ideas they could from the Brahmanic civilization. They lived not as members of towns or villages but of hamlets of their own, and were shunned by the Brahmanized peoples. Apart from their desire to imitate Brahmanic ideals as interpreted by other castes, their bond of social solidarity with other groups was the economic gain that resulted from an exchange of their economic activities with them. More or less similarly circumstanced were another half a dozen or a dozen of nomadic castes. About five to fifteen groups, mostly artisans and special traders, were peculiar to the towns, where social coherence was the result of common government rather than that of the co-operation of the groups. The remaining castes were distributed among the villages, every village having about fifteen to thirty of them. And it was in the village that caste-society manifested its other aspects, viz. co-operation and inter-dependence. Village society was characterized by the possession of a number of permanent officials and menials, belonging to different castes, each having a definite status in the economic and civic life of the village. In India south of the Vindhyas, the system was very highly developed, and the number of such dignitaries varied from twelve to twenty-four belonging to as many different castes. These persons, irrespective of their caste-status, had not only a voice in civic affairs but were also sometimes consulted in purely social and legal matters affecting the private lives of the individuals of any caste, resident in the village. In Northern India the system of village servants, though not so highly evolved as in the south, yet served the purposes of harmonizing different groups, till the super-imposition of a dominant caste had lessened the importance of the village dignitaries that were there. These latter, because of the particular form of land-tenure and revenue system and of their almost servile tenure, had no status in civic affairs, much less were they consulted in the private affairs of the members of the dominant caste.[100] In its pristine glory, however, a village or a town had a council of elders chosen from all castes and representing all the avocations in the locality.

The whole village had to deal with the government of the locality in revenue matters. This had engendered a splendid sense of solidarity among the members of the village community who were dearly attached to their lands. The stability, co-operative spirit, and sense of solidarity seen in the village communities evoked the following remarks from Sir Charles Metcalfe, who fervently pleaded against the introduction of the system of collecting revenue directly from individual proprietors. He observes: "The village communities are little republics, having nearly everything that they want within themselves, and almost independent of any foreign relations. They seem to last within themselves where nothing else lasts. Dynasty after dynasty tumbles down; revolution succeeds revolution; Hindoo, Pathan, Mogul, Mahratta, Sikh, English, are all masters in turn; but the village communities remain the same. In times of trouble they arm and fortify themselves: an hostile army passes through the country: the village communities collect their cattle within their walls, and let the enemy pass unprovoked. . . . If a country remains for a series of years the scene of continued pillage and massacre, so that the villages cannot be inhabited, the scattered villagers nevertheless return whenever the power of peaceable possession revives. A generation may pass away, but the succeeding generation will return. The sons will take the places of their fathers; the same site for the village, the same position for the houses, the same lands will be occupied by the descendants of those who were driven out when the village was depopulated; and it is not a trifling matter that will drive them out, for they will often maintain their post through times of disturbance and convulsion, and acquire strength sufficient to resist pillage and oppression with success . . . all acting in union with a common interest as regards the Government, and adjusting their own separate interests among themselves according to established usage."[101]

The decisions of the village-councils that have come down to us from the Maratha country, bear the signatures of almost all the village-servants, including the untouchable Mahār and Māng.[102] An entry in the Private Diary of Anandaranga Pillay of the middle of the eighteenth century refers to a village-meeting called to consider a case of temple-desecration "in which people of all castes—from the Brahmin to the Pariāh—took part."[103] Matthai quotes the description of a meeting of a village Panchāyat in which both the Brahmins and the Shudras took part. The Brahmin school-master of the place was the accused, he having inflicted exceptionally severe punishment on one of the boys under his charge. The Brahmin members sat on a higher platform and the Shudras on a lower veranda, both the sections indulging freely in betel and tobacco-snuff.[104] In the diaries of the Peshwas of Poona and the Raja of Satara there are a few references to meetings of the whole village community, assembled to adjudicate quarrels between Brahmins or to offer authoritative advice in their domestic matters. A Brahmin Kulkarni had one son who had married two wives, one of whom had borne him only two daughters. On the sudden death of the son, his senior wife resolved to immolate herself. The whole village, including all the village dignitaries, was called in conference. In view of the old man's helpless condition the assembly proposed that the lady should adopt a son before burning herself. This decision was agreed to by the old man and his daughter-in-law. The whole assemblage further, in consultation with the persons concerned, selected the person to be adopted and made a request for him to his guardian.[105] A quarrel between Brahmin cousins in respect of some hereditary rights was referred for settlement to the whole village. The assembly that was to give the decision included Marāthā, Dhangar, Gurav, Sutār, Lohār, Kumbhār, Koli, Nhāvi, Chāmbhār, Mahār, and Māng.[106]

Ideas of status were quietly accepted and did not prevent healthy co-operation and neighbourly feeling among the various caste-groups represented in the various village communities of Southern India. In the case of Northern India we must remember that though, perhaps, village life did not lead to as much co-operation and fellow feeling, the system of castes was marked by a more lenient view and practice about food and social intercourse. The various castes, in so far as they contributed their respective services towards the common life of the village, were welded together and inter-dependent for the purposes of civic life. Inter-dependence of castes was such a deep-rooted principle that it prevented other exclusive aspects, inherent in the system, from getting the better of the idea of a common civic goal and human sympathy for co-residents and hardening into caste-spirit or caste-patriotism. If interdependence in civic and economic life of the village counteracted the centripetal forces of social restrictions of caste, certain special functions and occasions reminded some castes, ordinarily considered to be low, of their importance and even afforded them opportunities of enjoying temporary superiority.

In parts of Uttar Pradesh the barber often acts as a match-maker and is present at weddings. The Dom at the burning 'ghāt' in Benares is an important personage. "Some years ago the head of the caste used to be conveyed to the funeral of a wealthy client in his own palanquin." The first five logs of wood for arranging the pyre must be given by a Dom, who has also to lay the foundation of the pyre and to hand a wisp of burning straw to the chief mourner for lightning the wood.[107] In the Central Provinces, as a part of the marriage ceremony, the bridegroom's party takes the bride to the house of the Kumbhār (potter) for making the marriage propitious. The wife of the potter presents her with seven new pots which are to be used at the wedding. In return for this veiled blessing the woman gets a present of clothes.[108] Both the barber and the washerman are prominent in a Kunbi wedding. At a particular stage in the ceremony the barber and the washerman take the bride and bridegroom on their shoulders and dance in the marriage-booth, for which services they receive presents.[109] In Vidarbha "at the Holi festival the fire of the Mahārs is kindled first and that of the Kunbis is set alight from it." Some Telis (oil-pressers), Lohārs (blacksmiths), Kunbis and other castes employ a Mahār (one of the untouchables) to fix the date of their wedding. The Mahār also officiates at the slaughter of a buffalo at the Dasara festival.[110] The barber acts as the Brahmin's assistant at marriage, and to the lower castes he is even the matrimonial priest.[111] The officiating priest at the famous temple of Jagannath is a barber, food cooked for the deity by him being acceptable to all but the most orthodox amongst Brahmins. For some of the Vellālas (Tamil cultivators) he even acts as the marriage-priest.[112] "Some of the most celebrated and exclusive temples are thrown open to the Paraiyan (the Tamil unapproachable) on certain days of the year, and for the time he lords it over the Brahmin." At some festivals at the temples of Shiva or of the local goddess he sits by the side of the idol in the procession or ties the badge of marriage round its neck. "When there is a dispute about a boundary, it is a Paraiyan, or in other parts of India, a member of the corresponding caste, who has to walk the line with a pot of water, his own son, or a clod of his native earth, on his head".[113] These and other occasions, on which some of the groups, which are considered to be low castes, could feel their importance, relieved the monotonous depression of these groups, and gave zest to their life even in their degraded condition.

To sum up, in each linguistic area there were about two hundred groups called castes with distinct names, birth in one of which, usually, determined the status in society of a given individual, which were divided into about two thousand smaller units—generally known as sub-castes—fixing the limits of marriage and effective social life and making for specific cultural tradition. These major groups were held together by the possession, with few exceptions, of a common priesthood. There was a sort of an overall counting which grouped all of them into five or six classes, overtly expressed or tacitly understood. Over a large part of the country they were welded together for civil life in the economy and civics of village communities. Common service to the civic life, prescriptive rights of monopolist service, and specific occasions for enjoying superiority for some of the castes, considered very low, made the village community more or less a harmonious civic unit. Complete acceptance of the system in its broad outlines by the groups making up that system and their social and economic interdependence in the village not only prevented the exclusivist organization of the groups from splitting up the system into independent units, but created a harmony in civic life. Of course, this harmony was not the harmony of parts that are equally valued, but of units which are rigorously subordinated to one another.

References

Note: In this chapter I have quoted many authorities that are chronologically later, by half a century or more, than the period I have here in view. But other and older authorities are almost everywhere indicated. The reason is that the later authorities give more details and are easily accessible to most people.

1. Baines, p. 11. 2. Quotation from Megasthenes' account in Wilson, vol. i, p. 347. 3. P. 124, footnote. 4. *The New Statesman, Special Supplement*, 28th April, 1917, p. 38. 5. Gujarat Brahmins do have such councils. See Borradaile's *Gujarat Caste-rules*, translated into Gujarati by Mangaldas Nathoobhoy. 6. Hultzsch, i, No. 56. 7. *United Provinces Census*, 1911, p. 337; *Panjub Census*, 1911, pp. 420–21; also cf. Hamilton, i, p. 110; Kerr, pp. 316–19; Martin, vol. iii, pp. 179–80; and Steele, pp. 150–1. 8. The result of this fact is to be seen in the departure of the customs of many castes from the rules laid down in the Hindu sacred laws. See Steele, p. 124 and Appendix A. 9. *United Provinces Census*, 1911, p. 337.

10. *Bengal Census*, 1911, pp. 467–9. 11. Ibid., p. 487. 12. *Godavari Dist. Gaz.* vol. i, p. 48. 13. Russell, ii, p. 31. 14. Crooke, i, pp. 45, 109; ii, pp. 93, 219, 326; iii, 247, 332; iv, 33, 43. 15. M. R. Majmudar in *Ghurye Felicitation Volume*, p. 282. 16. *Madras Census*, 1871, p. 137. 17. M. G. Ranade in *JBBRAS*., vol. xx. p. 476. 18. *Madras Census*, 1871, p. 151 and footnote. 19. *Mysore Census*, 1901, p. 400.

20. Martin, vol. ii, p. 466. 21. *U.P. Census*, 1901, p. 227, 22. *U.P. Census*, 1911, p. 328. 23. *U.P. Census*, 1911, p. 212. 24. Risley, (2), p. 159. 25. *U.P. Census*, 1911, p. 329, E. A. H. Blunt, pp. 90–94. 26. *U.P. Census*, 1911, p. 331. 27. Risley (1), vol. ii, p. 270. 28. *Bengal Census*. 1901, p. 367. 29. Ibid.

30. Ibid. 31. Forbes, ii, p. 240. 32. Bhattacharya, p. 255. 33. Wilson, vol. ii, pp. 74–5. 34. *Ency. of R. & E.*, vol. x, p. 491 (b). 35. Slater, p. 38. 36. *Trichinopoly Dist. Gaz.*, vol. i, p. 81. 37. Thurston, vi, p. 16. 38. *Bellary Dist. Gaz.*, p. 58. 39. Mann, p. 108.

40. Russell, iv, p. 189. 41. Thurston, vi, p. 88. 42. Russell, i, pp. 72–3. 43. *Panjab Census*, 1911, p. 413. 44. Briggs, p. 231. 45. *Ency. of R. and E.* ix, p. 636 (b); also compare Forbes, ii, p. 238. 46. Ranade, p. 478. 47. Bhattacharya, p. 259. 48. Logan, i, p. 85. 49. Bhattacharya, p. 259.

50. Wilson, ii, p. 77. 51. Wilson, ii, p. 79. 52. *Madras Census*, 1891, p. 224. 53. G. W. Forrest, *Official Writings of Mountstuart Elphinstone*, 1884, pp. 310–11. 54. *Madras Census*, 1871, p. 129. 55. D. V. Potdar, *Marathi Gadyacha Ingraji Avatar*, Appendix, pp. 42–3. 56. Vad, *Sawai Madhavrao*, vol. iii, p. 280. 57. Ranade, p. 478; Vad, ibid., p. 287. 58. Ibid., p. 478. 59. *Madras Census*, 1891, p. 299.

60. Bhattacharya, pp. 19–20. 61. Ranade, p. 456; Vad, *Balaji Bajirao*, vol. i, pp. 306, 309, 337. 62. Ibid., p. 455. 63. James Forbes, *Oriental Memoirs*, vol. i, 1834, p. 256. 64. Holt Mackenzie in *Minutes of Evidence taken before the Select Committee on the affairs of the East India Company*, vol. iii, 1832, p. 216. 65. Rickards, i, p. 29. 66. Campbell, *Ethnology of India*, p. 216. 67. Wilson, ii, 151; also compare Martin, vol. i, p. 111. 68. Bhattacharya, p. 39. 69. Wilson, ii, p. 115.

70. Wilson, ii, p. 59. 71. Ibid., p. 188; also compare Malcolm, ii, pp. 122–3. 72. Wilson, ii, p. 67. 73. Bhattacharya, pp. 50–1. 74. Baines, p. 28. 75. *Madras Census*, 1871, p. 133. 76. Bose, ii, p. 27, quotation from *Ain-i-Akbari*. 77. *Salem Dist. Gaz.*, 139–64; *Tanjore Dist. Gaz.*, 81–88. 78. Baines, p. 59. 79. Russell, i, p. 9.

80. Quoted in the *Encyclopaedia Britannica* (11th Edition), vol. v, p. 465 (a). 81. p. 19. 82. *Ethnography*, p. 11. 83. Westermarck, ii, p. 59. 84. Baines, p. 59. 85. Compare Malcolm, ii, p. 162. 86. *Ency. of R. and E.*, vol. iii, p. 234. 87. Martin, i, p. 110. 88. *Panjab Census*, 1911, p. 417. 89. *Bengal Census*, 1901, p. 351.

90. *U.P. Census*, 1911, p. 333. 91. Ibid., p. 353. 92. Op. cit., vol. i, p. 10. 93. *Madras Census*, 1901, p. 128; also compare Kerr, p., 279: "You may sometimes hear a native say that he is a Brahmin. But not unfrequently when you ask him to name his caste, he mentions the minor sub-division, or perhaps the trade or profession, to which he belongs." 94. *Salem Dist. Gazetteer*, pp. 123–4. 95. Rev. M. A. Sherring, *Hindu Tribes and Castes*, vol. i, 1872, p. xxii. 96. *Madras Census*, 1891, p. 234. 97. Gait, op. cit., p. 232. 98. *U.P. Census*, 1811, p. 354; Gait's observation may apply only to Gujarat. 99. *Journal of the Asiatic Society of Bengal*, 1907.

100. Baden-Powell, p. 26; Altekar, p. 122. The letter's view, in my opinion, requires a little modification as in the text. 101. *Minutes of Evidence taken before the Select Committee on the affairs of the East India Company*, vol. iii (Revenue), 1832, 331–2 (Appendix 84). 102. Altekar, p. 43. 103. Ibid., pp. 35–6. 104. Matthai, p. 20. 105. Vad, *Madhavrao I*, vol. ii, pp. 339, 341. 106. Vad, *Shahu Chhatrapati*, pp. 174, 176; Ghurye (6) and (7), 107. Crooke (2), pp. 102–29. 108. Russell, iv, pp. 6, 10. 109. Ibid., p. 20.

110. Ibid., pp. 18, 131. 111. Ibid., p. 265. 112. Thurston, i, pp. 32–4. 113. Baines, pp. 75–6.

2

Nature of Caste-Groups

We have seen that in the Hindu caste-society there are a number of groups with distinct names. The nature of these names is likely to furnish us with a clue to some understanding of the process by which distinction between groups came to be formulated. Of the major groups called castes many bear names derived from the principal professions they followed or the crafts they practised and, in the majority of cases, are still engaged in. Brahmin means one who recites the prayer, the ritual formulæ or incantations, and designates a group that was once wholly composed of individuals so engaged, though now it is the appellation of a group whose members are engaged not only in the priestly function, but also in the allied functions of clerks and writers, and even in pursuits absolutely foreign to the original ideals.

Of the groups carrying on trade and commerce a large number bear the name of Vāni or Baniyā, which is derived from a Sanskrit word meaning a trader. The Tamil Chetti seems also to refer to the avocation of the group in that linguistic area. Jāt of the Punjab means cultivator, so also do Vellāla of the Tamil and Vakkaliga of the Kanarese country. Kurmi, Kanbi, and Kunbi perhaps signify the occupation of the group, viz., that of cultivation, though it is not improbable that the name may be of tribal origin. Kisān, the name of a cultivating caste of northern India, must be derived from the Sanskrit word for cultivation. Sometimes the connection of agriculture is brought out indirectly as in the name of the Lodha of the Central Provinces. The name is believed to mean 'clod-hopper' from 'loh', a clod.[1] The cattle-breeding group takes the significant name of Gauli, derived from a Sanskrit word for cow. Soni or Sonār, the name of the goldsmith, refers to the material in which the group specializes. Barhai, Tarkhan, Tachchan and Sutār, the designations of the carpenter-caste in the different linguistic regions, point to the material worked on, the mode of working or the special implement of the craft. The names of the metalworking castes—Lohār, Tāmbat, Kāsār, and Thatherā—come from the metal handled by these groups, viz., iron, copper, bell-metal, and brass. Bunkar, Joriā, Tānti, Koshti, Patwā, Pattānulkāran, and Sāle are the designations of the various weaving castes. The first two are derived from a root meaning 'to put the threads together',[2] and the others from Sanskrit words for silk-cloth.[3] Kumbār or Kumbhār, the name of the potter-caste, means one who makes pots. Tili or Teli, the oil-presser, means either one who presses oil or one who handles sesamum. The names of the barber-caste are either derived from the Sanskrit word for barber or signify those who cut the hair. Luniā and Āgri mean salt-workers. Bāri, the leaf-plate-making caste, derives its name from 'bār', a 'plantation', and Tamboli, dealers in betel-leaf, from the Sanskrit word for betel-leaf. Dhārkār means rope-maker and Bānsphor, the basket-maker, means the bamboo-splitter. Chamār or Chāmbhār, the name of the leather-working caste, is derived from a Sanskrit word meaning worker in leather. Kahār, name of a North-Indian caste, formerly engaged chiefly as water-carriers but now as general and domestic servants, means a water-carrier. Pāsi means a user of noose and is significantly the name of an aboriginal caste living by catching wild birds, small game and tapping palms. The names of the snepherd castes seem to be derived from words meaning sheep. Such is at least the case with Gadariā from 'gādar', an old Hindi word for sheep.[4]

Many others of these major groups called castes bear merely tribal or ethnic names. Such are for example: Ārorā, Gujar, Lohānā, Bhatiā, Minā, Bhil, Dom, Orāon, Mundā, Santāl, Koch, Ahir, Mahār, Nāyar, Marāthā, Gond, Khond, etc.

Religious movements have not failed to give their names to groups, which are now castes. The Bishnois and Sadhus, the Jogis, the Gosāins, and the Mānbhaos are some of the examples of sectarian castes. The first four of these began as orders emphasizing certain aspect of Hindu tenets, while the last group was the result of a reformist movement in the Maratha region.

A few of the groups have names emphasizing a peculiarity which is somehow regarded as specific, or are of the nature of nicknames. Musāhār, meaning mouse-eaters, is the name of a low aboriginal caste of Uttar Pradesh. Bhangi, one who performs the useful function of removing night-soil, is a term probably applied to the caste simply as a token of contempt—those who are broken or outcast[5] Bhuliā, an Uriyā caste of weavers, are so called merely because they are supposed to be a forgetful people—from 'bhulnā', 'to forget'.[6] Dāngi, the name of a cultivating caste of the Central Provinces, means merely a hillman, perhaps referring to the former marauding activities of the now peaceful and once dominant people.[7] The Pankas of the Central Provinces are a caste of weavers and general labourers; but their name is believed to be derived from a certain incident in their conversion to the creed of Kabir and means those who are 'from water', 'pāni kā'.[8] Dublā, one of the aboriginal tribes of Gujarat, are so called because they are weaklings,[9] 'dublā' means weak. Nāikdas of Gujarat are perhaps so designated in contempt, the term meaning "little Naik". Rāmoshi, a thieving caste of the Deccan, is supposed to be a short form of Rama-Vamshi, i.e., descendant of Rama, the epic hero.[10] Kallan, the name of a Madras caste, means in Tamil a 'thief'. Tiyan, the toddy-tapping caste of Malabar, means a 'southerner', as the Tiyans are believed to have migrated from Ceylon. Pariāh, the name of the great untouchable caste of Madras, is commonly derived from a word for drum, which instrument is played by them.

A smaller number of these major groups are definitely known to be the outcome of miscegenation. Some of the members of the higher castes of Orissa and the Kayasth immigrants into Orissa keep maids of Bhandāri and other clean castes and treat them as their concubines. The issue of such unions is known by the name of Shāgirdapesha.[11] The Bhilālas are well known to be the offspring of Rajput males and Bhil women.[12] Vidur, a Marāthā caste of the Central Provinces, is wholly formed by individuals of mixed descent.[13]

A close study of the names of the various minor units, the so-called sub-castes, within the major groups reveals the fact that the bases of distinction leading to the exclusive marking off of these groups were: first, territorial or jurisdictional separateness; second, mixed origin; third, occupational distinction; fourth, some peculiarity in the technique of one and the same occupation; fifth, sectarian difference; sixth, dissimilarity of customs; and last, adventitious circumstances, suggesting certain nicknames.

Sub-castes that bear the name of some ancient city or locality are to be met with in the majority of the castes. The Ahirs of the Central Provinces have among their sub-castes, the following groups: Jijhotiā, taking their name from Jajhoti, the classical designation of Bundelkhand; Narwariā from Narwar; Kosariā from Kosala, the ancient name of Chhattisgarh; and Kanaujiā from Kanauj.[14] The Barai have the following endogamous sub-divisions: Chaurāsiā, from the Chaurasi pargana of Mirzapur District; Panagariā, from Panagar in Jabalpur; Mahobiā from Mahoba; Jāiswār from the town of Jais in Rai Bareli District; Gangāpāri, coming from the other side of the Ganges.[15] The Brahmins of Bengal have among their sub-castes the following names: Pāschātya, from the western part of India; Rādhiya from Radh, the old name of Western Bengal and Barendra from the northern part of Bengal.[16] The names of the sub-castes of the Brahmin caste of Uttar Pradesh are most of them territorial in origin: Kanaujiā from Kanauj; Maithil from Mithila; Jijhotiā from Jajhoti; Sāraswat, named after the river Saraswati; and Gaur from an old name of a large part of Northern India. Most of the sub-castes of the Brahmins of the Maratha country bear names of localities: Konkanasth from the Konkan; Deshasth from the Desh, the Deccan plateau. The Sāraswat Brahmins have more than six sub-castes, all territorial in origin. Of the numerous sub-castes of the Gujarat Brahmins the majority bear territorial names, like Agarwal, from Agra; Deshvāl, Harsola, Jhārolā, Modh, Nāgar Osvāl, Porvāl, Shrimali, Sorathiā, all of them being derived from old names of localities once independent in their jurisdiction.[17] Many of the sub-divisions of the Smārta Brahmins of the Telugu country bear names derived from the old names of the various parts of that country: Velnād, Vengi Nādu, Kasal Nādu, Mulki Nādu, and Telaga Nādu. The sub-caste of the Kanara Kammā Baidika is formed by Brahmins who originally came from the Kanarese country but are now naturalized in the Telugu country.[18] Following are some of the other castes among which the sub-castes bear territorial names: Vaniā, Mochi, Kansārā, Sutāan, Chāran, Kumbhār, Dhed, Darji, Lohār, and Koli among Gujarat castes; Kāyasth, Baniā and Vaidya, among the North Indian castes; Chāmbhār, Gauli, Koli, Kumbhār, Kunbi, Lohār, Mahār, Māli, Nhāvi, Sutār and Vāni among the Maratha castes.

Many castes have divisions bearing names reminiscent of the ethnic origins of these sub-groups. Many tribes, either because some of their members followed a particular occupation or because some of them intermarried with the members of a particular caste-in-formation, have contributed their names to sub-castes. The professions and castes, which allowed or tolerated the infusion of tribal people, still distinguished the groups formed by such inclusion or mesalliance. This is how many of the occupational castes have come to possess sub-castes bearing tribal names. This process of infusion and left-handed marriage does not seem to have been restricted to tribes alone. In spite of the so-called rigidity of caste, it appears that many of the occupational and tribal castes, either permitted or connived at the intrusion of members of other castes. Only they tried to keep the progeny and the group formed by them distinct from their original group. Thus the sub-castes of some of the major castes have composite names derived from the names of other castes. The Barai, a caste of betel-vine growers in the Central Provinces, have a sub-division called the Kumbhārdhang, who are supposed to be the descendants of a potter. The Basors, workers in bamboo, have the following sub-castes: Dumar or Dom-Basors, Basors who are derived from the Dom-tribe; Dhubela, perhaps from the Dhobi caste; Dhārkār, which is the name also of a large caste of ropemakers in Northern India. The Chāmbhārs, leather workers of the Maratha country, have Ahir as one of their sub-castes. The Chamārs of the Central Provinces, have a sub-caste named Korchamārs who "are said to be the descendants of alliance between Chamārs and Koris or weavers."[19] The Sāli, a weaving caste of Maratha country, has Ahir, Marāthā, and Chāmbhār sub-castes, which announce their origins from the different ethnic and occupational groups. The Dhimārs, a caste of fishermen and palanquin-bearers of the Central Provinces, retain in the name of one of their sub-castes its traditional origin from the Gonds. Among the Dheds, as among many castes of Gujarat, is a sub-caste named Gujar, derived from a medieval tribe of that name. Among the Gaulis, cowherds of the Maratha country, are to be found sub-castes bearing the name of Ahir, Kunbi, Kuruba, and Marāthā. Gondhali, a composite caste of religious minstrels, has sub-castes bearing the names of other well-known castes of the Maratha country, like the Brāhman, Dhangar, and Kumbhar. The Kolis of the Deccan have Āgri, Ahir and Bhil among their sub-castes. Nesfield has found among some castes of Uttar Pradesh sub-castes styled after the Kol tribe, which seem to have taken to various occupations during the formative period of the caste-system.[20] Among the Kunbis of Nagpur is a sub-caste bearing the name Mānwā derived from the Mānās, who were once a dominant people in Chanda district. The Khandesh Kunbis have, as one of their sub-castes, Kumbhār, which is the name of the potter-caste. "Bodies of the Kori and Katiā weaving castes of Northern India have been amalgamated with the Mahārs in Districts where they have come together along the Satpura Hills and Nerbudda Valley," the latter caste still having Katiā as one of its sub-castes.[21] Kunbi is one of the sub-castes of the Nhāvis, the Marāthā caste of barbers. The Pardhāns of the Central Provinces have a sub-caste called Gandā, supposed to be the offspring of intermarriages between the two castes.[22] Among the Shimpis or Marāthā tailors, one finds Ahir and Marāthā as two of their sub-castes, derived from well-known castes. "The Teli-Kalārs appear to be a mixed group of Kalārs who have taken to the oilman's profession, and the Teli-Baniās are Telis who have become shopkeepers."[23]

The nature of many of the occupations is such that though from a broad point of view each may be regarded as distinct, yet on closer scrutiny it presents differences which are sufficient to distinguish one aspect of it from another. Thus, though leather-working may be regarded as one occupation by the society, the followers of that occupation may distinguish different branches of leather-working as shoe-making, sandal-making, or oilcan-making. Such detailed distinctions within an occupation have been thought to be adequate to designate the group of members following the particular branch of the occupation by the name of that branch. Sub-castes within many of the occupational castes bear names derived from the special branches of the occupations. Among the Chamārs of the Central Provinces there are many sub-castes whose names are derived from the particular articles of leather that their members are engaged in making. The members of the sub-caste Budalgir prepare 'budlās' or oilcans of leather. Jingars are saddle-makers. The Katwā sub-caste specializes in leather-cutting. The Dhimār caste of the Central Provinces has Bānsiā and Bandhaiyā as two of its sub-castes. The former term is derived from 'bansi', a bamboo fishing-rod, and the latter means those who make ropes and sacking of hemp and fibre. The Kunbis have a sub-caste called Tilole presumably because once they cultivated the sesamum (til) plant. Among the Lonāris of Belgaum there are two sub-divisions styled after their particular article which they prepare as Mith (salt) and Chune (lime). Phul Māli, Kachā Māli, Jire Māli, and Halde Māli, together forming the bulk of the Māli-caste, are sub-castes which take their names from occupational specialization. Thus the Phul Māli is a florist, the Kachā Mālis prepare the cotton braid, the Jire grow cumin seed (jire), and the Halde grow 'halad' or turmeric. The Koshtis of the Central Provinces have Patwi and Sutsāle as two of their sub-castes. Patwis make the braid of silk-thread and sew silk-thread on ornaments. Sutsāles weave mostly cotton-thread.

Many sub-castes, especially among the castes that are either of the nature of ethnic groups or carry on secondary undefined occupations, are named from the nature of their special economic activities. Singāriā, Tānkiwālā, Dhuriā, Sonjhārā, and Kasdhoniā are some of the sub-divisions of the Dhimār caste in the Central Provinces. Singāriās cultivate 'singārā' or water-nut. Tānkiwālās are sharpeners of grind-stones. Dhuriās sell parched rice. Sonjhārās wash for gold, and Kasdhoniās wash the sand of sacred rivers to pick coins dropped in them by devout pilgrims. The Garpāgari Jogi derives the name of his sub-caste from his occupation of using magic to avert hailstorms. The Manihāri Jogis are pedlars selling beads and the Rithā Biknāth are so-called because they sell 'rithā' or soap-nut. Khaire, Dhānoje, and Lonhāre are three of the sub-castes of the Kunbis of the Central Provinces. Khaires presumably used to make catechu from 'khair'; Dhānoje are those who tend small stock or 'dhān', and Lonhāre formerly refined salt. The Lonāriā sub-caste of the Mahārs of the Central Provinces is engaged in salt-making. The Dhangars have Mendhes and Mhaskes as two of their sub-divisions, named because they keep sheep (mendhi) and buffaloes (mhashi) respectively.

The Māng-gārudis, a sub-division of the Māng-caste, are so called because they are snake-charmers; the Tokarphodes take their name from their occupation of splitting (phod) bamboo (tokar); the Nādes are so called because they make 'nādas' or ropes. The Māngmochis are leather-workers. Kākars make ropes of untanned hide.[24] Nhāvis, the barbers of the Maratha country, have among their sub-castes Vājantri and Mashālji. The former are so called because they play music and the latter because they carry torches (mashāl) before processions. Among Mahārs of the Maratha country two of their sub-divisions are named Panyā and Bele, the former from their working with leaves for making umbrellas and the latter from their making mats from chips of bamboo. In the Central Provinces the Yerande Telis, who are a sub-caste of the Teli caste, take their name from the fact that formerly they pressed only 'erandi' or castor oil seed. The Salo Telis have given up oil-pressing and are now cultivators.[25]

Peculiarities connected with the apparatus or technique of an occupation have given their names to the sub-divisions of some of the occupational castes. The Kumbhār, potters of the Maratha country, distinguish those who make pots by hand without the wheel as Hātghades (hand-potters), those who use a big wheel as Thorchāke ('thor', big, and 'chāk', wheel), and those who use a small wheel as Lahānchāke ('lahān', small). In the Central Provinces the potter-caste has the first sub-caste, but not the last two. Instead they have Chākere and Kurere, the latter using a revolving stone slab instead of a wheel. In addition they have a sub-caste called Goria because the members of this sub-division make white pots only and not black ones. In the Nagpur district the Telis have two principal sub-divisions. Ekbaile are those who yoke only one bullock to their press while Dobaile yoke two bullocks.

Differences of religious schools or sects have given names to sub-divisions among some castes. The old distinctions on the basis of the *Veda*, which was traditionally followed by the members of a group have persisted among the Deshasth Brahmins of the Maratha country leading to endogamous restrictions. Among them the Rigvedis and Yajurvedis—the followers of the Rig-veda and of the Yajurveda—are so far distinct as to be sub-castes. Later creeds and reformatory movements have also left their marks on caste organization. Among the Deshasth Brahmins there is also an endogamous group, whose members are supposed to be the descendants of Eknath, a reforming saint of Maharashtra.[26] The South Indian Brahmins carry their religious differences to such an extent that generally the Smārtas and Vaishnavas are regarded as sub-castes. The Chamārs of the Central Provinces have amongst them a large sub-caste named Satnāmi because the members are followers of the Satnāmi sect. The Padam Sālis have Hindu and Lingāyat divisions which are endogamous. So also have the Gaulis, the Kumbhārs and Fālis, Lingāyat divisions among them. The Pankās, a Dravidian caste of weavers, have Kabirhā and Shāktaha as their principal sub-castes. The Kabirhās are the followers of the sect of Kabir and the Shāktahas profess to belong to the Shākta creed.[27]

Differences in customs and diet have been regarded as so important that some of the castes recognize groups with such differences as sub-castes, though the names of these do not necessarily take after the differences. The Berads of Bombay have two sub-castes, the difference between them being that the members of one eat the flesh of buffaloes, bullocks or pigs, and allow their women to follow prostitution, while the members of the other do not tolerate these practices. These latter are termed Bile, i.e. white or pure, and the former Kare or black. Dhor, one of the five sub-divisions of the Kātkaris, is so called because the members eat beef. Moger, a Kanarese fishing-caste, has three sub-divisions named according to their rules of inheritance: Aliyāsantānas, Makalasantānas, and

Rāndesantānas, i.e., those who inherit through females, those who inherit through males, and those who are progeny of re-married widows.[28] The Kunbis of the Central Provinces have a sub-caste called Gādhao because they formerly kept donkeys ('gādhav').

Many castes have sub-castes, whose names are derived from some real peculiarity now forgotten, or some adventitious circumstance to which importance is attached, and which is used to distinguish the members of the group, or, in the case of miscegenation, from the fact of mere illegitimacy of unions, the exact lineage not being attended to. The Basors of the Central Provinces have a section called Purāniā or Juthiā because they are supposed to be the illegitimate progeny of Ahir wet-nurses (dāi), employed in Rajput households. The Chungiā Chamārs are a branch of the Satnāmi Chamārs and are so called because, contrary to the rules of the sect, they smoke evidently by means of a leafpipe (chungiā). The Dāijanya sub-caste of the Chamārs is so called because their women act as midwives, though this business is practised by women of other sub-castes as well. The Dhimārs have a sub-caste which is merely named Nādhā or those who live on the banks of streams. Their Suvarhā and Gadhewāle sub-castes derive their names from their special association with two unclean animals, pig and ass. The Mahārs disclose a sense of humour by designating the group of descendants of illicit unions by the term Dhārmik (pious). The Pardhāns, on the contrary, apply a prosaic term to such a group among them. It is known as 'Thothiā' or 'maimed'. Though 'langoti' or a narrow piece of cloth is the loincloth of many poor castes, the Pārdhis have hit upon its use as the distinctive mark of their members and call one of their sub-castes Langoti. The Kumbhārs have Gādhere, Bardiā, and Sungariā as three of their sub-castes, these groups deriving their names from the animal they use or keep: ass, bullock, and pig respectively. The Dhangars of Bombay call their bastard brethren 'kadu', while the Gujarat Kumbhārs use the term Vataliā, i.e. polluted, to designate such members.

Such is the picture of caste-groups presented by facts mostly taken from the Central Provinces, Maharashtra and Gujarat, both of which regions are outside the centre of old Brahmanic culture. In the home of the Brahmanic culture, Uttar Pradesh, the same principles can be discerned from the nomenclature of the castes and sub-castes. One additional and important feature of the caste origination of the region is that the names of Rajput clans and those of some of the eponymous personages figure very largely in the names of the sub-castes of many major groups.[29]

References

1. Russell, iv, p. 113. 2. Nesfield, p. 21. 3. Russell, iii, p. 581, and iv, p. 386. 4. Nesfield, p. 11. 5. Enthoven, i, v. 105. 6. Russell, ii, p. 320. 7. Russell, ii, pp. 457–8. 8. Russell, iv, p. 324. 9. Enthoven, i, p. 341.

10. Enthoven, iii, p. 297. 11. Risley, (2), p. 83. 12. Enthoven, i, p. 153. 13. Russell, iv, p. 596. 14. Russell, ii, pp. 24–5. 15. Ibid., p. 193. 16. Bhattacharya, p. 35. 17. Enthoven i, p. 221. Some of the Gujarat castes are further sub-divided according to the cities in which they reside, e.g., Shrimāli Baniās of Surat and those of Ahmedabad, etc. 18 Bhattacharya, p. 99. 19. Nesfield, p. 106.

20. Nesfield, p. 106. 21. Russell, iv, p. 133. 22. Russell iv, p. 354. 23. Ibid., p. 546. 24. Enthoven, ii, p. 436. 25. Russell, iv, p. 546. 26. Enthoven, iii, 327. N.B.: It is a curious fact that among the Gujarat Baniās the religious differences have not led to rigorous interdicting of intermarriage. There is no serious objection to marriages between Jain and Vaishnav Baniās. Compare Malcolm, ii, p. 162. 27. Russell, iv, p. 325. 28. Enthoven, iii, p. 60. 29. W. Crooke, *The Tribes and Castes of the North-Western Provinces and Oudh*, vol. i, pp. clxiv-v.

3

Caste Through the Ages—I

I have here sought to give a picture of Hindu caste society as it was functioning before modern ideas affected its course. We have now to see how it came to be what it was. For the convenience of such historical treatment I propose to break up the history of India into four periods. First, the Vedic period ending about B.C. 600 and comprising the literary data of the Vedic *Samhitās* and the *Brāhmanas*; second, the post-Vedic period, extending to about the third century of the Christian era. In this period we have three types of literature which shed light on this subject. The sacred laws of the Aryans present the orthodox and the more or less idealistic standpoint while the epics testify to the contemporary practices. Buddhist literature, on the other hand, gives a glimpse of the institution as it appeared to those who rebelled against it and in part provides us with a natural picture of some aspects of caste. The third period may be styled the period of the *Dharma-shāstras* and ends with the tenth or eleventh century A.D. Manu, Yājnavalkya and Vishnu are the chief exponents of the social ideals of this age. The fourth period may, with propriety, be called the modern period, and it brings us down to the beginning of the nineteenth century. The customs and beliefs of contemporary Hindus are those that were mostly fixed and classified by the writers of this period. It was during this period that the present-day vernaculars of India were being evolved. A fresh religion and a somewhat different ethnic stock, accounting for many of our present-day political and social problems were also introduced during this age. The idealistic point of view is provided by writers like Parāshara, Hemādri, and Mādhava, while the inscriptions and travellers' accounts reveal some of the realities of the times.

It must be mentioned at the outset that all the literary accounts of the important aspects of caste centre round the four orders in society, namely Brahmin, Kshatriya, Vaishya and Shudra, and not the multifarious groups which are the present-day castes.

In the *Rigveda*, the earliest work of the first period three classes of society are very frequently mentioned, and named Brahma, Kshatra, and Visha. The first two represented broadly the two professions of the poet-priest and the warrior-chief. The third division was apparently a group comprising all the common people. It is only in one of the later hymns, the celebrated Purushasūkta, that a reference has been made to four orders of society as emanating from the sacrifice of the Primeval Being. The names of those four orders are given there as Brāhmana, Rājanya, Vaishya, and Shudra, who are said to have come respectively from the mouth, the arms, the thighs, and the feet of the Creator. The particular limbs associated with these divisions and the order in which they are mentioned probably indicate their status in the society of the time, though no such interpretation is directly given in the hymn.

This origin of the four classes is repeated in most of the later works with slight variations and interpretative additions. The *Taittiriya Samhitā*, for example, ascribes the origins of those four classes to the four limbs of the Creator and adds an explanation. The Brahmins are declared to be the chief because they were created from the mouth, punning on the word 'mukha' ('mouth' and 'chief'). The Rājanyas are vigorous because they were created from vigour. The Vaishyas are meant to be eaten, referring to their liability to excessive taxation, because they were created from the stomach, the receptacle of food. The Shudra, because he was created from the feet, is to be the transporter of others and to subsist by the feet. In this particular account of the creation not only is the origin of the classes interpreted theologically, but also a divine justification is sought to be given to their functions and status. The creation-theory is here further amplified to account for certain other features of these social classes. God is said to have created certain deities simultaneously with these classes. The Vaishya class, the commoners, must have been naturally very large, and this account explains that social fact by a reference to the simultaneous creation of Vishvedevas, all and sundry deities, whose number is considerable. We are told that no deities were created along with the Shudra and hence he is disqualified for sacrifice. Here again, the social regulation which forbade a Shudra to offer sacrifice is explained as an incidental consequence of the creation.[1]

The fact that the four classes are described as of divine origin, although in a later hymn, must be taken as a sufficient indication that they were of long duration and very well-defined, even though the exact demarcation of their functions, the regulations guiding their inter-relations, and the extent of their flexibility may not be referred to in the main body of the Rigvedic literature, which is avowedly of a liturgical nature.

The *Shatapatha Brāhmana*, lays down different sizes of the funeral mound for the four classes. The terms of address are also different, varying in the degree of politeness. In the 'Human Sacrifice' the representatives of these orders are dedicated to different deities. A passage in the *Aitareya Brāhmana* warns a Kshatriya to avoid certain mistakes in the sacrificial ritual. If he commits a particular mistake, it goes on to say, "one like a Brahmin shall be born in his line who in the second or third generation from his has the power of becoming a Brahmin, and likes to live as a Brahmin." Similarly for two other mistakes he shall have a Vaishya-like and a Shudra-like son capable of becoming a full-fledged Vaishya or Shudra in two or three generations. It is clear, that though the classes had come to be almost stereotyped by the end of the Vedic period, it was not altogether impossible for an upward or downward change to occur in a particular family in two or three generations.[2]

These classes or orders are regularly referred to in later literature as *varnas*, so much so that popularly Hindu religion has come to be defined as Varnāshrama Dharma. Yet in the *Rigveda* the word 'varna' is never applied to any one of these classes. It is only the Ārya varna, or the Aryan people, that is contrasted with the Dāsa varna. The *Shatapatha Brahmana*, on the other hand, describes the four classes as the four varnas.[3] 'Varna' means 'colour', and it was in this sense that the word seems to have been employed in contrasting the Ārya and the Dāsa, referring to their fair and dark colours respectively. The colour-connotation of the word was so strong that later on when the classes came to be regularly described as varnas, four different colours were assigned to the four classes, by which their members were supposed to be distinguished.

On the relations subsisting between the four classes the *Rigveda* has very little to say. The inferences that we can draw are also few. Rigvedic literature stresses very strongly the difference between the Ārya and the Dāsa, not only in their colour but also in their speech, religious practices, and physical features. The Brahmin class, by the end of the period, appears to have acquired almost all the characteristics of a caste. Though the general body of the Rigvedic evidence is not quite determinative, yet a stray reference to a false claim for being regarded a Brahmin, like the one contained in the seventy-first hymn of the tenth book of the *Rigveda* points to this conclusion. The Brahmin is definitely said to be superior to the Kshatriya, whom he is able to embroil with his incantations or with his knowledge of rituals. He is said to ensure a king's safety in battle by his prayers and the *Aitareya Brāhmana* lays down that a king's offerings are not acceptable to the gods unless they are offered with the help of a Purohita (chaplain), who, as we shall later on see, was generally a Brahmin. Wherever it is necessary, as in the Rājasūya sacrifice, for the Brahmin to pay homage to the king, the fact is explained in such a way as not to affect the superiority of the Brahmins. It is even suggested that the king rules by the authority delegated to him by the Brahmin.[4] The power of the king and the nobles to harass a Brahmin is recognized and as an antidote a speedy ruin is threatened. The necessity of co-operation between the Brahmin and the Kshatriya for the complete prosperity of both is often reiterated. The Brahmins are declared to be gods on earth. The *Shatapatha Brāhmana*, even sums up the rights and duties of the Brahmins, amongst which receiving gifts and observing purity of descent are mentioned. It is also said that no Brahmin should accept whatever has been refused by others, and the sanctity attaching to the Brahmin is carried so far in the *Panchavimsha Brāhmana* as to foreclose any inquiry into his claim to Brahminhood. It appears from a passage in the *Shatapatha Brāhmana* that property of a Brahmin was exempt from the royal claim. The remains of the sacrificial food must be eaten by nobody but a Brahmin. According to the *Shatapatha Brāhmana* the murder of a Brahmin is alone a real murder, while the *Yajurveda* declares it to be a more heinous crime than that of killing any other man. It could only be expiated by a heavy ritual. In a legal dispute between a Brahmin and a non-Brahmin an arbitrator or a witness must speak in favour of the former. Though the *Shatapatha Brāhmana* enumerates freedom from being killed as a privilege of the Brahmins, the *Panchavimsha Brāhmana* declares that a Purohita might be punished with death for treachery to his master. According to a legend in the *Shatapatha Brāhmana* the Brahmins regarded themselves as the spreaders of civilization.

The functions of a Brahmin may be said to be teaching and officiating at sacrifices, and his aim was to be pre-eminent in sacred knowledge. To achieve this, a student's life (Brahmacharya) was enjoined. To this course, it seems, only Brahmins were generally admitted. The story of Satyakāma Jābāla makes this quite clear.[5] This youth went to a famous Brahmin teacher, requesting to be admitted as a pupil. The teacher asked him to give particulars of his lineage, whereupon Satyakāma is represented to have told the sage that he did not know the name of his father as he was born to his mother when she was overburdened with work. The teacher thereupon acclaimed him as a Brahmin because he told the truth, and allowed him to be his pupil. It must be inferred from this anecdote that according to this teacher at least, only Brahmins could be admitted to Brahmacharya-studentship, because Satyakāma was accepted as a pupil only when the teacher was satisfied that the boy was a Brahmin. The test of lineage was subordinated here to the criterion of the moral characteristic of truth-speaking. Incidentally it may be pointed out that according to the ideas of the age only Brahmins could be expected to speak the truth. This inference fundamentally conflicts with the general comment on this story that it proves the possibility of a non-Brahmin being allowed to acquire the sacred lore. That members of other classes could be admitted to studentship as special cases must be inferred from the fact that in the *Kāthaka Samhitā* a rite is referred to for the benefit of a person, who has mastered the lore, though himself not a Brahmin. The priest's profession was perhaps hereditary, as we read of a Brahmaputra in a few passages as the son of a Brāhmaṇa (a priest) and also of a Brahmabandhu (a priest in name only). Nevertheless there are indications, corroborated by later tradition, that members of the Kshatriya class could also be priests. The expression 'Brahmapurohita', meaning "having a Brahmin priest as Purohita", suggests the possibility of a non-Brahmin priest. Vishvāmitra, the chaplain of Sudāsa and the famous rival of Vasishtha, according to the tradition, was a Kshatriya. Yāska tells us that Devāpi, who officiated as priest at his brothers' sacrifice, was a prince of the Kuru family. The *Shatapatha Brāhmana* regards a Brahmin as impure if he follows the profession of a physician.

Whether marriage among the Brahmins was hemmed in by endogamous restrictions is not quite clear from the literature of this age. According to tradition, Chyavana and Shyāvāshva, two Vedic sages, married Kshatriya girls. On the other hand, the importance of pure descent was appreciated in so far as stress was laid on being a descendant of a Rishi. In the *Aitareya Brāhmana*, Kavasha is taunted with being the son of a female slave and in the *Panchavimsha Brāhmana* Vatsa is represented as having cleared himself of a similar charge.

The second order in society, the Kshatriya, is known in the later portions of the *Rigveda* as the Rājanya. The class seems to have included only the chiefs and the nobles as the word 'rājanya' points to the ruling activities, and thus brings out the functional origin of the class.[6] Usually the class is represented as inferior to the Brahmin, but a solitary reference in the *Kāthaka Samhitā* raises the Kshatriya over the Brahmin. In another text, 'rājakula' or the king's family, is ranked after the Brahmin family. The phrase, "claiming falsely Kshatriya's rank," occurring in the *Rigveda* (vii, 104, 13), raises the presumption that the Kshatriyas constituted a compact class.

The occupations of the class, as we have mentioned above, must have consisted in administrative and military duties, though the rank and file of the army might have been formed even by the commoners. In the prayer for the prosperity of a Kshatriya, he is said to be an archer and good chariot-fighter. That members of this class could follow other occupations is rendered probable by the mention of a Rājanya as playing on the flute in the *Shatapatha Brāhmana*. According to later tradition, some of the composers of the hymns of the *Rigveda* belonged to this class. The few examples of Kshatriyas acting as priests are mentioned above. It is clear from Upanishadic literature that some of the kings of the age were not only the patrons of philosophers but were themselves well versed in the profound philosophical speculations of their times. Janaka of the Videhas, Pravāhana Jaivali, Ajātashatru, and Ashvapati Kaikeya are some of the conspicuous names of philosopher-kings. It seems that some of the Kshatriyas, though as a class they followed other professions, had kept themselves quite alert and abreast of their Brahmin brethren. The forward and daring spirits amongst them tried to assert their equality with the Brahmins both in priestcraft and in philosophical disquisitions. The conclusion seems to be legitimate, therefore, that only when the ritual later on became too elaborate, and the Kshatriyas, on the other hand, became engrossed in the work of conquest, and progressively lost intimate contact with the older dialect, that they receded from the competitive field though only to rise in open rebellion against the Brahmins.

While there are a few traditional examples of Kshatriya girls being married to Brahmins, there is not a single example among the personages of this age where a Brahmin girl has married a Kshatriya. Though the Kshatriyas sometimes gave their daughters in marriage to Brahmins yet they seem to have had an objection to marry girls from even prosperous families of the two lower orders.

The third order in society, namely the Vaishya, figures singularly little in Vedic literature. The *Aitareya Brāhmana* describes him as tributary to another, "to be lived upon by another", and "to be suppressed at will". Representing the common people, both the composition and the functions of this class are shadowy. According to the *Taittiriya Samhitā*, the greatest ambition of a Vaishya was to be the 'Grāmani' or the village headman. "The son of a Vaishya woman is never anointed a king," so says the *Shatapatha Brāhmana*.[7] Though, in comparison with the higher classes, the Vaishyas' position was rather insignificant, yet the class definitely marked off from the Shudras.

The name of the fourth class, the Shudra, occurs only once in the *Rigveda*. It seems the class represented domestic servants, approximating very nearly to the position of slaves. The Shudra is described as "the servant of another", "to be expelled at will", and "to be slain at will". The *Panchavimsha Brāhmano* defines this position still more precisely when it declares that the Shudra, even if he be prosperous, cannot but be a servant of another, washing his superior's feet being his main business. Yet according to the same work some of the king's ministers were Shudras. The milk to be used for fire-oblation was not allowed to be milked by a Shudra. He was not to be addressed by a person consecrated for a sacrifice. He is declared to be unfit for sacrifice and not allowed even to be present in the hall where the sacrifice was being offered. The *Shatapatha Brāhmana* goes to the length of declaring that the Shudra is untruth itself.[8] Illicit connection between an Āryas male and a Shudra female is mentioned, and the uneasiness felt by the Shudra husband whose wife is a mistress of an Āryas is also hinted at.[9] In this connection we may mention that Vasishtha quotes a Brāhmana text to the effect that a woman of the black race, meaning the Shudra people, was meant only for enjoyment and not for furtherance of any higher motives.[10]

We have seen that in the *Rigveda* a marked distinction was drawn between the Ārya and the Dāsa. In the later Vedic literature this demarcation tends to be drawn between the Ārya and Shudra, who is being described as of dark colour. As if to preserve the memory of this change, as a part of sacrificial rites a mock-fight between an Āryas and a Shudra, in which the former necessarily wins, is prescribed. This change is perhaps due to the increasing association between the Aryan people and the Indian aborigines resulting in illicit unions not only between Āryas males and Shudra females but also between Shudra men and Ārya women.

Besides the four orders are mentioned in the *Rigveda*, occupations like blacksmith, leather-worker, barber, physician, goldsmith, merchant, and chariot-builder. We do not know which of these occupations were comprised in any of the four orders, nor can we say that each of them constituted a separate class. We know for certain that the status of the Rathakāra—the chariot-builder—was high enough to preclude his being classified with the Shudras. The formulæ for placing the sacrificial fire include one for the Rathakāra, indicating his high status even in religious matters.

It is not only the variety of occupations that is striking, but also the fact that one and the same occupation bore different names. The husbandman and potter have each more than one appellation. We have seen above that two groups, following the same occupation, have different names and are recognized as independent castes or subcastes. Naming is the first step towards distinction. We should, therefore, attach due significance to the fact of one and the same occupation being given different names, either through individual or provincial peculiarities, in the Vedic literature.

That some of the occupations at least had become hereditary is probable. The use of the patronymic, derived from the name of an occupation, lends support to this view, 'kaulāla', 'dhaivara', 'paunjishtha', and 'vanija' are used in the sense of the son of a 'kulāla' (potter), of a 'dhivara' (fisherman), of a 'punjishtha' (fisherman), and of a 'vanij' (merchant).

Four names occurring in the Vedic literature, viz., Āyogava, Chanḍāla, Nishāda, and Paulkasa, deserve more than passing notice. A king, named Marutta Āvikshita, is called the Āyogava. The meaning of the word is doubtful, but it must be pointed out that in the literature of the next period it is regularly given as the name of one of the mixed castes. The references to the Chandālas in the Yajurveda clearly show them to be degraded people. In the next period, it will be seen, Chandālas are described as the offspring of a Shudra father and a Brahmin mother. Whether their degraded position in the Vedic period was due to such mixed descent is more than can be ascertained. At the same time the possibility of such an explanation must not be wholly overlooked, inasmuch as illicit connection between a Shudra male and an Aryan female is sometimes hinted at. But the more plausible explanation would be that the Chandālas were a degraded group of aborigines. In the first place, it is difficult to see how a whole people could be the outcome of illicit unions between Aryan females and Shudra males. Secondly, they are not the only group described as degraded people in the Vedic literature. The Paulkasas and Chandālas are referred to as a despised race of men in the *Brihadāranyaka Upanishad*. This use of a derivative noun from Pulkasa shows the fixity of the group. The term also occurs in later literature as the name of the offspring of a Nishāda or Shudra by a Kshatriya woman. Such a connection of Kshatriya females, as a regular feature, is much more than can be believed. It is more reasonable to hold that both these groups, Chandāla and Paulkasa, were sections of the aborigines that were, for some reason or another, particularly despised by the Aryans. The Nishādas, on the other hand, seem to have been a section liked by the Aryans, probably because they were amenable to their civilized notions. The Vedic expression 'panchajanāh' is explained by tradition, belonging to the latter part of this period, to mean the four varnas and the Nishādas, a fact which shows that these people had, by this time, become quite acceptable to the Aryans. This conclusion is also borne out by a text of the *Kaushitaki Brāhmana* requiring the sacrifice in a particular rite to reside temporarily with Nishādas. It seems that the Vedic Dasa, by constant association and slow assimilation, had been partially differentiated into the Shudra and partially into the Nishāda, while the refractory and incorrigible elements were specially despised and styled Paulkasa and Chandāla.

We have seen that the three classes of the early portion of the *Rigveda* were later solidified into four groups, more or less compact, with three or four other groups, separately mentioned. Though these groups were very nearly exclusive units, upward or downward march of individuals was not altogether an impossibility, though it must have been an infrequent occurrence. Only the first three orders may be said to have been recognized as far as religious and ritualistic life was concerned. The Shudra, though he was received within the precincts of the Aryan fold, was systematically debarred from following the religious practices of the Aryans. Nay, the ideas of untouchability were first given literary expression in connection with the Shudras and the sacrifice. There were also various inequalities in the matter of religious practices between the other three classes. The impression is clearly gained that only the Brahmin and the Kshatriya were the two important orders in the society. The former was steadily gaining exclusive influence with the increasing complexity of the sacrificial ritual, while the latter produced, only off and on, individuals capable of keeping themselves abreast of the former. It was in keeping with this that the third order, Vaishya, was spoken of as the taxable group, and the fourth order, Shudra, was denied any justice. Each order seems to have been habitually endogamous though occasionally Brahmins married Kshatriya females, and all the three higher orders now and then might have kept Shudra mistresses. There was a variety of specialized occupations about which we have no means of ascertaining whether they were included in one or the other of the four orders. They seem to have been hereditary rather by custom than by regulation. The prohibition of dining in the company of others is not laid down in connection with these orders, though the general idea is there. It is only those who were performing a certain rite or who believed in a certain doctrine that were forbidden to dine in the company of others.[11]

The Brahmanic literature of the post-Vedic period, while reiterating that there are only four varnas, mentions certain mixed castes (sankara jāti) and also a group of out-cast classes (antyāvasāyin).

The sacred laws of the Aryas are designed to expound 'varna-dharma', i.e., the duties ostensibly of the four orders. The text-books of the different schools may broadly be analysed into four parts. The first part, generally very short, deals with the 'āshramas' (four stages in individual life) and their duties; the second part, forming a large portion of the book, really deals with 'varna-dharma'. Much of the law proper is treated in this section under the heading, "duties of the Kshatriya". The two other parts deal with expiatory acts and inheritance. Though the main bulk of the law is treated under 'varna-dharma', yet the 'Shudra' does not figure much in these texts. The 'varna-dharma' of the 'Shudra' is such that it does not require elaborate regulation. It may justly be said that the 'Shudra' was left to himself as far as his internal affairs were concerned. Mandlik observes, "The non-regenerate class thus seems to form a group by itself, and its internal economy is not specially provided for by the ordinary Ārya writers on law."[12] Their case is provided for by the general dictum, fathered on Manu, that the peculiar laws of countries, castes, and families may be followed in the absence of sacred rules.[13] The other classes are considered derivative, and therefore so much beneath notice that only four-fold humanity is always alluded to and prevention of the confusion of these castes (varna-saṅkara) is considered as an ideal necessity.[14] Mixtures of castes is regarded to be such a great evil that it must be combated even though the Brahmins and the Vaishyas have to resort to arms, a function which is normally sinful for them.[15] As the out-castes were deprived of the right to follow the lawful occupations of the twice-born men, and after death, of the rewards of meritorious deeds,[16] it follows that the lawgivers had no concern for them. They were enjoined to live together and fulfil their purposes, sacrificing for each other and confining other relations to themselves.[17] Of mixed castes those that were the outcome of hypergamous unions, were proposed to be treated in two different ways. Gautama excludes from the Brahmanic law only the issue of a Shudra female by males of the first three orders.[18] It is not clear how he would like to treat the remaining three possible groups. Persons born of unions in the inverse order of castes—technically known as the 'pratiloma' (reverse) castes—are, of course, outside the pale of the sacred law, with the possible exception of one, viz., the 'Suta'.

Among the four varnas, the old distinction of Ārya and Shudra now appears predominantly as Dvija and Shudra, though the old distinction is occasionally mentioned. The first three varnas are called Dvijas (twice-born) because they have to go through the initiation ceremony which is symbolic of rebirth. This privilege is denied to the Shudra who is therefore called 'ekajāti' (once-born).[19] The word 'jāti' which is here used for 'varna', henceforward is employed more often to mean the numerous sub-divisions of a 'varna'. It is also the vernacular term for a 'caste'. A rigorous demarcation of meaning between 'varna' and 'jāti', the former denoting the four large classes and the latter only their sub-divisions, cannot, however, be maintained. The word is sometimes indiscriminately used for 'varna'.

This period sees a great consolidation of the position of the Brahmin class, while the degradation of the Shudras comes out in marked contrast to the growing superiority of the Brahmins. The discomfiture of the Kshatriyas is complete, and the Vaishyas, at least the general mass, have progressively approximated to the Shudras. The first indication of the appreciation of the Brahmin's position is to be found in the implication underlying the sacred law that in strictness its dictates are meant primarily for the Brahmins. Vasishtha quotes some Vedic texts to inculcate the view that a Brahmin is born with three debts, viz., to the gods, to the manes, and to the sages. The discharge of these debts was to be achieved through sacrifices, progeny, and Vedic studies. These are fulfilled through the life of a student and of a householder. According to the philosophy of life current in this period, these debts should have been common to the Kshatriya and the Vaishya, yet it is only the Brahmin that is singled out as pre-eminently the one varna on whom the discharge of these debts was incumbent. The three lower castes are ordered to live according to the teaching of the Brahmin, who shall declare their duties, while the king is exhorted to regulate their conduct accordingly.[20]

The importance of sacrifices and ritualism had been growing and with it the prestige of the priest. The privilege of officiating at sacrificial sessions and other religious rites was exclusively preserved as a divinely appointed and hereditary function of the Brahmins. As the monopolist of ritual procedure, the Brahmin naturally became important. In another way also, he gained in respect because he fulfilled a very fundamental function in the general philosophy of life of these times. As the *Mahābhārata* has it, "sacrifice sustains both the manes and the gods",[21] and the Brahmin alone could ensure the proper performance of sacrifices. He was further represented as very beneficial to the political head of the society. Vasishtha quotes a Vedic text, declaring that the king obtains the sixth part of the merit which Brahmins accumulate by means of their sacrifices and good work.[22] Gifts had been praised since the Vedic times, and in the literature of this period, they were enjoined as a moral duty, the performance of which brought merit to the giver. "He who, placing on the skin of a black antelope, sesamum, gold, honey, and butter, gives it to a Brahmin overcomes all sin."[23] Āpastamba declares that a king, who without prejudice to his servants gives land and money to deserving Brahmins, gains endless heavenly worlds. The Brahmin alone could rightfully accept the gifts. As a channel of easy acquisition of merit he thus gained added importance. "The offering made through the mouth of a Brahmin, which is neither split nor causes pain (to sentient creature) nor assails him (who makes it), is far more excellent than an agnihotra."[24] All these circumstances and the growing unintelligibility of the scriptural language conspired to make the Brahmin almost a god on earth. The preeminence of the Brahmin was so great that the *Mahābhārata* declared that really speaking there was only one 'varna', viz., the Brahmin and the other varnas were merely its modifications.[25] Though Gautama quotes the Vedic texts which declare that the Kshatriyas assisted by the Brahmins prosper, and that the union of the two alone upholds the moral order, yet he lays down that when a king and a Brahmin pass along the same road the road belongs to the Brahmin and not to the king.[26] Vasishtha declares that the Brahmin's King is Soma.[27] The *Mahābhārata* goes even further, and emphasizes the subordinate position of the Kshatriya, whose only support is pronounced to be the Brahmin. It explains away earthly sovereignty of the Kshatriya by a social analogy. Just as a widow takes to her deceased husband's brother, so has the earth resorted to the Kshatriya in default of the Brahmin. Between a hundred year old Kshatriya and a ten year old Brahmin the latter is said to be like father.[28] And this in a society where age was the greatest consideration for respect.[29] The superiority of a child-Brahmin over an aged Kshatriya is also supported by Āpastamba.[30] It is thus clear that the union of the Brahmin and the Kshatriya that was advocated by Gautama must be understood to mean not an alliance between two equals but a tacit domination of the former over the latter.

This pre-eminence of the Brahmin had secured him many social privileges. According to Gautama, all varnas must serve their superiors,[31] which meant that the Brahmin, as the most superior among the varnas, was entitled to the services of the others. Naturally the Brahmin recognized no teacher who was not a member of his varna. It was only in times of distress that he was allowed to study under a non-Brahmin teacher, whom he surpassed in venerability on the completion of his studies.[32] This was against the general notions of respectability according to which the teacher must always be venerated by his pupils. The Brahmin might follow no gainful activity, yet as long as he continued the study of the Vedas, he was said to have fulfilled his purpose.[33] The Brahmin was exempt from the usual taxes.[34] If a Brahmin, who followed his lawful occupation, found a treasure, he had not to hand it over to the king.[35] Both the person and the property of the Brahmin were absolutely inviolate. Stealing the gold of a Brahmin and killing a Brahmin were regarded as heinous sins (mahāpātaka).[36] Raising one's hand or weapon in anger against a Brahmin, actually striking him, causing blood to flow from his body, unintentionally killing him, and wilfully murdering him were offences in the ascending order of their heinousness.[37] Wilful murder of a Brahmin was, of course, inexpiable. The Brahmin was exempt from corporal punishment.[38] The estate of heirless persons of the Kshatriya, Vaishya, and Shudra varnas went to the king, who had to distribute it among learned Brahmins, while the estate of an heirless Brahmin belonged directly to them.[39] The property of a Brahmin is described as the worst poison destroying him who takes it.[40] On the other hand, in order to defray the expenses of a marriage or of a religious rite, he may help himself to the money of a Shudra by fraud or by force. He may do the same with the property of those members of the other varnas who neglect their religious duties.[41] Even to accuse a Brahmin of a crime that he might have committed is a sin.[42] He must not be forced to be a witness at the instance of a non-Brahmin unless he is already mentioned in the plaint.[43] Even as regards the highly lauded and essential duty of a householder, viz. hospitality, the Brahmin has his privileges. He need not treat a non-Brahmin as his guest unless he comes on the occasion of a sacrifice.[44]

Though the various privileges of the Brahmins are sanctioned by the lawgivers, they insist from time to time that the Brahmin shall keep to the moral discipline of his class and conscientiously perform the duties laid down for him. They declare that a Brahmin who deviates from this path is equal to a Shudra and as such there can be no harm in neglecting him.[45]

The statement that God created the Shudra to be the slave of all is repeated and he is given the name 'pādaja' (born from the feet). He is to be supported, to be fed, to be clothed with the remnants and castaways of food and raiment by the three varnas.[46] He is contrasted with the Ārya, who, though younger than he, must be respected by him by rising from his seat.[47] Whereas in the Vedic period, as we have seen, the Dāsa was described as the black race, in this period the Shudra is given that appellation.[48] Vasishtha declares him to be a burial ground. The Veda must not be recited in his presence, no advice must be given to him, nor the remnants of the offerings to the gods. Holy law must not be expounded to him, nor must he be asked to perform a penance.[49] He shall use the old shoes, discarded garments, etc., of the members of the other varnas, and eat the leavings of their food.[50] So great was the feeling against the Shudra performing a sacrifice that Gautama exhorted a person to cast off his father if he either sacrificed with the money given by a Shudra or officiated at his sacrifice.[51] It is well known that in the story of the *Ramayana* Rama is represented to have killed a Shudra who was practising austerities.[52] The Shudra was regarded to be so despicable, that a Brahmin, when, out of sheer necessity, he had to take up the Shudra's occupation, was asked not to mix with them.[53]

It is clear that the Shudra could not perform a sacrifice, could not listen to or recite the Vedic texts, nor could he practise austerities. He was categorically denied the right of initiation and consequently the first stage of individual life (āshrama) the studentship. Out of the other sacraments marriage is the only one, which is explicitly applicable to the Shudras. While laying down their duties Gautama observes: "For him (Shudra) also (are prescribed) truthfulness, meekness, and purity. Some declare that instead of sipping water (the usual method of purification) he shall wash his hands and feet. (He shall also offer) the funeral oblations."[54] Āpastamba opines that the Shudra is not entitled to the rite of initiation, the study of the Vedas, and the kindling of the sacred fire. His works (rites) are declared by implication to be unproductive of rewards either in this world or in the next.[55] According to Gautama, the Shudra, if permitted, may use 'namah' (obeisance) as his 'mantra' (holy incantation). He states that some allow him to offer Pākayajnās[56] (minor sacrifices to be offered in the fire kept at home, as distinguished from major sacrifices offered in the Shrauta or Vedic fire). The *Mahābhārata* also takes the same view of the Shudra's religious duties. A Pākayajna may be offered on his behalf without his being initiated for it. Ample Dakshinā (fees) seems to be a prominent feature of such sacrifices offered by the Shudras, of whom one named Paijavana is said to have given away by thousands.[57] It is apparent from these data that the Shudra had no right to perform any of the important sacraments. As he could not kindle the sacred fire, his marriage was certainly not regarded as a sacrament, intended for the fulfilment of religious duties but only as a sexual union. As the minor sacrifices called the Pākayajnas were to be offered in the domestic sacred fire, and as we have seen above the Shudra had no right to kindle this fire, we cannot attach much significance to the permission given to the Shudra to offer these sacrifices. It only means that the Brahmin was not entirely unwilling to open up certain channels through which fees might flow to him, even though the donor might be a Shudra. It may be mentioned that even the Dasyus were encouraged to offer such sacrifices.[58] The utter indifference shown to the Shudras is further brought out by the fact that out of the eight forms of marriage the two forms recommended for the Shudra are entirely devoid of religious content. In fact, one of them may be termed rape as consummated marriage, and the curious justification offered for this prescription is that the Shudras are not particular about their wives.[59]

I cannot agree with Professor Max Müller when he says that the *Grihya Sutras* never expressly exclude the Shudra from the rite of initiation.[60] The ages at which this rite was to be performed are laid down only for the three classes and not for the Shudra. To me it appears that this is sufficient evidence that the *Grihya Sutras* did not contemplate the initiation of the Shudra. The initiation ceremony opened the door to the study of the Vedas. The Shudra has, throughout, been debarred from that study. He has never been allowed to hear Vedic recitations. How possibly could the *Grihya Sutras*, under these circumstances, even dream of the Shudra being initiated? The fact appears to be that undeserving as he was of this rite, he was simply ignored.

The *Mahābhārata* says that the Shudra can have no absolute property, because his wealth can be appropriated by his master at will.[61] If the master of a Shudra has fallen into distress, the latter shall be placed at the disposal of the poor master.[62] The king is enjoined to appoint only persons of the first three classes over villages and towns for their protection.[63] Shudra trying to hear the Vedic texts shall have his ears filled with molten tin or lac; if he recites the Veda his tongue shall be cut off, and if he remembers it he shall be dismembered. If he assumes a position of equality with twice-born men, either in sitting, conversing, or going along the road, he shall receive corporal punishment.[64] A Shudra, committing adultery with women of the first three castes, shall suffer capital punishment, or shall be burnt alive tied up in straw.[65] If he intentionally reviles twice-born men or criminally assaults them, the limb with which he offends shall be cut off.[66] Āpastamba, too, lays down the same punishment, but only in the case where the assault is directed against a Brahmin.[67] On the other hand, a Shudra can be abused by a Brahmin without entailing any punishment.[68] A Snātaka (a Vedic student) is exhorted not to go on a journey alone in the company of a Shudra.[69] For a Brahmin to eat the food given by a Shudra is a sin that must be expiated; and to avoid taking it is one of the few things the practice of which assures a Brahmin of bliss in heaven.[70] Gautama goes further and forbids a Snātaka to accept water given by a Shudra.[71] Though, as we shall see later on, marriage between a Brahmin male and a Shudra female is contemplated, yet it is said that such a wife is espoused merely for pleasure and not for the fulfilment of a religious purpose.[72] Cohabitation with a Shudra female is a sin, which a Brahmin must wipe out.[73] A Brahmin who marries a Shudra wife and dwells for twelve years in a village, where only well-water is obtainable, becomes equal to a Shudra.[74] A Shudra committing adultery with an Aryan woman shall have his organ cut off and his property confiscated.[75] Altogether so unworthy is the Shudra, that, if he comes as a guest, he shall be fed together with one's servants and that, too, perhaps after getting some work out of him.[76]

The Shudra, thus, had no civil or religious rights. Nevertheless, there are sentiments of compassion about him expressed here and there. A master is exhorted to support his Shudra servant when he is unable to work,[77] and to offer funeral oblation for him in case he dies childless.[78] Rarely, as in one case given by Āpastamba,[79] he is allowed to cook food, even though meant for a religious function, under the supervision of members of the other three classes. This extraordinary tolerance towards the Shudra might have been dictated by the peculiar conditions prevailing in the south during the early migration of the Indo-Aryans.

Though theoretically the position of the Shudras was very low, there is evidence to show that many of them were well-to-do.[80] Some of them succeeded in marrying their daughters in royal families. Sumitra, one of the four wives of king Dasharatha, was a Shudra.[81] Some of them even worked their way up to the throne. The famous Chandragupta is traditionally known to be a Shudra. The Ābhiras who ruled over the Deccan for some time were, according to Patanjali's counting, a caste by themselves not included among the Shudras, though they were not Kshatriyas.

The Vaishya, though traditionally classed with the first two 'varnas', is grouped on many occasions with the Shudras. As we shall see later on, the occupations ordained for these two classes are almost identical. Gain by labour is mentioned as a special mode of acquisition, both for Vaishya and Shudra.[82] Apart from this increasing similarity of occupations, the special occupations of the Vaishya were such that they could not be well defined. "The humblest tender of cows for a master may be of this caste, or the work may be done by one outside the Aryan ranks."[83] The Vaishyas are understood to consist of labourers.[84] Kautilya leaves no doubt as to the equality of occupational status between the two castes. The *Bhagavadgitā* proudly proclaims that its religious doctrines can lead even the Vaishyas and the Shudras to salvation.[85] In this matter these two classes stand in marked contrast to the other two classes. We are led to believe that the Vaishya, in spite of the injunction of the Brahmins that he should fulfil the duties prescribed for him in the sacred law, had so much fallen off that a less rigid and elaborate way of working out one's salvation was necessary for him. Out of the eight forms of marriage, the two prescribed for the Vaishyas are the same as those recommended for the Shudra. According to Vasishtha when a Brahmin marries outside his varna, his sons by a Vaishya and a Shudra wife shall inherit equal shares.[86] Similarly only one common formula of welcome need be used for a Vaishya and a Shudra guest. Both of them are to be fed together with one's servants.[87] In the chaos that is supposed to have ensued after Parashurama had slaughtered the Kshatriyas, we are told that both the Shudras and the Vaishyas discarded the Brahmanic rules of discipline and violated Brahmin females.[88] The moral of this story is clear. The Vaishyas, like the Shudras, were ready, as soon as the strong ruling arm was off, to rebel against the Brahmanic rules of conduct. And the growth of Jainism and Buddhism, particularly their quick appeal to the Vaishyas, fully corroborates this inference.

The theory of the divine origin of the four castes is off and on repeated with special stress on the origin of the Shudra from the feet of the Creator. In the *Mahābhārata* once at least a slightly material change is introduced in this theory, where we are told that the first three castes were created first, and the Shudra created afterwards for serving the others. Evidently this divine origin did not prove as comforting to the lower classes as could be desired in the interests of social order. Salvation of self had come to be the outstanding problem of the philosophy of life. If the performance of religious rites, as laid down by the sacred law, could alone lead to salvation, there was no hope for the Shudra nor even perhaps for the Vaishya, because the former was emphatically forbidden to perform these religious rites and the latter had progressively lost their practice. A philosophy of caste, guaranteeing individual salvation to all, through the performance of duties alone, had to be formulated. Such a theory was calculated to allay the unrest and quell the rebellion against caste that might arise owing to the unsatisfactory nature of the theory as far as salvation, which had become the most absorbing human interest, was concerned. The Buddhistic religion, however much its followers stood by caste was ready to declare that Brahmin, Kshatriya, Vaishya, Shudra, and Chandāla would be all equal in the world of the gods, if they had acted virtuously in this life, and that a person's worth in life was determined by his right conduct and knowledge. The necessity of closing up the ranks against the onslaught of Buddhism and of assuring individual salvation for all led to the formulation of two slightly differing philosophies of caste.

Gautama observes: "Men of the several castes and orders who always live according to their duty enjoy after death the rewards of their works, and by virtue of a remnant of their merit, they are born again in excellent countries, castes, and families endowed with beauty, long life, learning in the Vedas, virtuous conduct, wealth, happiness, and wisdom. Those who act in a contrary manner perish, being born again in various evil conditions."[89] According to Āpastamba, sinful persons are born as low castes and even as animals. A person, for example, who steals a Brahmin's gold will be reborn as a Chandāla if he is a Brahmin, as a Pulkasa if he is a Kshatriya and as a Vaina (a mixed caste) if he is a Vaishya. Men of the lower castes are reborn in higher castes if they have fulfilled their duties, while men of the higher castes are born in the lower ones as a result of their neglect of the prescribed duties.[90] It is clear that according to this law-giver conscientious practice of the duties proper to one's own varna, led to a birth in a higher varna and thus to salvation. Failure to act according to one's varna duties meant birth in a lower caste and finally spiritual annihilation. In the *Mahābhārata*, the upward march from one caste to another in succeeding births till a person is born a Brahmin is described in detail.[91]

In the *Bhagavadgitā* the Creator is said to have apportioned the duties and functions of the four castes according to the inherent qualities and capacities of individuals.[92] Of course, this theory fails to explain how the individuals at the very beginning of creation came to be possessed of peculiar qualities and capacities. This theory of origin, though it slurs over the above difficulty, tries to provide a rational sanction for the manifestly arbitrary divisions. God separated the people into four varnas, not merely because they were created from different limbs of his body nor again out of his will, but because he found them endowed with different qualities and capacities. In so far as a justification is sought to be given for a social phenomenon, which was hitherto taken for granted, the *Bhagavadgitā* records a remarkable change in attitude. In conformity with this the life-philosophy preached in the book furnishes us with the other philosophy of caste referred to above. The whole episode which made the occasion for the enunciation of the new philosophy, the philosophy of duty, ends with the burden that an individual must do the duty proper to his varna. Arjuna, the hero, is dismayed and refuses to fight, and thus to do the duty proper to his Kshatriya varna. The work is a supreme effort to drive home the truth that man must perform the duties to his social state faithfully and truthfully and then salvation shall be his without doubt. No work is bad, impure, or sinful. It is only the way in which work is done that determines its worth. The peculiar way in which all work must be done is the way of dedicating it to God. The philosophy is beautifully illustrated in two episodes of the *Mahābhārata*: the one about Jājali, the trader, and the other about Vyādha, the butcher. We may compare a similar phenomenon from the social history of medieval Europe. R. H. Tawney observes: "The facts of class status and inequality were rationalized in the Middle Ages by a functional theory of society."[93]

This philosophy of caste takes the sting off the institution and thus skilfully stereotypes it. During the later ages, therefore, this theory of caste has been rightly harped upon. The differences between the *Sutra*-theory of caste, detailed above, and this theory is significant. The Brahmin authors of the *Sutras* promised salvation to the Shudra only through the intermediary of births in higher castes. In plain words it was tantamount to asking him to wait till doomsday. The mark of inferiority was permanently impressed on him, and his low status was declared by implication to render it impossible for him to work out his salvation in his own person. The concession granted testifies only to the liberalism of the writers on Dharma. The *Gitā*, on the other hand, disarms opposition on more counts than one. First, it tries to provide a rationale for the original division into four varnas. Secondly, it unequivocally asserts the virtual equality of these divisions as far as the value of their distinct work and their inherent capacity for working out individual salvation are concerned.

We have seen that in the Vedic age Kshatriyas sometimes discharged the priestly functions and preached the higher philosophy. Vishvāmitra is one of those Kshatriyas who, according to later tradition, officiated as a priest. In the *Rigveda*, he and Vasishtha, the Brahmin, are said to have been the priests of king Sudāsa at different times.[94] In the Epic literature, Vasishtha, the Brahmin, and Vishvāmitra, the Kshatriya, figure as opponents in many a story.[95] The principal cause of quarrel between them appears to be the desire of Vishvāmitra to reckon himself a Brahmin. On the one hand, wonderful powers of enabling his royal patrons to lead their sacrifices to a successful finish, are credited to Vishvāmitra and on the other great valour and military skill are attributed to him. Vasishtha is described as a perfectly peaceful and learned Brahmin, able to complete the most difficult sacrifices as well as to meet the most deadly weapons of Vishvāmitra in the characteristic way of the Brahmins, viz, with the help of Brahmanic lustre. Reading these stories one cannot fail to get the idea that in the quarrel of these two individuals is epitomized the history of the rivalry between the first two castes. Though, in the end, Vishvāmitra won Brahminhood, yet Vasishtha is represented as having defeated him on every count, not excepting even his martial skill. It seems to me that these stories were designed to teach a lesson to the Kshatriya that his physical prowess was futile before the spiritual force of the Brahmin. Vishvāmitra is made to remark, "Fie on the Kshatriya's strength. By the single Brahmanic mace all my weapons are destroyed."[96] While the Brahmins of the Vedic age were content with making pious declarations that they were above the power of the king and addressing fervent exhortation that the Kshatriyas should work in union with the Brahmins, those of the later age were emboldened enough to draw a concrete picture of the utter futility of the Kashatriya's weapons against the spiritual prowess of the Brahmin. Though Vishvāmitra becomes a Brahmin in the end, the Kshatriya is crestfallen. His right to act as priest is very hard won. Vishvāmitra is allowed to become a Brahmin on the one condition that he renounces once for all his ways of the Kshatriyas, and through and through resorts to the methods of the Brahmins. No doubt he entered the Brahmin fold, but he could not open up the closed door to his erstwhile associates.

The Brahmins, as if not being content with showing the superiority of Brahmanic lustre over martial prowess, created in Parashurāma, a Brahmin, who overpowered the Kshatriyas not by the usual Brahmanic weapon of spiritual force, but by their own military weapons. Parashurāma is the champion of the Brahmins and avenges his father's murder on the Kshatriyas. He is represented as having destroyed the Kshatriya race in twenty-one campaigns. Though he wrests the control of the earth from the hands of the Kshatriyas, he is not prepared to rule over it. Everywhere chaos ensues, and the need for the strong arm to govern the people is keenly felt. According to one version of the story, on the retirement of Parashurāma some of the Kshatriyas, who had stealthily escaped him, were encouraged to multiply and rule. According to another account, the Kshatriyas of the post-Parashurāma age were all a mixed progeny of Kshatriya females and Brahmin males.[97] Two of the most skilled of the Kshatriya heroes of the *Mahābhārata*, namely, Bhishma and Karna, were reputed to be the most favourite disciples of Parashurāma, the Brahmin teacher of the Kshatriya's art. It is clear that the story of Parashurāma owed its origin—and there are many discrepancies in this story to prove this contention—mainly to the desire of the Brahmins: first, to show that the Brahmin's wrong would not remain unavenged; second, to impress the fact that the Brahmins, if they took to arms, would prove themselves immensely superior to the Kshatriyas in warfare and last, to humiliate the Kshatriyas.

I conclude from my discussion that the Brahmin was, during the period, very strongly entrenched and that he had sufficiently subdued the Kshatriya. Henceforth the Kshatriya as a serious competitor of the Brahmin vanishes from the field. Nevertheless he has been mortified. And it is my contention, that having succumbed in the age-long struggle within the fold, he breaks away and raises the banner of revolt. Both Jainism and Buddhism appear to me to be movements started by Kshatriyas of exceptional ability preaching a new philosophy which were utilized by their immediate followers for asserting the social superiority of the Kshatriyas over the Brahmins. The Brahmin has a fresh cause for grudge. He comes forward as the saviour of the Vedic Brahmanic culture. It is the Brahmin general of the last king of the dynasty of Ashoka that murders his king and proclaims himself the ruler. His family, the Shungas, not only ruled over a large part but offered stubborn resistance to the invading foreigners. The next dynasty, that of the Kānvas, too, was a Brahmin family. The feeling of wrath is cherished long in the Deccan, where nearly three centuries after the first Shunga revolt a Brahmin king proudly records that not only did he uproot the foreigners but also did he humble the pride of the Kshatriyas.[98]

Whatever be the express statements about caste in the original preachings of Mahāvira and Buddha, a close student of the early literature of these religious movements will feel convinced that the chief social aim of the writers was the assertion of the pre-eminence of the Kshatriyas. It is a well-known fact that no Jain Tirthamkara was ever born in any but a Kshatriya family. In Buddhist literature there are several examples where the enumeration of the four castes is headed by the Kshatriya, the Brahmin coming next. Many a time the Kshatriyas aggressively put forward claims for prior recognition over the Brahmins. E. J. Thomas observes: "The claim of the Shākyas to belong to the best caste, that of the warriors, is well-known; and though in the discourses the Brahmins are treated respectfully, their claims are criticized and rejected."[99] To Buddha himself is ascribed the saying that along with the Kshatriyas the Brahmins take precedence over the other castes in the matter of marks of respect to be shown to one's social superiors.[100] A legend tells us that Buddha, in one of his previous incarnations, wavered as to whether he should be reborn as a Brahmin or a Kshatriya and decided in favour of the latter alternative as the Kshatriya class was then regarded as higher than the Brahmin. In one of Buddha's discourses there is a dialogue between Buddha and Ambattha, Brahmin student, in which the latter is represented as having acknowledged the fact that a Kshatriya's son by a Brahmin wife would be recognized as a Brahmin by the Brahmins but not by the Kshatriyas, because the latter accorded equal status only to the full-blooded Kshatriyas.[101] Though the work *Lalitavistara* falls in the third period, some of its traditional statements may be taken as valid for this. According to it Bodhisattvas are not born in low families like those of Chandālas, Rathakāras, Venukāras or Pukkasas. They take birth only in families of the two classes of Brahmins and Kshatriyas. They choose either of the two classes for their birth according as the ruling order of the age prefers a Brahmin teacher or a Kshatriya one. Buddha's age being decidedly the age of Kshatriya teachers, he chose a Kshatriya family.[102]

The express ideas in the Buddhistic literature voice the feeling that caste has nothing to do either with material success in life or with reward after death. High caste is not protected from the effect of wrong doing, and to an ascetic caste ought to be a matter of utter indifference. One of the *Jātaka*-stories ends with the declaration from the Bodhisattva that the virtuous do not ask one about his birth if his piety is well known. A person's worth in life is determined by right conduct and knowledge.[103] Nevertheless, in the various anecdotes about Buddha's former lives an individual's status is regarded as fixed by his conduct and even sometimes by his birth. In a dispute between two youths as to whether a person is a Brahmin by birth or by his action, Buddha is said to have given his decision in favour of the latter alternative.[104] Thus Buddha is represented as being inclined to accept the divisions, basing them only on the individual's actions and not on his birth. That he meant these divisions to be status groups and not mere names is evident from another saying attributed to him, where the highest marks of social respect are claimed for the Kshatriyas and the Brahmins.[105] In actual practice it seems that birth determined an individual's status in society much more than the general remarks lead us to expect. Nay, I am inclined to look upon this theorizing about the futility of caste-ideas as mere exhortations, similar to the theorizing of the Brahmins recorded in the *Upanishads* and the epic literature. Buddha, in one of his former lives, had a child by a courtesan who proposed that the child should be given the name of Buddha's father. Buddha is said to have thus reflected: "A child which is born of a low woman cannot possibly be given the family name."[106] A king was fraudulently made to marry a girl born of a Kshatriya father and a slave mother as if she were a blue-blooded Kshatriya. When the king perceived the deceit practised on him he complained to Buddha, who, while consoling him, observed: "The family of the mother does not matter; the family of the father alone is important." Buddha's attitude as typified in this remark is not radically different from the Brahmanical doctrine. The king evidently does not seem to have been satisfied. He is represented as having divested his low born wife of all queenly honours. It may be interpreted to be the general rule of the times that the daughter of a Kshatriya male and a slave female could not be recognized as a Kshatriya.[107] It is narrated in the introduction to one of the *Jātakas* how a Shākya-chief—the Kshatriya family in which Buddha himself was born—had great scruples about dining in the same plate with, or taking the food brought by his daughter by a slave woman.[108] In this connection it may also be pointed out that, according to later works dealing with Buddha's life, Buddha is never represented to have chosen any but the families of the two higher castes for his previous birth.[109] In the opinion of the great majority of the monks, caste distinction had value even after persons had joined the brotherhood. Buddha does not countenance this view or practice.[110] From these facts we conclude that in the matter of caste-restrictions the preachings and actions of Buddha had only a general liberalizing effect. He does not seem to have started with the idea of abolishing caste-distinctions, nor do his actions, as described in the *Jātaka*-stories, demonstrate an utter indifference towards the accident of birth; much less do they evince any conscious effort to annihilate caste. Fick has rightly observed that it is wrong to look upon Buddha as a social reformer and Buddhism as a revolt against caste.[111] And Sir Charles Eliot has summed up his judgement in the words "though he (Buddha) denied that Brāhmans were superior by birth to others he did not preach against caste."[112]

Whatever might have been Buddha's own views and practice, it is indubitable that his early followers believed in the time-honoured restrictions of caste, and being most probably Kshatriyas themselves, utilized the opportunity, offered by Buddha's revolt, to establish Kshatriya preeminence among the four castes. The complete discomfiture of the Kshatriya within the Brahmanic fold had made this course inevitable. Measuring their strength with the Brahmins and failing in the contest, they naturally turned their attention to the masses. In their appeal to the masses to recognize them as the real leaders of society, they must have availed themselves of the general opinion against the Brahmin and made an excellent use of the art of ridicule in drawing a ludicrous picture of the wide contrast between the Brahmin's professions and his practices.[113] Use of a language, better understood than Sanskrit by the populace, immensely helped them in their cause. It is just because this must have been the probable genesis of Buddhism that the largest bulk of its early followers were Kshatriyas and other well-to-do non-Brahmins who were dissatisfied with their low position within the Brahmanic fold.

References

1. Muir, i, p. 16. 2. Ibid., p. 439. 3. *Vedic Index*, ii, p. 247. 4. Compare *Shatapatha Brahmana*, v, pp. 3, 4, 20. 5. *Chhāndogya Upanishad*, iv, 4. 6. Macdonell and Keith observe: "It is significant that Rājanya is a variant to Kshatriya, and an earlier one" (Vol. I, p. 203). 7. Eggeling's translation, pt. v, p. 326. 8. Eggeling's trans., pt. v, p. 446. 9. Ibid., p. 326.

10. Infra, p. 84. 11. *Vedic Index*, ii, p. 257. Note: The above discussion is principally based on facts collected in the *Vedic Index*. Special attention may be drawn to the articles on Ārya, Brāhmana, Chandāla, Dāsa, Kshatriya, Nishāda, Paulkasa, Shudra, Vaishya, and Varna. 12. Mandlik, p. 432. 13. Vasishtha, p. 4. 14. Gautama, p. 212. 15. Baudhāyana, p. 236. 16. Ibid., p. 277. 17. Baudhāyana, p. 220. 18. Gautama, p. 197. 19. Vasishtha, p. 9.

20. Vasishtha, pp. 7, 8, 56. 21. *Mahābhārata, Shānti Parva*, 23–5, 72. 22. Vasishtha, p. 8. 23. Vasishtha, p. 135. 24. Vasishtha, p. 139. The agnihotra has been the most fundamental and important ritual function that was enjoined on the first three castes since early Vedic times. 25. *Mahābhārata, Shānti Parva*, 50, 59. 26. Gautama, p. 235. Āpastamba, pp. 124–5. 27 Vasishtha, p. 8. 28. *Mahābhārata, Anushāsana*, 12, 21–3. 29. Gautama, p. 208.

30. Āpastamba, p. 53. 31. Gautama, p. 231. 32. Ibid., p. 209. 33. *Mahābhārata, Shānti Parva*, 14, 59. 34. Vasishtha, p. 8. 35. Vasishtha, p. 18. 36. Vasishtha, p. 5. 37. Baudhāyana, p. 212; Gautama, p. 279. 38. Gautama, p. 242; Baudhāyana, p. 201. 39. Gautama, p. 305; Baudhāyana, p. 179.

40. Baudhāyana, p. 180. 41. Gautama, p. 270. 42. Gautama, p. 279. 43. Gautama, p. 243. 44. Gautama, pp. 204–5. 45. Vasishtha, pp. 16–18, 46; Baudhāyana, p. 248. 46. *Mahābhārata, Shānti Parva*, 34, verses 31, 34, 36, 38, 59, 310. 47. Gautama, p. 206. 48. Āpastamba, p. 87; Vasishtha, p. 96. 49. Vasishtha, p. 96.

50. Gautama, p. 230. 51. Ibid., p. 274. 52. *Rāmāyana* (Nirnayasagar Ed.), *Uttarakānda*, vii, 4, 76. 53. Gautama, p. 211. 54. p. 230. 55. pp. 1–2. 56. p. 231. 57. *Mahābhārata, Shānti Parva*, 59, 40–2. 58. Ibid. 59. Baudhāyana, p. 207.

60. *A History of Ancient Sanskrit Literature* (Panini Office edition, 1912), p. 106. 61. *Mahābhārata, Shānti Parva*, 39, 59. 62. Gautama, p. 231. 63. Āpastamba, pp. 161–2. 64. Āpastamba, p. 165; Gautama, p. 236. 65. Āpastamba, p. 165; Vasishtha, pp. 109–10; Baudhāyana, p. 233. 66. Gautama, p. 236. 67. Āpastamba, p. 165. 68. Gautama, p. 237. 69. Baudhāyana, pp. 217, 243.

70. Baudhāyana, pp. 224, 313. 71. Gautama, p. 76. 72. Vasishtha, p. 96. 73. Baudhāyana, p. 313; Āpastamba, p. 84. 74. Baudhāyana, p. 244. 75. Gautama, p. 236. 76. Gautama, pp. 204–5; Baudhāyana, p. 239. 77. Gautama, p. 230. 78. *Mahābhārata, Shānti Parva*, 59, 38. 79. Āpastamba, p. 103.

80. Compare the allusion to Paijavana and other wealthy Shudras in the *Mahābhārata*. 81. loc. cit., I, 2, 72. 82. Gautama, p. 229. 83. *JAOS*., vol. xiii, p. 82. 84. Ibid., p. 83. 85. *Bhagavadgitā,* ix, 32–3. 86. p. 89. 87. Gautama, pp. 204, 205. 88. *Mahabharata, Shanti Parva*, 48, 70. 89. p. 235.

90. pp. 102–3, 125. 91. *Mahābhārata, Anushāsana Parva*, 4, 6. 92. *Bhagavadgitā*, iv, 13. 93. *Religion and the Rise of Capitalism*, p. 22. 94. Muir, vol. i, p. 375. 95. Ibid. 96. *Rāmāyana* (Nirnaysagar Edn.), 56, 23. 97. Muir, i, p. 452. 98. Sarkar, p. 199. 99. Fick, pp. 17–19, 81–7; also vide Fausboll's translation of *Sutta-Nipāta*, pp. 23, 52, 75, 192; op. cit., p. 174.

100. Fick, p. 209. 101. *Ambattha-sutta, Dīghanikāya*, No. 3. 102. *Lalitavistara* (Lefmann's ed.), p. 20. 103. Fick, pp. 19–20, 28, 30. 104. Fick, pp. 220–1. 105. Fick, p. 209. 106. Fick, pp. 20–1. 107. Fick, pp. 56–7. 108. Fick, pp. 45–6. 109. Fick. p. 86.

110. Fick, p. 33. 111. Fick, p. 32. 112. loc. cit. I, XXII. 113. *Sutta-Nipāta* (Fausboll's translation), pp. 46–51. N.B.: The greatest of the exponents of the *Bhagavadgitā*, the saint-poet-philosopher Jnāneshwar, towards the end of the 13th century, expanded the divine theory of caste in appropriate terms in his exposition of BG imagery of this universe as a great banyan tree, with roots above and branches all over. The four varnas or castes are described by him as the side and oblique branches of the main branch of the grand tree, viz., the human species (BG, XV, 2, comment verse no. 156).

4

Caste Through the Ages—II

The post-vedic period testifies to the rigid stratification and internal solidarity of the four varnas. Each group was recognized as distinct, almost complete in itself, for its social life. Among the laws that were valid, provided they did not contradict the sacred precepts, are those of castes. "Cultivators, traders, money-lenders, and artisans have authority to lay down rules for their respective classes."[1] It may be inferred that many of the sub-divisions within each varna—and undoubtedly by now there must have existed in each varna numerous sub-divisions—had rules of their own for their internal management. The word 'jāti' is applied by the great grammarian Patanjali to such ethnic groups as the Ābhīras, whom he declares to be other jati than the Shudra. By implication the Shudras too were a 'jāti'. 'Varna' and 'jāti' would thus appear to be interchangeable terms. It is clear that other groups than the four traditional ones were not only in existence but had come to be recognized as jātis.[2]

The four castes were even supposed to be distinguished by their origin and particular sacraments.[3] When officers were chosen from all castes, their positions were to be so adjusted as not to disturb the caste-order of precedence.[4] A number of major and minor offences are also enumerated as leading to loss of caste.[5] Social intercourse, eating, and intermarriage seem to have been the visible marks of an individual's assimilation in his group.[6] Clearly these groups and sub-divisions must have had each its own internal organization to carry out effectively the avoidance of social intercourse, eating and intermarriage with their defaulting members. Adherence to prescribed duties was neither wholly left to the sweet will of the individual, nor was it only to be enforced by the group. It was the duty of the king to see that the prescribed duties were performed by the proper individuals. If a man always neglected his prescribed duty and did what was forbidden, his property, with the exception of what was required for food and raiment, would be attached till his reformed his ways.[7]

The rules and regulations governing social life and individual conduct differed according to the orders in society, only the four 'varnas' being taken into account by the law-givers. Others, like the mixed castes and outcastes, are mentioned, but their status in the eye of law and morals is not clearly defined. Even the Dharma was apportioned according to 'varna'. The Brahmin was entitled to the practice of the whole of it, the Kshatriya to three-fourths of it, the Vaishya to half, and the Shudra only to a quarter.[8] A Brahmin was to be initiated in his eighth year, a Kshatriya in the eleventh, and a Vaishya in the twelfth.[9] A student, while begging alms, must use different formulae varying with his caste.[10] Of the eight forms of marriage only specific ones are enjoined for each caste. Where water is drunk for purification it must reach the heart, the throat, and the interior of the mouth in the case of the first three orders respectively. In case of the Shudra it need touch only the extremity of the lips.[11] The higher the caste the shorter was the period of impurity to be observed at birth and death.[12] If a man of a lower varna carried the corpse of one of a higher caste or vice versa, the period of impurity was determined by the caste of the deceased. The higher castes had their cremation-grounds in different localities from those of the lower castes.[13] While asking a guest about his health, the terms to be used, according to the caste of the guest, were "kushala" in the case of a Brahmin, "anāmaya" in the case of a Kshatriya, and "ārogya" in that of a Vaishya and a Shudra. A Brahmin must feed his Kshatriya guest after his Brahmin guests have had their meals. Other guests were to be fed together with one's servants.[14] In certain cases where a woman's husband had emigrated, the period of waiting prescribed for her varied according to her caste, being the shortest for a Shudra and the longest for a Brahmin female.[15]

Baudhāyana allows a sane man of any of the four castes to be a competent witness in a legal proceeding.[16] Vasishtha's opinion is less decided. He observes: "Shrotriyas, men of unblemished form, of good character, men who are holy and love truth (are fit to be) witnesses. Or (men of) any (caste) may give evidence regarding (men of) any (other castes). Let him make women witnesses regarding women; for twice-born men, twice-born men of the same caste (shall be witnesses), and good Shudras for Shudras and men of low birth for low caste men."[17] If a Shudra committed theft, he had to pay back eight times the value of the property stolen. In the case of a Vaishya thief, the penalty was doubled. A Kshatriya had to pay twice as much as a Vaishya and a Brahmin four times. If a learned man committed theft, the punishment was very much increased.[18] A man committing adultery with a woman of his caste had to undergo a certain penance.[19] Adultery with a woman of higher caste entailed punishment, the severity of which increased with the caste-status of the woman violated.[20] It seems that illicit intercourse with females of lower castes by males of higher castes was not regarded in the nature of a serious offence. Only adultery with a low-caste woman was condemned as a heinous crime, the punishment for which was either banishment or degradation to the caste of the woman.[21] If a Brahmin killed a Brahmin, he was to be banished from the kingdom with the mark of a headless trunk branded on his forehead; but if a man of any of the other three castes committed the same offence, the punishment was death and confiscation of all his property. For slaying a Kshatriya, a Vaishya and a Shudra the fine was a thousand, a hundred, and ten cows respectively with a bull for the expiation of the sin in each case.[22] Even in the matter of taxation there seems to have been much inequality on the basis of caste. From Buddhist literature we gather that both the Kshatriyas and the Brahmins, though they owned the greater portion of the land, were free from taxes.[23]

The Shudra generally was regarded as so low that his food might not be accepted by the Brahmin. There is one exception to this attitude of the lawgivers, and that is the permission given by Āpastamba for food being prepared by a Shudra under the guidance of the higher varnas.[24] As I have suggested above this relaxation of the usual rule must have been necessitated by the special conditions of South India from which Āpastamba hailed. The same author lays down very strict rules in the matter of acceptance of food by a Brahmin student, who has completed his studies but has not yet entered the life of a householder. In his opinion such a person shall not eat in the houses of people belonging to the three lower castes. He quotes, but evidently does not approve of, the view that he may take food offered by persons of the two castes, next in order, who follow the prescribed rules.[25] Baudhāyana exhorts such a person to beg only uncooked food from the members of the first three castes and from the carpenters[26] (lit. chariot-makers). He enjoins a Brahmin to eschew Shudra's food. A Brahmin observing this rule is said to be the worthiest object of gifts. If the injunction is broken, dreadful consequences will follow both for the recalcitrant individual as well as for his progeny. Recitation of the Veda or offering of sacrifices cannot obliterate the evil effects of such action. A person who dies with a Shudra's food in his stomach will be born again as a pig or a Shudra. If after partaking of such food a Brahmin be so unwise as to have a conjugal intercourse, the offspring will belong to the Shudra, and the Brahmin cannot ascend to heaven.[27] In another passage Vasishtha gives a list of persons whose food must not be eaten. They are the outcaste, the Shudra, the physician, the carpenter, the washerman, the cobbler, etc.[28] Gautama is more strict in his rule, and allows a Brahmin to eat the food, evidently cooked food, given only by such of the twice-born persons as are praised for the proper performance of their duties. But he differs from others in this that he recognizes the claims of some people, who are of the Shudra class, for special treatment. The food offered by a herdsman, a husbandman, an acquaintance of the family, a barber, or a servant may be accepted.[29] A Brahmin may also accept food at the hands of a trader who is not at the same time an artisan,[30] the latter's food being forbidden by Apastamba to a Brahmin student returned home.[31] According to Gautama the food of a carpenter is also taboo to a Brahmin.[32]

The idea that certain persons defile, while others sanctify the company, if they sit down to a meal in one row, is present in the *Sutras*.[33] In this idea may be discerned the origin of the later practice not to dine in the same row with people of other castes than one's own. Apastamba enjoins a Brahmin student, who has returned home, not to eat sitting in the same row with unworthy people.[34]

The idea that an impure person imparts pollution by his touch and even by his near approach to a member of the first three castes finds definite expression in the law-texts of this period, generally with reference to the persons who are outcasted and even specifically in relation to a class of people called Chandālas. According to Gautama a man who is guilty of the crime of killing a Brahmin, must live outside the village, entering it only for alms. When he thus enters the village he must step out of the road on meeting a member of the first three castes and make the way clear for him.[35] On touching a Chandāla or one who has touched a Chandāla one must immediately bathe with one's clothes on.[36] If a Brahmin unintentionally eats the food or accepts the presents given by a Chandāla he is outcast. But if he does so knowingly he becomes equal to a Chandāla.[37] The position of the Chandālas must have been very degraded. A householder is exhorted to throw some food for them and the outcastes along with that for crows and dogs outside the house, after all the members of the household have taken their meals.[38] In marked contrast stands the practice of people about the 2nd century or even the 5th century B.C. For no less a careful student of linguistic usage than Patanjali, while explaining a rule in Panini's grammar, imparts us the valuable information that the Chandālas were considered to be a variety of Shudras, not necessarily the last. That they were not outcast in the sense of having to live outside the limits of town or village is implied; and that they were outcast only as far as the use of their food-vessels by members of the twice-born orders was concerned is explicitly stated. They were the 'apapātra Shudras' or simply 'apapātras', a term later used by Manu, too, about the Chandālas. The vessels used by them for taking their food could not be cleansed by any process to make them fit for use by the twice-born. This definite and clearcut information supplied by the great grammarian writing in about 150 B.C. is impliedly corroborated by the clever administrator Kautilya a few centuries later. The latter forbids the Chandālas follow the custom of the Shudras. By implication one may conclude that the Chandālas were for sometime at least following the customs of the Shudras, because they were actually considered to be a variety of them.

Three of the Dharma Sutra writers have used the term 'apapātra', but in such a manner as to imply that the people designated are different from Shudras and sometimes from the Chandālas. But almost always they are exhorted to be treated like dogs and outcastes.[39] Āpastamba regards it as an offence even to speak to or to look at a Chandāla.[40] The outcastes are to live by themselves as a community, teaching each other and marrying among themselves. Association with them by pure men is prohibited on pain of ex-communication. By association is meant either a matrimonial alliance, officiating at their sacrifice, or even touching them.[41] It seems that the ideas of pollution had progressed further than these examples lead us to believe. Continued use by the Shudras of the water in a well rendered it unfit for religious purposes. This at least seems to be the opinion of Baudhāyana who says that a Brahmin, who marries a Shudra wife and dwells in a village where only well-water is available, becomes equal to a Shudra.[42] There are many stories in the *Jātakas*, illustrating the scrupulous avoidance of the proximity of persons belonging to a despised or even a very low caste. The fear of pollution was not entirely confined to the Brahmins, but sensitive females like the daughter of a merchant in the story showed it in an excessive degree. The impurity of a person could also be imparted to objects touched by him.[43] The Chandālas lived outside the town in a hamlet of their own, and it seems that the other low castes, mentioned together with them, like Pukkasa, Rathakāra, Nishāda, did likewise.[44]

The ideal theory of castes laid down certain duties as common to all of them and some as specific to each. Out of these some were prescribed as the authorized modes of gaining livelihood, and were generally peculiar to each caste and ordinarily forbidden to the others. The Brahmin must subsist on teaching and officiating as priest at the sacrifices of the castes that were entitled to offer such religious worship and by accepting gifts. The Kshatriya was to live by administration and the profession of arms. Agriculture, trade, and pastoral pursuits were to be exploited by the Vaishya, while the one occupation prescribed for the Shudra was service of the other castes.[45] In times of distress one might follow the occupation peculiar to the lower orders, but never that of the higher, and preferably the one prescribed for the caste next in status to one's own.[46] Gautama is more lenient than other lawgivers and allows a Brahmin to take to agriculture and trade as lawful occupations, provided he employs servants to carry on the actual business and does not do the work himself.[47] That the Brahmins engaged themselves in occupations other than the lawful ones, either out of necessity or even ordinarily, is clear from the injunction not to entertain at a Shrāddha-dinner Brahmins who follow the profession of Kshatriyas, or live by trade or by handicrafts.[48] When a Brahmin practises trade he is enjoined to abstain from dealing in certain articles. If he engages in agriculture, he must not yoke to his plough bullocks whose noses are pierced, nor must he plough after breakfast.[49] A few occupations like that of the carpenter, the charioteer, and the bard are assigned to some of the mixed castes that are described as the result of mesalliance between the four castes. It will be noticed that the theory of occupations as proper pursuits of specific castes does not accommodate the artisans. It is not that there were no artisans in the society but that their status does not seem to have been definitized. Indeed, Gautama distinguishes the artisans from those who live by personal labour, the latter expression being understood by the commentator to denote labourers like carriers.[50] Nay, crafts were so much advanced that pure artisans, who did not deal in their handiworks, were distinguished from artisan-traders.[51] That even members of the Kshatriya caste did engage in agriculture and other pursuits, not proper for their class, is proved by the Kambojas and Saurāshtras, who, though they are described as corporations of warriors, lived by agriculture and trade as much as by the profession of arms.[52] In view of the later degradation of the artisans it is to be noted that Kautilya already describes them as of naturally impure character.[53]

In the Buddhistic literature many of the occupations are represented as having been hereditary and some of the classes like that of the Brahmin and the Gahapati, the representative of the Vaishya, had definitely come to be regarded as such rigid castes that, though their members followed other occupations than those customary for their classes, they remained the members of their castes.[54] The *Jātakas* mention villages each of which consisted wholly of the followers of one occupation. Thus there were smiths' villages and potters' villages.[55] Some of the crafts are spoken of as low, e.g., that of the barber, who is also referred to as of inferior caste.[56] Though the Buddhistic evidence as regards the actual professions taken up by the contemporary Brahmins must be taken with some discount—it was but natural for the Buddhist writers to hold up to ridicule their opponents by depicting them as violators of their own precepts—yet it must be pointed out that the cultivating and cattle-rearing Brahmin is an oft-recurring figure in the Pāli texts and once even a Brahmin carpenter is mentioned.[57]

Though the orthodox theory of caste is stated in terms of only the broad categories of occupations, yet there are enough indications that in daily life further distinctions based on specialization were recognized. Traders and craftsmen are mentioned in specific relation to their special merchandise and craft. Giving directions for laying out the plan of the environs of the royal palace within the fort, Kautilya enjoins the localization of trades and crafts in various quarters; and in this connection he mentions, as separate groups, dealers in grain, purveyors of liquids, dealers in cooked rice, those who sell flesh, manufacturers of cotton threads, workers in bamboo, workers in hides, makers of gloves, ironsmiths and artisans working in precious stones.[58] From the evidence of the *Jātaka* literature,[59] we may conclude that these specific occupations were hereditary in this period, though the Brahmanic theory of castes referred only to the larger categories. The *Jātakas* further bear testimony to the then incipient practice of naming sub-divisions of artisans on the basis of differences in the methods employed in carrying on the craft. Thus the fishermen who used nets and baskets were called 'Kevattas' in contradistinction to 'Bālistikas' who were angling fishermen.[60]

The lawgivers look upon marriage in one's own caste among the four orders as the most ideal and in a way the only sanctified practice, though they are prepared to recognize marriages outside the caste as perfectly lawful. Vasishtha and Gautama exhort a person about to enter on the life of a householder, to marry a female of one's own caste and the latter opines that it is only the virtuous sons, born of wives of equal caste, who are married in accordance with the approved rites, that sanctify their fathers' family.[61] Baudhāyana recognizes only the son by a wife of equal caste as a 'sapinda', sons by wives of other castes being not so reckoned.[62] But, probably in conformity with the practice of their day, these lawgivers allowed males of higher castes to marry females of lower castes, though they refused to allow the issue of such marriages equal rights with the sons of equal marriages. In the matter of inheritance, for example, the share of a son in his patrimony varied according to the caste-status of his mother.[63] The offspring of such unequal unions are said to belong neither to the caste of the father nor to that of the mother but are relegated to separate classes, called the intermediate castes. The names of these castes as given by Gautama do not correspond to those given by Baudhāyana except in the case of the issue of the marriage of a Brahmin male and a Shudra female.[64] In the case of the first three castes Baudhāyana declares that the offspring of a male of the higher caste and a female of the next lower caste are 'savarnas' or of equal caste. Consistently he gives the name of the issue of the marriage of a Brahmin with a Kshatriya female as a Brahmin, and that of the union of a Kshatriya male and a Vaishya female as a Kshatriya. This seems to represent the old practice, when marriages between males of higher castes and females of castes next in order were regarded as perfectly regular and entailed no disqualification in the issue. For even Gautama calls the issue of the union of a Brahmin male and a Kshatriya female 'savarna', though refusing to give a similar name to the progeny of a Kshatriya male and Vaishya female. Kautilya's nomenclature of the mixed castes agrees with that of Baudhāyana except in the case of the issue of a Vaishya male and a Shudra female. But he designates the children of the unions of males of the Brahmin and Kshatriya castes and females of the Kshatriya and Vaishya castes respectively as 'savarnas', and does not explicitly speak of them as Brahmins and Kshatriyas.

That restriction on such marriages was being newly put during this period is rendered probable by the fact that the rule clearly enunciated in the works of the next period, viz., that only a wife of equal caste can be a full and lawful participant in the religious ceremonies of her husband, does not find its counterpart in the legal literature of this period. The lawgivers, as we shall note below, disquality for religious rites only a Shudra wife. Nay, we have reason to believe that the still older practice contemplated unrestricted marriages of the males of the two highest castes with females of the two lower castes—Kshatriya and Vaishya. It is said in the *Mahābhārata* that the sons of a Brahmin born of wives of the first three castes are Brahmins.[65]

We may conclude that in olden days Brahmins could marry females from any of the first three castes and Kshatriyas from their own and from among the Vaishyas without any stigma. The lawgivers of this period restricted this custom. While some of them recognized marriages of males of higher castes with females of the next lower caste as unobjectionable, others confined this attitude to the marriage of a Brahmin with a Kshatriya female and regarded the marriage of a Brahmin or a Kshatriya with a Vaishya female as outlandish. This view of marriage with a Vaishya female might have been due to the progressive assimilation of the Vaishya caste to the Shudras.

Marriage with a Shudra female, though theoretically, allowed for all the castes, is discountenanced in many practical ways. First, even Baudhāyana, who looks with no disfavour on the marriage of a male of a higher caste with a female of the next lower caste, does not concede the social status of its father to the child of a Vaishya by a Shudra female. He calls it Rathakāra. Vasishtha expressly forbids any of the first three castes to marry a Shudra female. Such a union according to him leads to the degradation of the family in this life and to loss of heavenly bliss in the next.[66] He forbids a householder, who has built the fire-altar for a Shrauta sacrifice, to approach a Shudra wife, for she is meant for pleasure and not for the fulfilment of the sacred duties. He quotes an opinion that the issue of a Brahmin male and a Shudra female is as impure as a corpse.[67] Gautama places the claims of such offspring on a par with the rights of persons that are the issue of marriages between lower caste males and females of the higher castes because both of them are outside the pale of the sacred law.[68] Thus the lawgivers definitely set their face against the marriages of men of the first three castes with Shudra females. This is the first pronounced restriction on marriage of the nature of endogamy in Hindu society.

The unions of males of lower castes with females of higher castes are contemplated and specifically treated. Yet they are not at all countenanced. As a matter of fact, they are not marriages at all. The progeny of such unions is declared to be without the pale of the sacred law,[69] though the names of the different groups formed by them according to the difference in the caste of the father and the mother are given.[70] Such unions are so despised that their offspring, though their actual parentage may be unknown, are held capable of being singled out, because such persons certainly are destitute of virtue and good conduct.[71] Chandāla—the untouchable and unapproachable class of this period—is represented as the issue of the union of a Shudra male with a Brahmin female.

The fresh groups, formed by the offspring of the unions of males of higher castes with females of the second lower castes, and those resulting from their unions, may intermarry and give rise to other castes. But these last mentioned mixed castes must marry among themselves.[72]

It seems reasonable to conclude that endogamy was being sought to be rigorously prescribed and was followed to a large extent, and that the writers were at great pains to explain the origin of so many different castes, which had sprung up either by miscegenation, local segregation, occupational specialization, or tribal incorporation, because the orthodox theory mentioned only four castes.

Fick summarizes the evidence of the *Jātakas* thus: "Marriage within one's own 'jāti' (caste) was the rule. Everywhere in the *Jātakas* we meet with the effort to keep the family pure through marriage confined to people of one's own standing and profession, and not to allow it to degenerate through mixture with lower elements. When the parents desire to marry their son, they seek a maiden of the same caste for him." Yet there are instances in the *Jātakas* where the barriers of caste against intermarriage are surmounted. Endogamy was rather a universal custom than a rigid rule of caste.[73]

Gautama is the one amongst the lawgivers who recognizes the possibility of a change of caste, which can only come about by marriage.[74] If a Brahmin male married a Vaishya female the progeny formed a separate caste. If a girl of this caste was married to a Brahmin male, and if their daughter again was married in the same way, and if such unions were continued for five or seven generations from the girl of the original mixed stock then the issue would be regarded as Brahmins. Evidently only the progeny through a female could thus be raised to a higher caste. The male issue of such mixed marriages could marry either among themselves or in the caste of their mother. The progeny in the fifth or the seventh generation, if the males continued to marry in the caste of their mother, was reduced to the caste of the female of the original mixed stock. Suitable marriages, continued through generations, alone could effect a change in caste. That this elaborate rule should have led to any practical results is more than doubtful.

The epics contain some examples of intercaste marriages, but they illustrate the practice prevailing among the aristocracy and the sages. We will leave out the sages as their stories are shrouded in much mystic lore. As for the aristocracy we have already mentioned that Dasharatha had a Shudra female as one of his wives. But the *Ramayana* does not drop any hint that the children of the union were regarded as in any way different from the Kshatriya. Shantanu married Satyavati, the daughter of a fisherman. In the story of the *Mahabharata*, no suggestion is made that the issue would be considered lower than the Kshatriyas. The girl's father extorts a promise from the king that the son of Satyavati by him shall be the heir to the throne to the exclusion of his other son, not because he feared that the status of the son of his daughter would debar him from his right to the throne, but because the other son of the king, being the eldest, would be entitled to it. As a matter of fact, the Kauravas and the Pāndavas, the heroes of the *Mahābhārata*, are represented as the descendants of the line of Satyavati. Though the Kshatriyas were willing to marry females of lower castes and bring up the progeny as their equals, yet they could not tolerate their daughters marrying men of faulty descent. Thus Draupadi at her choice-marriage raised an objection against Karna on the ground of his low birth.

Apropos of this treatment of the Shudras the information regarding the various classes of Shudras furnished by the grammarian Patanjali is very significant. There were recognized at least five varieties of Shudras. First, there were the Shakas and the Yavanas who resided outside Āryāvarta, the home of the Āryas. Second, there were the Chandālas and the Doms, who resided within the limits of towns and villages of the Āryas but whose foodvessels could not be used by the latter even after purification. Third, there were groups like the carpenters, the washermen, the blacksmiths and the weavers, whose foodvessels could be used by the Aryas after appropriate cleansing but who could not be permitted to attend sacrificial sessions and rituals. Fourth, by implication there were the Shudras, the specific illustrative groups being not named by Patanjali who could attend even sacrificial sessions and rituals. Fifth, there were those who lived beyond the limits of Āryan villages and towns.[75]

The third period of Indian history, as I have conceived the periods, is marked by two developments in the ideals of the Hindu Dharma, which had an important bearing on the theory and practice of caste.[76] The glorification of gifts to Brahmins, which became so absorbing a feature of later Hinduism, was largely the contribution of this age. True it is that certain hymns in the *Rigveda* praise the giving of gifts, and are known as 'Dāna-Stutis', but they remained outside the main currents of the Upanishadic age, which was seething with philosophical discussions. Nor are they so definitive in their tone as the dictum of Manu that gifts alone—and by gifts Manu unequivocally means gifts to Brahmins—is the supreme duty of man in the Kali age.[77] Another noteworthy development is the schematic growth of imaginary hells as punishments for certain offenders and the progressive application of the doctrine of rebirth. Penances have been always ordained for specific breaches of sacred rules. If these are not performed by the offenders, then the picture of torments in hell is held before the sinners. The dread of these imaginary hells was a new and perhaps a more effective method of seeing that penances were scrupulously performed. Unhesitating faith in the penances naturally adds to the importance of the Brahmins. The theory of rebirth is sought to be skilfully employed as a sanction for certain rules of conduct. The perpetrator of a particular offence, it is declared, will be born in such and such a low station. The murderer of a Brahmin will be reborn not as man but only as some beast. Those who relinquish without necessity their divinely ordained occupations will become the servants of the Dasyus. A Shudra who has fallen from his duty becomes an evil spirit feeding on moths.[78] Dread of horrible future births must have helped to uphold the proper practice of at least some of the rules connected with caste. The total result of the pronounced developments of these tendencies in this period is to be seen in the preposterous claims put forward in favour of the Brahmins.

According to Manu the Brahmin is the lord of this whole creation, because he is produced from the purest part of the Supreme Being, namely the mouth. Both the gods and manes have to receive their offerings through them. They are, therefore, the most exalted amongst men, so much so that, by his mere birth as a Brahmin, a person is the living embodiment of the eternal law. The function that fire performed in Vedic worship is now discharged by the Brahmin. He replaces, so to say, fire as an intermediary between man and the gods. A Brahmin alone can become one with Brahman for only he of all the varnas is entitled to enter the fourth stage of life, viz. asceticism. Feeding the Brahmins is one of the acknowledged ways of gaining religious merit.[79] Inscriptions of this period testify to the fact that this was not a mere pious wish of the Brahmins, but a living reality acted up to by contemporary men and women.[80] A Brahmin is entitled to whatever exists in the world. In fact, the whole world is his property, and others live on his charity.[81] So sacred are they that not to wait on them is one of the causes leading to the degradation of the Kshatriyas. In purity they are compared with fire and water, the two pre-eminently purifying agents. Whatever forbidden acts they do in adversity do not, therefore, contaminate them.[82] Vishnu is more audacious than Manu in asserting the worth of the Brahmins. He is not satisfied with claiming that they are intermediaries between man and the gods, but would like to enthrone them as the equals of gods, nay even as their master. He observes: "The gods are invisible deities, the Brahmins are visible deities, The Brahmins sustain the world. It is by the favour of the Brahmins that the gods reside in the heavens; a speech uttered by Brahmins (whether a curse or a benediction) never fails to come true. What the Brahmins pronounce, when highly pleased, (if they promise sons, cattle, wealth, or some other boon to a man) the gods will ratify; when the visible gods are pleased the invisible gods are surely pleased as well."[83] Even the level-headed administrator Kautilya suggested that in order to avert such providential calamities as fire, flood, and pestilence, the people should worship gods and Brahmins.[84]

Naturally many are the privileges that are claimed for the Brahmin. Kautilya exempted him from torture to elicit confession and from corporal punishment except it be for high treason.[85] While in the last period it was only the Shudra who was enjoined to serve the varnas and particularly the Brahmin, now all the three varnas are exhorted to serve the Brahmin, the theory being that each lower caste owes subservience to all the higher castes.[86] Nārada exhorts a king to be constantly showing honour to the Brahmins for "a field furnished with Brahmins is the root of the prosperity of the world." The king must show himself first in the morning to the Brahmins and salute them. To them belongs the right to collect flowers and such other things, to converse with other men's wives without any restraint, and to cross rivers without paying any fare for the ferry. If engaged in trade, they may use the ferry without paying any toll.[87] Yet with all his exaltation a Brahmin is exhorted to follow the rules of conduct laid down for him lest he should miss the fruit of his Vedic studies. And the old saying, applauding the union of the Brahmin and the Kshatriya, is glibly paraded forth.[88]

The Shudra gets socially more degraded, though ways and means are discovered for his religious emancipation. In the latter connection, the later division into 'sat' and 'asat'—good and bad—Shudras first makes its appearance. And the rules regarding social and moral life, evincing greater degradation of the class, must evidently have been devised for the use of the latter class, viz. the 'asat' Shudras. Servitude is proclaimed to be a permanent condition of a Shudra, whether he be actually bought or not. A Shudra must not acquire wealth, because thereby he causes pain to the Brahmins. Manu roundly declares that a Shudra cannot commit an offence causing loss of his caste, so degraded was he.[89] Where some kinds of spirituous liquors are forbidden to the members of the twice-born castes, the Shudra is left to himself.[90] Evidently the Shudra was regarded beyond the pale of moral influence. The Brahmin did not even condescend to expect of him an adherence to his high moral precepts. A householder, when sipping water for personal purification, must not use it if brought by a Shudra. A member of the first three castes must not travel in the company of Shudras. It seems that the Shudras were considered to impart some sort of defilement to objects like bed and seat by their touch.[91] According to Kautilya, a Shudra calling himself a Brahmin shall have his eyes destroyed by poison or shall pay the heavy fine of eight hundred 'panas'. If he violates a Brahmin female he shall be burnt to death. If he intentionally reviles or criminally assaults a Brahmin the offending limb shall be cut.[92]

In the sphere of religion the tendency is to forbid to the Shudra the use of the most efficacious formulae and rites on the one hand, and to exhort him to perform most of the daily rites and the obligatory sacraments prescribed for the other castes. The doctrine of salvation through the conscientious discharge of the duties proper to caste is, indeed, mentioned here and there. But evidently the Brahmin lawgivers of this period did not feel fully satisfied with that method of salvation. They had come to possess too much faith in the efficacy of the rites and sacraments to allow them to be neglected even by the Shudra. The liberalizing influence of the Buddhist revolt and of Vaishnava compassion led the Brahmins to devise ways and means of assuring spiritual betterment to the Shudra in the Brahmanic way of rites and sacraments. It must also be mentioned that the performance of the Brahmanic rites and sacraments by a large section of the people had a selfish interest for the Brahmin, which he could not have entirely lost sight of. Rites and sacraments require the services of a Brahmin. The Shudra caste—the largest section of the people—was the only one which was denied knowledge. If the Shudras wanted to perform the Brahmanic rites and sacraments they would invariably have to requisition the services of a Brahmin. To allow the Shudra the privilege of these sacred performances was thus to ensure a large clientele for the Brahmin. Yet neither the genuine desire to widen the scope of his religious regulations so as to make it possible for the lowly Shudra to work for his spiritual uplift in the Brahmanic way, nor the selfish motive of procuring mass clientele was strong enough for the Brahmin to override completely his supreme faith in the sanctity of his lore or his high regard for ceremonial purity. He began to make a distinction between the Shudra who behaved properly according to the Brahmin's ideas, and the Shudra who was slovenly enough not to come up to this standard of conduct—the 'sat' and the 'asat' Shudra. Only the former class of Shudras was allowed the privilege of the practice of rites and sacraments though without the use of the Vedic formulae.

Yājnavalkya opines that the usual sacraments are accompanied by the recital of 'mantras' only in the case of the first three castes. The Shudras, by implication, were to perform them without the use of Vedic formulae. They had to use the ordinary formula of "namah" (obeisance). They may offer in the same way the daily sacrifices on the domestic fire and also the annual offering to the manes.[93] According to the *Shukraniti*, a Shudra must perform all the sacred duties incumbent on him with the help of the "namah" formula, which is here explained in the terminology, usual in the next period, as the mantras given in the Purānas.[94] Atri, Laghushankha, and Likhita draw a distinction between the Shudras and the other castes by enjoining the Shudra to undertake only charitable and welfare works and to eschew the Vedic performances.[95] Manu is more rigorous in his refusal of the right of the Shudra to fulfil the sacred law of the Āryas. But even he is prepared to make a concession in the case of those Shudras who are desirous of gaining merit, and exhorts them to initiate the practices of the virtuous.[96] Yājnavalkya also seems to recognize the higher claims of those Shudras whose conduct is proper according to the Brahmanic ideas.[97] Ushanas, Brihadyama, and Laghuvishnu classify the shudra into a 'sat' and 'asat'.[98] The most potent agent for personal purification that the Brahmins have thought of, viz. the liquid made up by the mixture of cow's milk, curds, ghee, urine, and dung is, however, considered so sacred a thing that if a Shudra drinks it, he commits as heinous a sin as a Brahmin who drinks spirituous liquor.[99]

The approximation of the Vaishya to the Shudra, already noticed in the last period, is carried further in this. In the account of the creation of the four castes from the body of the Supreme Being, Manu groups the two castes together as being produced out of that half of the body, which is less sanctified than the other half, above the navel, from which the Brahmin and the Kshatriya are represented to have emerged.[100] While dealing with the question as to who should be treated as his guest by a Brahmin, Manu and Vishnu recommend that a Vaishya and a Shudra guest may be allowed to eat with one's servants, out of compassion.[101] Yājnavalkya prescribes for the Vaishya the same period of death-impurity as the one he recommends for a good Shudra.[102] We have seen that a Brahmin could not generally accept food offered by a Shudra, though he could eat what was given to him by a Vaishya Some writers of this period extend this privilege to the good Shudras, thus putting them on a par with the Vaishyas.[103] According to Kautilya the issue of a Vaishya by a Shudra wife is a Shudra.[104]

Of the castes that are supposed to spring from mixed marriage the offspring of hypergamous unions among the first three castes are allowed by Manu the rites and duties of the twice-born. The other mixed castes, according to him, are entitled only to the religious privileges of the Shudras.[105] Yājnavalkya's view is clearly stated only in the case of the Chandāla, whom he describes as outside the pale of the sacred law.[106] *Shukraniti* strikes a different note, more in consonance with the religious feelings of the later period, when worship through muttering the name of god came to be believed to be the universal and easy method of spiritual uplift. The issue of the mixed marriages of a hypergamous nature, excepting perhaps the offspring of a Brahmin male and a Kshatriya female, are to be treated as Shudras. This view is in marked contrast with that of the Dharma literature, but in perfect conformity with that of the *Arthashāstra* of Kautilya, who lays down that such mixed castes shall take to the occupations and practise the religious rites of the Shudras. Progeny of unions in the inverse order of castes is assigned to a new category, to be met with in the caste-organization of the later period. They are the lowest of the Shudras and must practise their duties for their religious uplift by repeating only the name of god.[107] Thus the 'pratilomas' (offspring of unions of females of higher and males of lower castes) are no doubt outside the pale of the Brahmanic law, as they were in the last period; but the general tendency of liberalizing religious regulations, as we observed, has effected a change in the attitude towards the necessity of spiritual betterment for these groups. And the newer method of religious worship is thrown open to them.

The solidarity of a caste as a unit of social organization is more acknowledged. It is the duty of the king to see that the various castes observe their own rules and regulations, and to bring back the erring members to their path of duty. He has also to differentiate between different castes by appropriate marks of distinction.[108] The king must inquire into the laws of castes before settling disputes. When enacting any law he must see that the proposed law is not at variance with the customs of castes.[109] Jāti or caste had come to be a very important feature of social organization. Both the plaintiff and the defendant in a lawsuit had to register their jāti. Defamation of one's nation or village was punishable with lower amercement than the one for the defamation of one's caste or guild. Kautilya prescribes differential rate of interest for debts according to caste, a Brahmin being charged 2 per cent, a Kshatriya 3, a Vaishya 4 and a Shudra 5 per cent. He lays down the use of four separate formulae for addressing witnesses of the four castes and for swearing them in.[110] Nārada recognizes the right of a member of a caste to succeed to the property of the deceased in case he has no near heirs entitled to succession.[111] Yājnavalkya requires a suitor to mention his caste in his plaint.[112] And that was quite natural in a society where a writer on administration laid down that among persons who might be suspected to be murderers, etc., were those who misstated their caste and 'gotra'. Generally persons of low caste and avocation were to be suspected of such serious crimes.[113] The solidarity of the Brahmin caste is very pronounced. Members of the caste owe certain duties to fellow-members on certain occasions. One of them is that of inviting certain neighbours of the caste to a dinner-party, at which twenty Brahmins are entertained.[114] It appears that specific quarters of towns and cities were occupied by certain castes and occupational groups. Thus Chārudatta, the Brahmin merchant, was living in the quarter of the 'shreshthis' or merchant princes. Bāna, the author of *Harshacharita*, had his residence in the Brahmin-quarters ('Brāhmanādhivāsa').

What constitutes effective association between members of a group is important from the point of view of the development of caste. Vishnu's views on association, though they govern the outcastes and the 'mlechchhas', are very much like the ideas that regulated social intercourse between caste and caste or between the members of a single caste in later times. Sitting on the same bench, riding in the same carriage, lying on the same couch, or eating in the company of a person proves such close relations that if a person happens to be an outcast, the person associating with him in the ways indicated above, becomes himself an outcast after a year. One who habitually drinks water from or bathes in a pool situated in a foreign country reduces himself to the status of the inhabitant of that country.[115] We can clearly recognize in these ideas, once they were applied to social behaviour, the potency to create, in course of time, newer and newer castes.

Food offered by a Shudra is generally forbidden to a Brahmin as in the last period; but with this difference that, in addition to the specifically privileged Shudras, there is the class of the good Shudras whose food may be accepted. The general tenor of the detailed regulations leads me to believe that this permitted food was to be either uncooked or specially prepared in milk or ghee. According to Vishnu, a member of the first three castes has to undergo a penance if he takes food offered by a carpenter, a blacksmith, a goldsmith, a dealer in molasses and other liquids, an oil-presser, a weaver, a dyer of cloth, a cane-worker, or a washerman. The later distinction between food prepared without the addition of water and that in which water is used is mentioned by Atri. He allows a Brahmin to accept from a Shudra anything that is prepared in ghee and articles like milk, buttermilk, curds, etc. Consistently with this distinction in food the same writer forbids a Brahmin to take water from a Shudra. The food offered even by a Kshatriya or a Vaishya was not considered to be perfectly innocuous.[116]

The origin of the later practice for members of different castes not to sit in the same row for taking meals must be discovered in an idea expressed by Angiras. He opines that if, among persons taking their meals sitting in a row, one of them happens to have committed any sin, all the others share it. This possibility of guilt can, however, be evaded by the interposition of doors, posts, ashes, and water.[117]

We have already noticed that Vishnu enjoins the householders of the first three castes not to travel in the company of the Shudras. The reason for this injunction was that probably the Shudra was considered to impart pollution by contact. As a matter of fact, according to the interpretation put by the commentator on another rule, the Shudra's touch defiled objects like vehicles and seats and thus rendered them unfit for use unless water was sprinkled over them.[118] Angiras requires a Brahmin to sip water for purification if he comes in contact with a washerman, a leather-worker, a fisherman, or a cane-worker. Manu declares the Chandālas and others like them to be worthy of being settled outside the town-limits. They were to be treated as 'apapātras', i.e. the vessels used by them were not to be used by other castes.[119] This disability we know to be very old. And Manu's exhortation to keep them on the outskirts marks a further deterioration in their position. Kautilya upholds Manu's position by prescribing that the Chandālas shall live beyond the burial grounds. A simile used by him makes it quite clear that the Chandālas had their own reservoirs of water which the other classes would not use.[120] A Brahmin, drinking water from the vessel of a Chandāla, has to undergo the penance of living on cow's urine for a number of days. Nay, Laghushankha goes even further and prescribes this penance if a Brahmin happens to drink water from a well from which a Chandāla has drawn water. Samvarta's opinion is still more stringent inasmuch as he regards even running water as defiled, if it is used by the 'Antyajas' or outcastes. From Bāna's argument it becomes clear that this was an extreme view. He is definite that fruits offered by a Chandāla could be accepted by others. Even water from the vessel of a Chandāla could be used provided it was first poured out of it on the ground.[121] Much more therefore must running water have been proof against pollution by a Chandāla. Atri declares a washerman, a leather-worker, a cane-worker, a fisherman, and a Bhil to be Antyajas or outcastes. Vedavyāsa adds to this list several other castes. According to Ushanas, the Chandāla was to enter a village for sweeping, etc., in the first half of the day, carrying a broom under his armpit and a small pot hanging at his neck.[122] These regulations remind one of Poona life in the days of the Peshwas, and establish the early existence of unapproachability.

The later theory of pollution by contact and its limits finds its first mention in Vriddhahārita who observes that the effect of contact is limited to three persons, the fourth person if touched being free. A regulation of Atri about touch-pollution fully breathes the later spirit. In sacrificial sessions, in religious and marriage processions, and on all festive occasions there is no question of untouchability.[123] Hemachandra has listed the words 'khikkhiri,' and 'jhanjhari', as non-Sanskritic, meaning a stick carried in their hands by such untouchables as Chandālas and Dumbas in order to warn people of their approach.[124]

The traditional scheme of occupations of the four castes is laid down as usual, but with some modifications, quite in keeping with the changed attitude towards the status of some of these groups. Thus, Yājnavalkya allows a Shudra, in case of necessity, to engage in trade, which was erstwhile regarded as the sole preserve of the Vaishyas.[125] Agriculture, again, in the opinion of some, was a proper occupation for the Shudra. Further, it was more and more regarded as a suitable occupation for all castes.[126] Nevertheless, Manu, as usual, represents the more orthodox view. Remarking that some regard agriculture as an excellent occupation, he contends that it is blameworthy because the plough injures the earth and the living organisms.[127] There are indications that the ideal occupations prescribed for the four castes were not necessarily followed by them. The Brahmins particularly seemed to have taken to many of the occupations that were entirely forbidden to them or allowed only in straitened circumstances. This is the only legitimate inference we can draw from the long lists of unholy Brahmins who must not be invited to a Shrāddha dinner.[128] Chārudatta, a Brahmin by birth, is represented in the play *Mricchakatika* as following the occupation of a Vaishya. It has descended to him from his father's father. In spite of this occupation his Brahmanic conception about ceremonial purity required him to give directions to his friend that the ornaments deposited by the courtezan Vasantasenā should not be taken into the inner quadrangle of the house for fear of polluting the sacrosanct precincts of Brahmin females.[129] That the occupation of the Kshatriya was often usurped by other castes is abundantly clear from the accounts of some of the ruling houses of this period. Harshavardhana of Kanauj, by contemporary account, was a Vaishya,[130] while the Kadamba rulers of Banawasi were Brahmins.[131] A Sanskrit inscription of the middle of the 5th century A.D. discovered at Mandasor in the Gwalior territories of Malwa records how some families of silk-weavers migrating there from Central Gujarat adopted different occupations as chance offered itself, varying from that of an archer and a warrior to that of an astrologer, an exponent of religious doctrines and an ascetic. Another from Indapur (Indore) registers the taking up of the conventional profession of a Vaishya by Kshatriyas. Still another inscription from further west, i.e. from the former Sirohi State, dated A.D. 625, describes a gentleman as "merchant or trader by birth."[132]

We have seen above the reason advanced by Manu why agriculture should be regarded as an unworthy occupation for the Brahmin. In regard to other occupations we do not know the grounds on which the status of an occupation was determined. Yet there is no doubt that there was some defined scheme of status of different occupations which depended not so much on their lucrativeness as on their ceremonial purity. Nārada distinguishes all work as either pure or impure, and mentions the following as impure work: sweeping the gateway, the privy, and the road, rubbing the master's limbs, shampooing the secret parts, and gathering and putting away the leavings of food, ordure, and urine.[133]

There is still permission for the three castes to marry outside their 'varna' excepting from among the Shudras. But a wife of lower 'varna' is declared to be unfit for the performance of religious rites.

The number of new groups, formed by unions between the members of the four castes, and by further intermarriages between these groups and so on, is no longer the limited number that it was in the last period.[134] With all this multiplicity, however, to each group is ascribed some more or less definite occupation. It appears that in reality new occupational groups having the characteristics of castes had arisen, and the Brahmanic account of their origins was a mere theory based on permutations and combinations of the four original castes which bounded the Brahmins' mental horizon.

That intercaste marriages were not absolutely out of vogue even to the end of the period under review is proved by epigraphical and other data. But it seems that except in the case of a Brahmin marrying a Shudra female the issue of such marriages were not singled out for special treatment, proper for a class different from that of the father or the mother. The Imperial Guptas who were Vaishyas had given one of their princesses in marriage to a Vākātaka prince of the Brahmin dynasty of the Deccan. It is recorded by a Chinese traveller that the daughter of King Harsha, who was a Vaishya, was married to a Kshatriya, and it does not appear that the children of the union were regarded as anything else than Kshatriyas.[135] A Jodhpur inscription of the latter half of the ninth century mentions the case of a Brahmin, who had two wives, one of whom was a Kshatriya lady. The children of this lady were classed as Kshatriyas.[136] In the tenth century, Rajashekhara, a Brahmin, took a Chāhamāna lady to wife.[137] An inscription from Bengal, ascribed to the seventh century, describes a certain individual as 'pārashava' and makes him the issue of a Brahmin father and a Shudra mother, which is in conformity with rules of the sacred laws.[138] Bāna in his *Harshacharita*, also tells us that his father, a Brahmin, had a Shudra wife besides a Brahmin one, and describes her issue as his 'pārashava brothers'.

The state of caste-organization as revealed by literature and the inscriptions of the fourth period is strikingly similar to that which we noticed as prevailing about the middle of the nineteenth century. The leading authorities of this period are Parāshara, Mādhava, and Kamalākara. The traditional account of the total extermination of the Kshatriyas by Parashurāma, strengthened by their defection to Buddhism, had already given rise to the theory that the Kshatriya race had ceased to exist with the Nandas. The rout of the older Kshatriya families, caused by the inroads of the Hunas, further lent support to the theory. Finally the rude shock that was given to Hindu sovereignty by the early Muslim conquerors so far convinced the Pandits of the extinction of the Kshatriyas that we find Kamalākara only grudgingly acknowledging their existence as a rare phenomenon.[139] This shadowy existence of the Kshatriyas rendered it unnecessary for the Brahmins, even if they wished it, to curtail their privileges excepting in very few particulars which touched the interests of the Brahmin caste. We, therefore, find the old scheme of four castes mentioned *in toto* in the literature of this period. Yet hypergamy is forbidden in favour of endogamy by Hemādri.[140] The use of spirituous drinks is sinful only for the Brahmin and not for the Kshatriya and the Vaishya as formerly. A Brahmin may take the food prepared either by a Kshatriya or a Vaishya in their own houses only on certain religious occasions, provided these persons have lived according to the sacred law.[141]

We have already noticed the progressive assimilation of the Vaishya with the Shudra, and we find Kamalākara, the latest authority of this period, openly declaring that the Vaishyas are hardly known to exist in the Kali age. In the regulations of this period it is becoming more and more clear that writers on religion treat both the Vaishyas and the Shudras as almost indistinguishable. The occupations prescribed by Parāshara, who is par excellence the mentor of the age, for both of them are the same, viz., agriculture, trade and crafts, with the usual addition of service of the Brahmins in the case of the Shudras.[142] Vaishya's food is almost as much taboo to the Brahmin as that of the Shudra.[143]

In the treatment of the Shudras, it seems that the distinction made in the last period between 'sat' and 'asat' Shudra was acted upon locally in Northern India, and did not appeal to writers on sacred law, hailing from Southern India. To them a Shudra was a Shudra, and as such untouchable, except in name. Mādhava exhorts a Brahmin to avoid living in the same house with a Shudra or accompanying him in a carriage. Nor must he take food ordinarily cooked by him. But food that is prepared in oily substance or in milk may be accepted, provided it is eaten not in the house of the Shudra but on the banks of a river.[144] Hemādri even goes further and impresses upon a Brahmin the sinfulness of eating one's food in a Shudra's house though prepared by oneself with the raw materials supplied by the Shudra.[145] Even the food of the few privileged Shudras that was formerly acceptable to the Brahmin is ruled out by Mādhava as a custom unsuited for the Kali age.[146] So determined has the opposition to the Shudra's food become, that Kamalākara is at pains to explain away ancient texts by all manner of fanciful interpretations.[147]

In the field of religion the Shudra has not only retained the rights that were conceded to him but finds them now evermore well-defined and codified beyond all cavil by Kamalākara, who even upholds his right to the use of the all-purifying mixture, 'panchagavya'.[148] As already observed, this religious emancipation of the Shudra does not by any means put him on an equal footing with the higher castes. Even within the folds of new creeds like devotional Vaishnavism, where, perfect religious equality may, naturally, be expected the Shudra's inferiority is taken for granted and even acted upon. It is precisely because Rāmānanda, one of the apostolic successors of Rāmānuja, the founder of perhaps the most catholic form of Vaishnavism, was insulted by his brethren for his social inferiority that he travelled northwards and established a new sect. He asked his followers not to inquire about anyone's caste.[149]

The religious upheaval in Maharashtra which began about the beginning of the thirteenth century, produced considerable appreciation in the religious position of the Shudra. We have already seen that the Shudra was exhorted to mutter the descriptive names of God for his salvation. This method of spiritual betterment was gradually becoming an integral part of the developing creeds of Shaivism and Vaishnavism. About the beginning of this period or a little earlier, Nāmamāhātmya or the importance of muttering the names of God was freely acknowledged in the Brahmanic works. In the period under review, there flourished in Maharashtra a number of Shudra saints of outstanding personality. They explored and perfected this easy method of salvation for the Shudras. The special method of preaching by means of peripatetic sermons delivered in temples with the accompaniment of some simple music was carried to perfection by two non-Brahmin saints, Nāmdev and Tukaram. The traditional history written by Mahipati in the middle of the eighteenth century makes this quite clear. Further, of the saints who contributed to the new religious forces a large majority was formed by the non-Brahmins. Of the Brahmin saints, many cannot be regarded as being wholly in a direct line of this movement. They still laid much emphasis on the philosophic aspect of religion. Jnāneshwar with his brother and sister and Ekanāth seem to be the outstanding Brahmin saints who had the greatest sympathy with the new doctrine of salvation through the muttering of the names of God. The former were the children of a Brahmin ascetic, returned to the living of a householder and as such much despised by the Brahmins. Ekanāth ventured to feed the untouchables at a Shrāddha-dinner (dinner in honour of the manes) before the invited Brahmins had had their meals. For this sacrilegious act, even though God had performed a miracle in favour of Ekanāth, the local Brahmins insisted on his undergoing a purificatory rite which Ekanāth duly performed. This intrepid Brahmin even dared to dine at a Mahār's house. Almost everywhere the Brahmins figured as opponents of the new movements which appeared to them to upset the good old Brahmanic way of salvation through proper rites and ceremonies and to undermine the system of caste.[150] By their poetic ability, their capacity for religious experience, and by their pure life, these Shudras impressed their contemporaries—irrespective of caste—so much so that they were enthroned as saints and adored by all. These saints of Maharashtra produced a revolution without the uproar of a rebellion. The Shudra, who was accustomed to look upon it as a great privilege to be allowed to practise the Brahmanic rites, though only with the accompaniment of the Puranic mantras, now produced individuals who struck out a new path and established themselves as teachers. And the Brahmin, who was doubtful whether a Shudra was even capable of profiting by his religious teachings, had to accept some of these Shudras as his religious masters. Devotional schools of religious sects produced a more or less similar change in the other parts of India.

These Shudra saints, though they exploited the easy method of salvation and thus freed the Shudras from the Brahmanic domination in their spiritual life, upheld the old order of the four castes including their own status of inferiority in the scheme. There was another contemporary movement which proclaimed a wholesale revolt against caste. It was the sect of the Mānbhāvas.[151] It proved to be an unsuccessful attempt, giving rise to a new caste. The followers of this sect were contemptuously treated and even bitterly hated by all classes of the population.

In Bengal Ramāi opened up the initiation ceremony for the 'thirtysix castes' which like the Dom were denied initiation. When the Sahajiya sect grew into importance in the 17th and 18th centuries its followers declared themselves against caste system and declined to accept the superior position of the Brahmins. If the Sahajiya sect was rather a revolt, Vaishnavism could not be looked upon as such. Yet its attitude to caste was not far different. Srinivāsa, a Brahmin, Rāmachandra, a Vaishya, and Narotam, a Kshatriya were all Vaishnavas and as such were not afraid to take their meals from the same plate.[152]

In the treatment of the outcaste section of the society this period witnesses a development which is in keeping with the ideas of ceremonial purity. Untouchability is graded according to the supposed impurity of the object. A Brahmin should keep a distance of one 'yuga', two, three and four 'yugas' between himself and a degraded person, a woman in her period, a parturient woman, and a Chandāla respectively in order that he may not catch pollution from them.[153]

In the sphere of religion the lot of these people is sought to be improved for the first time in the history of Hinduism. It was Rāmānuja, the Brahmin, who took bold steps for the religious betterment of these people. He secured for them the privilege of visiting the temple one day in the year and devised something which they might put on corresponding to the sacred thread of the Brahmins.[154]

In Maharashtra and other parts of India also the untouchables produced some saints who were not only adored by their own caste but in course of time came to be highly respected by all.

The traditional assignment of occupations to the four castes is very largely modified. We have already noticed that the Vaishyas and the Shudras are given common occupations, viz. trade, agriculture, and crafts. The Brahmin is allowed to live on agriculture provided he employs Shudra labourers to do the actual work. Mādhava candidly observes that it is not possible in the Kali age for the Brahmin to maintain himself on sacrificial fees. The economic aspect seems to have affected the writer to such an extent that he allows all the four varnas to trade and to practise crafts.[155] The ancient profession of the Kshatriyas we find taken up by other castes as well. It is well known that the Peshwa rulers of Poona were Brahmins. The Chera, Chola, and Pāndya kings belonged to the caste of the Vellālas,[156] a cultivating caste of Madras. The Nāyak kings of Madura and Tanjore were Balijas, traders by caste.[157] In some parts even the so-called aborigines ruled over petty principalities. The Gonds provide perhaps the best example.[158] The occupational diversity was far greater than the one contemplated in the old scheme and is frankly recognized both by Mādhava and Kamalākara in their treatment of mixed marriages.

As regards the regulations of marriage, the four castes and the other groups are regarded as completely endogamous units, hypergamy being positively discouraged. The list of groups considered to have been the result of mixed unions becomes very large and includes almost all the groups, occupational or otherwise, known to the authors, as behaving like unit castes. Kamalākara's list, for example, includes such groups as Kolhāti or Bahurupi, Kandu, Sāli, Mochi, Burud, Ghāsi, and others.[159] Mādhava tries to explain the origins only of about sixty groups and characteristically observes, "Innumerable are the caste-like groups that are produced by miscegenation."[160] It is clear that whatever element of reality this theory of the origins of the numerous caste-like groups, besides the four ancient castes, possessed at the outset, by now it was merely a hypothetical explanation of the increasing caste-groups in the society. The Brahmin writers could not rid themselves of the idea of the four original castes. To them numerous further groups could have been only produced as a result of unions between the members of the four castes, just as these latter were created from the body of the Supreme Being. In fact, this is Brahmanical theory of the origins of the numerous castes. Mādhava makes a frank and rare admission that the practices and regulations about the four castes have been changing from age to age.[161]

Caste as a group comprised within a larger class and with no necessary connection with occupation, is contemplated by the commentators and Nibandha-writers of this period. According to them, out of the many tribunals designed for justice one consisted of persons living in the same place following different occupations, and belonging to different castes, while another consisted of people carrying on one type of occupation but belonging to different castes.[162] Nilakantha explains a regulation of Yājnavalkya about witnesses to mean that they shall be according to the castes and 'varna' of the litigants. If the castes of the parties differ, then witnesses belonging to the 'varna' in which the castes are comprised should be called in.[163]

Thus by the end of this period we visualize the caste-organization, as revealed in the literature of the period, to be not at all different in any essential point from the one which I described as prevailing in the middle of the nineteenth century. Perhaps it may be contended that there is not the same multiplicity of groups described in this literature. I have opined that the theory of mixed castes, as expanded by the contemporary writers, marks the numerous groups that had come into existence. Now I propose to present some data from literary records, inscriptions and travellers' accounts bearing on the names and the variety of contemporary groups which corroborate my view.

Hemachandra mentions the Nāgara Brahmins under the appellation Nāgareyaka.[164]

In a Prakrit inscription of an early date of the Brahmanic king Shivaskandavarman of Kānchi are mentioned "Vallave" (herdsman) and "Govallave" (cow-herdsman).[165] In an inscription of the tenth century from Lalitpur district, occur the following names of professions or castes in combination with the proper names of individuals: "Vānika" (merchant), "Nemakavānika" (salt-merchant), "Tāmbulika" (beter-seller) and "Sutradhāra" (carpenter). In the same place is mentioned the shop of a brazier (Kamsāra) and that of a Brahmin betel-seller.[166] In a South Indian inscription the boundaries of a particular piece of land are fixed in reference to the lands of a blacksmith (Karumān),[167] "Vellālan" (cultivator) so-and-so or of such and such locality.[168] Ilavas (toddy-tappers) are referred to in another inscription.[169] In the ancient city of Conjeevaram certain quarters were mostly inhabited by weavers, "who were patronized by the king and consisted of two sections of Pattasālins," which correspond with the identical divisions of the present day Sāliyans (weavers) of Madras.[170] Venkayya has observed that many names of individuals occurring in some of the South Indian inscriptions have as their second portions names of "profession or caste to which the individual belonged, with a complimentary epithet, the whole title meaning, the great dancing master . . . carpenter, goldsmith, brazier, Brāhmana, etc., of the king whose name is prefixed to the title."[171]

A "Gauḍakaraṇika" (writer from the Gauda country) is mentioned in a North Indian inscription of the end of the tenth century.[172] In an inscription from Dharwar district belonging to the eleventh century occurs a clear reference to the division of the non-Brahmin castes of Madras into those of the right hand and those of the left.[173] Another reference to this well-known but not properly understood distinction occurs in a Madras inscription of about the same time.[174] Another inscription mentions some persons who refer to themselves as Shiva-Brāhmanas.[175] Kanmālar (artisans of Madras) are allowed certain rights, which were evidently not enjoyed by them previously. They may blow double conches and drums at their marriages and funerals; they may wear sandals, and cover their houses with plaster.[176] In an inscription from Chingleput district, ascribed to the middle of the twelfth century, a witness to a document refers to himself as "I, the carpenter so-and-so, who possesses the better half of the land of the carpenters in the village".[177] Nāgar Brahmins are mentioned in an inscription from Gujarat belonging to the middle of the twelfth century. An inscription from Orissa, ascribed to the end of the twelfth century, mentions a class of Rādhiya Brahmins.[178] Maga or Shākadvipiya Brahmins were known as such about the same time.[179] Jaina inscriptions from Mount Abu of the first and second quarters of the thirteenth century mention the following castes: Prāgvata, Dhārkatta, Shrimāla, Oswāla, Modha, and also Guguli Brahmins, who are found at present chiefly at Dwarka.[180] Two Maudgala Brahmins are mentioned in one inscription of A.D. 1240 as ministers of one of the Yādava kings. They also served their master in a military capacity.[181] A family of Kayastha race, whose occupation is that of writing, is referred to in a North Indian inscription belonging to the end of the thirteenth century. Some members of this family distinguished themselves as warriors, while one was the governor of a fort.[182] A 'Mochi' (shoemaker) built a temple of Vishnu at Raipur in Madhya Pradesh in about A.D. 1415.[183] In a Sanskrit inscription at Chitorgarh belonging to about A.D. 1429, the composer of the eulogy described himself as the son of one Vishnu Bhatt of the Dashapura caste.[184]

Duarte Barbosa speaks of eighteen castes in Malabar, each with customs and idol-worship of its own. The Brahmins serve the kings in almost any respectable capacity but in arms. Some of them even act as courtiers. Though the main occupation of the Tiyans is that of tapping toddy yet many of them are found as quarrymen, as soldiers, and even as agrestic serfs.[185] Domingos Paes tells us that there were many Brahmins in the service of the King of Vijayanagar as officers of the towns and cities, while others lived by trade or cultivation.[186] Abul Fazal remarks that the Vaishya and the Shudra are divided into numerous branches. He actually mentions the following castes: Kāyasth, Bhār, Bachgoti, Chandel, Chauhān, Gaharwāl, Gautami, Ghelot, Kausik, and Raghubansi evidently as sub-divisions among the Rājputs, Ahir, Lodh, Gujar, Kurmi, Bāgri, Minā, Meo, Mehtar, Bhil, Koli, Gwālia, Garāsiāh, Khāsiā, Bāoriyā, Bisen, Bais, Khand, and Khāri, a division of the Gaud Kāyasths.[187] Moreland rightly summarizes the position of caste at the end of Akbar's reign in the following words: "Among the Hindus the caste system existed substantially as it exists today and the differences among castes and races were such that we find travellers speaking of the Baniyās of Gujarātis as 'nations' distinct from Brāhmans or Rājputs."[188] In the time of Jehangir, the Baniyās of Gujarat had numerous sub-divisions neither of which would eat nor drink with others.[189] Hamilton, in the middle of the eighteenth century, mentions sixty-five divisions of the Baniyās of Surat.[190]

The impact of Islam was too strong to work as a leaven in the Hindu community. The culture and religious practices of its followers were so different that, as noted by Alberuni, the Hindus and the Muslims looked upon each other as contraries and natural enemies. Yet the doctrinal liberalization in the matter of contact and food which we noticed in some movements and even the doings in this line of some of the outstanding personalities of their time must be credited to the influence of Islamic doctrine and practices. The two cultures were too separate to settle down to a great rapprochement in times, when a death-struggle was being fought by the valiant sons of Ind for self-preservation of a cultural entity.

References

1. Gautama, p. 234; also compare *Arthashāstra*, (2), p. 203. 2. *Vyākaranamahābhāshya*, I, 2, 72. 3. Vasishtha, p. 25. 4. *JAOS*, vol. xiii, p. 95. 5. Baudhāyana, pp. 217–18. 6. Cf. Āpastamba, p. 5. 7. Gautama, p. 238. 8. *Mahābhārata Shānti Parva*, 34, 32–3. 9. Baudhāyana, p. 150.

10. Baudhāyana, p. 151; Vasishtha, pp. 56–8. 11. Baudhāyana, p. 167. 12. Vasishtha, p. 29; Gautama, p. 246. 13. Gautama, p. 250; *Arthashāstra*, (1), p. 56. 14. Gautama, pp. 204–5. 15. Vasishtha, p. 92. 16. Baudhāyana, p. 204; Gautama, p. 243. 17. Vasishtha, p. 82. 18. Gautama, p. 237. 19. Baudhāyana, p. 232; Āpastamba, p. 165.

20. Vasishtha, pp. 109–10; cf. *Arthashāstra*, (2), p. 285. 21. *Arthashāstra*, (2), p. 285. 22. Baudhāyana, pp. 201–2; Āpastamba, pp. 18–9; cf. *Arthashāstra*, (2), p. 270. 23. Fick, p. 119. 24. Āpastamba, p. 103. 25. Ibid., pp. 66–7. 26. p. 156. 27. Vasishtha, p. 38. 28. Ibid., p. 69. 29. Gautama, p. 262.

30. Ibid., p. 263. 31. Āpastamba, p. 67. 32. Gautama, p. 264. 33. Vasishtha. p. 19. 34. Āpastamba, p. 61. 35. p. 280. 36. Gautama, p. 250; Baudhāyana, p. 171. 37. Baudhāyana, p. 235. 38. Vasishtha, p. 50. 39. *Vyākaranamahābhāshya*, II, 4, 10; Āpastamba, 1, 7, 21; 1, 5, 16; II, 7, 17; Vasishtha, XX, 16; Baudhāyana, I, 21, 15; II, 2, 13. N.B.: R. G. Bhandarkar first drew attention to the important passage in Patanjali's *Mahābhāshya* in his *Social History of India* in 1901. He commented on it thus: "Patanjali mentions carpenters and blacksmiths as belonging to the Shudra class. The lowest of them, the Chandālas were in the same degraded condition as they are now" (*Collected Works*.), vol. II, p. 450). V. P. Kane in his *History of Dharmashastra*, vol. II—pt. I (1941) observes: "Therefore it follows that Pānini and Patanjali included candālas, and mritapas among Shūdras" (p. 168).

40. p. 103. 41. Baudhāyana, p. 220; Vasishtha, p. 5. 42. p. 244. 43. Fick, pp. 39, 43. 44. Ibid., pp. 318, 323. 45. Vasishtha, p. 11; Gautama, pp. 224–30; Āpastamba, pp. 122–3. 46. Vasishtha, p. 12; Gautama, pp. 209, 211; Baudhāyana, pp. 225–34. 47. P. 225. 48. Apastamba, p. 144; Gautama, p. 255. 49. Vasishtha, pp. 12–13; Baudhāyana, p. 236.

50. Gautama, p. 228. 51. Ibid., p. 263. 52. Ibid., p. 437. 53. Ibid., p. 221. 54. Fick, pp. 180–1, 255, 276, 278. 55. Ibid., p. 280. 56. Ibid., pp. 327–30. 57. Ibid., pp. 241, 246. 58. *Arthashastra*, (2), pp. 58–9. 59. Fick, pp. 276, 278–9.

60. Ibid., p. 302. 61. Vasishtha, p. 42; Gautama, pp. 194, 197. 62. p. 178. 63. Baudhāyana, p. 225. 64. Gautama, pp. 195–6; Baudhāyana, pp. 197–8; cf. *Arthashāstra*, (1), p. 164. 65. C. V. Vaidya, *Epic India*, p. 59. 66. Vasishtha, pp. 5–6. 67. Ibid., pp. 95–6. 68. Gautama, pp. 197, 306. 69. Ibid., p. 197.

70. Baudhāyana, pp. 197–8; Vasishtha, pp. 195–6; cf. *Arthashāstra*, (2), pp. 202–3. 71. Vasishtha, p. 94. 72. cf. *Arthashāstra*, (2), p. 203. 73. Fick, pp. 51–3. 74. pp. 196–7. 75. *Vyākaranamahābhāshya*, II, 4, 10. N.B.: P. V. Kane in his *History of Dharmashāstra* (vol. I, pt. I, p. 121), observes on this passage: "Shudras were divided into numerous sub-castes. But there were two main divisions. One was 'aniravasita shudras' (such as carpenters and blacksmiths) and the other 'niravasita shudras' (like candālas)". 76. Data which are common to the last period and the two succeeding ones are not repeated. Only such details as shed light on the development of the institution are collated. 77. Manu, i, 86. 78. Manu, xii, 54–80; also cf. Yājnavalkya, pp. 1243–58. 79. *Collection of Smritis*, p. 423.

80. R. G. Bhandarkar, *A Peep into the Early History of India*, p. 53. 81. Manu, i, 93–101. 82. Manu, x, 43, 103. 83. Vishnu, p. 77. 84. *Arthashāstra*, (2), p. 419. 85. Ibid., pp. 270, 277. 86. *Collection of Smritis*, p. 122. 87. Nārada, pp. 218–19. 88. Manu, ix, 322. 89. Manu, viii, 413–14; x, 126.

90. Vishnu, pp. 95–6. 91. Vishnu, pp. 198–9. 92. *Arthashāstra*, (2), p. 238, 275–6, 285. 93. Yājnavalkya, pp. 11, 86. 94. *Shukraniti*, p. 163. 95. *Collection of Smritis*, pp. 11, 124, 182. 96. Manu, x, 126–128. 97. Yājnavalkya, p. 1165. 98. *Collection of Smritis*, pp. 48, 101, 122. 99. Vishnu, p. 15; *Collection of Smritis*, p. 23.

100. Manu, i, 92. 101. Manu, iii, 112; Vishnu, p. 216. 102. Yājnavalkya, p. 1165. 103. *Collection of Smritis*, p. 122. 104. *Arthashāstra*, (1), p. 164. 105. Manu, x, 41. 106. Yājnavalkya, p. 67. 107. *Shukraniti*, p. 164; op. cit., (1), p. 165. 108. Yājnavalkya, p. 218; Nārada, p. 215; *Shukraniti*, p. 164. 109. Manu, viii, 41, 46; *Shukraniti*, p. 187.

110. *Arthashāstra*, (1), p. 176; (2), pp. 236–7. 111. *Nārada*, p 201. 112. Yājnavalkya, p. 247. 113. *Arthashāstra*, (2), pp. 105, 183, 260–1, 267. 114. Manu, viii, 392. 115. Vishnu, pp. 133, 255. 116. Vishnu, pp. 163, 164; *Collection of Smritis*, pp. 3, 4, 16, 20, 122, 392. 117. *Collection of Smritis*, p. 5. 118. Vishnu, p. 99. 119. Op. cit. X, 51.

120. *Arthashāstra*, (2), pp. 27, 59. 121. *Kādambari* (N. S. P. Ed.), p. 595. 122. *Collection of Smritis*, pp. 1, 16, 18, 22, 46, 125–6, 357, 421. 123. *Collection of Smritis*, pp. 20, 314. 124. Vide *Deshināmamālā*. 125. Yājnavalkya, p. 85. 126. *Collection of Smritis*, pp. 173, 273; *Shukraniti*, p. 151. 127. Manu, x, 84. 128. Manu, iii, 150–66. 129. *The Little Clay Cart*, translated by A. R. Ryder (1905), pp. 138, 151.

130. Vaidya, vol. i, pp. 61–2. 131. V. A. Smith, *The Oxford History of India*, 1923, p. 199. 132.Sircar D. C., pp. 292, 311; Ep. Ind., ix, 192. 133. Nārada, pp. 131–2. 134. Manu, x, 8–40; *Collection of Smritis*, pp. 46–8. 135. Vaidya, vol. I. pp. 61–2. 136. Quoted in R. C. Majumdar's *Corporate Life in Ancient India*, (1922), pp. 372–3. 137. Vaidya, vol. ii, p. 180. 138. *Epigraphia Indica*, vol. xv, pp. 305, 310–11. 139. *Shudra-Kamalākara*, p. 279.

140. Hemādri, vol. iii, pt. ii, p. 667. 141. Parāshara, vol. ii, pt. ii, pp. 78–9; vol. ii, pt. i, p. 410. 142. Parāshara, vol. i, pt. ii, pp. 15–16. 143. Hemādri, vol. iv, p. 382. 144. Parāshara, vol. ii, pt. ii, p. 29; pt. i, pp. 410–11. 145. Hemādri, vol. iv, p. 382. 146. Parāshara, vol. i, pt. i, p. 136. 147. *Shudra-Kamalākara*, p. 279. 148. The five products of the cow. 149. Hemchandra Raychaudhuri, *Materials for the Study of the Early History of Vaishnava sects*, (1920), p. 117. Nicol Macnicol, *Indian Theism*, (1915), p. 115.

150. Vide *Bhaktavijaya*, by Mahipati (Marathi), edited by L. B. Gokhale, 1888. 151. V. L. Bhawe, *Mahārāshtra Sāraswat* (Marathi) vol. i, pp. 70–1. 152. Dāsagupta, pp. 206, 214–15. 153. Parāshara, vol. ii, pt. ii, p. 38. 154. J. N. Farquhar, *Outline of the Religious Literature of India*, (1920), pp. 244–5. 155. Parāshara, vol. i, pt. ii, pp. 3–5, 15–16. 156. Kanakasabhai, p. 113. 157. Madras Census, 1901, p. 144. 158. *Imperial Gazetteer of India*, vol. x, p. 13. 159. *Shudra-Kamalākara*, pp. 289–92.

160. Parāshara, vol. i, pt. ii, p. 125. 161. Ibid., pt. i, p. 139. 162. *Vyavahāra-Mayukha* (Kane's edition, 1926), pp. 5, 215; compare also Medhātithi's comment on Manu, viii, p. 219. 162. *Vyavahāra-Mayukha*, loc. cit., notes, p. 69. 164. *Dvyāshrayakāvya*, II, p. 520. 165. *Epigraphia Indica*, vol. i, p. 5. 166. *Epigraphia Indica*, vol. i, pp. 173–7. 167. *South Indian Inscriptions*, vol. iii, p. 106. 168. Ibid., pp. 21 and 253. 169. Ibid., p. 437.

170. Ibid., p. 268. 171. *Archaeological Survey of India, Annual Report*, 1906–7, p. 243, f.n. 5. 172. *Epigraphia Indica*, vol. i, pp. 77, 85. 173. *Epigraphia Indica*, vol. xv, p. 81. 174. *South Indian Inscriptions*, vol. iii, pp. 114–17. 175. Ibid., pp. 470–1. 176. Ibid., p. 47. 177. Ibid., p. 82. 178. *Epigraphia Indica*, vol. i, pp. 299, 303, 304; vol. vi, p. 203, and f.n. 3. 179. Ibid., vol. p. 331.

180. Ibid., vol. viii, pp. 205, 208. 181. *Archaeological Survey of Western India, Report*, vol. iii, p. 86. 182. *Epigraphia Indica* vol. i, pp. 331–3, 336. 183. Ibid., vol. ii, p. 229. 184. Ibid., vol. ii, pp. 409, 420. 185. *The Book of Duarte Barbosa* by M. Longworth Dames, vol. ii, (1921), pp. 7, 37, 60. R. Sewell, *A Forgotten Empire*, ed. 1924, p. 245. 187. *Ain-i-Akbari*, translated by Jarrett, vol. iii, (1894), p. 118, and vol. ii, pp. 129, 131, 161, 162–3, 164–8, 177, 182, 184, 187, 189, 191, 198, 204–5, 255, 290. 188. *India at the Death of Akbar* (1920), p. 23. 189. *Jehangir's India*, by Moreland and Geyl, (1925), p. 76.

190. *A New Account of the East Indies*, by Capt. Alexander Hamilton, vol. i, (1740), p. 151.

5

Race and Caste

Caste is such an obtrusive factor of Indian social organization that since the time of Megasthenes it has never failed to attract the attention of the foreigner—be he traveller, administrator, or student of Sanskrit literature. The application of the sociological method to the explanation of caste, i.e., a systematic attempt to elucidate the genesis and growth of the institution of caste, by a comprehensive study of the contemporary castes, however, may be said to begin with the works of Denzil Ibbetson and J. C. Nesfield. Both of them, in general, endorse the view[1] that caste is mainly occupational in origin, i.e. occupations which were organized into guilds slowly became exclusive and stratified into castes. Nesfield went further and, affirming the essential unity of the Indian race, emphatically denied that racial distinction was the basis of caste.[2] This extraordinary statement of Nesfield led Herbert Risley to use anthropometry for a solution of the riddle of caste, for that alone could decide questions of racial affinity.[3] He carried on extensive measurements on many of the castes of Northern India and published the result of his splendid work in two volumes entitled *Anthropometric Data from Bengal* (1891). The bearing of these data on the theory of caste he discussed in the introduction to his *Tribes* and *Castes of Bengal*, and later in *The People of India*. His work further led to a succession of monographs on the anthropometric data from other Indian Provinces as a part of the ethnographic survey of India.

In any anthropometric work the student is, at the very outset, faced with two problems. The first is the question of the unit. What shall we take as a unit on which measurements may be taken and compared? Shall we take a geographical or political area as our unit and compare one with another? Or shall we take a whole people, and take our measurements on them and then analyse them? The solution of this problem is fundamental to anthropometric work. But as our main purpose is to institute comparisons between castes this problem need not engage us here. We may take one caste as a unit and compare it with another. This procedure does not involve the acceptance of Risley's view about the isolation of castes which, as pointed out by his learned annotator, W. Crooke,[4] requires much modification. We may thus take our measurements on Brahmins and compare them with those on Chamārs. But the data show us that neither Brahmins nor Chamārs among themselves have a uniform physical type. We ask ourselves the reason of this, and we are led to the question of the origins of the different physical types. Thus we have to deal with the general ethnology of India as, indeed, Herbert Risley did. We have to analyse racial mixture as well as compare different castes.

N.B.: This chapter is an adaptation of the author's paper "The Ethnic Theory of Caste", published in *Man in India*, 1924.

This procedure opens up the second problem, viz. what is the method by which we can detect racial affinities and compare groups? For such comparisons the average has long been in use. Risley principally used the average for his work, rarely bringing in the seriations and still more rarely the absolute measurements.[5] Seriations, like the frequency curve, only serve the purpose of showing the actual distribution and cannot be conveniently used for purposes of comparison, a fact which explains the rare use of these by Risley when dealing with the types, though they are given in the appendices. The average without the standard deviation is an abstraction which tells us almost nothing. The standard deviation is very useful both as serving the basis of the formula that we have utilized for comparison, as well as giving us an idea of the actual range of variation. "A range of six times the standard deviation usually includes 99 per cent or more of all the observations in the case of distributions of the symmetrical or moderately asymmetrical type."[6] I have therefore given in the appendix the means and their standard deviations for selected castes.

It will be observed that for the Punjab and Gujarat we have very meagre data: for Sindh proper we have none. For Madras, E. Thurston[7] has given us a long list of averages but very few individual measurements. Hence in the case of Dravidian India we can compare only two castes, data for which are taken from the paper of Sir Thomas Holland. Though we accept Thurston's averages for the general ethnology of India, yet we must point out that they are very crude in so far as the absolute measurements seem to have been recorded in centimetres.[8] For more scientific conclusions about Dravidian India we require fresh measurements taken on typical Dravidian castes.

When we compare two groups, what we want to know is not merely the differences between the two groups as regards the cephalic index or nasal index separately, but we want an expression which conveniently sums up all the differences in the various attributes that we may like to compare. Such an expression was used by T. A. Joyce in 1912. In order to compare two groups he starts with one character, say, the cephalic index, and works out the fraction

$$\sum \frac{M_1 - M_2}{\sqrt{s_1^2 - s_2^2}}$$

where M_1 and M_2 are the means for the cephalic indices of the two groups, $M_1 - M_2$ is their difference without regard to sign, and σ_1, σ_2, are the standard deviations. Similar fractions are found for as many characters as one likes, and all of them are added together. This sum is called the 'Differential Index'.[9] The expression is a convenient quantity showing the actual differentiation of two peoples and can be fruitfully used for comparisons. Another great advantage of this expression is that by its help we can include for comparison absolutes like the cephalic length which have, unfortunately, been too much neglected in anthropological work. Further this item is of special importance in the field of Indian ethnology; for here we have sometimes to deal with two dolichocephalic peoples whose absolute measurements of the head are essentially different. Thus the Brahmin of U.P. has a cephalic index of 73.29, while his cephalic length and cephalic breadth are 187.56 and 137.42 respectively. The Kurmi, on the other hand, with a cephalic index of 73.25 has the cephalic length of 184.05 and the cephalic breadth of 135.13. The cephalic indices of the Kurmi and the Musāhār of Bihar are respectively 75.82 and 75.79. Their cephalic length and cephalic breadth are 186.97 and 183.17, and 141.55 and 138.69 respectively. The Bhil of Khandesh with a cephalic index of 72.56

has the cephalic length of 182.92 and the cephalic breadth of 132.61 but the Kāyasth of U.P. with the cephalic index of 72.48 has the cephalic length of 186.62 and the cephalic breadth of 135.42. I have given in the appendix the differential indices for selected castes. In this chapter I have attempted to study the problem of caste with the help of this index.

I have said above that it was Risley who, under special circumstances, applied anthropometry to the solution of the problem of caste. But owing to the method which he followed, the light he was able to throw on the subject was not as decisive as was expected. Again he devoted more attention to the classification and origins of the various physical types of India than to the problem of caste proper.

It may be taken to be an historical fact that people calling themselves 'Āryas' poured into India through the north-west somewhere about 2000 B.C. It is equally clear from our discussion that an institution closely akin to caste has been very often described in Sanskrit books, which are the works of either the Aryans or the Aryan-inspired aborigines. Can we trace a close connection between the immigration of the Aryans and the rise of the institution of caste? We have seen that the Brahmins, who were the moral guides and legislators of the immigrant Aryans, tried to keep their blood free from any inter-mixture with the lower classes, though they had no objection to the members of their own class having progeny from females of lower class, provided these were not admitted into the Brahmin class. Can anthropometry shed any light on this aspect of caste? It appears to me that anthropometry will furnish us with a good guide, provided certain assumptions about the physical types of the Indo-Aryans and of the aborigines of Hindustan can be plausibly made.

These assumptions are two: First, that the Aryan type may be described as long-headed and fine-nosed. The average cephalic index may be said to vary between 70 and 75 and the nasal index from 65 to 75. The ground for this assumption is that almost all the averages of the cephalic index and the nasal index given by Risley[10] for the castes of the Punjab and Rajputana fall within these ranges; and these are the regions which, from their geographical position, must have been the home of Aryan settlements. We may reasonably hold, therefore, that the predominant physical type of the Punjab and Rajputana represents the Aryan type. The second assumption is that the aboriginal type may be deduced from such peoples as the Musāhār, who, not being within the pale of Hinduism, are like the jungle-tribes of Southern India. Their chief characteristic is the broad-nose, the nasal index being above 80. Very often the head is long. The broad nose seems to have been noticed even by the Vedic poets as a characteristic of the aborigines, whom they sometimes describe as "noseless".[11]

I can now proceed to set out the conclusions we get from our anthropometrical inquiry. Taking the Brahmin of the United Provinces* as the typical representative of the ancient Aryans we shall start comparisons with him. If we turn to the table of differential indices we find that he shows smaller differential index[12] as compared with the Chuhrā and the Khatri of the Punjab than with any caste from the United Provinces except the Chhatri. The differential index between the Khatri and the Chuhrā is only slightly less than that between the Brahmin of the United Provinces and the Chuhrā. This means that the Brahmin of the United Provinces has closer physical affinities with the Chuhrā and the Khatri of the Punjab than with any caste from his own province except the very high caste of the Chhatri. The Brahmin is as much akin to the Chuhrā as the latter is to the Khatri of the Punjab. The only valid conclusion is that the United Provinces Brahmin does not materially differ from the physical type of the Punjab, i.e. on the assumption, previously explained, that

* Now known as Uttar Pradesh.

he fairly represents the physical type of the Aryans. The reality of this close affinity between the United Provinces Brahmin and the Punjab Chuhrā is more clearly brought out if we look at the table of differential indices between the United Provinces Brahmin and the Brahmins of other regions. They are very high as compared with that between the Chuhrā and the United Provinces Brahmin. Even the differential index between the United Provinces Brahmin and the Bihar Brahmin, who from what we know about the history of the spread of Aryan culture, is expected to be very nearly allied to the former, is just twice as high as that between the United Provinces Brahmin and the Chuhrā. This ought to serve as a conclusive proof of the fact that the United Provinces Brahmin has essentially retained the same physical type as that of the Punjabis and of that ancient Aryans.

I must now examine in what relation the United Provinces Brahmin stands to the other castes of his province. From the table of differential indices for the United Provinces we see that in physical affinity with the Brahmin, the Kāyasth and the Kurmi stand next to the Chuhrā, while at the other end of the scale come the Pāsi and the Chamār. In the scheme of social precedence, the Kāyasth belongs to the fourth rank, the Kurmi stands at the head of the eighth, while the Pāsi and the Chamār take the eleventh and the twelfth rank.[13]

The true significance of this gradation in physical affinity with the Brahmin can be demonstrated by the study of the other provinces. On historical grounds we expect Bihar to approximate to the United Provinces. On referring to the table we find that the Kurmi comes near to the Brahmin, and the Chamār and the Dom stand much differentiated from him. But the Chamār in this case is not as much distinct from the Brahmin as the United Provinces Chamār is from the United Provinces Brahmin. The social status of the Kurmi is defined by stating that he ranks third while the Chamār and the Dom rank fifth and sixth.[14] Thus in Bihar the state of affairs in some way corresponds to that which we have tried to demonstrate for the United Provinces. The table for Bengal shows that identical conditions do not prevail there. The Chandāl, who stands sixth in the scheme of social precedence and whose touch pollutes,[15] is not much differentiated from the Brahmin, from whom the Kāyasth, second in rank, can hardly be said to be distinguished. The gradation observed in the United Provinces is thus absent in Bengal. Still more is this the case in Bombay. Here the Deshasth Brahmin bears as close an affinity to the Son Koli, a fisherman caste, as to his own compeer, the Chitpāvan Brahmin. The Mahār, the untouchable of the Maratha region, comes next together with the Kunbi, the peasant. Then follow in order the Shenvi Brahmin, the Nagar Brahmin and the high-caste Maratha. These results are rather odd. Stated in a generalized form they mean that there is no correspondence between social gradation and physical differentiation in Bombay. I venture to think that the results from Bengal would have been equally striking if we had data for the various sub-castes of the Brahmins. This contention is rendered plausible by some measurements published by Rai Bahadur Ramaprasad Chanda.[16] The following are the means and their standard deviations:

	Cephalic Index		*Nasal Index*	
	M.	*St. Dev.*	*M.*	*St. Dev*
Brahmin (31)	78.84	3.64	75.61	10.31
Pāshchātya Vaidik Brahmin (50)	79.83	3.56	71.97	8.62

With such differences between the two sub-castes of the Brahmins of Bengal we have reason to expect more startling results than we have, though these are quite insignificant.

Our survey of the regions of India other than Hindustan has made it abundantly clear that Hindustan is unique in this respect that here we have the Brahmin at the head of the physical hierarchy; then follows a high caste or two, hardly differing from him in physical type; then comes a group of castes, slightly differentiated from the Brahmin; low castes like the Chamār and the Pāsi, whom we may look upon as the Hinduized representatives of the aborigines, stand far removed from him.

I shall now turn to the conclusions arrived at by Risley. Believing in the "marked divergence of type that distinguishes the people of the Eastern Punjab from the people of Western Hindustan", to account for the people of Hindustan he brings in a second wave of the Aryans with few or no women. They married aboriginal women and thus modified their original type; "but a certain pride of blood remained to them, and when they had bred females enough to serve their purposes and to establish a distinct *jus connubii* they closed their ranks to all further intermixture of blood. When they did this, they became a caste like the castes of the present day."[17] I have shown that as far as the published data go the Hindustani Brahmin does not materially differ from the physical type of the Punjabis. An acute observer of Upper India, W. Crooke, remarked that a traveller from the Punjab glides into Hindustan without marking any change in the physical type.[18] It is, therefore, not necessary to postulate a second invasion of the Aryans, who could not bring their womenfolk with them.[19] Nor need we propose a theory entirely contradictory to the literary records of the Brahmins.

There is another proposition of Risley's which I must examine more minutely, for it is one which, if true to facts, affects my conclusion. He observes, "If we take a series of castes in Bengal, Bihar, the United Provinces of Agra and Oudh, or Madras, and arrange them in the order of the average nasal index so that the caste with the finest nose shall be at the top, and that with the coarsest at the bottom of the list, it will be found that this order substantially corresponds with the accepted order of social precedence".[20] In the argument elaborated above it is evident that we depend upon the uniqueness of Hindustan amongst the provinces of India as regards the gradation of the physical type for our explanation of the origin of endogamy. The statement of Risley in a way challenges that basis. For Bengal and Bombay I think I have made a good case, and my figures will speak for themselves; but as regards Madras, for lack of material, I have not been able to apply the formula for differential index. It may be urged against me that as far as nasal index, without the absolute measurements of the nose, can be an indication of racial mixture, Madras seriously damages my argument. I shall therefore examine the association between nasal index and social status province by province.

Risley, after comparing the nasal indices of some of the castes of Hindustan, says that the order of gradation established by means of the nasal index is "substantially" the same as that of social precedence.[21] This mild statement has been reproduced in an exaggerated form in an authoritative book on ethnology. It is said in Keane's *Man, Past and Present*[22] that the Hindustani type of the United Provinces has "a nose index exactly corresponding to social station". I shall presently show that Risley's statement is only partially true, and that Keane's generalization has no ground. The following is the order in which some of the typical castes of the United Provinces stand according to their nasal index as given in my table for the province: Bābhan, Brahmin, Chhatri, Kāyasth, Kurmi, Thāru, Baniā, Bhār, Kol, Lohār, Dom, Pāsi, Musāhār and Chamar. The order of social precedence as given in the Census Report of 1901[23] is as follows: Brahmin, Bābhan, Rajput, Kāyasth, Bania, Kurmi and Lohār, Mallāh and Bind, etc., Bhār and Thāru, etc., Kol and Muchi, etc., Pasi and Doadh, etc., Chamar, Musahar and Dom, etc. To these I may add Kachhi, Lodha, and Koiri.

Risley's[24] averages for their nasal index are: 82.9, 83.4, and 83.6. In my list the first two will rank after Kol and the third after Lohar. But in the scheme of social precedence they are grouped together with Kurmi. These comparisons prove that the statement of Keane is baseless and that of Risley is true only in a broad sense. For Bengal, Risley's[25] averages give us the following order: Brahmin of Eastern Bengal and Kāyasth, Brahmin of Western Bengal, Chandāl and Sadgop, Goala, Muchi, Pod, Kaibart, and Rajbansi Kochh. These castes may be arranged according to social status as: Brahmin, Kāyasth and others, Sadgop and others, Kaibarta and Goala, Bhuiyā and others, Kochh, and Pod, Chandal, Muchi and others.[26] It is evident that these lists disprove Risley's statement. On Risley's[27] averages for Orissa some of the castes rank as below: Shāshan Brahmin, Panda Brahmin and Teli, Khandait, Mastān Brahmin and Guria. and Chasa, Karan, Pan, Kewat, and Bāuri. The social order of precedence is: Brahmin, Karan, Khandāit and others, Chasā, Guriā and others, Goālā and others, Teli and Kewat, etc., Chamār, Bāuri and others, Pān and others.[28] I leave out Bombay, as it is not included in Risley's observation. By looking at the table the reader can satisfy himself that the figures for Bombay are more telling than in the case of the provinces so far dealt with. Finally we come to Madras. Here we must treat of the different linguistic areas separately for the schemes of social precedence in the various areas are different. I shall begin with the Telugu region. According to the averages given by Risley (p. 398) and by E. Thurston (vol. i, pp. lxviii–lxiii) the order of castes is as follows: Kāpu. Sāle, Gollā, Mālā, Madigā and Togātā, and Komāti. According to their social status they are ranked as below: Brahmin . . . Komāti, Gollā and Kāpu and others, and Sāle, Togāta and others. Mālā and Madigā occupy the lowest rank, being the Pariāhs of the Telugu country.[29] In the Kanarese region the nasal index gives the following order: Karnatak Smārta Brahmin, Bant, Billava, Mandyā Brahmin, Vakkaliga, Ganiga, Linga-Banajiga, Panchāla, Kuruba, Holeyā, Deshasth Brahmin, Toreyā, and Bedar. In the scheme of social precedence the castes take the ranks as under: Brahmin . . . Bant and Vakkaliga, Toreyā, etc., Kuruba and Ganiga, Badaga and Kurumba and Solaga, Billava, Bedar and Holeyā.[30] The significance of the comparison is enhanced when we remember that the nasal index of the Holeyā, the untouchable of the Kanarese region, is 75.1, that of the highest sub-caste of the Brahmin being 71.5, while those of the jungle Kurumba and the Solaga, who when Hinduized, occupy the rank allotted to them in the list, are 86.1 and 85.1 respectively. The ranks of the Linga-Banajiga and the Panchāla cannot be determined, as they do not recognize the authority of the Brahmin. The Tamil castes may be arranged according to their nasal index as follows: Ambattan, Vellāl, Idaiyan, Agamudaiyan, Tamil Brahmin, Palli, Malaiyāli, Shānān, Paraiyan, Irula, and Malāsar. The social ranking of these castes is: Brahmin, Idaiyan and Vellāla, Agamudaiyan and Palli, Ambattan and others, Irula and Malasar and Malaiyāli, Shānan and others, Paraiyan.[31] The nasal indices of four typical Malayalam castes are: Tiyan, 75: Nambudiri Brahmin, 75.5;[32] Nāyar, 76.7; Cheruman, 77.2. The order of social precedence among these is: Nambudiri, Nāyar, Tiyan, and Cheruman. The nasal index of the Kanikar, a jungle tribe of Travancore, is 84.6. Thus the Cheruman belongs to the same race as the Brahmin rather than to that of the Kanikar. I hope these comparisons will have made it abundantly clear that the proposition of Risley has almost no basis in fact outside Hindustan.

Outside Hindustan in each of the linguistic areas we find that the physical type of the population is mixed, and does not conform in its gradation to the scale of social precedence of the various castes. The Brahmin is not so far distinguished in his physical features from other castes as to stand out apart from them and at the head of the physical hierarchy. Some of the castes, very low in their social status, actually stand higher in physical features than some of the higher castes. In Hindustan, on the other hand, the gradation of physical types from the Brahmin downwards to Musahar corresponds very closely to the scheme of social precedence prevailing among the Hindustani castes. The state of things can be the result only of such regulations that prevented the possibility of Brahmin blood being mixed with aboriginal blood but allowed the mixture of blood of the other groups in varying proportions. As we have seen, this was just what the Brahmins attempted to do by their rules of conduct. The Brahmin kept himself pure by decreeing that only those persons both of whose parents were Brahmins were to be regarded as Brahmins. Thus the Brahmins were the first to be endogamous with reference to their class. We have also seen that the Brahmins of each of the linguistic areas show greater physical affinity with other castes of their region than with the Brahmins of other areas and of Hindustan. It is clear from this that the Brahmanic practice of endogamy must have been developed in Hindustan and thence conveyed as a cultural trait to the other areas without a large influx of the physical type of the Hindustan Brahmins.

The treatment of the subject cannot be complete without an investigation of the physical types of India and their origins.[33] In this field also a lead has been given by Risley. It is best to start with a statement of his view. He distinguishes seven types: (1) The Turko-Iranian of Baluchistan and North-West Frontier Provinces. We do not discuss this type, because we think that it essentially lies outside cultural India. (2) The Indo-Aryan type of Kashmir, Punjab, and Rajputana. It is dolichocephalic with a narrow nose. We leave out other physical characteristics as they are far too vague. (3) The Mongoloid type of the Himalayas, Nepal, Assam, and Burma. (4) The Dravidian type extending from Ceylon to the valley of the Ganges and pervading the whole of Madras, Hyderabad, and the Central Provinces, most of Central India and Chota-Nagpur. It was "probably the original type of the population of India". It is dolichocephalic with a "very broad nose". (5) The Aryo-Dravidian type of the United Provinces, Bihar and Ceylon. It is also found in parts of Rajputana. The head-form is long with a tendency to medium. (6) The Mongolo-Dravidian type of Lower Bengal and Orissa. "The head is broad; nose medium with a tendency to broad." (7) The Scytho-Dravidian type of Western India. "The head is broad; nose moderately fine."[34]

The Indo-Aryan Type: The first objection against this type is that the term used to denote it in the scheme proposed by Risley is unsatisfactory. In the case of the other types the names are compound terms composed of the names for the two physical types from which the particular type is supposed to be derived. Thus what is meant by the term Aryo-Dravidian is that the type is considered to be a mixture of the Aryan type and the Dravidian type. But in the case of the Indo-Aryan type no such mixture is meant. The Indo-Aryan type is not to be understood to be a mixture of the Indian and Aryan but to be a pure type. Indo-Aryan means nothing more than the Aryan of India as opposed to the Aryan of Iran. Thus it will be seen that in Risley's scheme the term is rather misleading. Nevertheless, as in my treatment of the subject I wish to avoid all compound terms I shall retain the term Indo-Aryan to denote the Aryan type of India. Instead I cannot use the term Aryan, for in philology it is generally applied to the Iranians as well as to the Indians. By Indo-Aryan, then, I mean the physical type to which the Vedic Indians largely contributed. The physical characteristics of this type are solely inferred from those of the present population of the Punjab. I have no reason to think that after the Aryan immigration into India and before Darius' dominion there was any considerable influx of foreigners. When Darius held sway over a part of the Punjab the country appears to have been already very populous and prosperous.[35] The physical type of the Punjab is so uniform as to preclude any possibility of large mixture. Hence we can reasonably assume that a large bulk of the present inhabitants of the Punjab are the descendants of the Vedic Aryans. Their number might have swollen by later immigrants whose physical type must have been similar to theirs but whose cultural affinities we may not be able to trace. Secondly, an objection has been levelled at Risley's classification of the Rajputs as Indo-Aryans.[36] It has been contended that some of the clan-names of the Rajputs are the same as those of the Gurjara tribe or caste and that the reigning dynasty of Kanauj during the ninth century and after was of the Gurjara stock. Hence it is argued that some of the Rajput clans are of non-Aryan decent.[37] Even the Minas and Meos of Rajputana are not physically much differentiated from the Rajputs.[38] The Rajputs are thus of the same race as the other peoples of Rajputana.* We cannot hold that Rajputana was untenanted before the foreign tribes entered it in the sixth century A.D. Perhaps it will be said that the Gurjaras were of the same physical type as the population of Rajputana and hence their presence cannot be detected by physical anthropology, though they had come in large numbers and produced the present population of Rajputana. This supposition is not tenable; for the Gurjaras are believed to be allied in blood to the White Huns,[39] who seem to have been a brachycephalic people.[40] It is reasonable therefore to assume that a few ruling families of the Gurjaras with a small band of followers succeeded in gaining ascendance and imposing their culture over the then population of Rajputana. It is also urged that some of the Rajput clans "are descended from the so-called aboriginal tribes—Gonds, Bhārs, Kols and the like",[41] apparently because both the Rajputs and the aboriginal tribes have certain clan-names in common. In physical characteristics these tribes are sharply distinguished from the Rajputs, and yet we are asked to believe that they are essentially the same because some features of social organization are common to both. The common clan-names can better be explained as a borrowing by the lowly castes or tribes from the dominant Rajputs. Thus there does not appear to be any serious objection to the Rajputs being classed as Indo-Aryans. Thirdly, there does not seem to be any foundation for Risley's classification of the Kashmiris as Indo-Aryans. The Kashmiris appear to be a mesaticephalic people, perhaps a mixture of the Alpine folk of Central Asia and the Indo-Aryans of the Punjab. Lastly, I have made it clear that Risley was not right in restricting the type to the Punjab and Rajputana. The type includes one or two high castes of Hindustan as well.

As regards the affinities of Indo-Aryans outside India, Haddon would perhaps see in them modified Proto-Nordics.[42] But it is better to connect them with the tall variety of the Mediterranean Race.

The Mongoloid type: Here we have no comment to make except to draw attention to a mistake of Risley,[43] repeated in *Man, Past and Present*.[44] Both the Kanets of Kulu and Lahoul are there classed as Mongoloid. A glance at the table for the Punjab will show that whereas the Kulu Kanets are very much akin to the Khatri of the Punjab, the Lahoul Kanets are quite distinct from them. The Kanets of Kulu are Indo-Aryans, while the Kanets of Lahoul are a mixture of the Kulu Kanets with the Mongoloid folk. Indeed, it was to elucidate the process of racial mixture between the Kanets of Kulu (who show marked points of contact wth the Punjabis) and the Mongoloids that Holland, our authority on the subject, undertook a study of these two peoples.[45]

The Dravidian type: Here we come upon the weakest part of Risley's great work. The type is supposed to spread from Ceylon to the valley of the Ganges, the best representatives of it being Nāyars, Paniyans, Santāls, and others.[46] This view has been repeated in *Man, Past and Present*,[47] where though the jungle tribes like the Paniyans are classed apart as Pre-Dravidian, the Nāyars and the Santāls are given as the typical representatives of the Dravidian type. Now even if we leave aside complexion, the Santāl stands as far apart from the Nāyar as the Paniyan. The nasal index of the

* Now known as Rajasthan.

Nāyar is 76.7; that of the Santāl, 88.8; that of the Paniyan, 95.1. The close connection of the Santāl with the jungle tribes of Southern India comes out more clearly if we take into account other tribes like the Irula and the Kanikār. It may be broadly stated that the nasal index of the jungle tribes ranges from 30 to 90. I have therefore to connect the Santāl with the jungle tribes and separate the Nāyar and others like him from them.

I propose to break up this composite group into four distinct types:

(a) The Pre-Dravida type. (b) The Mundā type.
(c) The Dravida type. (d) The Western type.

Before dealing with the types I must make a note about the use of certain terms. The Malayalam and the Tamil regions seem to have been collectively referred to by Sanskrit writers as 'Dravida desha', i.e. the Dravid country, as opposed to the 'Andhra desha' or the Telugu country. The type that I propose to designate Dravida is predominant only in the Malayalam and the Tamil regions. Hence it should be reservedly called the Dravida type. 'Dravidian' is only an anglicized form of the word 'Dravida'. But in philology it has been used to denote not only Tamil and Malayalam but Kanarese, Telugu, and kindred languages. It is also employed to designate a culture different from the Aryan culture. It is convenient to retain this word to denote a culture which in its social organization was characterized at one end by such practices as cross-cousin marriage and at the other by dual organization and matrilineal descent.

The Pre-Dravida type: The characteristic representatives of this type inhabit mostly the jungles of Southern India. They are also found in Western India, in the hilly country of Central India, in Rajasthan and Uttar Pradesh, everywhere penetrating like a wedge. Such a distribution makes it probable that these people were the first occupants of Southern India. Being pressed by later immigrants they seem to have taken to the hills and jungles, or again managed to become low members of the social polity of the immigrants. The immigrants who pressed upon them were the people of the Dravida type. Hence the name of the type under consideration. If we regard the Irula, the Kadir, the Kanikar, the Paniyan and the like as the best representatives of this type, its physical characteristics may be thus summed up: the head is long, the cephalic index being generally below 75; the nose broad, the nasal index being always above 80. The Bhil and the Kātkari of Western India are members of this racial stock. The Musāhār, the Pāsi, the Chamār, and the low castes in general of the United Provinces belong to the same type. From the fact that among the Kanikārs of the hills the system of inheritance is from father to son, only a portion of the personal property being given to the nephew, while among those of the plains an equal distribution of one's self-acquired property is made between the sons and the nephews,[48] it is reasonable to assume that the pre-Dravida people were essentially patrilineal. When they moved northwards they seem to have imbibed many of the items of the Dravidian culture. They carried with them the practice of raising megalithic tombs and monuments, which are found in Madhya Pradesh, Eastern Rajasthan and the Mirzapur District of Uttar Pradesh. They spoke Dravidian languages; for some of the names of the villages in the Central Provinces end in a Kanarese termination[49] and some village-names in the districts of Gaya and Mirzapur are distinctly Dravidian.[50] As for social organization they seem to have carried the practice of cross-cousin marriage, which now exists among them for the most part as a survival.[51]

This type has till now been known as pre-Dravidian. Some authorities connect these people with the Sakāi of the Malay Peninsula and the Australians.[52] They might have been the autochthones of India. That there is a negrito strain in this type is rendered probable by the researches of B. S. Guha.[53]

The Mundā type: Peoples having a very slight tendency towards mesaticephaly and a broad-nose, nasal index above 80, are massed together in Chota-Nagpur and Western Bengal. They are also found in Bihar, but not in Uttar Pradesh.[54] In this region Mundā culture seems to have originally flourished.[55] Hence it is best to designate the type as the Mundā type. Some of the peoples belonging to this type speak Indo-Aryan and Dravidian languages. In culture the Mundā peoples have affinities with the Indonesian and the Melanesian regions. That this Mundā culture had a far wider distribution than at present is certain because "Mundā languages must once have been spoken over a wide area in Central India, and probably also in the Ganges Valley".[56] Further, some of the names of villages in the districts of Gaya and Mirzapur are Mundā in origin.[57] The Mundā languages are closely related to the Mon-Khmer languages spoken by the Sakāis and Semāngs of the Malay Peninsula and are further connected with the languages of Indonesia, Melanesia, and Polynesia in such a manner as to allow us to group them together as one family.[58] A survival of a peculiar custom, viz., the marriage of grandfather with his grand-daughter, is confined only to this part of India. The existence of it among the Oraons was first made known by Rai Bahadur S. C. Roy. A counterpart of it is known from Melanesia.[59] Roy has also noticed certain practices from Bihar which are reminiscent of this survival.[60] Another sort of survival of this curious custom is reported from Ganjam, where even now a Mundā language is spoken. Among the Sollokhondiā section of the Gaudo caste if a girl fails to secure a husband before puberty she has to go through a nominal marriage with an old man, "preferably the girl's grandfather."[61] A similar practice prevails amongst the Kurumo of Ganjam.[62] The custom of marriage between the grand-daughter and the grandfather must have formed part of the Mundā culture. A neolithic artefact known as the "shouldered celt" is peculiar to the highlands of Bengal and Assam. Identical tools are found in the Malayan region.[63] The limited distribution of this implement in India lends support to the conclusion that the people who brought it to India must have come from the Malayan region. Further as the tool is not found west of the area characterized by the Mundā culture it is reasonable to suppose that the Mundā people were responsible for the introduction of this artefact. The conclusion about the origin of the Mundā type is that the people of this type came into India from the Malayan region when they were in the Neolithic Age.

The typical representatives of this type are the Mundā the Santāl, the Musāhār, and the Chamār of Bihar.

The Dravida type: This type is characterized by a long head, the cephalic index being below 75, and by a medium nose, the nasal index being less than 77. It is restricted to the Tamil and Malayalam countries.[64] Matrilineal descent seems to have been the chief characteristic of the social organization of the peoples of this type. A statement of Megasthenes is construed to refer to this peculiarity of the social organization of Malabar.[65] A physical trait which we have not so far taken into consideration is the hair. It is of special importance in connection with the inquiry of the affinities of this type. Most castes of Malabar excepting the Nambudiri have little or no hair on the cheeks and the chest. They are clean-shaven, and the Nambudiri imitating them shaves all his body excepting the top-knot. "Amongst the people of good caste in Malabar, to speak of one as a hairy man is to speak of him reproachfully."[66] This lack of hair on the cheeks definitely connects the Dravidas with the Brown Race as it is characterized by Elliot Smith.[67] When they came to India from Mesopotamia or Arabia, cannot be ascertained. They might have brought with them the matrilineal type of social organization from these countries; for there is some evidence for thinking that both the Arabs and the Babylonians practised mother-right.[68]

The best representatives of this type are: The Nāyar, the Tiyan, the Badaga, the Agamudaiyan, and the Vellāla, I exclude the Nambudiris from this type because their cephalic index is above 75, and they are extremely hairy The Todas are a problem. Their cephalic and nasal indices are such as to include them under this type; but their hairy system is particularly well developed. Rivers connects them with the Malabar castes and attributes their hairiness to their environment.[69] Against this explanation R. Chanda has justly urged that the Badagas, another tribe of the Nilgiris, do not seem to be hairy.[70] In view of the fact that "of all the castes or tribes of Malabar, the Nambudiris perhaps show the greatest number of resemblances to the customs of the Todas"[71] it is not unlikely that they might have some connection with the Nambudiris.

The Western type: I shall deal with this type in connection with the Scytho-Dravidian type of Risley.

The Aryo-Dravidian type: As the discussion so far must have made it clear we cannot speak of any Aryo-Dravidian type. I have shown that the high castes of the United Provinces (and perhaps also of Bihar) must be classed as Indo-Aryan. The lower castes of the United Provinces (and perhaps also of Bihar) must be classed as Indo-Aryan. The lower castes of the United Provinces must be referred to the pre-Dravidian type and those of Bihar to the Mundā type. That we must separate the low castes of Bihar from those of the United Provinces is made clear by the differential index. The differential index between the Brahmins of the two provinces is 2.05; that between the Kurmis is 3.49; and that between the Chamārs is 4.01. The intermediate castes of the United Provinces must be considered to be the result of a mixture between the Indo-Aryan and the pre-Dravidas, while those of Bihar that of the Indo-Aryans and the Mundās, with perhaps a pre-Dravida strain.

The Mongolo-Dravidian type: This type, according to Risley, is a mixture of the pure Mongoloid and Dravidian types and comprises the population of Lower Bengal and Orissa. He describes the head of this type as broad, but I think it would be better to describe it as medium. Of the fourteen castes of Bengal measured by Risley the cephalic indices ranged from 74.9 to 78.8, the lower castes like the Bāuri, Māl Phariā, Bagdi, Goāla and Māl, Kaibart and Muchi having the lower indices and Sadgop, Chandāl of the lower castes and Kāyasth and Brahmin of the high ones having the higher ones. Only the Rajbansi Māghas of the Chittagong Hills show a cephalic index of over 79; and they are essentially Mongoloid. The nasal indices of the above fourteen castes range between 70.7 to 94.7. The lower indices are shown in the ascending order by Kāyasth, Brahmin, Sadgop and Chandāl, etc. The Bagdi has the nasal index of 80.8 and the Bāuri, the Māl Phariā and the Māl follow in the ascending order.[72] The nasal index of the Mongoloid type in India is in most cases above 78.[73] Nor does the orbito-nasal index support any idea of a Mongoloid mixture.[74] In three lower castes of Bengal—the Pod, the Bagdi, and the Chandāl—the figures are, 111.5, 112.2, and 114.0. In Orissa the orbito-nasal index varies from 112 to 117. We do not wish to imply that there is no Mongoloid mixture in this part of India, but only to point out that the published data of anthropometry do not give us any clue. The Savaras of Ganjam are distinctly Mongoloid.[75] Again some of the castes of the United Provinces show marked cultural affinities with the Mongoloid peoples. Among the Baheliās, Dhangars, Dharkārs, Dombs, Dusadhs, and Nāis, marriage is permitted in the line of one's mother's sister.[76] Everywhere else in India such marriages are strictly prohibited; hence the permission for such marriages among these castes is very unusual. We can explain it only as a borrowing from the Mongoloid people, the Bhotiās of Sikkim. Among them one can marry one's cousin on the maternal side, either mother's brother's child or mother's sister's child.[77] I think that the Bengalis are only an extension of the Western type. Sailendranath Sengupta's[78] recent appraisal of the racial situation that "the brachycephaly among the higher castes can be reasonably supposed to be due to the admixture only of an adventitious element from the West," does not militate against this conclusion. The differential index shows that the Bengal Brahmin is more nearly related to the Shenvi and the Chitpāvan Brahmins of Bombay than to the Bihar Brahmin and far more so than to the United Provinces Brahmin. There is evidence to show that the people of Bengal have affinities with the Dravidian culture. The use in marriage of the Shank-bangles even by the Brahmins is an instance in point.[79] Risley thinks that there is "a strain of Indo-Aryan blood in the higher groups".[80] In view of the fact that the differential index between the Bengal Brahmin and the Chandāl is 1.11, while between him and the United Provinces Brahmin is 3.89, there does not seem any ground for this supposition. In Orissa there appears to be some mixture of the Mundā type, because the nasal index is sometimes very high. The people of Bengal and Orissa, therefore, would best be regarded as a mixture of the Western and the Mundā types slightly modified in some cases by the Mongoloid type.

The Scytho-Dravidian type: What Risley exactly meant by the term Scythian is not clear. He could not have meant Mongoloid, for then there would have been no point in distinguishing this type from the Mongolo-Dravidian. Perhaps he used the word as equivalent to the Shakas of Sanskrit writers. That there is no evidence of the Shakas having reached so far as this type stretches is amply proved.[81] We must, therefore, give up this designation of the type. I propose to call it the Western type, because it characterizes the Western Coast from Gujarat to South Kanara, and thence spreads inwards into Coorg, Mysore, the Deccan, and the Telugu country and through Orissa into Bengal. The head is mostly medium with a slight tendency towards broad; the nasal index in most communities is below 78. Representatives of this type are: Sāle, Bant, Vakkaliga, Coorga, Shenvi, Prabhu, Nāgar, Chitpāvan, Mālā, Madigā, and Holeyā. Chanda seeks to connect the Gujaratis, the Marathis, and the Bengalis with a people of the Alpine Race that, he supposes, came from Chinese Turkistan. And he has the support of no less an authority than Haddon, who first postulated an immigration of the Alpine folks to account for the "strongly marked brachycephalic element in the population of Western India."[82] Against this route of immigration it must be objected that if the Alpine people came through Kashmir and the Punjab, how is it that we have no trace of either brachycephaly or mesaticephaly in the intervening area till we come to Gujarat? Further, the highest cephalic indices are recorded from the southern part of the region characterized by this type, i.e., from Bellary. The distribution of the type sketched above suggests quite a different route of immigration, i.e., on the western coast by sea. Most of the castes are mesaticephalic and nine of the castes of the Marathi region, pooled together, give 77.84 as the mean cephalic index. It is therefore more reasonable to seek the origin of this type in a mixed stock rather than in purely Alpine one, for the latter has a very broad head, the cephalic index being often 85 and upwards.[83] Western Asia seems to provide us with such a people; for there we notice a prolonged process of mixture between the Brown race and the Alpine race.[84] Schoff sees in Cutch or Kachh reminiscences of the Kassites who migrated from Elam about 2200 B.C.[85] H. J. E. Peake thinks that about 2000 B.C. some of the Nordics had made their appearance in Asia Minor.[86] If some of them accompanied the people who landed on the western coast of India, we can explain the colour of the eyes of the Chitpāvans of Bombay. It is greenish grey rather than blue. Their eyes are known in Marathi as "cat-eyes".[87]

Giuffrida-Ruggeri has suggested the following classification of the ethnic elements in India: (a) Negritos. Apparently there are no representatives of these. He thinks that they survive in tribes like the Bhils, the Gonds, etc.[88] (b) Pre-Dravidians (Australoid-Veddaic); (c) Dravidians. They are connected with the Ethiopians, with the exception of the Somālis and Gallās.[89] Under the category he includes the mesaticephalic and the brachycephalic peoples of the Kanarese-Telugu regions.[90] Being afraid of sea migration—witness his gibe at Elliot Smith[91]—he brings the Dravidians into India from Iran, and explains the "elevation of the cephalic index among the inhabitants of the south by a mixture with the brachycephalic Negritos, the most ancient population between India and the Persian Gulf".[92] He entirely misses the significance of the distribution of the dolichocephalic and mesaticephalic types explained above. (d) Tall dolichocephalic elements (Todā),[93] (e) dolichocephalic Aryans. Under this class he includes Kafirs, Dards, Rajputs, and the Kanet of Lahoul,[94] (f) Brachycephalic Leucoderms. He accepts the hypothesis of Chanda,[95] about immigration of the Alpine folk. It will have been quite clear from my discussion that such a classification is untenable. The ascertained facts of Indian anthropometry are far better accommodated by the classification that emerges out of my discussion.

I should distinguish six main physical types among the Hindu population of India. These are: (1) The Indo-Aryan; (2) pre-Dravida; (3) the Dravida; (4) the Western; (5) the Mundā; and (6) the Mongoloid. The Indo-Aryan type is confined to the Punjab, Rajputana, and part of the United Provinces, and is mixed with the pre-Dravida and Mundā types in the last province among its lower classes. The Mundā type centres round Chota-Nagpur. The population of Bihar is formed by the mixture of three types, viz. the Indo-Aryan, the pre-Dravida, and the Mundā, while that of Bengal and Orissa combines the Western, the Mundā, and the Mongoloid types. The Mongoloid proper is confined to the Himalayas, Nepal, and Assam. The Western type is found on the western coast right up to the northern limits of Malabar, in Mysore and the Telugu country, and in the whole of Maharashtra. The Dravida type makes up the population of the Tamil and Malayalam speaking districts of the south, excepting the rudest hill-tribes. The jungle folks of South India generally represent the pre-Dravida type.

Von Eickstedt writing in 1933 came to the conclusion that six main racial types can be clearly distinguished and, though he named them rather fancifully, he showed their equivalence to my types mentioned above.[96] B. S. Guha's conclusion on the basis of his measurements taken as an accompaniment of the Census of 1931 cannot be taken *in toto* owing to serious defects in the conduct of the survey. As pointed out by me[97] the groups chosen were not proper, the individuals measured were not adequate in number and perhaps the individuals were not always representative of the group.

References

1. Risley, (2) pp. 263–5. Ibid., p. 265. 3. Ibid., p. 20. 4. Ibid., p. xvii. 5. Op. cit., p. 37. 6. Yule, *An Introduction to the Theory of Statistics*, 1916, p. 40. 7. Vol. i, p. xi 8. Ibid., pp. lv, lxi. 9. *J.R.A.I.*, 1912, p. 451. N.B.: Dr. B. S. Guha in his dissertation on the Racial Affinities of the Peoples of India (*Census of India*, 1931, vol. I, Part III, Ethnographical, 1933) used the more elaborate formula devised by Karl Pearson much after the time when I had to use the only formula then in existence. The new formula was called the Coefficient of Racial Likeness. Dr. Guha in using it further employed a correcting factor for the differing number of individuals as introduced by Pearson and called the Reduced Coefficient of Racial likeness (p. vii). In 1936 Prof. R. A. Fisher in his paper contributed to the *Journal of the Royal Anthropological Institute* criticized the use of the C.R.L. as a measure of affinity and distance and stressed the point that the formula only indicated divergence or otherwise from a particular universe. He remarked: "As has been explained above, it is the function of a test of significance to measure a probability, and not to afford an estimate of a metrical difference. It is, therefore, somewhat unfortunate that the name assigned to the Coefficient of Racial Likeness does suggest, to many who first hear of it, that it affords a measure of the differences, or inversely of the likenesses, between different races" (p. 60).

In 1949 Prof. P. C. Mahalanobis (*Sankhya*, vol. 9, pp. 237ff) levelled the same criticism against "the Pearsonian C.R.L." pointing out the main defect to be the fact that it does not take note of the differing sizes of samples, a point with he had already made in 1930 (*Biometrika*, vol. 22, p. 98). He does not refer to the above-mentioned paper of Prof. Fisher nor does he refer to the Reduced Coefficient of Racial Likeness used by Dr. Guha, in which correction for differing number is employed. He devised a new formula which he calls D^2 and used it in his work *U. P. Anthropometric Survey*, 1941 (*Sankhya*, vol, 9, pp. 111–202).

Further it has to be pointed out here that the results of the somatometric study of two Andhra workers refute Dr. Guha's confirmation of the dolichocephalic character of the Telugu head. In their paper read before the Anthropological Section of the Indian Science Congress in 1937 R. K. Rao and A. Ananthanarayan Iyer showed from the somatometric study of two hundred students representing mostly the intelligentsia of Andhradesha along with others that "the dominant head form is *mesaticephalic* with an average over 76 and that the mean nasal index is 73."

10. Op. cit., Appendix, iii, p. 396. 11. *Vedic Index, vide* Dasyu. 12. I have used only those differential indices which are based on six characters. 13. *United Provinces Census Report*, 1901 p. 248. 14. *Bengal Census Report*, 1901, p. 373. 15. Ibid., p. 369. 16. pp. 255–57. 17. (2), pp. 56, 274–5. 18. *Northern India*, 1907, p. 107. 19. The hypothesis of two or three Aryan inroads was examined by the author in his paper "The Ethic Theory of Caste", published in *Man in India* 1924.

20. Op. cit., p. 29. 21. Op. cit., p. 40. 22. p. 546. 23. p. 248. 24. Op. cit., p. 400. 25. p. 401. 26. *Bengal Census Report*, 1901, p. 369. 27. Op. cit., p. 401. 28. *Bengal Census Report*, 1901, p. 375. 29. *Madras Census Report*, 1901, pp. 130–7.

30. Ibid., pp. 136–9. 31. Ibid., p. 31. 32. Rivers, *The Todas*, p. 708. 33. In my discussion of the physical types I have confined my remarks to the Hindu population. 34. Risley, (2), pp. 33–4. 35. *Cambridge History of India*, vol. i, pp. 335–7. 36. V. A. Smith, *Early History of India* 1914, pp. 411–14. 38. Risley, p. 396. 39. Smith, op. cit., p. 321.

40. Keane, p. 326. 41. V. A. Smith, op. cit., p. 413. 42. *Wanderings of Peoples*, pp. 26–7. 43. p. 34. 44. p. 547. 45. *J.R.A.I.*, 1902, pp. 114, 120. 46. Risley, (2), 34–5. 47. p. 347. 48 Thurston, op. cit., iii, p. 169. 49. *Central Provinces District Gazetteers: Chanda*, p. 123.

50. *J.A.S.B.*, 1903, pt. iii, pp. 92–3. 51. *J.R.A.S.*, 1907, p. 626. 52. Keane, p. 422. 53. *Nature*, 1929, pp. 942–3. 54. Risley, pp. 399–440. 55. Haddon, p. 26. *Linguistic Survey of India*, iv, p. 9. 57. *J.A.S.B.*, 1903, pt. iii, pp. 92–3. 58. *Linguistic Survey of India*, iv, p. 14, and f.n. p. 21. 59. S. C. Roy, *The Oraons*, pp. 352–4.

60. Ibid. 61. Thurston, op. cit., ii, p. 276. 62. Ibid., vol. iv, p. 179. 63. *Journal of the Department of Letters*, Calcutta University, i, p. 165. 64. Thurston, op. cit., p. 41. 65. W. Logan, *Malabar*, i, p. 247. *Madras Museum Bulletin*, vol. iii, p. 38. 67. *The Ancient Egyptians*, pp. 50–62. 68. H. Schaeffer, *The Social Legislation of the Primitive Semites*, p. 3. 69. *The Todas*, p. 708.

70. *Journal of the Department of Letters*, Calcutta University, vol. viii, p. 300. 71. *The Todas*, p. 709. 72. *Sankhya*, I, pp. 76–105. 73. Risley, p. 402. 74. Ibid. p. 31. 75. Thurston, op. cit., vi, p. 312. 76. *U.P. Census Report*, 1911, p. 212. 77. *Bengal Census Report*, 1911, p. 326. 78. *Census, West Bengal*, 1951, *Tribes and Castes of West Bengal*, (1953), p. 383. 79. J. Hornell, *The Sacred Chank of India*, pp. 145–6.

80. Op. cit., p. 33. 81. Risley, (2), p. xx. 82. Op. cit., p. 27, and Map 1.83. Keane, p. 438. 84. Elliot Smith, op. cit., p. 136. 85. *The Periplus of the Erythrean Sea*, p. 134. 86. J.R.A.I. 1916. p. 172, and Map 2. 87. *Bombay Gazetteer*, vol. x, p. 111, f.n. 3. 88. *Journal of the Department of Letters*, Calcutta University, v, p. 226. 89. Ibid., p. 219.

90. Ibid., p. 222. 91. Ibid., p. 233. 92. Ibid., p. 216. 93. Ibid., p. 220. 94. Ibid., p. 256. 95. Ibid., p. 216. 96. L. A. Krishna Iyer, *The Travancore Tribes and Castes*, vol. ii, pp. xlix, liv. 97. *Quarterly Journal of the Mythic Society*, vol. xvii.

6

Elements of Caste Outside India

With the elements of Indian caste before us it will be instructive to see if any one or many of them in combination characterize any other community, civilized or tribal. In our quest for these elements we shall pass under review Egypt, Western Asia, China, Japan, America, and the tribal peoples on the one hand and Rome and tribal Europe on the other.

In Egypt during the Pyramid age there were three principal classes—the land-owners, the serfs and the slaves, the last two being distinguished from the first by the fact of their owning no land.[1] During the Eighteenth Dynasty, to judge from the classification made in an official census, there seem to have been at least four classes. They were the soldiers—who included among them all free persons of the middle class, not engaged in any of the other other callings—the priests, the craftsmen, and the serfs. The first two classes had so many common interests that they were clearly distinguished from the rest.[2] Yet in actual influence and possession of wealth the clergy were far superior to the soldiers.[3] And they had by then formed themselves into a huge sacerdotal organization.[4] The social situation is thus summarized by Petrie: "When we look at the various classes of the country, it is evident that there was, very naturally, a large amount of hereditary succession to office and to business. We see the same in England or any other country, although every one is free to change his occupation as he prefers. In Egypt, on the contrary, no artisan was allowed to have another trade or employment, or be reckoned in any other class. Hence, once in a trade, it was impossible to move out of it, and the natural facility of a boy learning his father's trade tended to fix each generation into the same line. Thus the impression which the Greeks received when stepping into such a society was that its structure was a group of genea or hereditary tribes."[5] It was not only the artisan who was prevented from attempting to enter another calling but it appears that a member of any of the other lower classes as well was not allowed to follow any other occupation than that of his father. As a result, offices often remained in the same families for many generations. Thus we are told in the inscriptions that the office of architect continued in a certain family for twenty-three generations.[6] The goldsmith's art as well as that of the painter and the sculptor was traditionally handed down from father to son. As regards the three middle-class professions, viz., those of a priest, a scribe, and a warrior, though generally they ran in the same families, yet there was no restriction against any one following any of these callings, even if one's father might not have professed that particular calling but had carried on one of the other two. Nay, one and the same man, on suitable occasion, could be a priest, a military or naval commander or could act as a scribe and an official.[7] "A general in the army could marry the daughter of a priest, and his children could be scribes, priests or public functionaries."[8] By the time of the early Ptolemies, however, and possibly earlier, only persons descended from priests could enter their profession. They had secured for the members of their class exemption from poll-tax.[9] Under the influence of their scribes, who were trying to exalt their own profession over the others, the Egyptians came to hold the agriculturists as well as the able craftsmen in light esteem.[10]

Among the Sumerians the aristocracy of the city was formed by the priests and the officials, while the free land-holding citizens formed the middle class, who worked their lands with the help of the slaves.[11] The fragments of Sumerian laws that have come down to us recognize no inequalities among these classes of the community.[12] But in the Code of Hammurabi, the nature and amounts of fine and punishments are mostly determined by the class-status of the offender and the sufferer.[13] The law of limb for limb was restricted to those cases only where the sufferer belonged to the highest class, physical injuries in other cases being generally compensated for by fines. For a physical injury inflicted by a patrician on a plebeian the fine was one-third that which a plebian would have had to pay if he had caused it to his equal. In the case of theft, the patrician paid thrice the fine that the plebeian had to pay. While divorcing a wife, for whom no bride-price was paid, the patricians had to pay her thrice the award that was demanded of a plebeian. The surgeon's fees depended on the status of the patient: the higher the status, the larger the fees.[14]

Woolley thinks that this class-system was military in its origin, and that was the reason why the lives of the patricians, who formed the regular army, were valued more than those of the non-combatant citizens.[15] This theory enables us to explain why in those cases where property was involved the higher classes had also greater responsibilities.

Whether all the males that were either descended from the same parents or were adopted in the family actually carried on the trade of the family is not quite clear. "Certainly many men who carried on a trade were 'sons' of the trade-father, but apparently not all."[16] And a clause in the code of Hammurabi lends support to the view that to enter into a particular trade, which was not followed by one's father, one had to seek legal adoption into a family that carried on that trade.[17] In some cities the trades had their distinct quarters.[18]

A slave could marry a free woman, the offspring being regarded as free. No disgrace seems to have attached to such a marriage, and such a free woman could bring with her a marriage-portion as if she had married in her own rank.[19]

In the earliest period of the Iranian civilization, i.e., before 700 B.C., three classes of society are often mentioned, priests, warriors, and husbandmen, but the fourth class, formed by artisans, is only once mentioned, though there is frequent reference to the work carried on by members of this class, viz., goldsmith, blacksmith, mason, etc. The origin of these classes is attributed to Zarathushtra.[20] According to the *Shah Namah*, however, the four classes were made by Yima.[21] In the Sassanian period, A.D. 226–651, we get more frequent references to these classes, and their relative position is also more well-defined. The priests are likened to the head of man, the warriors to his hands, the husbandmen to his stomach, and the artisans to his feet. Further, we are told that the members of the last class engaged also in trade and commerce. The four classes were credited with different virtues, good nature being that of the premier class, resourcefulness and manliness of the second, strenuous tillage of the third, and diligence and skill of the fourth. It is further observed that "the work of the priest is of the highest merit, and the lowest in the scale of usefulness is the work of the fourth class, more particularly their work of trade and commerce."[22]

The profession of the priest seems to have been hereditary from the earliest times when the classes began to be recognized. By the Sassanian period it was held to be the natural order to follow the occupation of one's ancestors. And if anyone wanted to try a profession other than the one of his class, he was allowed to do so only if, on examination, he proved to be a man of marked talent.[23]

It was only in the late period of Iranian history that there came to be any impediments to intermarriage between the different classes of society, the priestly class arrogating to itself the right of marrying girls from the laity, though refusing to give theirs to the lay youths.[24] Intermarriage of a Zoroastrian with a non-Zoroastrian was condemned in strong terms.[25]

In China it is supposed that society has from time immemorial, been divided into four orders, viz. gentlemen, agriculturists, artisans, and merchants. Gentlemen were all the members of the governing class, the members of the civil service, admission to which depended on a literary test, open to almost all who would like to try their luck and intelligence. "No profession except that of serving the State entitles a man to be called a 'gentleman'." Banker, barrister, physician, priest, merchant-prince, manufacturer, engineer, none of these could be styled a gentleman on the strength of either his profession or wealth. "The sole cachet of aristocracy is literary attainment which has given its proofs."[26] There was a slightly lower grade division of this class which was formed by those who had qualified for the civil service and yet had to be on the waiting list for lack of suitable appointments. These were known as the scholars.[27] Next in order stood the workers of the soil, agriculture being regarded, from very early times, a very noble calling. The social ladder was not quite complete with the traders. There still remained the barbers and their sons who were reckoned among the pariāh classes and were debarred from competing for the civil service.[28] According to Confucius, the people were divided into five classes, which in the descending order of social prestige were scholars, farmers, artisans, merchants, and servants, soldiers being always included in the last group.[29] In ancient times soldiers and scholars were grouped together under one term.[30]

Ranks were distinguished by different head-dresses, garments, badges, etc.[31] None whose parents were engaged in one of the degrading occupations, like menial service, play-acting or brother-keeping, was allowed to compete for the civil service.[32] One of the emperors forbade the use of silk garments or carriages by merchants; and in order to render that calling unpopular he levied heavy taxes on them.[33]

Except the civil service, it appears that most of the other occupations were customarily hereditary. One of the Chinese books lay it down as a rule that "the sons of officers ought always to be officers, the sons of artisans ought always to be artisans. The sons of merchants ought always to be merchants, and the sons of farmers ought always to be farmers".[34]

Marriages between officials and actresses or singing girls were not allowed. In the case of nobles of hereditary rank, for entering into such a union the penalty was degradation to a lower class.[35] Play-actors, policemen, and boatmen had to marry women of their own class. No slave could marry a free woman.[36] Officials were included under the scholar class and were loath to intermarry with merchant families. "Chinese society has been characterized by a remarkable minimum of hard and fast class divisions." observes Latourette.[37]

In Japan during her military age—twelfth century to the middle of the nineteenth century A.D.—society was divided into five distinct groups. Hereditary sodiers, the Samurai, were the foremost of these. Farmers, artisans, and traders followed next in order. The fifth class was formed by two groups called the Etā and the Hinin, who were the Pariāhs and outcastes of the community.[38] Every occupation that brought a man into contact with unclean things, such as the corpses of human beings, the carcasses of animals, and offal of all descriptions, was degraded.[39] Occupations that catered for the sensuous side of man as well as those that did not carry a fixed scale of remuneration were regarded as low.[40] The degrading calling, and some others like stone-cutting and casting of metal, were relegated to the outcastes.[41] After the Revolution, 1867–78 a change was brought about in the social classification and at the present day* there are three classes established by law. These are the nobility, the gentry, and the common people who include farmers, artisans, and merchants. The first two classes constitute only five per cent of the population, the rest being commoners. Every householder is required to nail up over his door a ticket with his name and class inscribed thereon.[42]

During the eight centuries of military feudalism preceding the Revolution the Samurai was a being apart. His conduct was governed by special canons, and special tribunals judged his offences. If he was temporarily imprisoned and had to be presented at a court, he was carried in a closed sedan-chair, while a common prisoner was marched through the streets.

The tribunal that adjudicated on matters relating to temples and shrines was distinct from that which had jurisdiction in the case of artisans, merchants, and others, and the agriculturists. During the latter part of the seventeenth century separate jails were built: one for the Samurai and priests, another for the merchants and common people and a third for the farmers. Till the latter part of the seventeenth century it had not been usual to send a Samurai to jail for any crime.[43] The Etā had to live on the outskirts of towns and villages and were governed by their own headmen. Prejudice against this unfortunate class of people was so great that it long survived the removal of their legal disabilities in 1871. serving as a theme for novelists.[44]

The outcasts could not marry persons of the higher classes.[45] During the feudal age intermarriage among the various recognized classes of society required special permission.[46]

In Mexico, as a result of its conquest by the Europeans, the population is divided into three main well-marked groups with numerous sub-divisions. The highest class is formed of members who have a more or less pure Spanish descent, the half-breed coming next, and the pure Indians forming the lowest class.[47] When the Spaniards captured Mexico they found that the sons generally learned the trades and entered the professions of their fathers. "The different trades were arranged into something like guilds, having each a particular district of the city appropriated to it, with its own chiefs, its own tutelary deity, its peculiar festivals."[48]

In spite of the great cultural differences, mixture of the Spaniards and the Indians has proceeded apace, largely it would appear because of the half-breed, called mestizo, being more active and adaptible than the Indian. In 1921 the pure Whites formed only 19 per cent of the total population, pure Indians 38 per cent, and the mestizo 43 per cent. According to a calculation made about 1940 the respective percentages had changed to 17, 19 and 54. The half-breed is almost invariably the result of the mating of a Spanish male with an Indian female. It is interesting to note that the White man though very properly was called *espānol* yet was otherwise known as *gachupin*, 'one who wears shoes'. In Peru too, where the Spaniards mixed with the Indians, the half-breeds, known as mestizo, have been on the increase. The half-breeds, living on the coastline, have special terms for all degrees of colour and race.

In Brazil, where the native Indians are not known to have developed a pre-Columbus civilization, and which was colonized by the Portuguese, the latter are described to have given the country "its language and basic racial type". This first half-breeds, known as mestizo or mameluco, were the progeny as elsewhere of the White male and the Indian female. Later the Negroes were introduced.

---

* This was written in 1930.

Intermarriage was not forbidden. Today* with Brazil's population standing at little over 40 million, the pure Indians and the mestizo form only 2 and 18 per cent of the population. The Whites are about three times the Negroes, among whom too the half-breed, called mulatto, shows greater growth. It is the old families of Portuguese descent that form the aristocracy, and being wealthy they have not allowed themselves to be superseded by the new rich from among the mixed population. "Exclusiveness is something unknown in Brazil, and in both the racial and social spheres, the process of assimilation continues", observed Zweig. In view of the figures given above this assimilation does not appear to be much different from annihilation of the Indian. In real assimilation one expects the half-breed to grow in preponderance.[49]

Among the Kayans and Kenyaks of Borneo there are three classes, the upper, middle and the slaves.[50] The Maoris distinguish the following orders in their society: the sacerdotal chiefs of smaller tribal divisions, the skilled artisans and other professionals, the bulk of the comparatively poor population and lastly the slaves taken captive in war.[51] The Samoans recognize six classes: The chiefs, priests, landed gentry, large landowners, commoners, and slaves, the first not being wholly uniform.[52] But the most distinct and unbridgeable gulf lies between the patricians and the plebeians—the two main divisions of society comprising the above classes.[53] Tahitian society was divided into classes that were insuperably distinct from one another. The privileged class was composed of the reigning king, the chieftains, and their relations. Next in rank came the gentry, the farmers, artisans and fishermen forming the next class. The lowest class comprised servants and slaves.[54] Among the Hawaiians, society was marked by an exclusive class-division, all persons belonging by birth to one of the three classes. The Ariis or the nobles, the Hakuaina or land-proprietors and the priests, the Canakamowree or the common people, comprising the small farmers, artisans and professionals, fishermen and labourers.[55]

In some parts of Fiji the people are divided into small independent bodies with smaller groups within each, these latter being called Matanggali. In some cases the Matanggali of a tribe have different functions, and some of these groups among the ordinary people are differentiated by the possession of special occupations.[56]

The people of Borneo nearly always marry within their class, though persons of the middle class sometimes do marry females of the slave class.[57] In the Carolinas, apart from the slaves, there are two classes, the lower of which is forbidden to touch the higher on pain of death. Further they are not allowed to carry on fishing and seafaring, nor to marry with members of the higher class.[58] Africa provides us with a very interesting case of obligatory endogamy. The smiths often form a social group kept distinct from the rest of the community, to which they belong, by having to marry within their group.[59] Though totemism is generally associated with exogamy yet there are totemic groups both in Africa and elsewhere that are more or less endogamous.[60]

In South Arabia there are two classes of Pariāhs. One class, comprising the artisans, was regarded as the subordinate menials of the dominant class. Its members were required to live on the outskirts of the towns, and though admitted into the mosques were not allowed to visit Arab houses. The other class of Pariāhs was regarded as still inferior, and its members were not allowed to enter even the mosque, though they were devout Muslims.[61]

There is enough evidence to show that the Arabs had no law of endogamy. But they did not like to intermarry with people who had different tastes and customs.[62]

* This was written in 1950.

In ancient Rome the populace was for a long time divided into three groups—the patricians, the plebeians, and the slaves. Of these the first two classes comprised all the free men. It is a matter of common knowledge that the evolution of political institutions in Rome was largely the result of a conflict between the patricians, the politically privileged class, and the plebeians who were politically insignificant. Up to the time of Servius Tullius the patricians alone ranked as citizens. Their marriage was regarded as sanctified and lawful. They had the special powers of testamentary disposition. None but they could consult the gods of Rome by a specially sacred procedure.[63] The plebeians were the artisans and craftsmen of Rome. Their marriages were not celebrated with the religious ceremony to which the patricians were accustomed, and were looked upon by the latter as not involving the legal consequences of marriage.[64] The disparity between the class and the mass in their political as well as socio-religious rights was gradually removed, so that by 287 B.C. the two groups were placed on a footing of equality.[65] Yet the old spirit found new embodiment in social matters. The great economic development resulting in many new and varied occupations fostered some which came to be looked upon as degraded *ipso facto*.[66] The development of economic life had advanced so far that even specialized arts and crafts had formed guilds. Thus the shoe-makers had amongst them various divisions like boot-makers, sandal-makers, slipper-makers, and ladies' shoe-makers. Workers in the same craft and trade congregated at Rome and elsewhere in Italy in special districts. There was a guild of anything and everything, each with its special deity and an annual festival. In the annual procession of the patron deity the guildsmen marched through the streets with their regalia and flag.[67] Roman laws of the fifth century of the Christian era reveal the upper class as cut off from the masses. Every social grade and occupation was "practically hereditary, from the senator to the waterman on the Tiber, or the sentinel at a frontier post." There was a tendency to stereotype social life by preventing free circulation among different callings and grades in society.[68] The Theodosian Code compelled a youth to follow the employment of his father.[69]

In prehistoric Rome endogamy existed to this extent that marriage was arranged within the limits of the gens.[70] Generally marriage could take place only between parties that were equal in their political rights. Thus a free man could not wed a freed woman without the special permission of the Senate.[71] A man of the senatorial rank could not contract a marriage with a woman born in one of the degraded occupations.[72] In the fifth century A.D. men were not permitted to marry out of their guild. If the daughter of a member of the baker caste married a man not belonging to it, her husband had to adopt her father's calling.[73] These provisions about marriage and occupation were more in the nature of financial adjustments than social development.

The Celts occupied Ireland in the fourth century B.C. and soon supplanted the aboriginal Pictish speech and culture. Macalister is convinced from his study of both the literary and archaeological remains of the immediately succeeding ages, that there was a marked contrast in the physical make-up and appearance between the new comers and the aborigines. He finds that in the literature of the period "every person spoken of with respect" is described as tall and fair, while "every person who for any reason is spoken of with disdain is described as being short, dark, and with close-cropped hair." He concludes from this that the physical contrast was "maintained by restrictions on intermarriage."[74]

In Anglo-Saxon England society was divided into three well-marked classes of people: the nobleman, the common freeman, and the slaves. There seems to have been also a fourth class called the 'Laet'. It represented a class "intermediate between freemen and slaves, which was rather infrequent in England though very common among the Teutonic peoples of the Continent.[75] This class, which was a feature peculiar to Kentish society, seems to have had three sub-divisions differing in their wergelds, with wergelds of 80, 60, and 40 shillings respectively.[76] The first class had two divisions, a higher and a lower order, the higher order, whose immediate overlord was the king, being subject to higher charges and heavier fines. The membership of the class was partly inherited and partly acquired. Possession of a certain amount of land by a family continuously for three generations bestowed permanent nobility on the members of that family.[77] The second class comprised all the free persons of English blood who were not members of the first class. Though there were many subdivisions in this class we find no evidence of any difference in wergeld,[78] "the fixed sum with which a person's death must be atoned for to his kindred or which he might in some cases have to pay for his own misdoing." The nobleman's wergeld was six times that of a commoner's; and his oath also was worth as much.[79] The slave being unfree was not a legal person and as such had no wergeld.

The clergy seem to have been regarded as members of the nobility; yet there was a special scale of wergeld for them. A priest, who was a nobleman previous to his taking orders, could have the option of demanding either the wergeld that was proper to his original rank or one that was due to him because of his ecclesiastical rank.[80]

If a slave stole the property of a freeman he had to pay twice the amount as compensation, while if the theft was committed by a freeman he paid thrice. If it was the priest's property that was stolen, nine-fold compensation had to be paid.[81] If a man's servant killed a nobleman, whose wergeld was three hundred shillings, the owner had to surrender the servant and pay the price of three men; but if he killed a commoner, whose wergeld was only a hundred shillings, then the owner paid the price of only one man in addition to surrendering the homicide. If a priest killed a man—any freeman—he was ejected from the monastic order and his property confiscated.[82] Fornication with a nobleman's serving maid was to be compensated for by double the sum of money that had to be paid in the case of the same offence being committed in respect of the serving maid of a commoner. If a man committed adultery with the wife of a servant, he had to pay compensation, while if he did the same with the wife of a freeman he had to procure a second wife in addition to compensation. If a betrothed woman of the commoner class was guilty of fornication, she was ordered to pay 60 shillings as compensation to the surety of the marriage; if she belonged to the higher class, this amount was to be greater in proportion to her wergeld. "If anyone rapes the slave of a commoner, he shall pay 5 shillings to the commoner, and a fine of 60 shillings. If a slave rapes a slave, castration shall be required as compensation." For illicit union a nobleman had to pay double the commoner's compensation.[83] Breaking into the premises of a nobleman had to be atoned for by thrice or six times the fine that had to be paid for the same offence against a commoner. In the scale of compensation that a man had to pay for fighting in the house of another the same proportion had to be maintained between the two classes.[84] A priest could clear himself of any charge by a simple declaration; a clerk had to place his hand on the altar accompanied by three men of his class, while a commoner was required to clear himself by the collective oath of himself and of three of his own class.[85] "If a nobleman who holds land neglects military service, he shall pay 120 shillings and forfeit his land; a nobleman who holds no land shall pay 60 shillings; a commoner shall pay a fine of 30 shillings for neglecting military service."[86]

By the thirteenth century the law of status had become relatively insignificant, and the law of tenure had risen into prominence. Accordingly, the law-books have very little to say about the ranks of men and a great deal about tenures. "In the main all free men are equal before the law. Just because this is so, the line between the free and the unfree seems very sharp." And even this distinction is very apt to appear in practice as a difference in tenures. The clergy was gaining in importance. Every ordained clerk was subject to special rules of eccelesiastical and secular law. If he committed any of the crimes known as felonies, he could be tried only by an ecclesiastical as well as by the temporal tribunals.[87]

By the fifteenth century commercial spirit had grown so much that the dwindling ideas of status had come to be replaced by social distinctions based on the possession of wealth, even land being regarded as a mere manifestation and a source of wealth. The failure of the sumptuary laws of this period is a measure of the futility of keeping the old class division.[88]

In Scandinavia during the early Middle Ages the following scheme of social classes was in force: high-born men comprising the kingly families and their immediate liegemen; the nobles; the great landed middle class, including all grades of freeholders; freed men and their descendants of many generations; and slaves. It was possible for members of lower rank to rise to the superior grade both by marriage as well as by accumulation of wealth. Yet the social stratification made its mark on social etiquette, and legal and sacerdotal affairs. Thus, in the great banqueting halls seats were so arranged that the lowliest members might be accommodated nearest the door. "Class discrimination was, however, felt most in connection with legal and governmental matters, in determining the amount of wergeld which must be paid if a member of the population was wronged or killed, in the composition of the juries, and in the exercise of legislative and judicial power at the political assemblies." In the public cemeteries of the Christian church the nobles were buried in the most sacred ground, nearest to the church, while the other classes had their burying places at further distances in the descending order of their rank, the slaves being relegated to the ground nearest the wall of the churchyard.[89]

During mediaeval times all over Europe trades and crafts were highly organized. There was a certain lack of freedom, therefore, about the choice of a trade or a craft. Thus in England, where smithcraft was held in special esteem, no villain was allowed to carry on that craft without his lord's permission.[90] When the important crafts came to be organized into guilds, anyone who desired to practise a particular craft had to join the guild as a journeyman to take his training in that craft. At first, it seems admission was unrestricted and the conditions fairly light, thus making the guilds more or less free associations of persons, engaged in crafts and pledged to instructing the new generation in the means of getting their livelihood. But in later times, about the thirteenth century, they degenerated into family coteries. The widow of a guildsman might carry on the trade of her husband, or could confer the freedom of the guild on her second husband if he was following the same trade. But if she married a man not belonging to the same craft, not only could she not confer the freedom of the guild on her new husband but she herself was excluded from the guild. In the fifteenth and sixteenth centuries the restrictions on admission to a craft guild became more and more rigorous, and the handicrafts became practically the monopolies of a few families.

About the same time, in Germany a candidate for admission into a guild had to furnish proof of pure birth in order to be worthy of the admission. Whole classes of people were being excluded from the guilds on the pretence of some infamy attaching to their birth, so much so that, after the sixteenth century, legislation had to be passed to remedy this growing evil. Apprentices, who proved the purity of their birth, had to undergo heavy expenses and during their probation had to undertake long travel, extending over as many as five years, before they could set up as masters of their crafts. Further, before a craftsman could set up independent practice, he had to prepare a masterpiece, which generally was a very costly and a useless article. The sons of master-craftsmen were, on the other hand, free from all these prohibitive conditions. In effect the guilds became clubs of families, hereditarily carrying on the particular crafts.

"The punishments decreed by the craft-guilds consisted in the payment of fines, or in earlier times in certain quantities of wax, or of beer or wine to be drunk at their feasts." Offences like forgery led to exclusion from the guild and withdrawal of the right to practise the craft.[91] The members of each craft usually occupied the same locality. Thus in London, the weavers concentrated in Cannon Street, smiths in Smithfield, and so on. "Such a grouping must have enormously strengthened the sense of corporate life in each craft."[92]

Though the crafts, the practice of which was from very early times hedged in by many restrictions, had become more or less hereditary, the learned professions and commerce had begun to offer fresh fields for the intelligent youths. "The church had always provided clever youths with an opportunity of rising in the world." Towards the end of the fourteenth and throughout the following century, it seems, the clergy were largely recruited from the middle classes and even from serfs, the economic changes rendering the profession less attractive to the members of the upper classes. In the fifteenth century the legal profession also opened up possibilities of a brilliant career.[93]

In the cities of Europe guilds were ranked according to the recognized importance of their trades. The principle on which the occupations were rated was evidently not the vital importance of the needs which were supplied by them. "The status of a profession seems to have depended on whether it was more or less honourable, lucrative or ancient. The place of honour was reserved for those crafts in which brain-work took precedence over manual work. They were regarded as honourable, evidently because in the dualistic conception which governed Christian societies, spirit was placed above matter, the intellectual above the animal part of man." The occupations demanding intellectual work alone came to be designated 'liberal' professions, as contrasted with those involving manual labour, these latter being termed 'servile'. In the university towns the professors occupied the first rank and shared with the nobles the privilege of walking on the wall side of the pavement. The doctors also belonged to this category, though their brethren of lower origins, the surgeon-barbers, were relegated to a lower status on account of their partiality for surgical operations. Though craftsmen usually were rated low, the goldsmiths had secured a high rank. Dealers in articles that were to be brought from distant countries, like spices and furs, were ranked very high. Bankers, money-changers, and wholesale dealers were distinguished not only because their professions required quickness of perception, complicated calculations, wide range of vision and rare thought, but also because of their show of wealth. "It is easy to see that in the priority accorded to the great industrial and commercial guilds, the second of the principles we have mentioned was at work, namely, that a craft was considered more or less honourable according to the wealth it yielded. . . . It was undoubtedly for this reason that the butchers, who had numerous assistants working under their orders and who made considerable profit, sometimes managed in Paris to be included among the 'Six Guilds'." Home crafts suffered from internal competition and thus were ranked rather low. At Florence the baker and the bread-maker came last in the list of the twenty-one official guilds.[94]

It was in keeping with these ideas of occupational dignity that in France a member of the nobility had his noble state suspended if he carried on trade or handicraft, incompatible with the profession of arms.[95]

The laws of the Anglo-Saxons laid it down that none was to seek in marriage a mate outside one's class, so that if a person of lower status married a woman of a higher class he was to perish.[96] By the fifteenth century, in England this rule of endogamy had almost vanished, so much so that one of the usual methods by which the needy nobles replenished their empty purses was by marrying the daughters or widows of rich merchants. Such marriages went a long way in fusing the upper and the middle classes.[97] In France, in the later period of the Roman Empire, the workmen, employed in the manufactures of the State like that of arms, were not allowed to marry their daughters outside their group.[98] In the eyes of the tribal law the only legal marriage that could take place was between free-born people of equal status. The free woman who married her own slave lost her freedom, and had her property confiscated, and the slave was killed on the wheel. Where a free man married either his slave or a freed woman, neither the wife nor the issue of the union attained the rank of the man.[99] During the feudal age, however, legitimate children took the status of their father, the principle that gentility came from the father being gradually recognized. If a free woman married a nobleman she attained his status but not so a servile woman.[100] In Germany "the consequences of equality of birth in private law made themselves felt in the law of family and inheritance. Only an equal-born member of the estate had the right of exercising guardianship over minors and women. And only between those equal in birth was there a right of inheritance". Originally members of different status-groups could not contract a legal marriage. A free woman's marriage with a slave meant loss of freedom to the woman or of life to the slave. Under the influence of Christianity the rigour of laws against the unequal marriages was much lessened, such unions being regarded as only inferior marriages and the issue as quite legitimate. But the higher status of one of the parties could not be conferred on the other, the issue being naturally relegated to the status of the lower-born. Exceptionally the children of a union, where the wife was a free woman and the husband half-free or unfree, were allowed to inherit the natural freedom of their mother. In the newer grouping of society on the occupational basis "the principle of equal birth was less and less heeded." Only the higher nobility clung to it.[101]

To sum up, distinction by birth has been usually recognized by many primitive peoples and almost all the major civilizations of ancient times. The primitive peoples, in so far as their arts and crafts are neither many, nor highly specialized, have few classes whose status is fixed. But wherever status is recognized, privileges and restrictions in the matter of the choice of avocation are very common. Restriction on the choice of one's mate based on birth is comparatively infrequent among them. In tribal England, in Rome, and in Asian civilizations, occupations not only tended to become hereditary but were actually prescribed to be followed by specific classes and graded in certain order as high and low. Specialized occupations had come to form themselves into units of community life. Society was divided into two, three, four, or five well-marked status-groups, intermarriage between which was often prohibited. The Chinese civilization, before it was influenced by Indian ideas, seems to have been the most free in its social grouping.

Well-marked status-groups within a society, distinguished from one another by rights and disabilities, separated from one another by the absence of freedom of intermarriage, may, therefore, be considered to be a common characteristic of the mental background and social picture of the Indo-European cultures. Specialization of occupations, accompanied by solidarity within specified occupations and great unfreedom about their choice, was a feature common to the ancient and mediaeval times. The circumstances that led to the abolition of distinctions, based on birth and occupation, in Rome and in England are peculiar to each and cannot be gone into here. Suffice it for us to remember that in each case it was the special conditions, making for political unity and commercial aggrandisement, that slowly killed the ideas of status by birth and removed the unfreedom of occupation. G. M. Trevelyan's observation about Chaucer's England illustrates the point. Trevelyan remarks: "National self-consciousness is beginning to dissolve the local loyalties and rigid class divisions which had characterized the cosmopolitan society of the feudal age."[102]

References

1. Breasted, (2), p. 67. 2. Breasted, (1), p. 246. 3. Maspero, p. 35. 4. Breasted, (1), p. 247. 5. Petre, pp. 11–12. 6. Spencer, iii, p. 422. 7. Erman, p. 460. 8. Wilkinson, i, p. 159, a note by Dr. S. Birch. 9. A. M. Blackman, in *Ency. of R. and E.*, vol. x, p. 299 (b).

10. Erman, p. 446, Breasted, (1), p. 169. 11. Breasted, (2), p. 119. 12. Brooks, p. 88. 13. Jastrow, p. 293. 14. Johns, p. 74. and pp. 44–63 of *The Code of Hammurabi* edited by him. 15. Woolley, p. 97. 16. Johns, p. 121. 17. Brooks, p. 44. 18. Johns, p. 121. 19. Ibid., pp. 75, 136.

20. Dhalla, p. 65. 21. Ibid., p. 7. 22. Ibid., p. 295. 23. Ibid., p. 296. 24. Ibid., p. 78. 25. Ibid., p. 304. 26. Brinkley, xi, pp. 202–4. 27. Douglas, p. 116. 28. Ibid., pp. 120–46. 29. Bash-ford, p. 43.

30. Latourette, II, p. 206. 31. Werner (1), Table I. 32. Brinkley, x, 132. 34. Spencer, iii, p. 422. 35. Mollendorff, p. 20. 36. Werner (2), p. 40. 37. Op. cit., II. pp. 204–206. 38. Longford, pp. 69–70. 39. Brinkley (2), vol. ii, p. 41.

40. Ibid. 41. Ibid., p. 49. 42. Chamberlain, p. 95. 43. Brinkley, iv, pp. 64–6, 76. 44. Chamberlain, pp. 149–150. 45. Brinkley (2), vol. ii, p. 50. 46. *Ency. of R. and E.*, viii, p. 459 (b). 47. Spencer, p. 25. 48. Spencer, vol. iii, pp. 422–45. 49. *E.B.*, XVI, pp. 381–382; XVII, p. 628; Zweig, pp. 136–7, 149, 150, 155; *E.B*, IV, pp. 50–51; *Condition of Life & Work of Indigenous Populations of Latin American Countries* (I.L.O. Publication, 1949), p. 17.

50. Hose and McDougall, i, p. 68. 51. Lowie, pp. 346–7. 52. Ibid., p. 347. 53. Ibid., p. 349. 54. Featherman, ii b, 37. 55. Ibid., p. 244. 56. Rivers, pp. 264–5. N.B.: The account of the Fijian and the Samoan classes given by A. M. Hocart makes it quite clear that these systems are copied from the Hindu caste system. See the summary appearing in *Nature*, 7th April, 1928, p. 551. 57. Hose and McDougall, pp. 71–2. 58. Hobhouse, *Morals in Evolution*, (1916), p. 274, f.n. 5. 59. Rivers in *Ency. of R. and E.* viii, p. 424 (b).

60. *E.B.* XXII, p. 315. 61. Featherman, v, p. 424. 62. Smith, W. Robertson, pp. 74–5, and f.n. 2. 63. Muirhead, p. 6. 64. Ibid., pp. 11–12; Louis, pp. 48–9. 65. Leage, p. 14. 66. Tucker, p. 295. 67. Friedlander, vol. i, p. 147; Tucker, p. 254; Dill (2), p. 265. 68. Dill, (2), pp. 228–33. 69. Lambert, p. 12.

70. Warde Fowler, in *Ency. of R. and E.*, vii, p. 463 (a); cf. Ghurye (2), pp. 210–11. 71. Leffingwell, p. 39. 72. Tucker, p. 295. 73. Dill, (2), p. 233, Louis, p. 261. 74. *E.B.* XII, p. 618. 75. Attenborough, p. 177. 76. Chadwick, p. 112. 77. Ibid., pp. 79–84. 78. Ibid., p. 85. 79. Pollock and Maitland, p. 33.

80. Ibid., p. 34. 81. Attenborough, pp. 5, 17. 82. Ibid., pp. 19–75. 83. Ibid., pp. 7, 9, 15, 25, 73, 75. 84. Ibid., pp. 81–3, 85. Ibid., p. 29. 86. Ibid., p. 53. 87. Pollock and Maitland, pp. 407, 412, 439, 441. 88. Abram, p. 72. 89. Williams, pp. 35–6.

90. Trail, vol, i, p. 104. 91. Toulmin Smith (Lujo Brentano in), pp. cxxvi–vii, cxxxii, cxlix–cli; Huebner, pp. 104, 129. 92. Ashley, p. 96. 93. Abram, pp. 99, 106. 94. Renard, pp. 57–61. 95. Brissaud (2), p. 300. 96. N. K. Sidhanta, *The Heroic Age of India*, pp. 136–7. 97. Abram, p. 89. N.B.: Compare the practice of the Japanese Samurai, in the middle of the eighteenth century, of adopting into their families the sons of rich commoners to replenish their treasury: Yosoburo Takakoshi, *The Economic Aspects of the History of the Civilization of Japan*, (1930), vol. ii, pp. 452–3. 98. Brissaud, (2), p. 48. 99. Brissaud, (1), pp. 158–9.

100. Brissaud, (2). pp. 291, f.n. 6, 298. 101. Huebner, pp. 92–4, 99. 102. Op. cit., p. 3.

7

Origins of the Caste System

Social differentiation with its attendant demarcation of groups and of status of individuals is a very widespread feature of human society.[1] In by far the larger number of communities this status depends on the individual's achievement in those fields of activity which are prized by those communities. They range from capacity for certain types of supernatural experience to ability to acquire wealth. The visible marks of this differentiation are, as we have seen, special rights for some groups and disabilities on others in the matter of dress, occupation, and even food. In other communities the status of an individual is determined by birth. People, speaking Indo-European tongues, carried this theory of status of birth to a farther extent than any other peoples, both in the matter of the number of differentiated groups within a society as well as in the matter of their rights and disabilities. Some of them even enjoined that members of a group shall marry in their own group. Thus it would be seen that the Hindu system is unique only in this that it alone classified some groups as untouchable and unapproachable.[2] In other respects it only differs in the thoroughness with which the scheme is worked out and in the number of differentiated groups.

Of the many cultures that flourished in India the literary records of the Indo-Aryan culture are not only the earliest but contain the first mention and a continuous history of the factors that make up caste. The only other culture whose records are intelligible is the Dravidian; but when that culture put forward its documents that are extant, it had already been immensely influenced by the Indo-Aryan tradition. The Brahmanic variety of this Indo-Aryan civilization—it is the most widely and deeply spread aspect—was developed in the Gangetic plain. I, therefore, conclude that some of the important aspects of caste originated in this region. The people, who are known here and elsewhere as Indo-Aryans and whose earliest literary records have furnished us with information about the institution of caste and class, belong linguistically to the larger family of peoples designed either as Indo-Europeans or as Indo-Germans. They comprised the Celts, the Anglo-Saxons and the Teutons, the Romans, and the Iranians among others. The Spanish and the Portuguese too belong to the same family. In prehistoric times about 5000 B.C., the ancestors of all these peoples seem to have occupied one fairly defined region and to have been in close cultural contact with one another. When for some reason they dispersed from their centre of characterization, various groups started in different directions and had varying adventures. Their separate languages diverged yet retained sufficient common structure and content to enable the 19th and 20th century philologists to group them together and reconstruct the primitive speech which must have been the stock-in-trade of their ancestors in their centre of characterization. One of the branches of these peoples which reached India about 2500 B.C. with the kind of religion represented in the early Vedic religion is called the Indo-Aryans.

As shown above their favourite word for certain groups and others of people was 'varna', 'colour'. Thus they spoke of the 'Dāsa varna', 'Dāsa colour' or more properly the Dāsa people. Iranian literature, though in the bulk very much later than the Vedas, has preserved the significant information that the Iranians spoke of the people, whom they found in occupation of certain areas which later they captured, as 'Dāha'. Iranian 'Dāha' is the exact equivalent of Vedic 'Dāsa', making allowance for the linguistic values of the sounds of the last syllable. Like the Vedic Aryans they spoke of themselves as 'Āryas' or 'Airya' whose identity with the Sanskrit word 'Āryas' need not be pointed out. The 'Dāha' are the predatory tribes of Turan, where before their bifurcation and further dispersal the ancestors of the Vedic Indians and Iranians lived together as one community, designating themselves by the term 'Arya'. Though 'Dāha' means enemies or robbers, their nationality is suspected to be Iranian. The Vedic Indians might well have applied the term to their enemies in India, the native population of the Punjab. It is further to be noted that though Iranian literature, perhaps because of its highly mutilated condition in which it has reached us, does not attest the use of the equivalent of the Sanskrit 'Anāryas', 'un-Aryan', applied to a people, the Greek geographers like Strabo have mentioned a people called 'Anariacae', 'Non-Arians'.[3]

The early Persians and their great monarchs show a catholicity and pliability which is not merely a diplomatic gesture of a world empire. As the great historian Eduard Meyer has observed: "In contrast with Judaism, Zoroastrianism did not enter the lists against all gods save its own, but found no difficulty in recognizing them as subordinate powers—helpers and servants of Ahura-Mazda." Darius, the Great, not only encouraged the efforts of the Egyptian priests in every way, but also built temples for their gods. Cyrus, Darius and Artaxerxes I between them enabled the Jews to re-establish themselves in Babylon. This spirit of tolerance and even of active sympathy and of selective assimilation of the early Persians stands in marked contrast with the exclusiveness and intolerance of their successors in the Sassanian period about 700 to 800 years later. The Neo-Persian empire, as the Sassanian kingdom is designated, showed itself to be a continuation of the national tradition of the Achaemenian period in almost all respects, excepting in that of the basic spirit of tolerance and of the practice of ceremonial purity. Something had happened to the Persians during this long interval. Prescriptions of ceremonial purity which could not be observed abroad were being diligently adhered to. In the words of Eduard Meyer, "the ritual and the doctrine of purity were elaborated and expanded, and there was evolved a complete and detailed system of casuistry, dealing with all things allowed and forbidden, the forms of pollution and the expiation for each, etc., which in its arid and spiritless monotony, vividly recalls the similar prescriptions in the Pentateuch. . . . In short, the tolerance of the Achaemenids and the indifference of the Arsacids are now replaced by intolerance and religious persecution."[4] These words of this savant and others too many to be quoted here, are very significant for a student of the development of the idea of ceremonial purity and its role in the growth of exclusiveness which are so fundamental in the Indian caste-society. And it cannot be a mere coincidence that, as we have seen, the four social orders of the Persian society, viz., the Athravan, etc., are positively enumerated and the few privileges and diabilities pertaining to them are specifically mentioned during the Sassanian period of Persian history. The Indian Aryans, as must have been plain from a perusal of Chapter III, began with moderate amount of both exclusiveness and tolerance. Having come across people, who were very dark in colour and had rather snub noses, they described the earlier settlers as 'dark colour', as people without noses, and applied to them the term 'dāsa' which in Iranian stood for 'enemy'. Their ideas of ritual purity, which we have come across in the fourth chapter, are very earlier in extant available literature. They are quite analogous too. In matters of religious faith and practice, though they began by stigmatizing that of the natives, they did not develop the extreme intolerance which the Persians of the Sassanian period show. Their tolerance of the varied faiths was based on the principle that religious and moral belief and practice were to be adjusted to the spiritual stature of individuals and groups. The Indian Aryans as later Hindus not only tolerated both beliefs and practices not harmonizing with their central doctrines but also assimilated a number in their own complex. Partially at least, on the social organizational side caste system was the *modus operandi* accommodating diversity of faiths and practices.

Limited and conditional exclusiveness and consequent practice of ceremonial purity show themselves as fundamental traits of culture and character of other and western branches of Indo-European peoples. The Greeks, even in the heyday of their philosophical thought, manifested this spirit. Their contempt of the slaves is almost proverbial; and the bulk of the slave population differed from them in both race and culture. Plato, the maker of ideal laws, offers the finest testimony of the depth of this feeling and perhaps of the extent of the practice. His penalty for the heinous offence of striking one's parent is the perpetual exilement of the striker from the city. In order that his exile and ostracism may be completely successful, Plato further lays down a rule, which is redolent of the caste penalties of the Hindus on their erring members. It runs: "And if any person eat or drink, or have any other sort of intercourse with him, or only meeting him have voluntarily touched him, he shall not enter into any temple, nor into the agora, nor into the city, until he is purified; for he should consider that he has become tainted by a curse."[5]

Just as the Vedic Aryans came across, in India, a civilized people, those perhaps who have left the traces of their culture in the mounds at Harappa in the Punjab and at Mohenjodaro in Sindh, the Greeks were confronted in their land of choice with the higher Aegean civilization. The interaction of the two cultures and its results are not adequately preserved for us. Some eight or ten centuries passed after the Greeks were face to face and in close contact with another civilization of much greater antiquity, stability and width, when they established a colony at Naukratis in Egypt. Some intelligible account of what happened then is available. It is very illuminating and may be presented here with advantage. It is well known that after Alexander's death when his vast empire was parcelled out among the various claimants, Egypt fell to the lot of Ptolemy. The social history of Ptolemaic Egypt in general and that of the cities like Naukratis and the newer Alexandria is instructive. Pride and exclusive spirit, which are so patent in the early Vedic literature, were exhibited by the Greeks even in their dealings with the Egyptians, from whose stable and old civilization their own had already received not only inspiration in general but also a few specific traits. They treated the Egyptians as a subject people, being themselves the conquerors. In spite of their appreciation of the high antiquity of the civilization of the Egyptians they showed themselves as the heirs and representatives of a higher one. One may well compare this situation with that prevailing in India during the better part of the 19th century, the British taking the place of the Greeks and the Indians that of the Egyptians. In the cities of Alexandria, Naukratis, etc., they seem to have segregated the populations. And marriages between them were not permitted. Even Greek males could not marry Egyptian females. But in the country, where there was no such bar, the Greek and Macedonian soldiers and ordinary settlers had no horror of intermarriage with Egyptian women. The Egyptians on their part had realized that in order to get on with the victors and rulers it was necessary for them not only to learn Greek but also to dress and behave like the Greeks. From this double process ensued a fairly continual mixture of blood. The racial difference too began to grow less and less, so that large numbers of people in Egypt, who later on called themselves Greeks were in reality mainly Egyptian in blood, refined or diluted by a slight admixture of the blood from Greek males. The distinction between the higher stratum of Greeks and the lower stratum of Egyptians did not cease. Yet if the Ptolemaic rule had continued longer and had not been cut short by the incursion of the proud Romans, the difference between the Greek and the Egyptian might have gradually faded away. Edwyn Bevan[6] who opines thus also informs his readers that the rule of the Romans further depressed the condition of the Egyptians, who thenceforward came third in rank and thus almost represented the castaway.

The impact between the Vedic Indians and the earlier settlers of India represents a situation only slightly different from that of the Greco-Egyptian one. First of all, it appears that the people of India who opposed the Vedic Aryans were preponderantly of dark colour. Second, however high the local civilization might have been the Indian Aryans had not derived theirs from the local variety. The Vedic people had thus much greater reason to show off their pride and exclusiveness. As we have seen in the third chapter they used rather strong expressions against the natives and though they did not mind using their women for sex-gratification they had a great prejudice against them. An Aryan woman demeaning herself by consorting with a native male was simply an anathema and as such a situation vehemently deprecated.

The doings of another branch of the Indo-Europeans, the Romans, seem to present a parallel in some respects to the Indian development of caste. And I have already drawn my readers' attention to these common elements. But the occupational endogamy and restrictions were largely an imposition during the period when fiscal arrangements required a steady flow of occupational activity and the social conditions and trends conspired to hinder it. If we, therefore, leave this apparent similarity engendered in the last period of the Roman Empire we shall find the social history of Rome helping us to understand the Indian development rather by contrast than by similarity. The Romans and the Greeks were peculiar among peoples of antiquity in having been almost completely free from priestly power.[7]

First, the small number of original Romans seem to have been divided into two classes, the patrician aristocrats and the plebeian commoners. The attitude of the former towards the latter is one of condescension. The latter are without rights. Among the patricians, who later came to be the senators, spirit of exclusiveness was rampant. They could contract legal marriage only among themselves. Their pride and exclusiveness led them to lay down that no Roman shall marry a non-Roman, unless he belonged to one of the special nationalities, taking of a bride from among whom was permissible. Thus the early Romans were hypergamous towards others and the patricians endogamous among themselves. This pride of birth and spirit of exclusiveness continued among the patricians and similar people for a long time. Even Cicero harped on the importance of birth; and stoic philosophers while toying with the brotherhood of mankind in the abstract went on detesting the plebs and the slaves and their lowly occupations. The plebs and others were far more interested in their political rights and their economic welfare than in social exclusiveness or its opposite, assimilation with the senators. The few aristocratic families settled in the city suffered great diminution in their numbers, through incessant wars, frequent infertility and repeated political massacres. Thus the aristocratic leaven did not find congenial medium. Nor was it large enough for vital action.[8]

Secondly, Roman religion, though a formal one and consequently one in which ideas of rigid procedure and of ceremonial purity should prosper, did not much develop in that line. And nothing marks so well the contrasting attitudes to life and the divergent fate of the Romans and the Indians as the vicissitudes of their original religion among the two peoples. From very early times religion in Rome becomes institutionalized and established, the college of pontiffs being charged with keeping the *status quo*. As almost everything else the religious field too is invaded by politics. If religion by being a kind of a handmaid of politics ceases to grow in its own line it runs to decay owing to the growth of the practice of business and consequent desire for gain. In this respect the condition reached by Roman religion before the beginning of the Christian era was entered into by Hindu religion only about the beginning of the twentieth century. There was no scope for the elaboration of the ideas of ceremonial purity and their application to social life.

Thirdly, the religion of the Romans was a religion of farmers. And the leading farmers got confined into a city. Their religion not having changed, it naturally got devoid of vitality. It soon fell an easy prey to various cults from the conquered Orient. Yet it could not offer a satisfying creed and practice to its adherents. And the final result of this growing situation was the more or less easy triumph of Christianity.[9] Small wonder that Roman religion failed to co-operate with the exclusive spirit of the Roman aristocrats.

Fourthly, the existence and the early great growth of slavery with its attendant occupational grading or degrading proved to be one of the most potent factors against the development of exclusive stratification. The number of slaves was so large even before the end of the Republic that the free population was almost swamped. The composition of the slave population was a significant aspect of Roman slavery. The slaves were largely either Greeks or Hellenized Orientals like the Egyptians, the Syrians and even the Jews or the Latins and the Western Barbarians. Most of them were not different from the Romans in external appearances of race. Many of them were even of superior mien. And quite a large number were well educated and cultured. The Syrians and Jews in particular were expert in business. We read of many slave-risings. The unrest of the slaves were helped by the policy of manumission, which because of its economic advantages to slave-owning Romans rapidly grew in practice. The freed men, as the manumissioned slaves were known, played a significant role in Roman economic system. Slavery of able and not ugly people was an effective check against discriminating stratification of ranks and classes within Roman society.[10]

We can see why the Romans, beginning their account with many of the characteristics common to a number of Indo-Europeans, ended during the course of some centuries on a different note. Their economic organization came to depend on what was called the colony system but was in reality the same thing as serfdom.[11] Their religion was supplanted by Christianity which in theory at least could not countenance exclusive spirit.

The Celts and the Anglo-Saxons, as is seen in the previous chapter, lacked in many of the special features attendant on the settlement of the Romans in their new habitat. They developed their original traits after the Hindu pattern more or less. Their civilization was rather rudimentary for a long time. During that period the Celts, who had retained their original religion, showed the exclusive spirit though not backed by the slight religious development that had taken place. The Anglo-Saxons, though they had accepted Christianity, exhibited the exclusive spirit. And the priests of the Celts, the Druids, had developed enough power and had devised rules and their sanctions which are reminiscent of the Brahmins of India. Caesar has preserved the important information that they interdicted recalcitrant persons from the sacrifices and that such excommunicated persons were looked upon as of the number of the impious and criminal. All persons shunned them and avoided not only their touch but also speech with them, lest they should be hurt by their contagion.[12]

One may safely conclude from the above account that the Indo-European people, of whom Vedic Aryans were but a branch, had early developed the exclusive spirit in social behaviour and had cultivated a partiality for ideas of ceremonial purity. Some of them in their separate development actually elaborated them into an exclusive social stratification, though of rather limited extent and depth.

It is very instructive to observe the behaviour of the European conquerors and settlers from the 16th century onwards. For these modern representatives of the early Indo-Europeans, of the Latins, of the Celts and of the Teutons or Anglo-Saxons, had by that time been imbibing the liberalizing tenets of Christianity for about eight to ten centuries, asking them to treat men as brothers and exhorting them to cast off pride and exclusiveness. In spite of the equalitarian and democratic preaching of centuries, wherever the Europeans went as conquerors they manifested exclusiveness varying from utter contempt and strictest barrier to condescension and hypergamous feeling and practice. Wherever they condescended they at most took the conquered women to wives but never even connived at their own women marrying the native males. Even in this hypergamous practice they took care to separate the progeny of half-breeds.

The behaviour of exclusive pride towards conquered peoples of whatever cultural status or racial mien met with in the doings of so many Indo-European peoples, whether under the continuance of their tribal religions or even under the acceptance of Christianity, appears in the attitudes and practices of the Aryans of the Gangetic plains of the Vedic or post-Vedic age in a particular context. Their conquered were a dark people. When they entered India they must have had among them at least three well-defined classes, intermarriage between whom must have been rather rare, though not positively forbidden. Their first regulations in this line began with the task of excluding the Shudras, which class must have been largely formed by the aborigines, from their religious worship. We have seen that the Shudra was represented as the lowest class in society. Very early in their Indian history the Aryans enjoined that the Shudra shall not practise the religious worship developed by them. They even forbade his presence in the sacrificial hall. The three first castes were first enjoined not to marry a Shudra female before any other restriction of an endogamous nature was tried to be promulgated. A Shudra male trying to marry a Brahmin female was the greatest sacrilege that could be perpetrated against society. The various factors that characterize caste-society were the result, in the first instance, of the attempts on the part of the upholders of the Brahmanic civilization to exclude the aborigines and the Shudras from religious and social communion with themselves. That the Shudra class was largely formed by those aborigines who had accepted the overlordship of the Indo-Aryans and had entered into their service is more than probable. It will have been noticed that in the earliest literature only the first three classes—the Brahmin, the Kshatriya, and the Vaishya—are postulated and that it is only in one place, which is regarded by most Vedic scholars to be chronologically one of the latest, that the Shudra class is mentioned as one of the four. It has not been found possible yet to give a satisfactory derivation of the word Shudra in terms of Sanskritic roots. Further, when this fourth class is definitely formulated the Brahmanic literature contemplates it as in contradistinction to the other three classes. Thus the Vedic opposition between the Āryas and the Dāsa is replaced by the Brahmanic classification of the 'dvijāti' and the 'ekajāti' (the Shudra), suggesting the transmutation of the Dāsa into the Shudra in the minds of the writers of the Brahmanic and later periods.

That the main ingredient of caste system, viz. the regulation of endogamy or rather its earlier form, permitted hypergamy, was the result of the desire on the part of the Aryans of the Gangetic plain to preserve their physical purity and cultural integrity is a proposition which finds almost unequivocal support in the distribution of physical types in Northern India. It is very instructive and even necessary to bear in mind that, even as late as 150 B.C. when Patanjali the great grammarian wrote, "the physical characteristics of a Brahmin were fair skin, and tawny hair", Patanjali declares them to be the intrinsic traits marking a Brahmin, and black colour of the skin that of a non-Brahmin.*

Basing my calculation on some of the physical measurements taken by anthropologists and using one of the statistical devices to gauge the nearness of distance of one caste from another in the totality of these measurements, I have established a general correspondence between finer physical type and high position in the caste-hierarchy. Taking the Brahmin of Uttar Pradesh (U.P.) as the typical representative of the ancient Aryans one finds that the group is physically more like the Khatri, a high caste, and even the Chuhrā, a low caste of the Punjab, than like any caste of Uttar Pradesh except the Chhatri, the next highest to the Brahmin in caste hierarchy. Thus the highest caste of Uttar Pradesh has greater physical affinity even with the low caste of the Punjab than with most castes of its own region. If the Punjab castes should be taken to represent in the main the old Aryan stock then the U.P. Brahmin as a good representative of the same stock should naturally show this relation. U.P. Brahmin's separateness from most of the lower castes of his region shows that he has succeeded in keeping his physical type as undiluted as possible under the circumstances. The physical likeness between the various castes of the Uttar Pradesh more or less corresponds with the precedence of caste. The Chhatri which is the next caste to the Brahmin shows the greatest likeness to him. The Kāyasth comes next and is followed by the Ahir and the Kurmi, the former a high caste of intellectual pursuits and the latter two artisan castes of high status. The Pāsi and the untouchable Chamār show much less likeness and in that order. In the scheme of social precedence the Kāyasth occupies the fourth rank, the Kurmi stands at the head of the eighth, while the Pāsi and the Chamār the eleventh and the twelfth ranks.[13] P. C. Mahalanobis concludes his survey of the U.P. castes thus: 'The Brahmins occupy the highest social position in Hindu society at the top of the picture, and have the largest build of face and body with tall stature, large facial breadth, and comparatively large nasal length and biggest nasal depth but narrow nasal breadth. As one goes down from the top to the bottom of the picture there is a steady decrease in both social status and physical size (except in the case of the degraded castes, Bhātu, Hābru and Dom)".[14]

The facts stated above acquire even greater significance when it is known that by the same method of comparison the Brahmin of Bihar is more distant in physical likeness from the Brahmin of Uttar Pradesh than are the Chhatri, the Kāyasth and the Kurmi from the latter.

Comparing the castes of Bihar among themselves the physical affinity grades some of the castes in the order Brahmin, Kurmi, Chamār and Dom, while social precedence not disturbing the relative order places the Kurmi in the third place and the Chamār and the Dom in the fifth and sixth.[15] Here again though the Brahmin is not the same as the Brahmin of the U.P. he has managed to keep himself at the top of the physical ladder.

Similar comparisons instituted in respect of the caśtes of Bengal and of Western India show a slightly different pattern. While many of the high castes standing in physical proximity of the Brahmin of Bengal establish the inference that inter-mixture with him "has varied directly as the cultural proximity of the caste concerned", the close resemblance of the Chandāl, whose touch pollutes is rather unexpected. Similarly in the comparisons instituted by Mahalanobis, the physical distance of the Bengal Brahmin from the Bihar Brahmin and the even greater distinctness from the U.P. Brahmin contrasted with his close likeness with the Punjab Khatri are equally disturbing. One of his conclusions may be quoted here for its great relevance. He observes: "The influence of the northern Indian

---

* Vyākaraṇa-mahābhāshya, Sutra II, 2, 6.

castes decreases and that of the aboriginal tribes of Chota Nagpur increases as we go down the social scale".[16] The Deshasth Brahmin of Maharashtra proclaims his physical affinity with the Son Koli rather than with his social compeer the Chitpāvan Brahmin. In Gujarat the data of the anthropometric survey of the 1931 Census of India reveal the close affinity of the Nāgar Brahmin with Baniā Jain. Another section of Brahmins, the Audich, however, shows a wider distance from the Nāgar Brahmin than even the Kāthi.[17] The Audich, as the name signifies, is a Northern immigrant group.

In general, in a linguistic region the castes are physically more related to one another than to similar castes outside the region. Outside Uttar Pradesh there appear to be some castes rather low in the social scale which are physically more akin to the highest caste than are the middle ones. The origin of endogamy in the earlier form of hypergamy may be placed in the Gangetic plain and attributed to the Brahmanic culture whose literature provides the earliest word picture of such a state of things. The idea of endogamy and other elements of caste were taken by the Brahmin prospectors with them. Hence in the other regions as much correspondence between physical type and social status is not met with. The prospectors could not disturb the physical mixture of the region where they went. They could only try to apply their scheme of occupational segregation and endogamy to various groups according to their receptive abilities. I may conclude that caste in India is a Brahmanic child of the Indo-Aryan culture, cradled in the land of the Ganges and the Jamna and thence transferred to other parts of the country.

This racial origin of the principal feature of the caste system is further supported by the early term 'varna' meaning colour used to specify the orders in society. Later on the word 'jāti' is specialized to denote caste, which is a group the membership of which is acquired by birth. The word 'jāti' etymologically means 'something into which one is born'. It is occasionally used by good ancient authorities as equivalent to 'varna'.

As an important constituent of the Brahmanic culture in connection with the sacrificial ritual the Aryan notions of ceremonial purity took on an exaggerated aspect. Not only the correct wording and pronunciation of the sacred formulae but also the strictest adherence to the minutest details of the ritual procedure were essential for the proper performance of rites. Distinctions began to be made between things pure and things impure. Whatever was unclean was of course impure And with the change of outlook on the animal world even some of the formerly honourable occupations came to be looked upon as degrading. How fastidious the Brahmanic ideal of ceremonial purity had come to be by the time of the *Sutras* is best illustrated by the meticulous rules laid down in them for purification and for general conduct.

The Brahmins, partly out of their honest desire to preserve the purity of Vedic ritual, partly being the victims of their own ideas of ceremonial purity, and partly also owing to their consciousness of superiority over the aborigines, first enacted rules for the guidance of their own members, which were intended to prevent the possibility of the Shudras in any way lowering their moral standard and introducing their low blood.

It is because the Brahmins put restrictions on the acceptance of food and drink from the Shudras during the second stage of the development of their culture that we find that in Northern India generally there is some leniency shown by them towards some of the higher castes, while in Southern India such an attitude and practice is considered a great sacrilege. As the taboo was laid against the Shudra, and as the Brahmin most probably continued to treat the other two castes as almost his own equals in this matter, even when in later times the taboo became stricter and was made widely applicable, by force of habit and tradition, he continued to take water from pure castes and specially prepared food from high castes. When the pioneers of Brahmanic culture progressed into Southern India with restrictions against food and water from the Shudra as one of the items of their tradition, as they had none of the other castes—the Kshatriya and the Vaishya—to whom they were accustomed, to think of in their new regions, they applied their rules against the Shudras to all the indigenous population of the Southern countries. And the seed fell on a very congenial soil. The Southern peoples before their contact with the Indo-Aryan culture most probably had beliefs about the sanctity and power of food to transmit certain qualities very much like those of primitive peoples.[18] This is why the restrictions on food and drink are so rigorous in South India, where, as I said, the Brahmin does not accept food or water at the hands of anyone but a Brahmin.

With the progressive assimilation of the Vaishyas with the Shudras the Brahmins enacted rules to keep their group free from admixture with them by assigning different status to the issue of the union of a Brahmin male and a Vaishya female. And with the march of time and particularly after the overthrow of Buddhism they stopped taking food at the hands of the Vaishyas. Owing to the peculiar position of the Kshatriyas, the king having belonged to that group, in theory at least the Brahmins did not prohibit food being taken at their hands. Yet they tried to preserve their racial purity by treating the offspring of a Brahmin male and a Kshatriya female as belonging to a separate group.

The restrictions on intermarriage and on food were thus in their origin the outcome of the Brahmins' desire to keep themselves pure. This desire was partly due to the exaggerated notions of purity, partly to the enormous importance that came to be attached to the perpetuation of Vedic lore without even the slightest change, and in part also to the pride of superiority, which the Brahmins had shared in common with the other Indo-Aryan classes in the beginning, and which they alone could keep unimpaired. The total discomfiture of the Kshatriyas and the complete dissociation of the language of the people from the old language of the scriptures made it easy for the Brahmins to have it all their own way.

It must, however, be said to the credit of the Brahmins that they did not quite forget the original solidarity of the first three classes. They tried to preserve the purity, on their model of course, of both the Kshatriyas and the Vaishyas at least in their ideal scheme, though they treated the latter for all practical purposes as equal to the Shudras.

This social pattern set for themselves by the most respected class in society could not fail to be imitated with fervid enthusiasm by all manner of groups that would claim respectability. Thus it must have been that the original restrictions on intermarriage and regulations about the acceptance of food, which contemplated only four classes in society, came to be the characteristics of each and every well-marked group.

Group solidarity and group prestige would soon assert themselves against marrying on unequal terms: the lower group would refuse to marry their females to the males of the higher classes only to create a new group giving itself superior airs. It was bound to close up its ranks and be endogamous.

With functional differentiation in society there came into being separate occupational groups with more or less distinct interests. We have noticed it as a widespread feature of ancient and medieval society that the occupation of each group tends to become customarily hereditary among its members. Only the Brahmins reserved as their monopoly the occupation of a priest. No doubt they were in the beginning inspired by the laudable motive of preserving the all-important sacred lore. But later on they looked upon their priestcraft as their monopolistic activity and rigorously kept it up, while the traditional occupations of the other two castes were progressively encroached upon by other castes. There is also a natural inclination for each occupational group, as we have already noticed, to be habitually endogamous. Both these tendencies became rules: the former more or less nebulous, and the latter very rigid, after the pattern of the Brahmins. Occupations thus became endogamous groups.

The attitude of respect for details that was first fostered in connection with ritual became the prevaīling attitude in social behaviour. Adherence to detail of social and customary etiquette became the distinguishing mark of membership of a group. Distinction in any detail tended to be translated into separateness of membership and hence of a group.

The lack of rigid unitary control of the State, the unwillingness of the rulers to enforce a uniform standard of law and custom, their readiness to recognize the varying customs of different groups as valid, and their usual practice of allowing things somehow to adjust themselves[19] helped the fissiparous tendency of groups and fostered the spirit of solidarity and community feeling in every group.

Both these circumstances conspired to encourage the formation of small groups based on petty distinctions.

Special rights for the higher classes and disabilities on the lower ones was almost a universal feature of class society; and the Brahmanic theory of four castes with their rights and disabilities does not call for any special explanation. Only the practice of untouchability is peculiar to the Hindu system. It will have been clear from the history of this factor of caste, narrated in the third and fourth chapters, that the ideas of untouchability and unapproachability arose out of the ideas of ceremonial purity, first applied to the aboriginal Shudras in connection with the sacrificial ritual and expanded and extended to other groups because of the theoretical impurity of certain occupations.

Multiplicity of the groups and the thoroughness of the whole system are due to the habit of the Hindu mind to create categories and to carry things to their logical end, a characteristic manifest in their literature, philosophy, and religious creeds.[20]

References

1. See C. C. North, *Social Differentiation*. 2. Untouchability in Japan can hardly be regarded as quite independent of the Indian ideas on the subject. 3. *E.B.*, XVII, pp. 565–66. 4. Ibid., pp. 568, 570, 580, 582. 5. Jowett's *Dialogues of Plato*, vol. V, p. 267. 6. Op. cit., pp. 80, 83–4, 86, 87, 98. 7. Russell, B., *Power*, p. 52. 8. Dill (1), pp. 1, 3, 38, 102–03, 104, 273, 282; Warde Fowler, pp. 43–44, 61, 97–99, 101; Louis, pp. 30–33, 110–11, 148–9; Duff, pp. 200–01, 207; Geer, pp. 161–3. 9. Dill (1), pp. 529–35, 537, 543–45; Warde Fowler, pp. 154, 320–23, 331; Louis, p. 151; Geer, pp. 173–75, 187–191, 279–89.

10. Dill (1), pp. 100–103; Warde Fowler, pp. 69, 204–07; Louis, pp. 37, 39, 42–3, 130, 135–7, 140, 144, 147–8; Duff, pp. 1–3, 5, 7, 9, 19, 188, 190–1, 202–04; Geer, p. 169. 11. Louis, pp. 214–15, 241–45, 252–57. 12. Seebohm, F., *Tribal Custom in Anglo-Saxon Law* (1911), p. 118. 13. *United Provinces Census Report*, 1901, p. 248. 14. *Sankhyā*, IX (1949), p. 199. 15. *Bengal Census Report*, 1901, p. 373. 16. *J.A.S.B.*, XXIII (1927), pp. 310, 311, 319; Ghurye in *Q. J. of the Mythic Society*, vol. XVII, Nos. & 4, p. 17 (of the Reprint). 17. G. S. Ghurye in *The Q. J. of the Mythic Socīety*, vol. XXVII, Nos. 3 & 4, pp. 34–35 (Reprint). 18. A. E. Crawley, *The Mystic Rose*, 1902, pp. 157–60. On p. 162 he thus summarizes the attitude towards food: "It is clear that men believe human properties to be transmitted not only by contact with the food of others, but by eating with them or in their presence." 19. See V. A. Gadgil in the *Journal of the Bombay Branch of the Royal Asiatic Society*, 1926, p. 161, for the connection of this practice with the village-organization of Northern India.

20. Professor C. G. Seligman attributes this mental trait to the Nordic race (see his presidential address to the Royal Anthropological Institute, *J.R.A.I.* 1924).

8

Caste, Sub-caste: Fusion or Fission?

The view of caste propounded in this book, quite clearly acknowledged the so-called sub-caste as the real caste, its essential characteristic being endogamy. Alternatively sub-caste was either referred to as smaller unit and the so-called caste as either caste, or major unit. Not rarely are the sub-castes referred to as divisions or sub-divisions, evidently of or within a major unit called caste. Their nature is analysed in the second chapter, wherein the reader is provided with the principles or the bases of distinction leading to the exclusive marking off of these 'minor units', or rather sub-groups, as deduced from a study of the nature of castes and sub-castes in the old Bombay Province and the Central Provinces, i.e., in effect in present Maharashtra. It is further affirmed that in Uttar Pradesh, the home of Brahmanic culture, the same principles can be discerned with the addition of Rajput clans and eponymous personages.

The discerning reader will perceive that the statement based on an analysis of the existing castes and sub-castes is no more a theory than the groups themselves but that it is a statement of facts. He will further draw support, if necessary, for this from the fact that the principles stated in the second chapter as the bases of sub-caste nomenclature are not used in the seventh chapter which states my view or theory of the origin of the caste-system I should emphasize the fact that I have formulated a theory of origins of the caste-system and I have not attempted to explain the origins of castes.

Since the publication of the first edition of this book in 1932 a large number of studies of caste have appeared; but they appeared to me to add facts and support my theory of the origins, and at least not directly attempt to contradict it, till Iravati Karve published her book entitled *Hindu Society: An Interpretation* in 1961. In particular Karve is positive and almost certain that the so-called subcastes, far from being either subdivisions or even specialized and differentiated subunits, are the actual castes, the so-called castes of the parlance, and of the written usage of most students of the Hindu or Indian caste-system, being really "caste-clusters" formed by a "fusion" of the so-called sub-castes (pp. 11–12, 19, 26–28, 61).

I shall begin with the views of E. A. Blunt based on and relating to the caste-system current in Uttar Pradesh, the original home of the system in my opinion. Blunt, who was the Superintendent of the 1911 Census of the United Provinces and later the Chairman of the United Provinces Banking Enquiry Committee, published his book *Caste System of Northern India* in 1931 late enough for it not to be received in the Bombay University Library before September 1932, i.e., four or so months

* This chapter was written in 1968.

after the *Times of India* review of my book appeared. His views thus are absolutely independent of any influence of my book, formed in utter ignorance of it, solely on the wide knowledge of the caste-system garnered during a District Officer's career of over two or three decades. And as the writing of the largest part of it was done, as the author informs us in his Preface, before 1927 and of the whole of it before the beginning of 1931, there is no possibility of the author's view having in any way been influenced by J. H. Hutton's dissertation on caste appearing in the *Census Report on India* which came out only in 1933.

It is instructive that Blunt not only speaks of sub-caste but also of sub-sub-caste (p. 49). He tells his readers that the "subdivisions of caste" were recorded in detail at the Census of 1891; and that the result was that the Jāts and the Ahirs "were each responsible for over 1,700 entries; the Kurmi for nearly 1,500". He naturally remarks that however much the number may be reduced by judicious scanning, the record "affords striking proof of the fertility of the caste system in the development of subdivisions". He thinks that "the name of a subdivision is generally the only clue that we possess to its [caste nomenclature] origin" and states that "nobody has ever attempted a detailed analysis of caste nomenclature". He, therefore, analyses its "principal features" and states: "There are, firstly, local, eponymous and occupational names"; secondly, there are "sectional names which are derived from castes". The fifth variety of names is totemistic; sixth, nicknames; seventh, based on some social custom; eighth, referring to origin; ninth, "referring to religious belief" and tenth, names "recalling castes of the Purānas" (pp. 37–42; 50–57; 236–38).

J. H. Hutton in his *Caste in India* first published in 1946—my references are all to the third edition of 1961—quite often uses the word and the concept and even speaks of the processes of segregation, separation and fission when writing about some of the castes and their subunits and contracts the processes of the formation of sub-castes of former times with those operating in recent caste. Formerly he states "fissions of this kind", i.e., as those seen in the subunits or sub-castes of the Khātik, a caste of butchers, viz., Bekanwālā,* 'pork butcher'; Rājgār, 'mason'; Sombattā, 'rope maker'; Mewā-farosh, 'fruiterer'; were due to migration or to political or social factors, but latterly they tend to be based on the upgrading of one's status. Mentioning with approval A. M. T. Jackson's statement based on castes of the Bombay Presidency that "a large proportion of subcastes bear geographical names he says that they could be added to without much difficulty by "parallel instances from all over India". Pointing out the favourable nature of the political condition of ancient India for "just this kind of fission" he concludes: "Clearly geographical, political and administrative considerations have not been unimportant in the development and operation of the caste system". He further used the concept and the fact of sub-caste to expound the nature and function of hypergamy (pp. 51–6, 113, 119, 181).

In the views of Blunt quoted above there is the sweeping mention of want of an analysis of caste and sub-caste nomenclature which is not quite correct. A. M. T. Jackson's contribution of 1907 has been incidentally noted above. Among the many points of credit due to Sir Herbert Risley in the matter of the study of caste the analysis of some caste or sub-caste names is one and it is but fair that in view of Blunt's assertion I should briefly describe it. In view of Karve's footnote remark about my sub-caste treatment a brief statement of Risley's contribution will do justice to me, too.

---

* E. A. Blunt wrote about this group as "in process of formation" and not actually formed. I wonder, when Hutton in 1946 turned it into a sub-caste already formed, if it was really so formed or was in the process of formation as when Blunt wrote fifteen years before him!

After describing types of tribes in the chapter on Social Types, Risley details types of castes distinguishing seven types which are: (i) Tribal castes; (ii) Functional castes—(occupational castes of other writers); (iii) Sectarian castes; (iv) Castes formed by crossing; (v) Castes of the national type; (vi) Castes formed by migration; (vii) Castes formed by changes of custom. In the fifth group of castes he draws upon castes with territorial names; but in view of the fact that the territorial principle or even the political principle of A. M. T. Jackson is seen operative in the nomenclature of the so-called sub-castes to an exceedingly large extent, Risley has to bring in the concept and fact of sub-caste, though he is concerned with distinguishing types of castes and not the so-called sub-castes. He says that people of some caste migrating to other regions than the one where their caste people in large numbers have been living, fairly soon found it necessary to effect marital alliance among the limited number in the new habitat and "in course of time the emigrants . . . become a sub-caste usually distinguished by a territorial name, such as Jaunpuriā, Tirhutiā, Bārendra and the like". Under the seventh group, too, Risley mentions the locality-based names alongside of names indicating the particular realm of social custom in which a change is effected. Thus he instances the Awadhiyā Kurmis and the Kanaujiā Kurmis as sub-castes of the great Kurmi caste (*People of India*, ed. 1915, pp. 75–94). Treating of endogamy Risley counted only six named categories. Without going into the discrepancies or the rationale of the categories, here I must point out that he dwells on territorial or local names of other groups as well as mentioning the Halia sub-caste of Kaibarttas and Duliā, Machhuā and Matiāl sub-castes of Bāgdis, both Bengal castes. Finally, he enunciates his views in general terms which are tantamount to stating the principles of sub-caste nomenclature thus: ". . . the tendency towards sub-division, which is inherent in Indian society, seems to have been set in motion by the fiction that men who speak a different language, who dwell in a different district, who worship different gods, who observe different social customs, who follow a different profession, or practise the same profession in a slightly different way, must be of a fundamentally different race." (pp. 156–88)

Of the recent students of caste in rural areas whose views are based on intensive investigation in a restricted locality I shall pick out A. C. Mayer. He of all others has discussed the question of the advisability and nature of the concept of sub-caste. And he has done so not merely on the background of the scene of his operations but has gone out much further afield. He has weighed the views about, and the contributions to, this topic of S. V. Ketkar, E. A. Blunt, J. H. Hutton, H. N. Stevenson, S. C. Dube, M. N. Srinivas, and has arrived at the conclusion which more or less wholly upholds my point of view. (Adrian C. Mayer, *Caste and Kinship in Central India*, 1960, pp. 4–9 and also pp. 152–60).

Another field investigator operating in the heart of Tamilnad, i.e., Tanjore District, Kathleen Gough (E. R. Leach, *op. cit.*, p. 16) mentions four "sub-divisions" of the Shaiva or Smārtha Tamil Brahmins and adds: "Each sub-division *is divided into small regional endogamous sub-castes each comprising the local communities of some ten to twenty villages*". About the four sub-divisions she says that they are "distinguished by minor differences in the performance of Vedic rites".

In the face of these verdicts Karve's objection to and criticism of my statement in the second chapter which is concerned with the nature of caste-groups is not only peculiar or partisan but both carping and ill-advised. To appraise fully this aspect of Karve's criticism it is necessary to state briefly her own view and also the views of S. V. Ketkar, the Indologist whose work on caste was published within a decade of Risley's book *People of India* and two decades before my book. While reading Ketkar's views the reader should bear in mind the fact that his book *The History of Caste in India*, published in 1909, deals with caste as can be studied in the Laws of Manu and that it is only the preliminary essay entitled *The Caste System*, forming not more than one-fifth of the whole book, that treats of caste in general.

Karve distinguishes three stages of groupings in the Hindu society; (i) Castes, i.e., 'jātis' in Indian terms, the endogamous groups; (ii) caste-clusters such as Brahmin, Kunbi or Maratha-Kunbi, Sonār, Kumbhār; and (iii) *varna*. She adds: "According to the older way of designation, each of the Kumbhār castes was called a sub-caste, while the caste-cluster of earthen pot-makers was called the 'Kumbhār caste'. This mode of naming the smallest endogamous groups created the impression that sub-castes were smaller groups derived through the sub-division of an entity called caste. A few examples were known of a split within a caste leading to the establishment of two new separate endogamous units; but such cases are exceptions rather than the rule". Illustrating her objection in the case of her "caste-cluster" called Kumbhār, she stated that Thor-chāke, Lahan-chāke, Kurere, Hātghade Kumbhār, Gadheriā Kumbhār, etc., are "names by which the endogamous castes" within it are known, and though it was "never expressly stated that an original Kumbhār caste split into various endogamous units owing to some people coming to use different implements and techniques or owing to the use of certain animals like donkeys for carrying the pots", "the way in which the whole caste system was described gave the impression" that they were sub-divisions which had come into existence through splitting up of a unit. She went further and asserted that "when caste was described as a social organization, the description and analysis made mention of castes bearing the same or similar names over very wide areas including many linguistic regions, sometimes over the whole of India and the impression was strengthened that either (1) the castes bearing similar names were products of fission of an original single body or that (2) each linguistic region having a single casteless society split into several endogamous groups called castes". (pp. 9–13, 19–20)

The basic groupings, it is clear from the so-called description of the caste system in Maharashtra, are the *'jātis'* and the *'varnas'*. Karve observes (p. 47), "the *'jāti'* system which allowed innumerable different endogamous groups to live separately is entirely different from the *'varna'* system which divided all society into four ranks. The *'jāti'* organization or something very like it was in existence in India for a long time, the author thinks, even prior to the coming in of the Aryans. The *'varna'* organization belonged to the society which brought the Vedas to India. In course of time the *varna* system was modified and the *varna* and *jāti* systems were interwoven together to form a very elaborate ranking system". She explains more specifically what she means by her assertion about *'jāti'* system thus (p. 66): "My contention that a caste in each linguistic region is separate from the other castes and was so for centuries, does not mean that there were two thousand separate entities to start with. There were in India tribal groups, as also different races . . . the names of many of these groups are recorded in India's literature."

In so far as Karve is positive that there are about 200 castes in each linguistic region giving "over two thousand castes in India" and in as much as she assures us that these two thousand, and therefore the language-centred 200, castes were not all there from the beginning, one naturally expects her to tell one how she proposes to explain the contemporary or recent existence of so many out of the few tribal racial groups named by her. The tag after the named tribal and racial groups which reads "and a hundred others", if taken seriously, as a measured expression will contradict Karve's affirmation that the two hundred or two thousand groups did not exist from the start. However, there is no further statement of hers, except the enunciation of what she calls her "second proposition", viz., "groups living apart and organized into a caste-like structure seem to have existed for a very long time in

India, were there before the Aryans came and persisted up to the present", and the statement "no tribal society in the world has as many cells within it as the Indian society". (p. 69)

In support of her assertion that she got the impression from my book that the so-called sub-castes "arose out of castes", she quotes the following passage as one that "suggests that sub-castes arose out of castes". "A close study of the names of the various minor units, the so-called sub-castes, within the major group reveals the fact that the bases of distinction *leading to the exclusive marking off* of these groups were territorial, etc." (Italics mine).

This passage in the second chapter of my book occurs after the enumeration of the nomenclature of the major groups called castes. As the chapter is devoted to an analysis of "the nature of caste groups", the passage under quotation introduces the enumeration of the nomenclature of the so-called sub-castes. It abstracts the bases which provide the names of the sub-castes. Whether the expression italicized by Karve means rigidly what she has taken it to mean must be decided by the expressions used in the illustrations following the passage seriatum. And I submit that the context does not uphold Karve's interpretation, though about many of these I am prepared to emphasize that they are differentiational separations from their main bodies or units.

Thus illustrating the principle of ethnic or other mixture I observe: "In spite of the so-called rigidity of caste, it appears that many of the occupational and tribal castes, either permitted or connived at the infusion of members of other castes". "Sub-castes that bear the name of some ancient city or locality are to be met with in the majority of the castes" is a mere statement of fact without the further implication as to either fission of the local caste or accretion from another region.

Lokamanya B. G. Tilak, so late as 1918, spoke of various Maratha castes as either "upajātis" or "potashākhās", i.e. sub-divisions, of one Maratha caste (see *Lokamanya Tilakanche Kesaritil Lekha*, pt. IV, p. 553).

Sub-castes, howsoever formed, are shown to be real castes by me. However, I have emphasized at the same time the distinct functions of the so-called sub-caste and the caste for the individual, and the different apperception of them by other groups in the society. And it is this feature of my treatment that led A. C. Mayer, on his having discovered the truth of it for himself in his area of fieldwork, to approve of it. He has dealt with the sub-castes and their functions in the village of his study at fair length (pp. 5–9; 151–161; 271–72) as the principal aspect of the "internal structure of the caste".

Karve in her criticism has mentioned me almost wholly to the exclusion of other well-known writers on the subject of caste. The critical portion of the quotation from her book made above, to give an idea of her views on caste, would naturally be taken to apply to my book, whether it was intended by her or not, especially as she has not specified any author in that criticism. So in regard to that feature which is not a part of her criticism but is offered as a contribution would be judged to be her own fresh contribution not contained in my work. I therefore shall quote here one or more passages which will make it clear that her criticism cannot apply to my work and also that her contribution is not new to me or to my work.

In the first chapter of my book there is the following passage: "Of the features of caste society dealt with so far three pertain to the caste as a whole; for the status in the hierarchy of any sub-caste depends upon the status of the caste, from which follow the various civil and religious rights and disabilities, and the traditional occupation is determined by the nature of the caste. The other three features, which are very material in the consideration of a group from the point of view of an effective social life, viz. those that regulate communal life and prescribe rules as regards feeling, social intercourse and endogamy, belong to the sub-caste." Then here is another:

"Each of these groups, major, as well as minor, generally known as castes and sub-castes, has a name. When any group of the same name happens to have a wide distribution, language delimits effective social intercourse....In any linguistic area there were from fifty to two hundred of these major groups divided into five hundred to two thousand minor groups. An individual's circle of community feeling was any of these minor groups, in which he or she was born; but as far as civic life was concerned it was the major group that decided the status of an individual." At the end of the first chapter after reiterating the approximate number of the major groups, the minor groups are mentioned as "generally known as sub-castes". The statement then proceeds: "These major groups were held together by the possession with few exceptions, of a common priesthood. There was a sort of an overall counting which grouped all of them into five or six classes, overtly expressed or tacitly understood."

It is seen from the above quotations from my book that I have not committed the offence of treating all castes of India together. I have very clearly expressed the view that castes are confined by linguistic barriers. In the case of Brahmins I have implemented my view so rigorously that I have eschewed all reference to the traditional account of Brahmins as one community divided into Five Gaudas and Five Dravidas. As regards Karve's insinuation that the three-tiered analysis of Caste system is her discovery or contribution, it is plain that I had arrived at that conclusion thirty years before she put it forward as a brand new discovery. I did not claim it as my contribution because it was suggested by J. N. Bhattacharya's treatment of caste and was the basis of the Risleyan classification of the 1901 Census. What is more, it is also explicitly stated by S. V. Ketkar in his work published in 1909. The work, though entitled *History of Caste in India*, is, as is made clear in the sub-title, almost wholly devoted to critical description of the caste system as envisaged in *Manusmriti*. The first thirty-three pages alone present the introductory dissertation on caste system in general. And it is in that essay that Ketkar has made statements which, in the context of Karve's implied claim of the freshness of her approach and carping criticism of my views, need to be carefully noted. I shall therefore transcribe the relevant portion here.

Ketkar (pp. 5, 15–6) says: "The two hundred million Hindus are made up of diverse racial elements... They are again divided into over three thousand castes, most of them having sub-castes. One of these castes, i.e. that of the Brahmins is divided over eight hundred subcastes. . . A caste is a social group having two characteristics. . . Each one of such groups has a special name by which it is called together under a common name, while these larger groups are but sub-divisions of groups still larger which have independent names. Thus we see that there are several stages of groups and that the word 'caste' is applied to groups at any stage. The words 'caste' and 'sub-caste' are not absolute but comparative in signification. . . When we talk of Maratha Brahmin and Konkan Brahmin, the first one would be called a caste while the latter would be called a sub-caste. Maratha Brahmins in their turn would be called a sub-caste of the southern or Dravidian Brahmins. These divisions and sub-divisions are introduced on different principles. In this way two hundred million Hindus are so much divided and subdivided that there are castes who cannot marry outside fifteen families. . . *these three thousand castes with their sub-castes put together make Hindu society*."* . . . When I say that Hindu Society is divided into many castes it should not be understood that so many thousand castes have split out of one united body. . . Numerous tribes which were living in different parts of India existed as different units, and after the custom of endogamy was introduced they did not fuse,

* Italics mine.

though scattered all over the country. . . But it should not be understood that castes are made only out of tribes. Originally united bodies were also divided into many castes."

It can be seen that Irawati Karve has carried over the dicta of Ketkar, made two decades before the publication of my book, as impressions and turned them into the bogey of castes being considered on an all-India basis. This facilitates her figuring as the champion of the correct approach. In the process, casual or purposeful silence is employed to castigate my work on caste as the culprit!

The truth of the matter is quite clear. And that is that I got clear of Ketkar's wrong views and propounded the correct view of confining the study of castes to their linguistic confines and had gone further than Karve almost three decades before Karve wrote on the subject. Inadvertently, or intentionally, Karve did not note that advance in clarification of the viewpoint and went on to state what is a drag over from the past.

The third and the widest grouping of castes is not 'varna' as Karve states but a nebulous one, 'varna' the older grouping being impressed into service regularly in the case of Brahmins and only occasionally in the case of two or three castes in each one of the linguistic regions. In the case of the two hundred or so castes other groupings, which are nebulous, have been the common mode for the last hundred and fifty years at least.

For Karve's criticism and statements, so much drawn from the contributions of Herbert Risley, Ketkar who wrote twenty to thirty years before me, of E. A. Blunt and Hutton, who wrote either contemporaneously with or just later than the first edition of my book, and of Mayer and Gough, who wrote almost contemporaneously with Karve's work and almost three decades after the first edition of my book, this will suffice.

I shall now turn to the positive side, the illustrations that Karve has given to support her contention that so-called sub-castes, which are really castes of the first grade, degree and stage, are not fissions but fusions or, as Blunt (p. 50, 236–38) said it in 1931, "accretions" or "affiliation".

Karve instances (pp. 22–25) the "variety" of castes "among the Brahmin caste-cluster of Maharashtra" by choosing "only a few major groups among Brahmins, viz. Sāraswat, Chitpāvan, Deshasth Rigvedi, Mādhyandina and Charak." By Sāraswat she clearly means all the groups of people who are known either as Sāraswat Brahmins or Gaud Sāraswat Brahmins. For she specifies their spread as "the western coastal region between Malwan and Mangalore." However, the characterization, through both food habits and language, refers only to the group which styles itself as Chitrāpur Sāraswats and is known among Gaud Sāraswat Brahmins as 'Shenāipaiki'.

There are at least seven groups of these people, who five centuries ago were confined mostly to Goa territory, who during the last three hundred years have spread not only on the western coast below Devgad but also north of it to Rajapur in Ratnagiri district, to Alibag in Colaba district and to Bombay. Since at least Shivaji's time some of them have been known to the ghauts and a little later to Baroda, Indore and Gwalior in the north and Nagpur in the east. The groups, the so-called sub-castes, are: (i) Bardeshkar, (ii) Bhalawalikar, (iii) Kudaldeshkar, (iv) Lotlikar, (v) Pednekar, (vi) Sāshtikar, (vii) Shenavi or Shenvi-paiki. Saraswat Vidyarthi Sahayak Mandal listed as No. 1425 in the *Directory of Public Trusts* (Greater Bombay and Bombay Suburban District) published in 1954 by the Charity Commissioner of Maharasthra"* specifies these seven groups as its beneficiaries.

---

* It is regretted that later data could not be availed of. Not finding any later published document I requested Professor D. N. Marshall, the Librarian of the University of Bombay, to inquire of the Charity Commissioner if there was any

Dr. Karve's mention of Sāraswats as one group of people in the Brahmin cluster, and her assertion that their language is Konkani, and that they are all Shaivites, furnishes the most telling substantiation of my statement that "sub-caste" is a grouping known mostly to the people of the caste while caste is the grouping known to the society at large. The Chitrāpur Sāraswats, to whom Karve's characterization of Sāraswats wholly applies, consider themselves to be a separate group. They are all Shaivites. Their language is Konkani, which is considered by many to be a sister language of Marathi. They mostly abjure fish in their food. The six sub-castes of Gaud-Sāraswats, with the possible exception of one of them, the Kaudāldeshkars, were and have themselves, for long, considered to be one caste. They started a movement for fusion in the first decade of the twentieth century. In short they, considered together, are on a par with the other four or five or six sub-castes of Brahmins, the Chitpāvans, the Deshasthās, the Karhādās, the Palshes, the Devrukhās, etc. These latter sections of Brahmins have been fusing together mostly during the last sixty years, though some of them attempted or expressed their desire to do so much earlier. Their endeavour is concretised in such institutions as the Brahmin Sabha of Bombay, while that of the former group, the Gaud Sāraswats, in the Gaud Saraswat Brahmin Samaj, also of Bombay.

Of the sub-castes of the Gaud Sāraswat Brahmins at least two, Bārdeshkar and Sāshtikar, are Vaishnavites, being the followers of the Madhva school of Dualistic Vedanta, and acknowledge the religious authority of the pontiff of the monastic centre of that school. The home language of the sub-castes of Gaud Sāraswat Brahmins is what is known as Mālwani or Kudāli speech. It is quite clearly a dialect of Marathi and not a sister language of it. At least during almost two centuries past the educated section of the caste has taken its education through standard Marathi. And whether the members of these sub-castes use Marathi as their home-tongue or not they almost invariably look upon Marathi as their language. In the Goa territory it is largely the members of these sub-castes that sponsored Marathi for their primary education for almost a hundred years and formed the spearhead of the movement to merge Goa territory with Maharashtra.

Karve mentions in her list of major groups forming the Brahmin cluster, Deshasth Rigvedi (pp. 22–23) whom she refers to later (p. 25) as Rigvedi Deshasth, and Mādhyandina. In the Public Trusts Directory mentioned above, Deshasth Rigvedi Brahmins figure in two Trusts at least, while the entry Mādhyandina Brāhmin by itself is not found. Instead there is at least one (no. 63) which reads "Mādhyandin Brāhman (Deshasth Shukla Yajurvedi)" and two (871 and 1631) which read "Mādhyandin Brāhman". The slight difference in nomenclature made by Karve, whether intentionally or not, is advantageous to her theory, removing a hurdle for her as it does! "Deshasth Rigvedi Brāhman" suggests another group of Deshasth Brahmins which is non-Rigvedi. It may be Yajurvedi or Shukla Yajurvedi or Krishna Yajurvedi or Sāmavedi. The naming of the group as Mādhyandin conceals the affiliation of the group with the Deshasth Brahmin. If on the other hand, the groups, the so-called sub-castes, are listed as they are commonly known in the society at large they would have to be named as Deshasth Rigvedi and Deshasth Yajurvedi or Deshasth Shukla Yajurvedi. This way of naming would require Karve to explain away the manifest division of the Deshasth Brahmin community which is rather difficult to do successfully. Naming the sub-caste as Mādhyandin enables Karve to put herself right with her

---

later publication of this or whether he could enable a research worker to have access to later data in any other way. Prof. Marshall was kind enough to write twice to the Officer but did not receive any reply!

reader in the context. The actuality of the situation, however, asserts itself and makes Karve herself name the caste later as "the Māhyandin Shukla Yajurvedi Brahmins" (p. 46).

However, her way of naming does violence to the current practice and notions prevalent in the society at large and the Deshasth Brahmin caste itself. The *Census Report on the Bombay Presidency*, 1911 (p. 245) records the caste as Deshasth and informs the reader that it has two main divisions, i.e. Rigvedis and Yajurvedis, which eat together but do not inter-marry. It also registers a third division, named 'Atharvans', evidently followers of the *Atharvaveda*, "though rather localised". It goes on to assure us that the Rigvedis are "subdivided into": (a) Smārtas and Madhvas or Vaishnavas. According to the same source of information, the Madhvas or Vaishnavas have eighteen "subdivisions which eat together but only three of them, named Satyabodhas, Rajendratirthas and Rāghavendras, inter-marry. The Yajurvedis, the same authority vouchsafes, are "split up into" those that follow the Black Yajus and those that follow the White, which do not inter-marry. The older sources of information, the *District Gazetteers* of Bombay published in 1884, testify to the correctness of the Census Report details and even add more. Thus we find in the *District Gazetteer of Ahmednagar* (p. 50), after the statement that the Deshasths have two divisions, i.e. Rigvedis and Yajurvedis, the further information that among the Yajurvedis there is "a further division called Kanvas": what a complex labyrinth in actuality and how grossly incorrect an over-simplification presented by Karve! Lokamanya Tilak advocating in 1881 intermarriage among Brahmin groups mentions, Deshasth, Konkanasth and Karhāde, as the "upajātis" or "potashākhās" which should freely inter-marry (*Lokamanya Tilakanche Kesaritil Lekha*, IV, pp. 1, 211, 553).

Karve expatiating on the nature of her Mādhyandina caste has done a sort of casual injustice to E. Thurston, the compiler of the seven volumes named *Castes and Tribes of Southern India*—she has not mentioned the book much less specified the page—and maligned "the southern Brahmins". She says (p. 25): "Thurston remarks that in the south these Brahmins are supposed to attain Brahminhood only after mid-day. Mādhyandina means 'of the mid-day'; it is also the name of a person, a pupil of Yājnavalkya, the founder of Shukla Yajurveda and followers of Mādhyandina are known by his name. Apparently the name was misunderstood or deliberately misinterpreted by the southern Brahmins."

Thurston (I, pp. 344–47) has devoted some pages to deal with one of the twelve subdivisions of Smārta Brahmins known in Tamilnad and the south as Prathamasāki. Prathamasākis being followers of the White Yajurveda are called Shukla Yajurvedis and are further "sometimes called Kātyāyana, Vajusaneya [Vajasaneya] and Madyandanas [Mādhyandinas]. *The last two names occur among their Pravara Gotra Rishis*. The Prathamasākis are found among all the linguistic groups [Kannada, Tamil, and Telugu]. Among Smārthas, Āndhras and Vaishnavas, they are regarded as inferior. Carnātaka Prathamasākis are, on the other hand, not considered inferior by the other sections of Carnātakas.* *In the Tanjore district, the Prathamasākis are said to be known as Madyāna* [Madhyānha] *Paraiyans*."

Thurston then records the two slightly varying versions of the traditional Puranic account explaining the origin of the name of these Brahmins and their Vedic 'Shākhā'. It is about the doctrinal difference that originated between Vaishampāyana, the promulgator of the *Yajurveda* and the preceptor of Yājnavalkya among others, and his pupil Yājnavalkya.

The difference relates to the penance, that Vaishampāyana had to undergo to expatiate the sin which he had incurred in *killing his sister's child* by accidental trampling over it. The difference

* This identity is not quite correct. M. N. Srinivas (*Marriage and Family in Mysore*, p 29) says about them: "For an unknown reason they are looked down upon by the other Brāhmans". Italics mine.

led to the schism between the Vedic school of Vaishampāyana and the one founded by his dissident but able pupil Yājnavalkya, the former school is known as the Black Yajurveda and the latter as the White Yajurveda. Followers of the fifteen traditional branches of the latter are together known as the 'Vājasaneyins'. Among them figure the followers of the Mādhyandina branch called so after its first promulgator Mādhyandina (Chitrāv, *Prāchina Charitrakosha* (Marathi), *vide* Pippalāda, Yājnavalkya, Vājasaneya, Vaishampāyana, Vyāsa). The followers of the White Yajurveda are called by the name under consideration, i.e. Prathamasākis, because perhaps Mādhyandina was the first of the fifteen branches of Yājnavalkya's recasting of the Yajurveda.

In one version of the story presented by Thurston four distinguished disciples of Yājnavalkya are mentioned, among whom figure "Mādhyandanār and Kātyāyanār". In both versions a curse is said to have been pronounced on Yājnavalkya. The curse condemned Yājnavalkya to become a Chandāla, outcaste. The Prathamasāki Brahmins, or the Mid-day Paraiyans as they are called, "are supposed to expatiate their defilement [being either themselves condemned to be Chandālas or because they are the followers of Yājnavalkya who was condemned to become a Chandāla] by staying outside their houses for an hour and a half every day at mid-day to bathe afterwards. . . . But few of them observe the rule; and orthodox persons will not eat with them."

It is seen that (1) Thurston has not done anything of the kind that Karve ascribes to him; (2) The Tamil Brahmins know that Mādhyandina, or Mādhyandanār as they called him, was a disciple of Yājnavalkya; (3) that a certain practice known to be current, though dwindling, among at least a local section of the Prathamsāki or Mādhyandina Brahmins of Tamilnad, must have provided justification for the designation given to them. It is further clear that the section was known as Mid-day Paraiyans and were Paraiyans only at mid-day or till mid-day. They were not as Karve would have her readers believe, Brahmins only at mid-day. The mid-day segregation and ablution practised by them can of course receive the appellation 'Mādhyandina'; but it does not necessarily justify the inference that it originated from ignorance of the fact of its having been the traditional name of an individual. And it is not only the Mādhyandina Brahmins of Tamilnad that have some special practice for the mid-day but nearer home in Maharashtra, too, they are known for one. *The District Gazetteer of Ahmednagar*, published in 1884, contains (p. 50) the following statement: "Yajurvedis are also called Mādhyandina because they perform their religious ceremonies, including the prayers or *sandhyā*, at noon instead of at dawn as is done by Rigvedis."

A curious feature of the lives of the great Vedic redactors recorded in the traditional accounts which acquires an uncanny significance in the context of Tamilnad, whose Brahmins like many non-Brahmins not only permit the marriage of a man with his sister's daughter but practise it in some measure even today, may be emphasized as perhaps contributory to the general disfavour shown to the Prathamasāki Brahmins. Vaishampāyana, the preceptor, had to perform a penance, which engendered the quarrel with Yājnavalkya, for having inadvertently caused the death of his sister's infant. Yājnavalkya, on the other hand, is credited with having married or mated with his own sister and given her a famous son, Pippalāda by name, who too, became the head of one branch of the White Yajurveda of Yājnavalkya!

I shall take only one other illustration of Karve's and that will be from the agricultural land-owner section of Maharashtrian society. She says (pp. 19–20): "The Maratha-Kunbi caste cluster comprises castes engaged in agriculture. . . . The word 'Kunbi' is applied to various groups of tillers of land. The word 'Maratha' used to be applied to a particular group in western Maharashtra.... The Maratha-Kunbi form over 40 per cent of the population of western Maharashtra. Of these the Marathas consider themselves as rulers and aristocrats and do not marry the Kunbis. . . . The Marathas of the districts of Poona, Satara, Kolhapur, Ahmednagar, parts of Khandesh and Sholapur marry among themselves."

The information provided in the older *Gazetteers*, the first editions of Districts Ahmednagar, Poona, Satara and Sholapur, record two or three other castes than Kunbis or Marathas under the heading 'husbandmen'. Among them Mālis figure, who numbered nearly 53 thousand as against Kunbis who numbered 397 thousand in 1881 in Poona District. The *Gazetteers* of Ahmednagar and Poona do not have a separate heading for Marathas, and that of Satara, though it has a separate section for the latter, does not number them separately. The *Sholapur District Gazetteer* treats of Kunbis, without of course numbering them, under Marathas who numbered 180 thousand in that district. The Census of 1881 recorded all Marathas under the heading Kunbi.

In the *Sholapur District Gazetteer* we find the following statements about the connection between Marathas, whose name furnishes the section-heading, and Kunbis who do not receive any separate treatment: "Kunbis are said to be bastards or *akarmashe* Marathas the offspring of a Maratha by a Maratha woman not his wife."

In Ahmednagar district the Kunbis, including of course the Marathas, numbered 304 thousand. The note in its *Gazetteer* is more ample and explains the relations between the two groups better. We are informed that among the Marathas there are "two classes", viz. (1) "God" or sweet, i.e. legitimate; and (2) "Kadu" (bitter) or "Akarmashe" (bastards) and that among the former some families of high social position allow their sons, but not their daughters, to marry into "ordinary Maratha" families. Further portion of the note curiously sounds like the injunction of the great lawgivers of old like Yājnavalkya become operative, reminding one of it and runs: "After four or five generations the bastard Marathas are allowed to become sweet or legitimate. While the Sholapur account plainly asserts that the Marathas and Kunbis eat together but do not inter-marry and thus supports Karve's statement, the Poona account emphasizing the assertion that Marathas and Kunbis inter-marry by adding that the two groups "do not differ in appearance, religion or customs" contradicts her.

Kunbis were thus considered and treated as a sub-caste of inferior status by the Marathas seventy-five years ago. And that sub-caste in part at least was believed to be formed through miscegenation. Despite what Karve says to the contrary on the basis of selective information, in both the Brahmin and the Maratha castes sub-castes were formed through separation or fission or segregation from the main group.

Evidently to emphasize her viewpoint Karve has brought in the 'evidence' of an old Marathi document. She says (p. 21, 31): "In Berar and Nagpur the dominant Kunbi group is called Tirole Kunbi. They differ from the western Kunbis in many respects . . . and they did not formerly lay claim to be fighters. From among the numerous other castes calling themselves Kunbis only one need be mentioned. This is called Mana or Manwa Kunbi. . . . In an old document a village of the Konkan coast (western Maharashtra) is described. In it are mentioned Brahmin, Kunbi and other castes. . . . But the writer of the document did not feel it necessary to mention any more caste names since the village contained only one caste each of Brahmins and Kunbis."

The Central Provinces and Berar Tirole Kunbis according to R. V. Russell (*Tribes and Castes of the C.P.*, II, 19) claim to be Rajputs. Karve's statement must be considered to be either wrong or based on esoteric information not amenable to verification. As for her assertion of their difference from the Western Kunbis it has to be pointed out that in 1880 when the *District Gazetteer of Khandesh* (p. 68) was published at least "eight classes" were recognised among the local, i.e. non-Gujar, Kunbis. One of them is Tirole (named in the *Gazetteer* as Tilole which according to Russell is an alternative spelling of the name) who numbered nearly 70 thousand in a total of less than 350,000 of Khandesh Kunbis. Another "class" is "Marāthe" who numbered less than 50 thousand and a third is "Akarmashe", bastards. The "Marāthe" Kunbis had the further subdivision into Khasas and Karchis, the latter being the progeny of the maid servants of the 'Marāthe' Khasa Kunbis.

As for the support of the document I have to point out that it is beside the mark. Among the castes mentioned in the document the Kunbis do not figure at all. The document mentions, on the other hand, the Marāthās. Karve has referred her readers for this document, to the autobiography of her late father-in-law Dhondo Keshav Karve. At page 536 of the book, named *Ātmavritta* (in Marathi) the reader will find a mention of the Marāthās but will search in vain for a mention of Kunbi. About fifteen months before the publication of Karve's book, *Hindu Society: An Interpretation*, had appeared a reference to this document in my book *After a Century and a Quarter* (p. xxiii). In the Introduction, which deals with the history of village formation and management in India, I have drawn upon this document to enlighten us on the process of village formation. I drew upon it from the writings of V. N. Mandlik who had brought the document to the notice of the public in 1865, a fact noted by D. K. Karve too. In *Mandlik's Writings and Speeches*, pages 201 to 234 are occupied by an excellent English translation of the document with explanatory notes by V. N. Mandlik himself; and any reader can satisfy himself by looking into it.

Having disposed of Karve's claims and contentions about the formation of the so-called sub-castes, I shall add a few examples where the people concerned like the Gaud Sāraswat Brahmins dealt with earlier, have considered themselves or the society at large has considered them to be the differentiated sections of a parent body.

To begin with the region of the origin of the caste system, the Sarwariyā Brahmins of U.P., as reported by Blunt (pp. 51–2), "ascribe their origin to the fact that when their ancestors were sent to perform the *jagiya* (purificatory ceremony)* for Rama after he had killed Ravana, they accepted 'dān' or part of the sacrificial offering; and, on their return *the Kanaujiyās, to whom*** they belonged, refused to receive them, and compelled them to settle across the Sarju river, whence the name Sarwariyā (Sarjupāriyā)". The 'Byāhut' sub-caste found in several castes such as the Kalwār, Lohār, Nāi and Teli is considered to be "the result of the abandonment of the practice of widow marriage" (Blunt, p. 53). The Sainthwar sub-caste of Kurmis has lately become a separate caste, chiefly because of the rise of its leading family: it has also given up widow-marriage (Blunt, p. 55).

In Malwa, Mayer (p. 258) has instanced a kind of split leading to the formation of a sub-caste among the Rājputs, his Rāmkheri Rājputs with at present a five-village circle, were formerly one of a much larger circle of sixty villages.

The cases of Sadgopās and Madhunāpits of Bengal provide additional examples of sub-caste and caste formation by change of occupation. The Gopās who numbered nearly 600 thousand and the Sadgopās 570 thousand in 1931 were one caste. The former who deal in milk and milk products are not acknowledged as 'good' Shudras. Those of the original Gopās who gave up their traditional occupation called themselves Sadgopās, and adopting cultivation as their new occupation, have succeeded in securing a better status. Though in the traditional list of the Navashākha caste-group the Gopa caste figures, in actual practice today only the Sadgopā receives the treatment proper

* 'Jagiya' appears to be a slovenly pronunciation of the word *'yagya'* which is again the Sanskrit word *'yajna'* (sacrifice).

** Italics mine.

for that group. The Nāpits, barbers of Bengal, have been accorded a better status there than their compeers receive in Northern India and elsewhere. The Madhunāpits, who are Nāpits who have turned sweetmeat-makers, however, claim even a higher status and have stopped marrying with the Nāpits (N. K. Dutt, II, pp. 128–30).

The Nāgar Brahmins of Gujarat, who are considered by many to be one of the foreign tribes that came into the country with Hunas in the fifth to the seventh century A.D., provide an example of a set of cases where the so-called sub-castes cannot but be considered to be the result of separation or fission. According to the *Bombay Gazetteer (IX) Gujarat Population* (p. 13) they have six main 'divisions' and they totalled 28,250 souls in 1891. The highest among them is undoubtedly the Vadnagrā Nāgars, food cooked by whom can be eaten by the rest of the sub-castes, except perhaps by the Prashnora sub-caste (G. H. Desai, p. 76). Desai has recorded: "The split in the community [the sub-castes of the Nāgar Brahmins] is attributed to Shiva's wrath whose temple (Hatkeshwar) was excluded from Vadnagar when the town was built." Another tradition, making the first fission give us the Visnagrā sub-caste, all the six units being named after cities or towns of mediæval Gujarat, associates it with the founding of the town of Visnagar by Vishāldev, a Chauhān king of Patna. Vishāldev while distributing *dakshinā* at the sacrifice he had performed on the foundation of his city offered it to those Nāgar Brahmins who were present there. The Brahmins, however, declined to accept it as it is not proper for a learned high-class Brahmin to accept such gifts off hand. The king practised a ruse to make them accept the same which conferred on them certain villages. The Brahmins thereupon settled themselves in their free villages. These grantees were, however, "ex-communicated by their castemen, who had remained behind at Vadnagar" and came to be known as Vishālnagar or Visnagar Brahmins. Among the Vadnagrās, the Visnagrās and the Sathodrās, which is one of the remaining four sub-castes, there is a subdivision which is considered to be an additional division or sub-caste of the Nāgar Brahmins. They are described as "those who, unable to have wives from their own community, married girls from other castes and lived apart". Till the middle of the 10th century A.D. there were only Nāgars without the further distinctions of sub-castes as a copper plate sent from Ahmedabad testifies (*Ep. Ind.* XIX, 241).

The Audich Brahmins as their name shows are northerners and must be considered to have migrated to Gujarat from the North. In 1891 they numbered, in Gujarat, just a few thousand more than 200 thousand forming 36 per cent of the total Brahmins of Gujarat. According to the *Gazetteer (Ibid.,* pp. 2–3) Brahmins of Gujarat totalled, in 1891, 570 thousand and had fifty-three named divisions, though eighty-four were mentioned of which seventy were traceable. In the *Census Report of Bombay* for 1911 (p. 240) the number of divisions among the Brahmins of Gujarat is recorded as ninety-three. Their main fission is associated with the reign of the Gujarat King Mulraj (A.D. 961–996). Some Audich Brahmins were drafted by him to help him carry out a sacrifice. On the completion of the sacrifice the King offered them inducement to stop in his dominions. Only one thousand Brahmins are believed to have accepted the offer, the rest forming a *toli* (band) refused to reside. But they, too, were later persuaded to stay on by the offer of further benefits. The first settlers naturally came to be known as Sahasra and the latter ones as Tolakiā. Strangely, however, the Sahasras are looked upon as superior in social rank. The Sahasras have among them two subdivisions which are purely geographical, i.e., Sihoras and Sidhpuriās named after the respective towns. Ten other sub-castes or castes are mentioned as having originated with the Audich Brahmins (Desai, p. 4). Among the registered Charity Trusts listed in the Charity Commissioner's Directory mentioned above not only

Audichya Sahasra (1164, 1427) and Audichya Sahasra of Sidhpur (1239) figure but also Dandhavya Audichya Brahmin (291) and Ghangoli Audichya (438) occur.

The Vāniās (Baniās) of Gujarat numbering 210 thousand in 1891 were said to have twenty-three divisions (*Gazetteer*, p. 70); but the 1911 Census Report on Bombay (p. 307) reported them as having forty-one "subcastes". Most of the divisions or sub-castes, except the Kapols, who number a little over 17 thousand are reported to have the standard subdivision—a subdivision which is widespread in Gujarat castes with the exception of the Brahmins and Rājputs and perhaps the Kanbis (Kunbis or agriculturists)—ov Visas "full-scores" as Sir Athelstane Baines (p. 34) renders it, Das as "half-scores" and "Panchās", "quarter scores". Among one section, that of the Shrimāli Vāniās, instead of the lowest subdivision being called 'Panchā' is known as 'Ladvā' (Desai, p. 103). And difference of nomenclature is accompanied by difference in social treatment. The 'Visās and the 'Dasās' of the Shrimāli, though they do not inter-marry, inter-dine but neither of them inter-dines with the Ladvā. More or less, similar is the case with the 'Panchās' of the Oswāls who call the section alternatively 'Letā' (Desai, p. 78).

Among the Modh Baniās, who are so named apparently from the mediæval Gujarat cultural centre, Modhera, and numbered almost 35 thousand in 1891, there are at least six sub-units, at least three of which, Adaljā, Goghvā, and Mandaliyā are named after towns, all located round about Ahmedabad (Desai, p. 74). Not only do these units do not inter-marry but even among each, intermarriage is not free but tends to be restricted to certain localised groups. Thus, the Goghvā Modhs of Ahmedabad do not marry with Goghvā Modhs of Surat, while the Broach Goghvā Modhs do not marry with the Kairā Goghvā Modhs. Similarly, the Visā Desavāls of Ahmedabad do not marry with the Surat Visā Desavāls, the total number of Desavāl Modhs being 17,411 (*Gazetteer*, p. 70). The 'Visā' and 'Dasā' divisions are so far integrated units that there are a number of charity trusts for each separately. Thus Dasā Disawāl, Dasā Gomathiā, Dasa Gujjar Vanik, Dasā Lad, Dasā Modh Adalji, Dasā Modh Mandaliyā, Dasā Porwād, Dasā Shrimāli and Dasā Zarolā Vanik are all represented in the Directory of Charity Trusts of the Charity Commissioner of Maharashtra mentioned above. Among these the Dasā Shrimāli claim at least sixteen such trusts in the Directory (see pp. 301–3, 881, 954, 966, 973, etc.).

The few features of the 'Visā' and 'Dasā' divisions in the Baniā or Vāniā community of Gujarat that are mentioned here quite clearly establish that they are endogamous subdivisions of the various sections, commonly called sub-castes and as such claim the appellation of sub-sub-caste. This is fission and multiplication of castes through it.

Mochis are leather-workers; but in Gujarat their subdivisions are restricted to the various specializations of their craft trade. Besides Dhālgar (shield makers), Jingars (saddlers), Pakhāri (makers of ornamental hangings for horses) and Sikligārs (grinders), there are Mochis who are Chandlagāras (makers of lac spangles), Chitāras (painters), Mingāras (workers in enamel), Pānagāras (gold and silver foil makers) and Rasaniās (electroplaters). The different subdivisions dine together but the last five have shown tendency to claim superiority and the Chandlāgāras, Chitārās and Rasaniās "have, of late, separated into separate castes and raised themselves to the level of bricklayers, carpenters, masons and artisans". (Desai, p. 72; *Bombay Census Report*, 1911, p. 203)

The functional, occupational or artisan castes are naturally to be accounted for by fission or separation through differentiation. The history of technological development dictates this mode of explanation of the multiplicity of castes and sub-castes as the reasonable one. The view propounded by Karve postulates the simultaneous existence of all the specialization and differentiation evinced by the nomenclature of the multitude of sub-units among the occupational castes. Technical development of that kind is at best a modern or a very recent phenomenon. The much longer period of pre-modern technology, on the other hand, shows slow and progressive adoption of differentiated methods of arts and crafts.

To insist, in spite of the varied examples of actual fission and the common view current among many castes regarding the origin of the sub-castes among them, is to emulate the Shri Vaishnavās of Tamilnad. Shri Vaishnavism started as a sect in the eleventh century A.D. or at least with Nāthamuni in the tenth century (Gopinath Rao in *Indian Antiquary*, 1919, p. 20). Before the tenth century there were Brahmins in Tamilnad. Students of society and the Tamilnad Society itself have looked upon the original Shri Vaishnavās as converts, i.e., dissidents or separatists, from the earlier Smarta Brahmins. The Shri Vaishnava Brahmins, on the other hand, insist that they co-existed as a separate caste of Brahmins along with the Smārtas (B. S. Baliga, p. 127). To make matters worse there is further division within the Shri Vaishnavās, giving us two sub-sub-castes, Vadagalai and Tengalai. J. N. Farquhar (p. 320) observes: 'Each sect has seized as many of the temples as possible and numerous lawsuits have resulted. So deep is the division that it prevents intermarriage." And the schism causing this division started with Vedānta Desika after the middle of the fourteenth century.

The Soliya Vellālas, one of the four main territorial sections of the great agricultural caste of Tamilnad, have the following three "subdivisions": (1) The Vellāla Chettis, Vellāla merchants; (2) the Kodikkals, 'betel-vine growers'; and (3) the Kanakilinättār, "inhabitants of Kanakkilinadu". The last unit is so small and "girls in it are getting so scarce, that its members are now going to other subdivisions for their brides", transgressing the rule of endogamy within the unit. The Konga Vellālas, another of the four territorial divisions, have the following intriguing endogamous units among others: (1) Sendalai ('redheaded men'); (2) Paditalais ('leaders of armies'); (3) Vellikkai ('the silver hands'); (4) Paralamkatti ('wearers of coral'); (5) Malaiyadi ('foot of the hills'); (6) Tollakātu ('ears with big holes'); (7) Āttangarais ('riverbank') (Thurston, VII, pp. 374–81).

The Shānārs of Salem district are divided into two endogamous sections. The Konga Shānārs who are believed to be the progeny of the first wife of a certain Muppan do not inter-marry with the Kalyāna Shānārs believed to be the progeny of the second wife of the person (*Salem District Gazetteer*, p. 183).

Earlier, in connection with Karve's charge against South Indian Brahmins, I have dealt with one sub-caste or division among Tamilnad Brahmins, the so-called Prathamasāki. The fact that the Brahacharanam section has among its nine 'subdivisions' a unit named Puthur Dravida, further supports the differentiation of Brahmin group later into subunits. So does the 'subdivision' among the Vattimas, one of the twelve or so main sections of the Smārta Brahmins of Tamilnad, named Pathinettu Grāmaththu ('eighteen villages') group and the one named Shatkulam (six families) among the four subdivisions of the Ashtasahasram section (Thurston, I, pp. 335–38).

Pandārams are a caste of Tamilnad priests who cater to the spiritual and semi-spiritual needs of a large section of the non-Brahmins. The caste-Pandārams distinguished from priestly mendicants "are said to have been originally Sozhiā Vellālas, with whom intermarriage still takes place" (Thurston, VI, p. 46).

I shall close this brief account of evidence of fission forming sub-castes with the interesting illustration recorded in a Privy Council case of over a century-and-a-half ago and that too among the so-called functional caste of traders and merchants. Some 'Comatte-Vaishyas' of Orissa filed a suit against a Brahmin organization which had declined to give them professional services of Vedic ritual, concluding that the so-called Vaishyas had been practising Shudra customs for two thousand years. *Inter alia* it came out that the adoption of the so-called Shudra customs had led to three divisions or sub-castes in the group; "Byri Comaties", "Borkka Comaties [?]" and "Nogaram Comaties" (*Moore's Indian Appeals* (1836–72) *with Complete Digest*, by P. Hari Rao, Vol. III, pp. 226–41).

The fact is that differentiation, specialization and schisms of varied nature have been going on in this land for a long long time. The great Maurya emperor, Ashoka, earliest to be concerned with integration of his people, noted this fact with poignancy in one of his edicts (D. C. Sircar, p. 35) and speaks about the religious sects and their bitter controversies, while in another (*ibid.*, pp. 51–54) he claims to have commingled the people or their religious or semi-religious sects. Separation or fission thus stands out as the most important of the factors, next to the theoretical groundwork of the notion of caste, that gave rise to the multiplicity of endogamous groups in the Hindu society.

9

Caste, Sub-caste and Kin

C. E. A. W. Oldham, the author of the then talked of book, *The Sun and the Serpent*, reviewing the first edition of this book in 1932, wrote in *Man* (November issue): "Risley, for example, laid stress on racial distinctions and *the influence of the idea of kinship*, and Nesfield on the functional basis of caste. Most authorities have referred to the powerful influence of the Brahman priesthood, at least in shaping the development of the system. Dr. Ghurye goes farther and holds that caste in India is 'a brahmanic child . . .' and that endogamy—the outstanding feature of the system—was first developed by the Brahmans in the plains of northern India and thence conveyed as a cultural trait to the other areas. We feel that this explanation is inadequate, and that account must also be taken of such phenomena as the *totemistic septs, the devakas of western India* and many other factors, of race, tribe, *kinship*, locality, religious and social usages and function that have contributed to the building up of this complicated structure, *the foundations of which go down to times anterior to the so-called 'Aryan' immigration*, the influence of which there has been a tendency to overrate."

To begin with the alleged emphasis on 'the influence of the idea of kinship' on the formation of the Indian caste-system laid by Herbert Risley, it has to be pointed out that the remark of Oldham is almost a hearsay statement. No doubt Risley devoted a whole chapter, entitled "Caste and Marriage", to the consideration of the institution of Hindu marriage *vis-a-vis* caste, but that did not lead him to analyse or to expound any connection between the two. He was concerned with the rages of the reformers of the time and of the British Liberal Civil Servants, viz., infanticide, infant-marriage, widow-marriage and the associated marital institutions of hypergamy, exogamy and endogamy, only the last of which was and has been for long a concomitant of caste. Says Sir Herbert:[1] "We have seen that endogamy restricts intermarriage in one direction by creating a number of artificially small groups within which people must marry. Exogamy brings about the same result by artificially enlarging the circle within which they may not marry." The nine conclusions that Risley has stated at the end of the chapter, entitled "The Origin of Caste", do not contain any mention of kinship. In one of them endogamous, exogamous and hypergamous groups are mentioned as sub-divisions of 'tribes and castes', and in another a large number of the exogamous groups are pronounced to be totemistic. Plausible origins of caste form the subject matter of the ninth conclusion. Calling them 'conjecture', he tells his readers that they are "based—firstly, upon the correspondence that can be traced between certain caste gradations and certain variations of physical types; secondly, on the development of mixed races from stocks of different colour; and thirdly, on the influence of fiction."[2]

There is nothing in all these and other observations of Risley which can justify Oldham's statement about Risley's emphasis on kinship in the genesis of the Indian caste system. The only mention of influence of kinship that Risley has considered it necessary to make is in connection with his valuation of E. Senart's criticism of Denzil Ibbetson's functional or occupational theory of caste. Says Risley:[3] "He (Senart) demurs, in the first place, to the share which he supposes it to assign to Brahmanical influence, and challenges the supposition that a strict code of rules, exercising so absolute a dominion over the consciences of men, could be merely a modern invention, artificial in its character and self-regarding in its aims. Secondly, he takes exception to the disproportionate importance which he conceives Denzil Ibbetson to attach to community of occupation, and points out that, if this were really the original binding principle of caste, the tendency towards incessant fission and dislocation would be much less marked: The force that in the beginning united the various scattered atoms would continue to hold them together to the end. *Both criticisms appear to miss an essential feature in the scheme, the influence of the idea of kinship, which is certainly the oldest and probably the most enduring factor in the caste system, and which seems to have supplied the framework and the motive principle of the more modern restrictions based upon ceremonial usage and community of occupation.*"* Risley, however, did not care to or does not substantiate his *obiten dicta* by any factual evidence of logical reasoning!

This is not to maintain that Risley eschewed all consideration of marital regulations of Hindu society, which are the fundamental basis of major part of kinship. On the contrary he devoted a whole chapter to them, heading it "Caste and Marriage". Of course, no student, however raw he may be, or no novice at the study of caste, can escape giving his attention to marriage, as marriage within a specified birth-group is the residual essence of caste. In the case of Risley, over and above his intensive knowledge of caste in India, was his special concern with the problems of female infanticide, particularly prevalent then and before in Rajasthan, and of what is called Kulinism in Bengal or with the woes of high caste Bengali reformers and publicists so obtruding themselves on the attention of the then District Officers.

Risley deals briefly with 'endogamy' and 'exogamy' and more spaciously with 'hypergamy', and also with 'polyandry'. His discussion of exogamy, in view of his dilating on polyandry of both types, is particularly brief and truncated. Thus with his special knowledge of Bengal, including of course Bihar which was then a component of Bengal, that he should not have mentioned the rather elaborate and highly restrictive rules of 'mul'-exogamy current among the lower castes in that region is an instance in point. This feature also exposes to us his inability to discover appreciable relation between exogamy and caste. The only observation that he makes actually demonstrates the utter extraneousness of Risley's treatment of the subject. He says about the relation between exogamy and caste or endogamy: "... endogamy restricts intermarriage in one direction by creating a number of artificially small groups within which people must marry. Exogamy brings about the same result by artificially enlarging the circle within which they may not marry." He states that an exogamous unit within some Brahmin castes is large enough to contain two thousand persons and that, even leaving out the fact of understatement, the number of persons prohibited by the law of prohibited degrees current among English people presents a striking contrast. Then he points out the need for an additional or supplementary rule to correct the utter one-sidedness of the exogamic rule.[4] Well, all this, even if it be all perfectly correct, is beside the point, if one's objective is to discover the relations, if any, that subsist between exogamy and caste.

Risley deals with hypergamy at great length; but his main objective is to bring out its relation with polygyny and female infanticide, though he speaks of it as having been "so intimately connected

---

* Italics mine.

with evolution of caste" and expresses his surprise that that old practice "should have escaped the notice of all modern writers on the early history of marriage."[5]

The connection of hypergamy with caste comes out in his discussion only when Risley speaks about its absence among "the Muhammadans and those Hindu castes which permit widows to remarry". He points out that among such castes such conditions as a change in occupation or "settlement outside the traditional habitat of the caste" instead of creating hypergamous sections tend to form endogamous sub-castes.[6] But surely this is a doubtful and extremely tenuous connection, if any, between hypergamy and caste!

It is in the origin of hypergamy that Risley brings in race and conquest as the two or combined factors and illustrates his view with the help of the "mixed or coloured races of America". He further illustrates Indian hypergamy by reference to the social stratification existing in Madagascar and "hazards the conjecture that matrimonial relations between patricians and plebeians in Rome before the Lex Canuleia (445 B.C.) may have been regulated by the custom of hypergamy".[7]

Perhaps W. Kirkpatrick was the first among writers on caste who spoke of exogamy and endogamy together in such a manner as to postulate their joint contribution to the making up of caste. In 1912 he wrote in his paper entitled "Primitive Exogamy and the Caste System" published in the *Journal of the Asiatic Society of Bengal, N. S.*, VIII (pp. cix-cx): "Each endogamous section is divided up into several exogamous sects or sub-sections. These facts surely point to a conclusion, which without any extravagant argument enables us to trace the present Hindu caste system back to the primeval laws which required and instituted and enforced a vigorous and rigid observance of the Exogamic law. . . . In short, the constant creation of separate connubial groups in modern Hinduism has its basis and origin in the instinct, which taught man to seek his bride and secure her forcibly if necessary from another camp—which is marriage by capture—which is Exogamy in its most primitive form."

It is seen from the above quotation that it is not only a mere assertion unsupported by any evidence or argument but also that it is hopelessly confused, exogamy as the operative form of marriage by capture being credited with the mysterious generation of caste-system.

B. R. Ambedkar was the next person to connect together exogamy and endogamy as the generating force of caste: In a paper read in a seminar at Columbia University and afterwards published in the *Indian Antiquary* in 1917, almost in the same mysterious vein as that of Kirkpatrick but with supposed intervening steps, rather verbosely put up, he propounded that endogamy superimposed on exogamy gave India her system almost automatically. Without going into the details or attempting to criticise or rather to brush aside Ambedkar's reasoning, I shall point out the essential feature of his theory to be the appreciation of the fact that exogamy is not only almost universal in India but is also demonstrably an older institution than caste-system. As Ambedkar emphasises, exogamy is also very much more widely diffused than any form of caste system, even many of the most primitive peoples practising it in a rigorous form.

The following quotation sums up Ambedkar's views: (loc. cit., p. 84) "One of the primitive survivals [in Indian society] . . . is the *custom of exogamy*. . . . The various *gotras* of India are and have been exogamous. So are the groups with totemic organization. It is no exaggeration to say that with the people of India exogamy is a creed and none dare infringe it, so much so that, in spite of the endogamy of the Castes [?] within them, exogamy is strictly observed and that there are more rigorous penalties for violating exogamy than there are for violating endogamy. You will, therefore, readily see that with exogamy as the rule there could be no Castes, for exogamy means fusion. But we *have* Castes; consequently in the final analysis creation of Castes, so far as India is concerned, means the super-imposition of endogamy on exogamy. However, in an originally exogamous population an easy working out of endogamy (which is equivalent to the creation of Caste) is a grave problem and it is in the consideration of the means utilized for the preservation of endogamy against exogamy that we may hope to find the solution of the problem. Thus *the superimposition of endogamy on exogamy means the creation of caste*."

E. A. H. Blunt, who was the Superintendent of the Census operations of 1911 in the United Provinces and later Chairman of the Banking Inquiry Committee in the same administrative unit, published his book entitled *Caste System of Northern India* towards the end of 1931. As Blunt tells his reader the book was a writing from 1913 out was mainly written to completion between 1927 and 1930. Blunt makes it quite clear that the caste-system studied and expounded in his book is that of the United Provinces of Agra and Oudh; and he has left no loophole for any reader to be led astray by adding an appropriate tag in small letters to the title of the book itself. In the preface he adds the correct justification for the title without the tag when he assures his readers that the Hindu social system of U.P. is the Hindu Social System of northern India and that "if there are variations, elsewhere, they are not in essentials".

Blunt's was the first, and I believe has remained the only, book which deals with the caste-system of one specific Province or State and as such claims the closest attention of the students of the institution. What is still more important from our special point of view is that, evidently following Risley, he devoted two chapters to the consideration of marriage and its impact on caste. He went at least a step further than Risley in that he added the middle term of sub-caste and headed these two chapters as "Caste, Sub-caste and Marriage". Detailing the restrictions on marriage in the five categories of endogamy, exogamy, prohibited degrees of kin, hypergamy and virgin marriage, he observes (p. 37): "Save for certain quite exceptional castes, the first of these restrictions is universal. Either the second or the third operates in every caste; generally both operate together. The fourth is common. The fifth [which forbids a man to marry a widow] applies to perhaps one-third of the population, i.e. to most higher castes."

Endogamy and exogamy are then taken up for consideration first as both of them "involve segmentation of the caste". From an analysis of caste names Blunt concludes (p. 41) that "the constitution of a caste is very liable to alternation", groups originally exogamous becoming endogamous and vice versa, though the latter process is "less common". The local section of an endogamous group is known as '*birādari*' and has generally a 'panchāyat' or caste-council of its own. A *birādari* or brotherhood of this kind is an exogamous group, its members being too closely related to one another. However membership of the *birādari* "depends not on the fact of the members' incapacity to inter-marry" but "on the fact that they all belong to an endogamous group, coupled, of course, with the residential qualification" (pp. 128–9).

The custom of hypergamy according to Blunt (pp. 46–47) works within the framework of the total exogamous units of a caste. The exogamous groups are classified "according to their social position [?]", a group of higher rank takes brides from the lower group but does not give bride to it. The only observation about its influence on caste that Blunt makes is that "the law of hypergamy greatly complicates the marriage system of the castes who observe it".

Endogamy, of course, "is a factor of the greatest importance in the caste system", marriage restrictions "generally speaking, governing all other restrictions" (pp. 47, 89).

The laws of prohibited degrees supplement the exogamic rules and in the case of castes without exogamous groups wholly regulates marital unions. The law of prohibited degrees bars an "unnecessarily wide" kindred, many of the forbidden relatives not being "available for matrimonial purposes" (p. 60).

Next comes J. H. Hutton writing in 1946.* In one chapter on the Structures of Caste, he deals with endogamy, hypergamy and exogamy in that order and also mentions other restrictions on marriage. Finally, however, he observes (p. 63) that, among restrictions on marriage which are varied, "many of the rules can hardly be said to be exactly relevant to the question of caste". The only relevance he points out is that of endogamy and of those marriage rules which when broken are taken note of by the caste council as breaches of the caste code of conduct, breach of the rule of endogamy commonly leading to putting out of the caste (p. 64). Later when dealing with commensal and other restrictions which "isolate or, rather, insulate one caste from another" he asserts that "the marital restrictions of caste . . . are vitally involved in the relationship of a caste to society as a whole" and that "caste endogamy is more or less incidental to the taboo on taking food cooked by a person of at any rate a lower . . . caste" (p. 71). Thus it appears that Hutton considers the connection of endogamy with caste as secondary, endogamy itself being incidental to the commensal taboo!

It will be noticed that neither Blunt nor even Hutton has to say directly anything about kinship and its influence, if any, on caste system. Nor did Risley before them do so. I think A. C. Mayer was the first student of the institution, who put the two, caste and kinship, together in one context and title, and thus gave clear and direct expression to the view that some connection subsists between caste and kinship. Mayer's book *Caste and Kinship in Central India*, prefaced in January 1958, was published in 1960. Leaving the two chapters, "Introduction" and "Conclusion", the book has eleven chapters, out of which at least five deal with kinship in its ramification and influence on caste. And characteristically, as it should be in a viewpoint that is kinship-oriented, 'marriage' does not start the series. The Pattern of Marriage comes for consideration only after levels of kinship have been dealt with and individuals forming the components of the system are, brought on the stage as ready for marriage. The natural sequence of marriage is the practical operation of the pattern of kinship behaviour. The whole plan of work and the treatment is such that, if anywhere, it is in Mayer's book one should find a clear picture of the connection between kinship and caste.

Mayer's conclusions on this point may be stated to be: (1) Every man is a member of three bodies—the kindred, the sub-caste and the caste (p. 5); (2) "the entire sub-caste may, in the last analysis, be a kin-group; but this is the anthropologists' abstraction, and would only in exceptional cases be a kin-group recognised as such by any single member". Normally its recognition proceeds from the common sub-caste name. It is, the people of a smaller region "composed of several score settlements" that form "the effective sub-caste group"; and "these people are at the same time kin". And it is this local sub-caste group therefore that can be properly defined as a kin-group (pp. 151, 248, 269, 271, 272); (3) Kin-ship provides the key to recognition as a caste or sub-caste member, a sub-caste member coming from a distance being treated as such only if his connection within certain recognised degrees of kinship with the local people is established (p. 213).

Many of the works dealing with specific ethnic groups or particular village societies published from 1955 onwards have provided material for an appraisal of the roles of both endogamy and exogamy in the integration of caste and Hindu society. Mayer's endeavour in that direction has been one of the very best. His specific contribution, however, in this behalf will have to be spoken of later in its proper context.

This general resumé of what writers on caste during the last sixty, more particularly thirty-seven, years have had to say regarding the connection between caste and kinship may be closed with the observation that the role of endogamy in relation to caste was most emphatically and comprehensively

* Page references are all to the third edition, 1961.

pointed out in the first edition of this book thirty-seven years ago and can be found so stressed in the earlier chapters of this edition too. It only remains for me to inform the readers of this edition, few of whom might have known the situation as current in 1932, that my view that endogamy is the core and soul of caste was not generally liked by intellectuals or by the reading public at large. And it is there still as the crux of the problem of caste!

What is necessary, therefore, is to seek to unravel the connections of exogamy and hypergamy with caste and focus all the new light on the nature and size of the endogamous unit.

The history of caste-elements presented in the earlier part of this book has shown that, before the fundamental element of the system, i.e. endogamy, marriage within one's caste or sub-caste, became an almost inexorable rule of social life, it was possible for intermarriage between members of the four 'varnas' or caste-groups. As a matter of fact since very early times, i.e. at least from about 500 B.C., it has been the practice of all texts on Sacred Law to account for a large number of named groups as a result of a these intermarriages, their permutations and combinations. Intermarriages between female members of the higher 'varnas' and males of the lower, called 'pratiloma', against the hair or grain, were however condemned. The other kind of intermarriages called 'anuloma', in line with the hair or grain, were, however, permitted to such an extent and continued to be in evidence, though only rarely, for such a long time that they must be considered to have been a common practice in early times. To put it in a generalised form, naturally much more simplified than the probable actuality, taking girls to wife from a 'varna' immediately lower than one's own, between Brahmins and Kshatriyas, on the one hand, and between Kshatriyas and Vaishyas, and Vaishyas and Shudras on the other, was one of the modes of social interaction and social assimilation going on for a long time before the social milieu hardened into the caste system as we know it.

Hypergamous practice is an age-old and almost universal trait of society of early and mediaeval civilized society not completely obliterated even in the highly sophisticated age of 'liberty, equality and fraternity'. And so-called hypergamy is only an institutionalised form of this hypergamous sentiment and practice. Hypergamy has not been and cannot be like endogamy a compulsory or exclusive form of marriage. No society, hardly any group, is known to have ordined that a male, if he marries, must marry a female from a group lower than his own, whether one step or more lower. What has been laid down in certain societies is that a female may be married to a male who does not come from a group lower than that of the female. She may marry a man of her own group; but if she is to go out of the group she can only be married into a higher group. Marrying away a female into a higher group may or may not bring some reward in the shape of increased social prestige or even status of the family that has succeeded in so doing but marrying her into a lower group is sure to bring obloquy and loss of status to the family whose female has been thus married.

There were at least four status groups or 'varnas' in the Hindu society of Vedic times. It was thus possible for a male of the first status group, the Brahmin 'varna', to marry a female from any of the three lower 'varnas', if there was no further regulation of marriage other than the one encouraging or exhorting or requiring a female of one of the lower status-groups to marry into a higher status group. And the hypergamous practice, it does not appear to have been a rule of hypergamy even of the strength or rigidity of the type we meet with in the later hypergamous practice under Bengal 'Kulinism' or status pattern envisaged by the writers on Sacred Hindu Law, from the authors of the *Dharmasutras*, who lived between 500 B.C. to 300 B.C., to the law-givers of the *Smritis* down to the sixth or eighth century A.D., permitted in theory at least the marriage of a female of any of the three lower 'varnas' with a male of the highest status group, the Brahmin 'varna'. A Kshatriya male could marry from any one of the two lower 'varnas' and the Vaishya could marry from the Shudra group, which of course had to find wives from among its own females, over and above supplying some at least to the members of the higher 'varnas' in the hope of bettering or heightening the prestige of the family and of seeing the progeny of their females forming members of a separate group, slightly at least higher in status than its own.

The institution was so far considered by the law-givers, from Gautama, about 500 B.C., to the liberal *Smriti*-writer Brihaspati in the sixth century A.D., that many of them provided for the contingency arising from the fact of there being sons of a deceased person born of wives from different 'varnas' and for the troublesome problem of adjusting claims with equity and fairness, consequent on the differential number of these sons, as between the deceased's wives of different '*varnas*'.*

Baudhāyana Dharmasutra lays down the rule which remains more or less the norm throughout. It runs: "If there are sons born of wives of different castes ('varna'), they should make ten portions of the ancestral property and take four shares, three, two (and) one, according to the order (of the castes)." In the *Vishnusmriti* we find a detailed treatment accompanied by illustrative cases of differential plurality of sons, the two guiding rules being: "If there are two sons by a Brahmana wife, and one son by a Shudra wife, the estate shall be divided into nine parts; and of these, the two sons of the Brahmana wife shall take eight ["two" in Jolly's translation being an error] parts, the one son of the Shudra wife, a single part. If there are two sons of a Shudra, and one son by a Brahmana wife, the estate shall be divided into six parts; and of these the son of the Brahmana wife shall take four parts, and the two sons of the Shudra wife together shall take two parts." This appears to have been the standard interpretation of the rule of inheritance in respect of sons of wives of different 'varnas', the division being made on the basis of specific shares to which a son is entitled owing to the status of his mother. The great jurist of the eleventh century, Vijnāneshvara, commenting on *Yājnavalkyasmriti* (II, 125) adumbrates the same principle. It does not base the partition on the basis of the mothers of the sons. If the division was made on the latter basis, in the first illustrative example of the *Vishnusmriti* the primary division of the estate would have been in five parts, and the single son of the Shudra wife would have received one-fifth of the deceased's estate, while each son of the Brahmin wife would have received two-fifths, i.e. double that of the Shudra wife's son, and not four-ninths as in the illustration of Vishnu.

Brihaspati of the sixth century, known for his liberal treatment of woman's rights, however, generalizes in a way which in ordinary cases of polygyny gives the rule of inheritance which has been known in Punjab customary law[8] as 'chundewand', inheritance or division according to 'chunda' i.e. braid of hair. It is known in Western U. P. as 'jorubant', division according to wife, and is referred to in Sanskrit works as 'patnibhāga', wifely division. Says Brihaspati (XXV, 15): "When there are many sons sprung from one father, equal in caste and number, but born of different mothers, a legal division (of the property) may be effected by adjusting the share according to the mothers." B. H. Baden-Powell, the most painstaking and penetrating student of village-life in Northern India, writing in A.D. 1900 (*J.R.A.S.*, p. 271) on village-life in far off Goa of the early sixteenth century, tells us that "the principle of division of property of a man when there are sons by two wives is to

* *Gautama*, XXVIII, 35–39 (*S. B. E.* series, II, pp. 308–9); *Baudhāyana*, II, 2, 3, 10–12 (*S. B. E.* series, XIV, pp. 225–6; *Vishnusmriti*, XVIII, 1–34 (*S. B. E.* series, VII, pp. 72–3), *Vasishtha*. XVII, 47–50 (*S. B. E.* series, XIV, p. 89); *Manusmriti*, IX, 149–53; *Brihaspati* (*S. B. E.* series, XXXIII), pp. 374–5; *Kautiliya Arthashāstra* (Eng. Trans, by R. P. Kangle, pp. 245–6) II, 6; 17–22.

divide *per-stirpes* (jorubant in N. W. India or Chundawand in the Punjab) and not *per capita*". The rule thus appears to have had a much wider spread than the Punjab and U.P.

The slight rise in status ensuing from a hypergamous marriage at least for the progeny—higher than that of the wife and the mother—is implicit in another provision made in the rather orthodox and uncompromising early law-book, *Gautama Dharmasutra* (I, 4, 18–19 or *S. B. E.* trans., p. 199): It reads: "In the seventh (generation men obtain) a change of caste either being raised to a higher one or being degraded to a lower one." The rule of seven generations was apparently the older law, and venerable teachers exhorted that it should be liberalized to the extent that only five generations should suffice to raise or degrade the progeny of 'anuloma', hypergamous marriage, or 'pratiloma', downward marriage, respectively. Haradatta, the great commentator of the early thirteenth century, has fully explained the operation of the rule which envisages the marriage of the female born of hypergamous marriage, marrying generation after generation in the same higher group into which the first female of the series had married. The progeny of such marriage series in the seventh generation from the first Brahmin marrying a Kshatriya female, would be full-fledged Brahmin.

The rule, in more or less identical wording, is laid down in *Yājnavalkyasmriti* (I, 96) of the second or the third century A.D., seven to eight hundred years after Gautama. What is even more interesting and even instructive is that the jurist Vijnāneshvara, commenting on it about the last decade of the eleventh century, illustrates it with examples which testify to the still greater liberalization of this anti-caste-rigidity provision. According to Vijnāneshvara, the female progeny of a Brahmin marrying a Kshatriya female would confer the status of full-fledged Brahminhood on the progeny of her great-granddaughter if in the intervening three generations the female progeny contracted marriage with Brahmins. Thus the rule envisages the fifth generation upgrading for a Kshatriya female's hypergamous marriage with a Brahmin and the seventh generation upgrading for a Shudra female's hypergamous marriage with a Brahmin. Without going into further discussion, leaving out all niceties and particulars, one can safely conclude that hypergamous marriage had such social repercussions that other institutions than marriage were being shaped to accommodate it. It was at the same time being encouraged through offering easier terms for upgrading of the progeny of such marriages. Needless to emphasize the fact that no attempt appears to have been made to restrict the hypergamous marriage to consecutive ranking groups only.

D. F. Pocock in his valuable study of hypergamy among the Pātidārs of Gujarat speaks of one type of hypergamy as 'free hypergamy'[9] (*Ghurye Felicitation Volume*, p. 196). Adapting his usage I shall speak of the hypergamy of the ancient Hindu law-givers, 'varna'-hypergamy as 'free' hypergamy. For there is no restriction regulating hypergamy either on the basis of a rank-order of the 'varna' or of the position of the marrying male in his family or again on whether the marriage is first or subsequent one of the marrying male. Hypergamy, requiring these latter points to be taken into account, being permissible under one set and forbidden under another, may be spoken of as 'restricted' hypergamy.

Free hypergamy in modern India appears to have been practised, outside the peculiar social milieu of Kerala, in the Punjab hills. "We are told of it in a proverb current among the hill peoples. It runs: "sātvi pidhi Ghirthni ki bhi Rāni hojāti", the daughter of a Ghirath woman can become a Rāni in the seventh generation. The Ghirath caste is the last of the rung of the social ladder of the Hills and the Rānās are the highest. A Ghirath girl, exceptionally endowed, may succeed in marrying up and if her female descendants keep on similarly marrying up and up, the sixth female descendant in the line can marry a Rānā and her daughter would be a Rāni in her own birth-right.[10]

Non-'varna' hypergamy or intra-caste hypergamy has been known to be a widespread phenomenon in modern India and has been associated with many social evils which are quite often credited to it. What is even more interesting and instructive from the viewpoint of understanding caste, sub-caste, multiplicity of groups, and the influence of marital regulations and kinship-system on caste is the fact that it has even been developing further during the last three quarters of a century.

The most notorious hypergamy has been what is known as Bengal 'kulinism', described by Risley. N. K. Dutt and D. C. Sircar have pointed out that the institution could not have been formulated by a king in the twelfth century as asserted by Bengal tradition.[11]

Rājputs, Baniās, Kunbis and Pātidārs and even Brahmins of Gujarat practice intra-caste hypergamy where there are divisions named 'visās', 'dasās', 'panchās' among them to indicate the hierarchical status of the groups within the caste or the sub-caste or there are only named or recognised 'gols' or territorial circles.[12]

Not only Khatris and Kāyasthas and Baniās but also Brahmins of U.P. are known to practise intra-caste hypergamy, the subdivisions forming the basis for it being in principle like those of Gujarat. They are, however, named differently as 'Dhāighar', two and half houses; 'Chāraghar', four houses,' 'Bārghar', twelve houses, and 'Bāwanjāti', fifty-two breeds, among the Khatris.[13] Among the Baniās the sub-divisions bear names identical with those of Gujarat like 'Dasā' and 'Visā' etc.[14]

According to one account of the organization of the Kanaujiā Brahmins—and their intricate organization appears to have borne different versions—"personally verified" by Burn, the Census Superintendent of 1901, "there are six or seven *gotras*, each of which is divided into ten or a dozen *kuls* or families, the names of which are mostly local. The *kuls* in each *gotra* are divided into three classes in order of social rank, one or two being called Khatkul, a few more the Panchadari, and the remainder the Dhakra. A Khatkul may marry only a Khatkul unless he is marrying for the second time after the demise of his first wife who must be a Khatkul. For his second marriage he may marry a Panchadari but not a Dhakra.[15] Pocock states that in Bengal hypergamy restriction on the basis of the seniority or juniority of the person marrying occurs (p. 196). He it is who informs us of the development in the hypergamy of the Pātidārs*. The villages which formerly were informally known to be members of a lower marrying circle gave themselves a formal look, calling their group 'ekadā', unity, and having a 'panch' for looking after the matrimonial affairs. The immediate result of this formalization is the widening of the hypergamous spread and the proximate consequence may well be the formation of a sub-caste. For as Pocock states any 'ekadā' family may take brides from lower families or marrying circles but may not give its daughters to the erstwhile higher marrying circle. The 'ekadā' is thus not incompatible with hypergamy and as Pocock (p. 203) observes "the rise of lower groups may lead to the formation of a series of endogamous sub-castes."

The theoretical consequences for caste and its solidarity, apart from the possibility and traditional assertion of multiplicity of castes or sub-castes, are very well generalized by Pocock in terms of kinship and I can do no better than quote his general conclusion. He says:[16] "We can say that while hypergamy is a factor disruptive to large kin-groups the factors making for their permanence are today impotent or destroyed."

---

* This development was clearly stated by G. H. Desai (op cit., p. 63) forty years before Pocock.

To turn to exogamy, which appears to have been an institution as old as family itself, it may be noted that it exists in two forms. The two forms may be distinguished as (1) Sept, or in Hindu terminology *gotra*-exogamy, and (2) prohibited degrees, or in Hindu terminology *sapinda*- exogamy. Both forms of exogamy tend to integrate the larger group, the endogamous unit, by requiring marital connections to be established among persons outside the smaller units of family, lineage and or sept as the case may be.

Sept or *gotra*-exogamy, requiring a person to seek his mate from outside his sept or *gotra*, which is handed, in patrilineal societies, from father to son, may be distinguished as far as India is concerned as (1) Brahmanic system and (2) Non-Brahmanic. As will be made clear soon there exists an apparently mixed hybrid form which in actual operation turns out to be only the second variety of exogamy.

The non-Brahmanic variety of exogamy may even be designated totemic exogamy, if one keeps in mind the extremely nebulous nature of totemic complex met with in India. As J. V. Ferreira[17] has recently made out, not only is totemism in India "almost entirely of the clan variety" but also is totem worship of relatively recent age and influenced by Hindu civilization. And as the same scholar points out "the extreme south and large areas in the north and north-west are non-totemic."

In his classic study of Hindu exogamy, S. V. Karandikar (*Hindu Exogamy*, pp. 220–82) has systematically listed the septs which form the basis of exogamy among non-Brahmin castes. We can distinguish six varieties of them as: (1) Septs which are territorial divisions; (2) Septs which are family sections; (3) Septs which are titular or nickname groups; (4) Septs which are based on the number of Gods worshiped; (5) Septs which are totemic or based on 'devaks' respected and (6) Septs which are eponymous divisions. The last variety in its purest form is also the Brahmanic form of sept exogamy.

We may speak of a seventh variety which is produced by a combination of any of the first five varieties with the sixth. But I prefer not to do so as it is the non-eponymous component of it which, as will be seen, regulates exogamy.

Of these varieties the first two and the last are the most important both because they account for a large number of castes and tribes and also because they bear the closest analogy with or reflect the greatest influence of the Brahmanic variety. Before proceeding with a brief analysis of these, it has to be pointed out that despite the common view that primitive exogamy is very wide-spread Karandikar was able to list no less than fifty-one castes as regulating their marriages only with the help of the rule of prohibited degrees or by 'sapinda' exogamy.

The best examples of local or family sections as exogamous units are provided by at least two castes of Maharashtra, the Kunbi and the Chamār. The exogamous sections of Kunbis are called 'Kuls' and they are nothing better than surnames or names of lineages, however received or formed. Marriage within the same 'Kul' is prohibited. We are informed that though the Kunbis favour the preferential mating of a man with his mother's brother's daughter, marriage is prohibited in the *kuls* of the mother's father, father's mother's father and mother's mother's father (?). Wherever there are the totemic sections known as *devaks*, they too are taken into consideration so that a man must avoid a girl whose father's either surname or *devak* is the same as his own. Among some Chamār sub-castes one cannot marry in one's family, in that of his mother's father's or in those of his mother's mother's father's and great-grand-mother's (?).

Ahirs, a caste found in the Punjab and U.P., particularly in strong concentration in the eastern districts, are said to have *gotra* exogamy in the western region; but in Bihar it is known to have exogamous divisions of the territorial type which are known as *muls*. We are further informed that when these 'muls' are discovered to be rather large, they are divided into conveniently smaller sections. These smaller sections are called *purukhs*. It is these 'purukhs' that form the basis of exogamy of the Ahirs wherever they exist. In the western areas whatever the 'gotras' may be, the exogamic rule based on them is very wide. A person has to avoid four *gotras*, that of his father, that of his mother's father, that of his father's mother's father and that of his mother's mother's father (Blunt, p. 62) Among the Bais, a man must not marry a woman of his *mul* or of his mother's father's *mul* or of his father's mother's father's *mul*. There is a further interesting extension of the exogamic rule which requires that similar restriction must be observed in respect of the *muls* on the bride's side. The *mul* of the girl's mother's father's and that of her father's mother's father also must be different from the 'muls' of father, mother's father and father's mother's father of the groom for the girl to be eligible (Risley. *Tribes and Castes*, I, p. 51).

The Dosadhs, being sort of untouchables, have been an enigma (Blunt, p. 101) and they have sub-castes which possess territorial or local sections and the rule of exogamy among some of them is very wide, barring seven sections, of the father, father's mother's father, father's father's mother's father, father's father's father's mother's father, mother's father, mother's mother's father and mother's mother's mother's father.

The Goālās of Bihar, have among them two sub-castes which provide an almost unique illustration of marital regulations other than endogamy influencing caste. They are named Naomuliā and Satmuliā respectively, because the former have to avoid nine *muls* or exogamous sections, while the latter only seven. The *muls* to be avoided are: (1) own *mul*, i.e. one's father's; (2) mother's father's; (3) mother's mother's father's; (4) mother's mother's mother's father's; (5) father's mother's father's; (6) father's father's mother's father's and (7) father's father's father's mother's father's. The Naomuliās have further to eschew the *muls* of their (8) father's mother's mother's father and (9) of father's mother's father's mother's father.[18] The Hajāms of Bengal go further in extending the rule as they have to apply the formula to the girl's identical relatives and to see that these 'muls' do not tally with his (Ibid, p. 306).

The Gujar is a pastoral and an agricultural caste concentrated in the western districts of U.P. and in the eastern ones of the Punjab. If the Census data recorded by Crooke (See Crooke, II, 443–440) are anywhere near being correct, they can and do vie with the standard Brahmin ramification of exogamous units. As will be mentioned later the number of Brahmanic *gotras*, as listed by John Brough from Baudhāyana's ancient text on the subject, is less than 900. The number of Brahmanic *gotras* in one of the latest of the Sanskrit-ritualistic literary endeavours, *Samskārakaustubha* (18th century A.D.) is about 1600. The *gotras* of the Gujar are said to number 1178! Most of them, however, are believed to be territorial in origin. It is to be carefully noted that the relation of exogamy with caste in this community is that its rule varies in different sub-castes. That some of these sub-castes avoid four *gotras* in marriage should incline one to discount any role of exogamy in creating or preventing fragmentation of a caste into separate endogamous units.

The Jāts have numerous exogamous sections, many of which are believed to have originated in village names. What is further important from the viewpoint of connection between caste and kinship is that some sections form together one exogamous group, as the sections are believed to be related to one another.

The recent work of Oscar Lewis in the village Rani Khera about fifteen miles from Delhi, i.e. in an area of Jāt concentration, is perhaps the only source of light on this feature of Jāt organization. Lewis tells us that Rani Khera is a constituent of a larger unit known as *chaugāma*, or 'four-village unit' and also of a still larger unit, significantly named bisgāma or 'twenty-village unit' as its constituents number twenty villages of which Rani Khera is one. These villages are so grouped together because they are known to contain the dominant community, the Jāts, who are descended from a common ancestor, the number of generations passed is, however, not specified by Lewis. Perhaps the Jāts or their genealogists do not remember the exact number of generations but only the tradition that they are the descendants of a great-grandson of "the famous ruler Prithvi Raj" (?) who came to live in Rampur in about A.D. 1200. These twenty villages together are known as "Dabas" villages, evidently because the common ancestor lived in the village of that name! Though Lewis goes on to observe that "these twenty-village units in turn are members of larger inter-village networks which culminate in a 360-village unit, all of whose ancestors were related in the distant past", it is quite clear from his exposition of the marital arrangements of the Jāts of Rani Khera that the twenty-village unit is the exogamous unit and not the larger one of 360-village unit or any middling one. *Dabas* is actually the name of an exogamous section, 'gotra' or sib or clan as Lewis calls it.[19]

The Jāts of Rani Khera evidently are members of that sub-caste among them which has to avoid four sections, septs or *gotras* in marriage. Lewis wrote about them, without letting his readers know the name of the sub-caste if any. These Rani Khera Jāts cannot marry into their father's section, sept or *gotra*, nor in that of their mother, nor again either in that of the father's mother's father or of the mother's mother's father.[20]

Some sub-castes of the Kāyasths of U.P. have local groups which they call *als* and base their exogamy on them. A person cannot marry in his own *al* or in that of his mother's father's or mother's mother's father's *al*.

Some castes have both the Brahmanic *gotras* and another type of exogamous sections and a few of them may now be instanced.

Among the Bābhans, a large landowning caste of Bihar, there exist two types of exogamous units, the Brahmanic *gotras* and territorial divisions; and we are told that the exogamic rule is based on both, so that when they "conflict the authority of territorial class overrides that of the eponymous or the Brahmanical class". It is noteworthy that the sections of both parents have to be avoided. The Bhumihārs of U.P., the counterpart of Bihar Babhans, have 84 of the standard Brahmanic *gotras*, like Bhārgava, Kāshyapa, Parāshara, Vasishtha, and also recognise territorial sections or *muls*. In case of conflict the 'mul' exclusion prevails over the *gotra* exogamy.[21] The Kāyasths of Bihar have both *gotras* and territorial sections known as *kuls*; but they base their exogamy on the 'kuls', avoiding only the 'kul' of one's own.

The Bhātiyās, a Rājput community of U.P., have Brahmanical *gotras*, each of which is sub-divided into several *nukhs* or 'families', which are named after some person, village or even occupation. The *gotras* apparently are prestige symbols not counting in the exogamic rule which is wholly based upon *nukhs*. We are told that each *nukh* is "separated by at least 49 generations, from all other *nukhs*".[22] It is intriguing that the number of generations separating a *nukh* from others should be identical with that of the 'pravaras' on whose basis, twenty-three hundred years ago, Baudhāyana is known to have arranged the *gotras* of the Brahmins!

About the Rājputs of U.P. and Bihar—all the Rājputs including those of Rajasthan, Punjab and Madhya Pradesh with these nearly equal the total number of Brahmins in India—have septs which appear to be of the territorial variety. They have also the Brahmanic *gotras*. Among some only the Brahmanic *'gotra'* exogamy is practised. Among others the original septs form the basis of exogamy. Among these latter the wider prohibition is in force, requiring a person to seek a bride not only from outside his own sept but also those of his mother's father, mother's mother's father and father's mother's father.

About the Rājputs of Rajasthan, the home of Rājputs, D. R. Bhandarkar has provided very interesting data regarding exogamous restrictions.[23] He tells us that as Kshatriyas they adopt the 'pravaras', the 'rishi'-based invocation formulas, of their priests but "it is not enough for them to avoid these *pravaras* as it seems was in the case of the Kshatriyas of the pre-Christian period." Besides these *pravaras* they have to take note of another division to which they belong, e.g. the *khamp* or "clan". Each *khamp* has further divisions or branches. Thus Chohān and Guhilots are *khamps*. As branches—the technical name for these, if any, we are not informed about—of the Chohān *khamp* or clan are mentioned: Chohān, Hada, Khichi, Songirā, Devdā, and of the Guhilot, Guhilot, Sisodiyā, Ahadā, Pāpadā, Mangalyā, etc. The branches of each *khamp* are exogamous so that one has to marry outside one's *khamp*.

Both the Devdā and the Sonagārā or Songiārā branches and others like Nadoliā and Sanchorā are known to have been named after the principalities founded or ruled over by the first important direct ancestor of the lineage.[24]

The Marwar Brahmin caste named Dahimā or Dadhich, so called after the name of their patron goddess Dadhimati, appear to possess both 'gotras' and 'khampas'. Some of the 'khampas' are: 'Gothecha', 'Mangalodya', 'Asopa'. 'Inanya', 'Khatoda', 'Borada', 'Didawanya', which, as Pandit Ram Karna informs us, are all named after localities or villages. An old record, dated about A.D. 610, from near Nagor in the former Jodhpur state, mentioning these Brahmins (fourteen of them), refers to them as having been of 'Vatsa-gotra'. It does not mention any of the 'Khampas'. And Pandit Ram Karna has drawn the important conclusion that the 'khampas' must have come into existence among the Dahima Brahmins after the seventh century A.D.[25] May it be that they were the creation of the royal Rajputs distinguishing their branches through their specific territories and using them as exogamous units based on locality? Anyway 'Khampas' of the Rajputs will have to be regarded as later than the Brahmanic 'gotras' and as in origin an appropriate reaction of the royalty, devoid of and denied the Brahmanic 'rishi-heredity' or rather heritage!

The Agrawālā, a sub-caste of the great trading caste of Bania, claim Brahminical *gotras* which as given by three different authors, writing within about twenty years of each other, do not tally; and their exogamy is based on them. A person has to avoid his own *gotra* as well as that of his mother's father.

The artisans of Tamil Nadu, Kammālans, who, as pointed out in the earlier part of the book, have contended for some centuries past that they are as good as or perhaps better than Brahmins, have five *gotras* which are said to be Brahmanical, though I do not find any of them in the long index of *gotras* appended by John Brough to his book. They are Ahima, Janagha, Janārdana, Ubhendrā and Vishvagu. There are said to be twenty-five sub-sections within each 'gotra' but they are hardly known to the common people of the community. The exogamy of Kammālans, therefore, is declared to be the Brahmanic variety, i.e. 'gotra' exogamy.

What is this Brahmanic exogamy or 'gotra-' or sept-exogamy and how old is it are the questions that claim our attention in order that we may be able to get some idea of the connection that marriage regulations and the consequent pattern of kinship may have had with caste. It cannot be too strongly emphasised that an analysis of the 'gotra' system, the date of its formation or implementation as also its dovetailing into the total social system are quite necessary to determine the nature and extent of any relation between caste and kinship. For the caste system, as we know it, in its essential features, was evolved in the Indo-Gangetic doab-region largely by the Brahmin intellectuals and law-givers before the sixth century B.C.

That this view of the origin of the essential features of the caste system put forward in the first edition of this book is the only correct view is the confirmed opinion of this writer after nearly forty years' more study of the subject through original sources and modern field-investigations carried out by many different students. For this view alone can accommodate properly the largest number of known historical facts and recent and contemporary data, the former of which have been marshalled in the first few chapters of this book and the latter have been utilised from the eighth chapter to the end of this book.

I shall put in only two fresh pleas and arguments to further support the theory of the Brahmanic and North-Indo-Aryan origin of the essential features of the caste system, before going on with a brief statement on the nature and date of Brahmanic or *gotra* exogamy.

The first point to be made out is about the recrudescence of the theory of indigenous, or rather Dravidian, origin of the caste system. It has to be emphasized in this connection that this theory is of fair age and was first put forward by one of the most versatile and deeply read and severely critical Indologists. It was Oldenberg who was the sponsor of that theory which I state from the references to it in Hutton's *Caste in India* (p. 179) Oldenberg criticised Senart's view that caste was an Indo-Aryan development on the basis of the incoming Aryans' complex of beliefs and customs and the prevailing social condition of the indigeneous people. He rejects the view that restrictions on commensality originated with the incoming Aryans and suggests that endogamy was more likely to have been the contribution of the local people. Earlier Hutton had written more positively in the *Census Report of India 1931* (p. 434): "Credit must also be given to Oldenberg for having seen as early as 1907, that tabus on commensality were pre-Aryan in origin."

The discovery of the Indus-valley civilization and its dubious affiliation with Dravidian or rather Tamil culture have led many to ascribe to Tamilians all kinds of early achievements, among which this one of caste figures in the counting of some. The fact, however, so far is that there is no literary evidence of Tamil culture before, at the earliest, first or second century B.C. And the evidence of the earliest available Tamil literature, that of the Sangam age, is the most relevant authority for the elements and traits of Tamilian culture.

N. Subramanian, a recent student, negatives any significant Tamil contribution to caste. He says[26]: ". . . the Brahmins as a caste was an Aryan gift to Tamiliham [Tamilnadu]: not the person but the concept". He further assures his readers that the *Velirs* and *Vellālars*, the real Tamils, "were non-Aryan North Indian immigrants". He further asserts that the Tamil caste system even of the Sangam age "depended entirely on the Brahmins" who were "such ideal priests, scholars and philosophers that not only were they themselves greatly venerated by all alike but it was possible for the caste system also to build itself up in their name and none found any reason for rejecting any of the implications of the caste system".

This squarely disposes of Hutton's contention (p. 153) that "there were Brahmans before the Rigvedic Aryans, and we must look for the origin of that caste partly no doubt in the priests of the presumably Dravidian speaking civilization."

The second point is concerned with the criticism which Hutton has offered regarding my views on the origin of caste.

First, I shall deal with Hutton's notion that a part of my theory is identical with that of Biren Bonnerjea and the suggestion implied in his specific mention of the dates of the two publications

(Hutton, p. 178). Says Hutton: 'Ghurye takes a rather similar line, and suggests that the southern Indian peoples, before their contact with Indo-Aryan culture, probably shared the ideas of primitive peoples about the power of food to transmit qualities, while ideas of untouchability arose from ideas of ceremonial purity first applied to aboriginals in connection with sacrificial ritual and the theoretical purity of certain occupations." In the next paragraph Hutton tells his readers that Ghurye's account of caste was published in 1932, "but before that Bonnerjea, in an article in *The Indian Antiquary* (April 1931) had explained caste as due to primitive belief in magic, with which he credits both Aryan and pre-Aryan."

Let me inform the reader, first of all, that the typescript of my book, as pointed out in the preface to its second edition—and this information was purposely included in the preface because two books on caste, those of N. K. Dutt and E. A. Blunt, were published a few months before the first edition of my book had appeared—was despatched to the London publishers early in 1931. A review of my book had appeared in the *Times of India* in its issue of 5th May 1932. Further, Hutton in his Census contribution (*Report of 1931*), where he paid me the compliment of quoting from or referring to my book, could mention Biren Bonnerjea's hypothesis only in a footnote (p. 434). He says: "This applies also to Dr. Bonnerjea's hypothesis published in the *Indian Antiquary*, 1931. While criticising Rice for regarding caste as predating the Aryan invasion he regards the system as introduced by the Indo-Europeans, but nevertheless ascribes the institution to primitive superstition and to a belief in magic. Dr. Guha advanced a similar view in a thesis before Harvard University in 1924. I agree in ascribing caste to a belief in magic, though I cannot accept the rest of Dr. Bonnerjea's hypothesis which appears to me to be contradictory. It may be added that the theory of caste here put forward was arrived at before I had seen either Rice's [1929] or Bonnerjea's [1931] articles and was independent of their conclusions."

And after all, what is Rice's or Bonnerjea's theory of caste? I shall let Bonnerjea himself tell the readers by quoting his estimate of Stanley Rice's theory, which he declares to be the totemic view of the origin of caste-system. Says Bonnerjea (*Indian Antiquary*, 1931, pp. 50 and 91): ". . . the totemic origin of caste presents some difficulties, although in our opinion this seems to be the likeliest of the three". The other two theories of the origin of the caste system according to Bonnerjea are: (1) Occupation; and (2) "Somatological" or Racial as Risley and I and some others would call it.

Secondly, I have to turn to Hutton's criticism of another part of my theory. Hutton (p. 175) says: "Mr. Hayavadana Rao and Dr. Ghurye likewise, [i.e. Prof. N. K. Dutt] regard caste as having arisen largely as a result of racial differences. Ghurye emphasizes in particular the factor of priestly manipulation by Brahmans attempting to maintain the purity of race of Aryan invaders. One cannot but believe, however, that for priestly interference of this kind to be effective in setting up so far-reaching and complicated a system as that of caste, it is necessary to assume the pre-existence of certain of the essential factors in that system which would predispose the population generally to accept the extension of them." Further he attributes to me as to the late S. C. Roy the acceptance of "Risley's test of nasal index as indicative of the position of a caste in the social scale" "as holding good in a broad sense for northern India" and asserts, without quoting examples, that "there are a number of striking exceptions to the general rule".

As far as nasal index and its close correspondence with social precedence as put forward by Risley is concerned Hutton has misrepresented my view. On page 108 of my book I began the discussion of nasal index as a test of social gradation with the sentence "There is another proposition of Risley's which we must examine minutely, for it is one which, if true to facts, affects our conclusion". I have then quoted Risley as stating, "If we take a series of castes in Bengal, Bihar, the United Provinces of Agra and Oudh, or Madras, and arrange them in the order of the average nasal index so that the caste with the finest nose shall be at the top, and that with the coarsest at the bottom of the list, it will be found that this order substantially corresponds with the accepted order of social precedence". And I have in the next sentence said: "In the argument elaborated above [by me] it is evident that we depend upon the uniqueness of Hindustan amongst the provinces of India as regards the gradation of the physical type for the explanation of the origin of endogamy. The statement of Risley in a way challenges that basis." In the next paragraph I have begun by pointing out that the view of Risley that "the order of gradation established by means of the nasal index is 'substantially' the same as that of social precedence" is turned in Keane's *Man, Past and Present* into the statement "that the Hindustani type of the United Provinces has "a nose index exactly corresponding to social station." And on it I have remarked: "We shall presently show that Risley's statement is only partially true, and that Keane's generalization has no ground". Then I have pointed out discrepancies by giving actual data and not left it to the reader to guess as Hutton does in spite of the fact that he had the material before him duly dressed up by me two decades before.* I shall not repeat them as they will be found on pages 109–111 of the first edition and pages 120–22 of the fourth. The whole discussion is then thus concluded: "We hope that these comparisons will have made it abundantly clear that the proposition of Risley has almost no basis in fact outside Hindustan. Outside Hindustan in each of the linguistic areas we find that the physical type of the population is mixed, and does not conform in its gradation to the scale of social precedence of the various castes."

Hutton's doubts and query regarding the success of the "priestly interference" and his demand for conditioning prerequisites in the local or indigenous population may now be answered. I should at the outset point out that as a student of culture Hutton should have considered and given due weight to the prestige-factor of an incoming or an intruding culture in the complex of the intellectual, emotional and social commerce that goes on and is named culture contact and acculturation. And it is a patent fact in the history of culture that a convert may, and tends to, outdo the original in rigidity, severity and thoroughness of implementation. As Hutton appears to have ignored this aspect of culture contact and culture transformation he must not have fully grasped the bearing of my treatment of caste through the ages, the historical development of caste in pre-British India. And now that the question has arisen I shall here make a special but brief resumé of the prestige-situation of the Brahmin in Indian society.

Far back in history, about 800 B.C., in a *Brāhmana* work, the *Shatapatha Brāhmana* (II, 2, 2, 6) of the later Vedic age, Brahmins asserted their supremely God-like importance in these words: "Verily there are two kinds of gods; for, indeed, the gods are the gods and the Brahmins who have studied and who teach sacred lore are the human gods." The acquisition of immense prestige through the knowledge of the sacrificial ritual was further augmented by the Brahmins' possession of the extremely esoteric and extraordinarily important knowledge about Brahma, the Reality, which in spite of very healthy, competent and extensive competition of the Kshatriyas, remained largely a Brahmin achievement. The extent and depth of this prestige may be gauged from the stories of Raikva (*Chhāndogya Up.*, IV, 2) and Yājnavalkya (*Brihadāranyaka Up.*, IV. 4). The latter may serve our purpose better and

* The material was used in my paper *The Ethnic Theory of Caste* which was duly abstracted in the 'Research Items' of *Nature* of 15th Aug. 1925 with the remark that it is "an important contribution to the discussion of the question of caste in India".

may be narrated. Janaka, the king of Videha, who figures in the *Upanishads* as perhaps the greatest of Brahma-realizers, only second to Yājnavalkya, was so much impressed and overpowered by Yājnavalkya's mastery of both the subject and its verbal expression that at one stage he offered his whole kingdom to Yājnavalkya if he would go on with his soul-stirring exposition of the subject.

A teacher, at the end of the scholastic career of his student, exhorted him, in what, in modern terminology, may be called his convocation address, among other things, about the source of authoritative conduct in cases of doubt. He told him to observe the conduct of Brahmins, who are thoughtful, conscientious, diligent, not harsh, and determined to do the right, and to follow it as the norm (*Taittiriya Up*., XI, 4). Two or three centuries later, i.e. about 400 B.C. the law-text of Baudhāyana (*Baudhāyana Dharmasutra*, I, 1, 1, 14) declared: "What Brahmins riding the chariot of 'Dharmashāstra' and wielding the sword of the Veda, propound even in jest, that is declared to be the highest law." The most authoritative conduct of course was that current among the Brahmins of the doab, the country of the Kurus and the Pānchālas (I, 1, 2, 15–6).

The *Grihya Sutras*, works that cannot be dated later than 500 B.C., further reflect the actuality of the Brahmin's prestige As a part of the total performance in most of the religious or semi-religious rites described in these works as taking place periodically throughout the year, Brahmins were required to be fed.

Added to this was the growing mystical view about that grand language Sanskrit, which was perhaps already dubbed the language of the Gods. The extraordinary significance of that language is perhaps best appreciated when one notes that the grammarian Pānini, who gave a scientific grammar to Sanskrit and made it fairly easy for anyone to study and master that cadenceful speech, and who must have lived before 400 B.C., very soon came to be referred to as Bhagawān Pānini, Pānini, the Divine or the God-head.

Manu's authority in matters of law and conduct is very ancient, though the extant text of *Manusmriti* may be ascribable to the second or third century A.D. And what Manu said was declared to be as beneficial as medicine and therefore to be implicitly acted upon.

Manu's emphasis (*Manusmriti*, I, 92–101) on the supremacy of Brahmins flowing from the fact of their having been produced from the highest and the best part of the body of the Supreme Being is well-known. He employed the deduction not only to establish Brahmins' claim to be the premier among the 'Varnas' (castes and classes) but also to govern the conduct of all, though through the proper channel of the royal civil authority. Manu went even a step further and declared that all men in the whole world should learn their proper duties from Brahmins of the Ganga-Yamuna doab, the Indo-Gangetic region.

Another ground, equally charged with religious content, for assigning to Brahmins a super-divine status is that all the offering made to gods and manes can reach their destination, the gods or the manes, principally or even exclusively through Brahmins and Fire. Brahmins, therefore, are as important and potent as Fire. Even the much-liked and liberal *Bhagavadgitā* (IX, 33) unequivocally affirms that Brahmins *sui generis* are pure and meritorious. With this background and with the royal and priestly power wielded by Brahmins from about 200 B.C., it is no wonder that we find the law-text *Vishnusmriti* pitching the Brahmin claims much further. We read in it (XIX, 20, 4): "The gods are invisible deities while the Brahmins are visible deities. They sustain the world. It is by the favour of the Brahmins that the gods reside in heaven. A speech uttered by Brahmins, whether a curse or a benediction never fails to come true. . . . When the visible gods are pleased the invisible gods are surely pleased as well."

That this claim of the Brahmin law-givers of the North was no vain boast or mere wish-fulfilment is attested by their estimation recorded in the Tamil literature of the Sangam age, i.e. of about a century or two earlier than *Vishnusmriti*, which I have quoted above from N. Subramanian's work, *Sangam Polity*.

What is particularly instructive and relevant in our present context, i.e. *vis-a-vis* Hutton's objections, doubts and queries, is the fact that in the third decade of the twentieth century, F. E. Pargiter (p. 308), a British Civil Servant of India of the generation senior to that of Hutton, had significantly observed: "Their [early Brahmins'] reputation rested on their claim to possess 'occult' faculties and powers and the popular belief that they possessed them. And an early illustration goes back to the time of the *Yajurveda* [1200 B.C.] at least."

I shall not multiply quotations from old texts but close this section of the high claims put by Brahmins of occult powers commonly ascribed to them and of superior treatment accorded to them with one reference which must be very telling. Brihaspati, a law-giver of the sixth or seventh century A.D., is known to have been an exceptionally enlightened and liberal thinker. For, regarding women's rights his teaching was appreciated by western students as of a generally "advanced character" (Julius Jolly in *Sacred Books of the East Series*, vol. XXXIII, p. 275). And even he has laid down (XXIII, 12) that "a man who has connection with a woman of higher caste than his own shall be put to death" and has included the worship of Brahmins along with that of the manes and Gods as a test of a united household (XXV, 6). In the matter of Brahmins' privileges even a liberal and an almost purely civil-law-giver could not give up very superior claims and rights of Brahmins.

From this evidence, most of it in hortatory, normative or ritual literature, we shall now turn to the actual state of affairs, and more particularly to the Dravidian south, to see if it supports the verbal claims or contradicts them.

The family of the Sātavāhana kings of the Deccan, who ruled over a large part of present Maharashtra and Andhra Pradesh during a century or two before Christ and two centuries after Christ, has left records which testify to the reverence Brahmins received from members of that family even though they were Buddhists. In their record we come across proud mention of performance of a number of Vedic sacrifices, some of which must have involved even animal sacrifices, apart from the fact that Vedic sacrifice as such was an anathema to Buddha and the Buddhists. The largess distributed to Brahmins as an incident of these sacrifices total up to a stupendous sum, besides whole villages granted tax-free. Gifts to Brahmins were thought to be such a meritorious act by members of the royal family that hundreds and thousands of coconut-palm trees besides hundreds of cows were presented to them. Bringing about marriages of Brahmins was a merit-earning activity just as much as a dinner to one lakh (one hundred thousand) Brahmins and both these types of pious activities find proud mention in these documents (Sircar, pp. 186–205). In one record at least one of the kings of the family is described as "the one Brahmin", i.e. the best of the Brahmins and more, an unparalleled one, as one who not only turned the tide of mixture of castes but also as one who had humbled the pride of Kshatriyas, a non-legendary and historical Parashurāma as it were, and even as the source of the knowledge of all Vedic lore (p. 199).

The Ikshvāku kings of the Krishna-Guntur region in their Nagarjunikonda, Guntur district, inscriptions, dated about the middle, or in the third quarter, of the third century A.D. (Sircar, pp. 219–31), have gone one better. For though they described themselves as under the special favour of god Mahāsena, the leader of the 'Virupāksha gana' of Shiva, not only have they begun their documents with a bow to Buddha but also declared him to be of their own lineage, the Ikshvākus (p. 225), they were proud to describe their princes and kings as performers of a number of Vedic sacrifices and as donors of crores of gold coins and lakhs of cows and ploughs to Brahmins in the very records which commemorated the dedication of some structure to the cause of Buddhists and Buddhism.

The records of the Vākātaka dynasty, ascribed to the fourth and fifth century A.D. and hailing from Vidarbha, bear eloquent testimony to the growing importance of Brahmanism and Brahmins. This Brahmin dynasty was the earliest to describe itself in pure Brahmanical terms mentioning the 'gotra', Vishnuvriddha, of their lineage. It, too, produced kings who prided themselves on the performance of a multitude of Vedic sacrifices. Their kings described themselves as Dharmamahārājas, the great magistrates of Dharma, which title D. C. Sircar[27] tells his readers "is found in the records of the Pallavas [of Kānchi], Kadambas [of Banvāsi] and Western Gangas". Sircar further enlightens the reader with his informative note that the title was apparently sported by these dynasties justifying their claim "to have purified Brahmanical faith from the influence of heretical doctrines like Buddhism" (pp. 406–25).

The Pallava dynasty of Kānchi in its records, dating from the fourth to seventh century A.D., equally proudly or rather much more ostentatiously mentioned its regenerative role in so far as the title was redoubled and spelled Dharmamahārājādhirāja, the Overlord of the Mahārājas of Dharma. The Pallavas also described themselves in terms of their Gotra as 'Bhāradvājasagotra', of the Bhāradvāja gotra. They further proclaimed their habitual performance of at least three of the Vedic sacrifices, including the Horse-sacrifice (Ashvamedha). Vishnugopa is described as intent on serving Gods, Brahmins, preceptors and old people, while his son Dharmamahārāja Shri Simhavarman as even ready to regenerate Dharma, whenever it is clouded or beset by defects and evils common to the Iron Age (Kali-age). Vishnugopa's father Shri Skandavarman is described as one who had increased his store of merit (Dharma) by giving away land, gold and cows in good measure or number.[28]

A Ganga king's record of the second half of the fifth century A.D. found at Penukonda in Anantapur district describes the donee Brahmin as one competent to curse and to bless owing to the powers acquired by him through restraint, regularity, penance, sacred study, sacrifice, teaching and officiating at sacrifices of others.[29]

A Guntur district Reddi inscription in Telugu dated A.D. 1413 attests the continuance of this belief in the magical competence of Brahmins when it registers the donee Brahmin, characterizing his father as the source of all the pure lores like the Vedas, "equally capable of cursing or conferring boons, master of the potent 'incantation of Lakshminarsimha' and the overlord sovereign of all poets".[30]

That Brahmins had gathered immense prestige for themselves on various counts, one of which was their supposed power to do good or evil by mere words, in South India, by the fourth Century A.D. and had continued to reap the fruits of their influence is thus clear from a large number of contemporary records. Mention of Brahmins for specification had also required the mention of their Brahmanical 'gotra' Such early specification of Brahmins by their 'gotras' in Tamil Nadu is a clear proof that Brahmins, whatever their number, from the Ganga-Yamuna doab region had acclimatized themselves to the South and had got the Tamilians accustomed to recognise them by their distinctive social organization, the 'gotra'.

We may then set aside Hutton's criticism of the Brahmanic theory of caste and proceed with full acceptance of the role of the Brahmins in the genesis and spread of the caste system.

Thus Brahmins occupied the pivotal position in caste and claim our attention to their social organization which was their characteristic and has been so treated in the early records of Tamil Nadu

Brahmins, again, who numbered 14.89 millions in 1901, formed 7.2 per cent of the total Hindus. Their social organization, that of *gotra* and *pravara*, the former of which has been for the last 2500 years at least the basis of exogamy, deserves to be scanned, however briefly, to complete the discussion of the connection of caste with kinship.

As observed earlier, 'gotras' number not less than nine hundred as enumerated by Baudhāyana in his *Pravarādhyāya* or *Mahāpravara*, an appendix to his *Shrauta Sutra*, about 400 B.C., and over sixteen hundred as listed in the eighteenth century work of a Maharashtrian writer in his book *Samskārakaustubha*. Every one of these 'gotras' is an exogamous unit, i.e. a person cannot marry—this has ceased to be a legal condition for a valid Hindu marriage since 1955 (see pp. 60–67 of K. Desai's *Indian Law of Marriage and Divorce*)—a girl whose father's gotra is the same as that of the person himself, i.e. of his father. But this is not sufficient. For the 'gotras' are believed or known to have certain relationships and affiliations. The principle on which these can be and are determined is known as 'pravara'. which means a 'rishi'-based invocation or announcement formula. This formula every Brahmin, recently and today only orthodox ones, who had his sacred thread ceremony performed, i.e. from about the tenth year of his life, till quite old, repeats twice every day when he performs his 'sandhyā' or 'dawn and dusk adoration'. So every orthodox Brahmin should know not only his 'gotra', which he repeats in the announcement formula, but also should be able to determine the relationship or affiliation of his 'gotra' with others.

The writers on the subject, however, have not left things to chance or to the faulty memory of man. Since Baudhāyana's time, and probably from a much earlier time in popular practice, these 'gotras' have been treated or listed only under their superior units by a reference to the 'pravara'.

The eight hundred or more 'gotras' are listed by one authority under seventy-one* superior units which we may conveniently designate 'gotra'-complexes. These seventy-one 'gotra'-complexes themselves are exogamous units. But the organization and exogamy do not end there, sixty-one of these 'gotra' complexes having relationships *inter se*. They are, therefore, further grouped in view of their relationship and affiliations into eight groups which we may designate 'super-gotras' and which in popular and technical language are known as the progenitors or the heads of 'gotras'. They are the eight famous 'rishis' or sages: Agastya, Atri, Bhāradvāja, Gautama, Jamadagni, Kashyapa, Vasishtha and Visvāmitra. The 'gotra'-complexes, classed under or included in each of these eight 'super-gotras', are also exogamous units. Thus the seven 'gotra'-complexes subsumed under Agastya, or to use the appropriate expression which by itself can proclaim the sept or clan-nature of the unit, the super-gotra Agastyas in the plural, form an exogamous unit. A person having any one of the seven 'gotra'-complexes of the Agastyas as his 'gotra' cannot marry a girl whose father has anyone of these seven as his 'gotra'. It follows that one having anyone of the twenty 'gotras' which form these seven 'gotra'-complexes cannot marry any girl whose father has anyone of the same twenty 'gotras'.

The remaining ten of the seventyone 'gotra'-complexes are also grouped under superior gotras or assigned to 'Gotra'-kāra 'rishis', four being grouped under Bhrigu or Bhrigus and six under Angirasa or Angirasas. But this grouping has no particular significance. For the four 'gotra'-complexes under Bhrigus can intermarry; only the 'gotras' under each of the 'gotra'-complexes cannot intermarry. Similarly the six 'gotra'-complexes under the Angirasas can intermarry, the 'gotra' under each 'gotra'-complex being alone exogamous.

---

* This is the total number as can be counted in the Tables of Pravaras given in John Brough's *The Early Brahmanical System of Gotra and Pravara*, pp. 31–37.

To illustrate with actual examples: In Bengal among Rādhi Brahmins a Ganguli man cannot marry a Ghosal girl or vice versa. Gangulis have 'Savarni' as their 'gotra' while Ghosals have 'Vatsa'.[31] 'Savarni' is one of the seventy-three 'gotras' coming under 'Vatsas', which is itself one of the seven 'gotra'-complexes going under Jamadagnis.

To further elucidate the 'gotra'-organization in its exogamic aspect and also to shed light on the relation between kinship and caste, I shall briefly describe the situation existing among the Chitpāvan Brahmins of Maharashtra. The task is not only rendered easy but even tempting by the splendid work of the late N. G. Chapekar* on the subject which he published in his book *Chitpāvan* written in Marathi (2nd edition, 1966).

The Chitpāvan Brahmins are said to number about two or two and a half lakhs. The surnames among them as collected by Chapekar number 360. There are only the following fourteen 'gotras' among them shared among these surnames. The 'gotra' along with the number of surnames which have them, so thoughtfully listed by Chapekar, are as in the table that follows.

Gotra			*No of contemtemporary surnames*	*No. of surnames (old, early or original)*
1. Atri	..	..	16	3
2. Bābhravya	..	..	2	2
3. Bhāradvaja	..	..	20	6
4. Gārgya	..	..	32	5
5. Jāmadagnya	..	..	4	2
6. Kapi	..	..	26	4
7. Kāshyapa	..	..	46	5
8. Kaundinya	..	..	7	2
9. Kaushika	..	..	42	5
10. Nityundana	..	..	7	2
11. Shāndilya	..	..	66	7
12. Vasishtha	..	..	61	12
13. Vatsa	..	..	22	1
14. Vishnuvriddha	..	..	9	4

It is believed, on some evidence which is of course not unimpeachable, that the Chitpāvans had only sixty surnames among them. Their distribution 'gotra'-wise is presented in the third column of the table. They are listed in the late *Skandapurāna*. That was perhaps ten centuries ago and it is possible that the immigrant Brahmins who became known as the Chitpāvans came in a batch of sixty families. Today Chapekar tells us that though he has been able to trace 'gotra'-wise only 360 surnames there are over 400 surnames among the Chitpāvans (pp. 64–7, 84–5).

Surnames only tell us the lineages but they cannot by themselves reveal the number of families bearing that lineage name and we cannot form any legitimate conclusion about the relative numbers of people having the different 'gotras'. We cannot, therefore, use the data for anything like a quantitative

* This indefatigable and keen student of society died in his 99th year in March 1968.

assessment of the nature and extent of caste integration that can be and was being brought about through 'gotra'-exogamy and 'gotra'-exogamy-based kinship.

The increase in the surnames cannot be due to infiltration or incorporation of new elements from outside the original group, i.e., the Chitpāvan caste, unless we can show, or choose to believe, that the sixty families came at a time when castes were not in existence. As we have attempted to show, and we think with very sound reasons and on strong grounds, that the caste system in a distinctly recognisable form, or of an image not much different from the later system in its fundamental features, must have existed before the seventh century B.C., we have also suggested that 'gotra'-organization had come into existence not later than the sixth or the seventh century B.C. The Chitpāvan families could not have had the 'gotras if they had come from Northern India before the seventh or the sixth century B.C. There is no evidence, that the Chitpāvans acquired their Gotras in Maharashtra. As a matter of fact we have to start with the assumption that a Brahmin, wherever south or east, found in India, went there with the 'gotra' and therefore could not have proceeded there much before 600 B.C.

The surnames were in reality only fifty-nine though the Gotras were fourteen, as one of the surnames figured under two 'gotras'. The situation is much more complicated than what one would be led to think to be the case from Chapekar's statement that making allowance for the repetition of certain surnames in more than one 'gotra' the total lineages are 304. For as he has pointed out in the case of the 'Kaushika gotra', out of the 42 listed surnames under that 'gotra' at least twenty-five have no living representatives (p. 284).

We can speak of the qualitative aspect of exogamic integration, only if we keep in mind always that that aspect is not a complete picture even in rough outline and that the restrictions on the score of prohibited degrees or 'sapinda'-exogamy may modify it, in terms of the number of surnames open for intermarriage.

Among the Chitpāvans, as among most of the Brahmins in other parts of India, a person cannot marry one whose father's 'gotra' is the same as one's own, i.e., as one's own father's. The sixty-six surnames of the 'Shāndilya gotra' of course must seek their mates from outside the sixty-six surnames. As the 'Kāshyapa gotra' is listed in the authoritative texts on the subject to be the 'gotra'-complex under which 'Shāndilya' is placed they cannot marry anyone of the 'Kāshyapa' gotra too. They have, therefore, to eschew in addition, the forty-six surnames of the 'Kāshyapa gotra'. Thus the 'gotra'-based exogamic rules keep open for intermarriage to the sixty-six 'Shāndilya gotra' and the forty-six 'Kāshyapa gotra' surnames only two hundred forty-eight out of the total of three hundred and sixty surnames. For the thirty-two surnames of the 'Gārgya'-gotra over and above their thirty-two, the twenty-six surnames of the 'Kapi'-gotra and the twenty surnames of the 'Bhāradvaja'-gotra are unmarriageable, the Bhāradvaja'-gotra being the 'gotra'-complex under which are listed both the 'Gārgya' and 'Kapi' gotras. The surnames of the 'Vishnuvriddha' and 'Nitundana' gotras, nine and seven respectively, can marry out of these sixteen surnames into anyone of the remaining three hundred forty-four surnames. Such are the potentialities of intra-caste integration under the 'gotra'-exogamy among the Chitpāvans.

The Mādhyandina Deshastha Brahmins of Maharashtra are a slightly larger community, perhaps numbering three hundred thousand. But there are among them, as Purushottam Shete (*Gotravali*, in Marathi) informs us not less than two thousand surnames and one hundred and thirty-eight (138) 'gotras'. At least ten 'gotras' out of the 138 have each more than 50 surnames under each. They are with the number of the surnames; Kāshyapa, 245; Bhāradvāja, 217; Vatsa, 168; Atri, 126; Gautama, 118; Parāshara, 87; Shāndilya, 78; Vāsistha, 77; Kaundinya, 73; and Gārgya, 72. Five other 'gotras', selected for their affiliation, show very low numbers of surnames in them. Thus: Upamanyu has 28; Kaushika, 10; Samkriti, 8; and Jatu-karnya, 7. One may note further that the 'Agasti-gotra' which appears to be rare anywhere, has twelve surnames under it.

The Mādhyandina Deshastha exogamic rules require a person not only to eschew the father's or own 'gotra' but also that of one's mother's father's gotra. With this complication the compulsory diversification of marital connections becomes greater, ensuing in the integration of a wider circle of families and persons belonging to the caste. Thus, supposing a Mādhyandina Brahmin man wanting to marry belongs to the 'Shāndilya gotra', he has not only to eschew all the surnames which have the 'Shāndilya-gotra' but also those 245 which come under the 'Kāshyapa-gotra'. This he has to do as the Chitpāvan and most other Brahmins have to, because though the 'pravaras' or the announcement-formulae of both the 'Kāshyapa' and the 'Shāndilya' 'gotras' have a common 'rishi' only in some texts, yet Shāndilya is definitely placed under the Kāshyapas by all the authoritative ancient writers on the subject of 'gotras' and their affiliation through 'pravaras'. But among the Mādhyandinas the intending bridegroom has also to avoid a girl whose father's 'gotra' is the same as that of his mother's father. Under the general rule of 'gotra'-exogamy the bridegroom's mother's father's 'gotra' must have been different from both Kāshyapa and Shāndilya. Let us suppose that it was Bhāradvāja. This particular intending bridegroom has, therefore, to eschew also a girl whose father's 'gotra' is Bhāradvāja. He has to choose a girl from any other surname group than the 323 surnames having either Kāshyapa or the Shāndilya 'gotra' and also the 217 surnames having the Bhāradvāja 'gotra'. The bridegroom has thus to avoid at least 540 surnames out of the 1,326 which are comprised under the fifteen 'gotras' I have picked out for calculations.

Another illustration will still further clarify the complicated situation regarding marriage on the score of 'gotra'-exogamy and enlighten us on the rather tenuous connection of exogamy-originated kinship with caste.

Another intending Mādhyandina bridegroom we shall suppose to have Vasishtha as his 'gotra'. Among the fifteen 'gotras' picked out there are three which are affiliated to the Vasishtha 'gotra' through a common rishi in the 'pravara' or the announcement-formula. They are Parāshara, Kaundinya and Upamanyu. This particular bridegroom of the Vasishtha 'gotra' has to avoid a girl from any of surnames falling under one or the other of these four 'gotras', i.e., he must seek for a bride from outside the group of 265 surnames comprised under the 'gotras', Vasishtha, Parāshara, Kaundinya and Upamanyu. Further, as his mother's father's 'gotra' must have been different from any of these four he has to avoid a 'girl' from the surname groups coming under that 'gotra'. Let us suppose that the groom's mother's father's 'gotra' was Kāshyapa and that he has to eschew a girl having anyone of the 245 surnames comprised under Kāshyapa 'gotra'. Thus the particular groom has to go outside the 510 surnames comprised under the five 'gotras', Vasishtha, Parāshara,, Kaundinya, Upamanyu and Kāshyapa. If the 'gotra' of the bridegroom's mother's father was Jatukarnya, as it well could be, then the situation becomes much more easy for the groom. For then he has to avoid only the seven surnames that come under the Jatukarnya 'gotra' in addition to the 265 surnames to be avoided under the general rule of 'gotra'-exogamy. This particular Mādhyandina bridegroom can marry, provided the rules of 'sapinda'-exogamy or prohibited degrees are satisfied, in any of the remaining 1,054 surnames out of the 1,326 comprised under the fifteen 'gotras' picked out for calculation. The choice of the previous bridegroom, the one whose mother's father's 'gotra' is Kāshyapa, is limited to only 816 surnames out of the same total.

The exogamic situation for the surnames under 'Atrigotra' illustrates still another facet of the 'gotra-pravara' organization and its impact on integration resulting from exogamic marriage and its kinship system. There are 126 surnames with 'Atri-gotra'. Among the fifteen 'gotras' and their 1,326 surnames there is no 'gotra' which under the Brahmanical organization is affiliated to it. The 126 surnames of the Atri-'gotra' therefore, can, other marital rules not barring, marry in any of the remaining fourteen 'gotras' and their 1,200 surnames. This I think is the widest circle open under the general rule of exogamy. But in this case, that of the Mādhyandina bridegroom, of course, his mother's 'gotra' has to be considered. If she came, say, from the Jatukarnya 'gotra', then the limitation of the circle would be so small as almost to be ignored, the bridegroom having 1,192 surnames open to him for his choice; but if she came, say, from the Kāshyapa 'gotra' his choice would be curtailed and confined to only 955 surnames.

One's mother's 'gotra' or comparable unit having to be taken into consideration while choosing a mate is a fairly wide-spread phenomenon in Northern India as we have seen; but as one can judge from the available material it is one which is more pronounced and perhaps even indigenous in the eastern districts and regions of Northern India. In U.P. as we have seen, the exogamic rule, at least among the higher castes, envisages the exclusion of one's own 'gotra' from the marriageable circle.

Among the U.P. Brahmins it appears the 'gotra' rule comprehends the 'gotra' in the general sense and does not extend to the inclusion of the identity on the 'pravara' principle. We do not get any reference to the 'pravaras' and their connection with 'gotra' and 'gotra'-based exogamy in the statements, for example, of the Kanaujiā Brahmins and even of the U.P. Brahmins in general. This is what E. A. H. Blunt says about 'gotras' and exogamy (p. 44): "The rule of *gotra* exogamy can now be stated thus. There are eighteen groups, of which eight consist of a 'gotra' plus its subsidiary *gotras*, and no man belonging to any one of these groups may marry a woman also belonging to it. Every law-giver insists on this rule, which Brahmans universally observe, save the hill Brahman who neglects his *gotra* for his *that*, a local sub-division."

The exogamic regulations of the Kanaujiā Brahmins[32] appear complicated but the complication is due to a combination of partial endogamy with partial hypergamy, and do not contradict the statement about 'gotra' being the unit of exogamy without reference to the 'pravara' or the announcement formula and its 'rishis'.

Among the Brahmins of Kashimer there are nineteen 'gotras'. Among them both Kāshyapa ahd Shāndilya occur and are intermarriageable. N. G. Chapekar who has vouchsafed this information in his book *Kashmir* (147, in Marathi), in a letter informed me that the Kashmiri Brahmins not only only do not apply the 'pravara' principle in the matter of 'gotra'-exogamy but they do not even know the 'pravaras'. I understand that among Gujarati Brahmins, too, 'pravara' affiliation is not considered in marriage. Narendra Vyas, Principal of the Tribal Research Institute at Udaipur, informs me that Rajasthani Brahmins, whether Paliwāl, Dadhich or others, would be hard put to it to name a 'pravara' and that 'pravaras' must be counted as non-existent for them.

D. R. Bhandarkar pointed out in 1932[33] that among the Vaidik Brahmins of Bengal, the 'pravaras' as stated are very varied and that there were many 'interlopers' among them. Yet he found that Banerjis and Chatterjis of the Rādhi Brahmins intermarry, though the 'gotra' of the former is Shāndilya and that of the latter Kāshyapa. Thus they resemble the Kashmiri Brahmins and fall apart from the Chitpāvan and other Mahārāshtriya Brahmins who generally consider the two 'gotras' as non-intermarriageable. In a recent study of marriage regulations in a sample of Rādhi Brahmins in Calcutta[34] it was found that nearly thirty-five per cent of the affinal families, i.e., the families with which marital relations had taken place, of the people of the Shāndilya 'gotra' were Kāshyapa-'gotra' families. Among the affinal families of the people of Kāshyapa gotra as many as forty-two per cent were of the Shāndilya gotra.

The percentage of affinal families of particular 'gotra'-families must depend to some extent on the number of families in various 'gotras', their relative distinguished status and in this particular, i.e., of the Bengal Brahmins, even more on the composition of the hypergamic sections, which have been in existence for more than four centuries and may be as much as eight hundred years old.[35]

It is an interesting fact that there are only eighteen surnames among the Rādhi Brahmins of this sample, but the 'gotras' among the Rādhi's as a whole are only eight.[36] According to Dutt's historical account we should have fifty-six surnames[37] among the Rādhis. Even then compared with the Chitpāvan Brahmins and more so with the Mādhyandina Deshastha Brahmins of Maharashtra, the Rādhi Brahmins, who are likely to number more than either of the Maharashtra Brahmin communities, is a compact community. This fact stands out clear even from the study of the marriage regulations of Calcutta Rādhis referred to above. There are eight surnames in the sample going under 'Bhāradvāja-gotra' with which none of the other four 'gotras' represented in the sample is unmarriageable. 'Kāshyapa-gotra' claims seven surnames. As Shāndilya is a marriageable 'gotra' in Bengal for even 'Kāshyapa-gotra', surnames under it numbering five can pick up marriageable mates from the other four gotras and the thirteen surnames under them. The 'Batsya-gotra' has six surnames under it in the sample and the 'Sabarnya' only three. But Batsya (Vatsa) and Sabarnya (Savarni) are affiliated 'gotras', the 'pravara' of the two being identical. The nine surnames under these two 'gotras' of the Rādhi Brahmins are, therefore, not intermarriageable. For them only the remaining nine surnames are open for choice.

From the way 'gotras' of Kannada Brahmins are summarily referred to both by L. K. Anantha Krishna Iyer in the volumes of *The Castes and Tribes of Mysore* and by M. N. Srinivas in his book *Marriage and Family in Mysore* (pp. 32–7), I feel that 'pravaras' are either absent or are not paid any heed in marital selection among them.

In a brief study of the inscriptional data for the elucidation of this interesting topic I have come across more than 1,000 Brahmin donees of Andhra Pradesh and Tamil Nadu, more than 300 of them being Tamil Brahmins. The records date from about A.D. 600 to about A.D. 1600. Among them there is not one whose 'gotra' is specified in terms of or by reference to the 'pravara'. This utter absence of 'pravara' in the specification of Brahmin donees of Tamil Nadu leads me to the conclusion that 'pravaras' if they are at all appended to the 'gotras' of Tamil Brahmins, have no significance in any important matter. Gotra-exogamy of the South Indian Brahmins, in particular of Tamil Brahmins, would appear to be based on 'gotra' alone without any consideration of affiliation through 'pravara' or the 'rishi'-based announcement formula.

More direct appraisal of the influence of exogamy cannot be attempted even theoretically without taking into account marital regulation by prohibited degrees and more particularly the rules, if any, prescribing or even encouraging preferential mating. Prescription or encouragement of preferential mating, i.e., requiring a certain relative to be married in preference to any other possible bride, has the effect of counteracting the dispersive effect of prohibited degrees and group-exogamy. It makes for in-marrying and tends to create a habitually endogamous unit much smaller than the original group, caste or sub-caste. Conceivably, such marital regulation persisted through and through may result in a new group which, for matrimonial purposes, even more than the 'ekadā' of Gujarat Pātidārs mentioned earlier, assumes the form and colour of a subcaste.

The most widespread preferential mating is the marriage of a person with his mother's brother's daughter, that with one's father's sister's daughter being another but less frequent and more restricted form of it. I have in the past dealt with the spread and the historical past of this form of preferential mating (see my papers in my *Anthropo-Sociological Papers* and in the appendix to the second edition of my *Family and Kin in Indo-European Culture*) and I shall not repeat the performance here. The most important question that arose in my mind,—I expressed it in my paper published in 1946, reproduced in the appendix to *Family and Kin in Indo-European Culture*—was that the behaviour pattern of the mother-in-law of a woman in North Indian folklore and kin-practices, where, cross-cousin marriage, as this form of preferential mating is significantly called, has been very much less in evidence, only figuring sporadically in non-elite or very special classes of people, has not differed materially from that in Maharashtra, a region where cross-cousin marriage has been in evidence among all castes excepting only two or three.

From the Dravidian-speaking regions, Mysore, Andhra Pradesh and Tamil Nadu, it has been recorded that the preferential form of mating of the cross-cousin marriage variety has greater intensity. In addition other forms of preferential mating involving relatives of even nearer consanguinity or affinity as the case may be are known to have prevailed and to be in evidence in contemporary times. One of them, near allied to the cross-cousin marriage variety, is the marriage of a man with his sister's daughter, preferably or even exclusively with the daughter of his elder sister, and is known to be practised or permissible among almost all castes, including the Brahmins.

The only exception to this rule, permitting or even requiring or encouraging marriage with a sister's daughter, is formed by those communities, mostly concentrated in the southern districts of Tinnevelly and Ramanathapuram, like the Maravans, the Kallans and a section of Vellālas, among whom, the *Kilai*, the exogamous unit, is matrilineal, children inheriting their *kilai* from their mother. A man and his sister's daughter belong, under this dispensation, to the same exogamous unit, *kilai*, and hence cannot marry each other.[38]

This preferential mating, marriage with one's sister's daughter, is met with sporadically among some Maharashtrian Brahmin castes and also in the Māli (gardener) caste.[39]

The mother-in-law of a woman in such society is either her father's sister or mother's brother's wife or mother's mother. That even, in these societies, at least in two of them, Kannada and Tamil, the strife between a woman and her husband's mother is as bitter as in the North-Indian society was known through the work of M. N. Srinivas,[40] when I wrote my paper on kin behaviour as reflected in Indo-Aryan literature; but naturally I had to leave it out as it pertained to Dravidian folk-literature and folk-practice.

The strife as depicted in a Tamil folk-song is more tragic and heart-rending than any known from other folk-literature, whether of the North or of Gujarat or of Maharashtra. The following remark of Srinivas will suffice to convince the reader: "A long tale described the fight between a sadist mother-in-law and her daughter-in-law, and how in the end the latter commits suicide. The girl's elder brother learns of his sister's death, puts the mother-in-law to disgrace, and finally throws her into a burning lime kiln. He also hacks the other daughters-in-law who probably aided in the conspiracy against his sister." The deeply rooted nature of this bitter antagonism between mother-in-law and daughter-in-law is concretized in village institutions as revealed in a recent village survey carried out under the scheme of the 1961 census. In the village of Thiruvellari in Tiruchirapally district (*Thiruvellari*, p. 86) there is a 'Swastik'-well, i.e., a well in the shape of a 'Swastik', called significantly "Māmiyār Marumagal Kulam" by the villagers. The expression means that the well is meant for a mother-in-law and a daughter-in-law. The reason for so naming the Swastik-shaped well, we are told, is that these two relatives who are always at loggerheads with each other can peacefully take their bath without being even seen by each other at this well!

This almost universal pattern of kin-behaviour led me to think of the quantitative factor as needing consideration. With all the permission and even encouragement of the preferential mating in actual practice such matings might not have adequate frequency to influence the standard type of behaviour which would appear to be not contraindicated in individual psychology. At the earliest opportunity of a specific and detailed field investigation, I decided to make a sample study of the actual extent of such marriages in any of these communities. Accordingly about 1952–53 I included the item in the two field studies that I then initiated. It is an interesting fact, worthy to be noted and pondered over by students of the sociology of knowledge, that almost exactly about that time investigations carried on by a number of workers in the field of Sociology in India had on their schedule, as is indicated by their publications between 1955 and 1963, similar queries. The data provided by the labours of these students, S. C. Dube, G. S. Ghurye, T. S. Epstein, W. McCormack, Dagfinn Sivertsen, combined with those made available through the 'Village Survey' of the 1961 Census, have rendered it possible to make a meaningful statement about the actual extent of the three kinds of preferential mating. The following tabular presentation of the data is made in furtherance of such a statement:

		Per cent with		
*Region**	*No. of Marriages*	*Mother's Brother's Daughter*	*Father's Sister's Daughter*	*Sister's Daughter*
Tamil Nadu	703	9.2	6.5	7.4
Andhra Pradesh	960	12.7	7.3	3.8
Mysore	620	7.4	5.5	11.3
Maharashtra	495	6.9	**	†

*Sources: (*Andhra Pradesh* 1961 *Census*, Vilalge Survey Monographs: *Jerrela* (Visakh. dist.), *Kondiba, Mantsala* (Kurnool dist.), *Pasarlapudilanka* (East Godavari dist.) and Telugus of *Nuagolabandh* (Ganjam dist.); Dr. Dube's Shamirpet data showed 18 per cent of the 380 marriages to have been between cross-cousins. (Maharashtra)—*Mahadev Kolis* and *After a Century and a Quarter*, by G. S. Ghurye; (Mysore)—W. McCormack in *Man in India*, 1958; *Nandigudi* (Harihar taluka) 1961 *Census*, Village Survey Monograph; T. S. Epstein, *Economic Development and Social Change in South India*, 1962; (Tamil Nadu)—Sivertsen, *When Caste Barriers Fall*, 1963; Census (1961) Village Survey Monographs: *Ayyangarkulam* (Chingleput dist.), *Athanagari* (Ramnathapuram dist.) and *Ravanasamudram* (Tiruneleveli or Tinnevelly dist).
**Only one case.
† Nil.

We see that in Maharashtra the frequency of marriages in which the mother-in-law of a woman happens to be her father's sister is so low that there need be no wonder if that relationship has not materially affected the standard pattern of behaviour between a woman and her mother-in-law, which approximates to that of Gujarat and North India. In the Mysore and Tamil Nadu regions, on the other hand, in more than 16 per cent of the marriages the mother-in-law of a woman happens to be either her mother's mother or father's sister. We should expect some influence of this fact on the standard pattern of behaviour. However, as there is no evidence of such, are we to conclude that the authoritarian mentality so rampant in the institution of the joint-family, and so ingrained in the total cultural milieu has been able to defy the other influence!

The extent of preferential mating, apart from its importance in the study of the behaviour pattern of certain kin, claims our serious attention as a force of making for integration of a sub-caste into smaller kin-groups and perhaps consequently aiding the formation of a multiplicity of sub-castes. The actual geographical spread of marital unions, which, of course, are the configurated result of sub-caste-hypergamic, exogamic and preferential regulations of marriage, can enlighten us on this aspect. And this aspect is the same as signified by the heading of this chapter, i.e., influence of kinship on caste or sub-caste.

The work of many of the students mentioned above has furnished data for an appraisal of the geographical spread of marital unions; and the following researchers have swelled the flow of materials in this behalf,* by their work during the same period: A. R. Beals, F. G. Bailey, K. Gough, Oscar Lewis, A. C. Mayer and Mckim Marriott.

For Tamil Nadu Gough's data for Kumbapettai in Tanjore district may serve as typical. She (I, p. 49) tells us that "each caste group of the village appears to have belonged to an endogamous sub-caste extending over some fifteen to twenty villages", the Brahmins at the time of enquiry belonging to eighteen villages "fairly widely scattered round the North Tanjore and Trichinopoly boundary", spread "within a radius of about thirty miles". She has further very thoughtfully enlightened us on the size of this inmarrying Brahmin unit. It comprised some five to six thousand persons (II, p. 829). Pallans, the untouchables are "still confined largely to villages within a radius of twenty miles" and "members of each of the several Non-Brahman caste groups have kin up to sixty miles away" (I, p. 49).

For Kannada-speaking region we have A. R. Beals' Namhalli, with its large circle of related villages, "many marriages" creating "connections as far as fifty miles away" (p. 96). In Epstein's Wangala, full 50 per cent of the extant inter-village unions were "restricted to villages within a radius of four miles" and marriages involving villages within a radius of ten miles amounted to 83 per cent (pp. 166–69). Marriages within a radius of six miles formed 69 per cent of the extant inter-village unions. In her other village, Dalena, such marriages formed 79 per cent of the extant inter-village unions (pp. 296–97). In the former village 54 per cent and in the latter according to Epstein 68.5 per cent of the marriages were unions with mates from outside the village. However, I find that the data of Table 21 in Epstein's book yield the very high percentage (85) for unions outside Dalena village!

For Andhra Pradesh Dube's Shamirpet near Hyderabad may suffice. Out of the 380 marriages 68 per cent connected the village with units within a radius of thirtyfive miles, 30 per cent with villages as far as sixty miles. It appears that among these 380 marriages there were 5.3 per cent in which both partners belonged to Shamirpet (p. 54), i.e. were within the village.

In the village Pasarlapudilanka in Razole Taluk of East Godavari district, of the 210 marriages 20 per cent were within the village itself and 51 per cent within a distance of ten miles from the village. Thirty-two (32) marriages were beyond ten miles but within the district and 79 within the Taluk (1961 Census, A. P. VI, No. 16, p. 27). Of the 391 marriages of the village Mantsala in Adoni Taluk of Kurnool district 36.8 per cent were within the village. Thirty-four and a half per cent (34.5) of the marriages were in villages lying between ten and twenty-five miles distant from Mantsala. Marriages involving a distance of twenty-six to a hundred miles formed 14.8 per cent of the total.

---

* 1) The works of the scholars already noted under the previous tabular presentation; (2) *Village India*, edited by McKim Marriott; (3) Gough in *American Anthropologist*, 1956; (4) Oscar Lewis, *Village Life in Northern India*, 1958; (5) A. C. Mayer, *Caste and Kinship in Central India*, 1960; (6) A. R. Beals, *Gopalpur,* 1962; (7) F. G. Bailey, *Politics and Social Change*, 1963 and (8) S. C. Dube, *Indian Village*, 1955.

The most noteworthy feature of marital pattern of Mantsala is the fact that of the 21 marriages contracted with mates from villages a hundred and one miles and more distant from Mantsala, 20 were Brahmin marriages!

Compare this with what I found in Lonikand, a village in Haveli taluk, about twelve miles northeast of Poona. In the father-generation, of the mothers of the heads, the fathers, 39 per cent were from the village itself; but among the wives of these heads the Lonikand women formed only about 22 per cent. Of the 62 married sisters of the heads, for which the villages into which they were married are known, about 42 were married in the villages of Haveli taluk and nearly 31 per cent in Lonikand itself. Of the 56 daughters of the heads or their brothers that were married 38 per cent had husbands from Haveli taluk and only 21 per cent from Lonikand itself. In both the groups of marriages, those of sisters and daughters, the contiguous taluka on the northeast, Sirur, had provided 38 per cent of the husbands (*After a Century and a Quarter*, pp. 77–8).

Surely marriage in Lonikand almost at the cultural centre of Maharashtra shows greater intensity of territorial in-marrying than in the southern regions including Tamil Nadu.

Passing on to the North I should draw upon the splendid work of A. C. Mayer in a Malwa village. Mayer has provided the most detailed statement about the territorial spread of the marriages of his Ramkheri people. The generalized view of the marital situation is thus stated (p. 212): "The affinal links of a village sub-caste group stretch out for an average of twenty to thirty miles, with the most distant up to fifty miles or so." The castewise particularized position is much more nebulous or fluid than the generalized average may lead one to think. Leaving out the Muslim 'cotton-carder'-marriages, in Table 2 at page 210 of Mayer's book, we have 264 marriages: Of these in 141 marriages the bridegrooms were of Ramkheri while in 123 Ramkheri girls were the brides. In both types of marriages the Rajput made the longest average distance from which either the bride or the bridegroom came, that in the former type being seventeen miles. The average distance from which the mate of a Rajput came was fifteen and a half miles, the next being twelve miles in the 'Farmer' caste. The number of Rajput marriages in the sample were 86 while that of Farmer marriages was 96.

Further north, in Oscar Lewis' village near Delhi the two hundred and sixty-six married women in the village had come from "two hundred" different villages at distances of up to forty miles, the average distance being twelve to twenty-four miles. As Lewis has not provided his readers with a further break-up of his marriage data it is not possible to say whether the general average distance from which a bride was brought into his village was eighteen or fifteen miles. However, this deficiency is made up for by the information provided about the Brahmins, Jāts, Nāis (barber caste) and Chamārs. Whereas Jāts and Brahmins had looked for their brides from villages distant only twelve to thirteen miles, Chamārs had gone out further and averaged twenty miles. Nāis, the barbers, rather strange to find, had travelled even further, averaging about twenty-four (p. 161). The village Kishan Garhi for which some data are made available by McKim Marriott about a hundred miles to the east in Aligarh district, in which though the main landlords are Jāts as in Lewis' village Brahmin tenant-farmers formed a numerous group possessing about one-half of the village lands. Marriott has given us but meagre data. He does not even reveal the total number of marriages, though it is clear that they must number more than three hundred. Much less does he, like Lewis and later Mayer, present us castewise data. He tells us that "half of the marriage ties of groups in Kishan Garhi connect them with places more than fourteen miles away, while 5 per cent connect them with places more than forty miles distant". We get no information, direct or indirect, about the remaining 45 per cent of the marriages (p. 174–5). In a later publication of his, *Caste Ranking Community Structure* (1965, p. 25), he modified the statement thus: "The effect of these rules [marriage] is to scatter out marriage ties to an average distance of more than fourteen miles on all sides of the village." This appears to me to be an understatement, which either distorts the original statement or casts doubt on it. However it may be, I do not think that Kishan Garhi people deviated much from the practice of Lewis' people in the matter of the distance over which they sought mates in marriage, which may be put down at an average of between fifteen and twenty miles.

It is thus seen that, perhaps with some exceptions in Kannada-speaking region, the territorial spread of marriages in South India and in particular in Tamil Nadu is not markedly different from that in the Indo-Aryan North of Madhya Pradesh and Uttar Pradesh. Preferential mating, therefore, does not materially influence the distance of affinal kin and the consequent regional or territorial integration of an endogamous group, caste or sub-caste.

This inference or conclusion is supported even by the limited information regarding the actual size of endogamous units which we can bring to bear on this problem. K. Gough has obliged us by stating that the Brahmins of her Kumbapettai belong to an endogamous group which, spread over eighteen villages, counts about 5 or 6 thousand.

In 1891, Brahmins of Gujarat numbered 569 thousand. They are said to have ninety-three sub-divisions among them (*Bombay Census*, 1911, *Report*, p. 240). The volume of Bombay Gazetteer entitled *Gujarat Population* (p. 3) which states the above number, however, speaks of only 54 'classes' though as many as 79 or even 84 non-intermarrying groups among them were said to have existed. One division among them or one caste, Audich Brahmins, was stated to have had a little over 200 thousand members. If we were to divide the remaining 369 thousand Brahmins equally among the remaining 53 sub-divisions or castes we would have just seven thousand persons in one caste, a number which is almost identical with that of the Brihachchharana Brahmin caste of Kumbapettai in 1951. Sixty years earlier of course the Kumbapettai Brahmin caste would have had less members than six thousand or so as it had in 1951. This means that among Gujarat Brahmins there must have been endogamous units which were slightly bigger than the endogamous unit of Kumbapettai Brahmins. On the other hand, some Brahmin castes of Gujarat could have been smaller; and we know from the same source of information that the caste known as Bhārgava Brahmin, actually counted as its members only 1884 souls (p. 8). The famous and leading Gujarati community, the Nāgar Brahmin caste, had only 28,250 members divided among its six 'main' divisions (p. 13). If the members were more or less evenly distributed among these six endogamous units each unit would have had a strength of about five thousand, again a number very near to that of the Brahmin caste of Kumbapettai: Further, unlike Kumbapettai Brahmins at least three of the sub-divisions of the Nāgars are divided in two classes, 'grihastha' (householder) and 'bhikshuka' (priest); and among one of these sub-divisions, the Vadnagarā Nāgara, the two classes do not inter-marry (Desai, G. H., p. 76). Thus even if Vadnagarā Nāgara Brahmins had numbered about eight thousand there would have been two endogamous units among them, 'Grihastha' and 'bhikshuka', each of which would have had about three thousand to five thousand members.

On the available evidence, which of course is not entirely free from defects, we may conclude that neither hypergamy, nor exogamy, nor again preferential mating appears to influence materially the extent of an endogamous unit or the multiplicity of such units.

References

1. *People of India*, 2nd ed., p. 161. 2. P. 277. 3. P. 264. 4. Op. cit. (2), pp. 161–63. 5. Op. cit. (2), p. 179. 6. p. 185. 7. Pp. 179–80. 8. Rattigan, W. H., *Digest of Punjab Customary Law* (3rd ed., 1883), pp. 7–8. 9. *Ghurye Felicitation Volume*, p. 196.

10. Rose, H. A.: II, p. 289. 11. Risley: (1) pp. 48, 66, etc.; (2) Pp. 163–71; Dutt: (II) pp. 5–16, 62–5; Sircar, pp. 498–500. 12. *Bom. Gaz.*, IX, *Gujarat Population*, p. 123; *Bombay Census Report*, 1911, pp. 118–20, 280–81; Pocock in *Ghurye Felicitation Volume*. 13. *U.P. Census Report*, 1901, pp. 209–10; Blunt, pp. 46–9. 14. Baines, p. 34. 15. *U.P. Census Report*, 1901, pp. 209–10; Blunt, p. 49. 16. P. 23. 17. *Totemism in India*, 1965, p. 283. 18. Risley, *T.C.*, I, pp. 285–6. 19. *Village Life in Northern India*, p. 23; McKim Marriott's *Village India*, pp. 155, 163.

20. Marriott, *Village India*, pp. 155, 163. 21. Blunt, p. 45. 22. Blunt, p. 45. 23. *Ep. Ind.*, LXI, 1932, p. 55. 24. D. R. Bhandarkar in *Ep. Ind.*, XI, pp. 26, 61, 79. 25. *Ep. Ind.*, XI, pp. 299–303. 26. Pp. 250, 254. 27. Pp. 406–25. 28. Sircar, pp. pp. 433, 47. 29. Sircar, pp. 456–57.

30. *Ep. Ind.*, XI, pp. 317, 325. 31. *Ep. Ind.*, LXI, pp. 71–2. 32. Blunt, p. 49. 33. *Ind. Art.*, p. 71–2. 34. Gangopadhay, p. 42. 35. N. K. Dutt (2), pp. 3, 5, 9–12. 36. Gangopadhay, p. 40. 37. Dutt, 4, 12. 38. *Dist. Gaz. Tinnevelly*, pp. 133–40; Thurston, III, p. 73; *Madras Census* 1961, *Village Survey Monographs; Kunnalur* (Thanjavur Dist.), p. 15; *Golwarpatti* (Ramnathapuram Dist.), p. 10. 39. *Bombay Census Report*, 1911, pp. 245, 288.

40. *Marriage and Family in Mysore*, pp. 191–98; 'Some Tamil Folk Songs' in the *Journal of University of Bombay*, vol. XII, 1943–44, pp. 61, 75–9.

10

Caste During the British Rule

We Have seen that the Brahmin was at the apex of the hierarchical organization of caste and that the Hindu kings upheld the institution with the help of their civil power. With the advent of the British as the political head of society things were bound to take on a different aspect. The British brought with them their own traditional form of government, and as Christians they could not have much sympathy with the institutions of the Hindus. As prudent foreigners wishing to consolidate their power over a strange land and people they decided to leave the peculiar institutions of the country severely alone except where they egregiously violated their cherished ideas of government. They introduced a system of education which did not demand of the learners any change of religion. Ideas and behaviour patterns, very different from those to which the people were accustomed, were thus presented as isolated from religion. The policy of comparative non-interference naturally gave scope for the revolt of the castes that were not quite comfortable under the Brahmin supremacy. Later on, with the incoming of the modern industrial organization and the growth of industrial cities, large numbers of peoples congregated in cities of mixed populations, away from the influence of their homes and unobserved by their caste or village people. This is the background of the picture of contemporary caste. In this chapter I shall trace the consequences of these circumstances on our institution.

Early in the history of the British rule the practice of the rulers over the three Presidencies was not uniform. In Bengal one of the Regulations, while recognizing the integrity of caste organization, allowed suits for restoration of caste to be entertained by the ordinary courts.[1] It was held that cases of expulsion from clubs or voluntary associations were of an entirely different nature from excommunication from caste.[2] In Bombay, however, the pertinent regulation expressly provides that no court shall interfere in any caste question, "beyond the admission and trial of any suit instituted for the recovery of damages on account of the alleged injury to the caste and character of the plaintiff arising from some illegal act of the other party."[3] Social privileges of the membership of a caste are held to be wholly within the jurisdiction of the caste. It is only when a complainant alleges that a legal right either of property or of office is violated by his exclusion from the caste that a suit may be entertained by a court of law.[4] This autonomy of caste, it is further held, exists only under the law and not against it. Hence caste-proceedings must be according to usage, giving reasonable opportunity of explanation to the person concerned and must not be influenced by malice.[5]

This recognition of the integrity of caste for internal affairs did not protect the institution from inroads on some of its very vital powers. The establishment of British courts, administering a uniform criminal law, removed from the purview of caste many matters that used to be erstwhile adjudicated by it. Questions of assault, adultery, rape, and the like were taken before the British courts for decision, and the caste councils in proportion lost their former importance. Even in matters of civil law, such as marriage, divorce, etc., though the avowed intention of the British was to be guided by the caste-customs slowly but surely various decisions of the High Courts practically set aside the authority of caste.

The first British administrators on the Bombay side employed, as early as 1826, officials like Borradaile and Steele, to make compilations of the various usages and customs of the many castes of the Presidency. These painstaking officers made useful compilations. But similar compendiums were not prepared in other provinces. The result was that the Widow-Remarriage Act of 1856 contained clauses practically violating the customs of some of the so-called lower castes. While legalizing the marriage of a Hindu widow, this Act deprived such a remarried widow of all her rights and interests in her deceased husband's property. Fortunately the courts have taken a reasonable view of these sections of the Act, and have decreed that the Act with its restrictive clause applies only to those widows who could not, without the aid of this Act, remarry according to their caste-usage. Widows of castes allowing remarriage forfeited their rights and interests in their deceased husband's property only when caste-usage enjoined such forfeiture.[6]

As early as 1876, the High Court of Bombay ruled that "Courts of law will not recognize the authority of a caste to declare a marriage void, or to give permission to a woman to remarry".[7] When any caste-council, in utter ignorance of its changed status, ventures to step in as a tribunal to try one of its defaulting members, it is promptly made to realize the force of law. It is well known that one of the most usual methods in the old regime of detecting an offence was to submit the accused person to an ordeal of varying intensity. Recently the caste-council of Pakhāh Rajputs of Ahmedabad submitted a man and his mother, both accused of witchcraft, to an ordeal usual in such cases. As one of the suspects failed to come out successful, the council demanded penalty for the alleged crime. A suit was filed for recovery of this penalty but was dismissed as being against policy. Thereupon one of the persons lodged a complaint for defamation against the persons who had complained against them to the caste-council.[8]

The hereditary and prescriptive right of the Brahmins to act as priests to all castes of the Hindus, with only a few exceptions, has been the one uniform and general principle inhering in caste-society through all its vicissitudes. Later on I shall describe the attitude of the people towards this question; but here I should like to point out how certain decisions of the High Courts have emboldened the non-Brahmanic castes to dislodge the Brahmins from their monopoly of priesthood. In Bengal and in North India generally it is now settled that there is no office of priest recognized as such in law, and a householder may employ anyone he likes for the performance of any priestly service and pay the fees to him. A similar view has been taken in the Madras Presidency.[9] When in the Maratha country the non-Brahmin reformists started the practice of performing their religious rites without the aid of the Brahmin priests, the latter lodged a complaint asking for an injunction against the persons so violating their rights. The High Court of Bombay decreed that people could engage any priest they liked, and were not at all bound to call for the services of the hereditary priest; but unlike the High Court of Madras, they decreed that the hereditary priest must be paid some fees by way of compensation.[10]

This opens the way to the dissolution of the only bond holding together the diverse castes, viz. the employment of common priesthood.

The Castes-Disabilities Removal Act of 1850 dealt another blow at the integrity of caste. The Act does not, as may be expected from its title, remove civil disabilities existing between caste and caste but facilitates conversion to another religion or admission into another caste. Notwithstanding any custom of caste disinheriting a person for change of caste or religion, this Act provides that a person does not forfeit his ordinary rights of property by loss of caste or change of religion.

Regarding the most important aspect, and almost the only surviving one, viz. that of prohibition against marriage outside the caste, the practice of the British courts has varied. In some early cases it was held that marriages between persons belonging to different divisions of the Brahmins or the Shudras were invalid unless specially sanctioned by custom; but recent decisions decree otherwise. In a Madras case when a Hindu, belonging to the Shudra class, married a Christian woman, turned into a Hindu, the marriage was accepted as one between members of different divisions of the Shudra class and therefore valid. Integrity of caste was so far recognized that the Court held that where a caste regards marriage as valid and treats the parties as its members, the Court cannot declare it null and void.[11]

Social reformers, however, were not satisfied with the existing state of affairs, and legislators tried to introduce bills legalizing intercaste marriages. The Special Marriage Act of 1872 made it possible for an Indian of whatever caste or creed to enter into a valid marriage with a person belonging to any caste or creed, provided the parties registered the contract of marriage, declaring *inter alia* that they did not belong to any religion. The clause requiring the solemn renunciation of caste and religion by the parties to a civil marriage was considered a great hardship and a moral dilemma by all progressive elements in the country. To add to this grievance, members of the Brahmo Samaj, who were regarded as outside the purview of this Act, were held, by a decision of the Privy Council to be Hindus for the purposes of the Act. Marriages of Brahmo-Samajists could no longer be valid unless the parties signed a declaration that they did not belong to any caste or religion. Continued agitation was carried on by reformers to liberalize the marriage law. Owing partially to the apathy of the Government and the hostility of the conservative section of the Hindus, both B. N. Basu and Vithalbhai Patel, one after the other, failed in their efforts in this direction. It was only in the Reformed Legislature that Sir Hari Sing Gour succeeded in getting a pertinent bill passed into law, though not in the original form intended by the first reformers. It is known as the Special Marriage Amendment Act of 1923. It applies only to Hindus including Jains, Sikhs, and Brahmos. Persons marrying under the provisions of this Act, to whatever caste they may belong, need not make the declaration prescribed in the Act of 1872. This advantage, however, is gained not without a substantial sacrifice. If two Hindus belonging to different castes marry under this Act they are not required to renounce their religion in declaration but have to forfeit certain of their personal rights as Hindus. They cannot adopt. On their marriage they cease to be the members of the joint family to which they previously belonged. Whatever rights in the property of the family would have accrued to them by survivorship under the Hindu Law cease. As regards their own property they will be governed by the Indian Succession Act and not by the Hindu Law.[12]

Under the old regime of caste certain sections of Hindu society which were regarded as untouchable were devoid of many of the civil rights. The question of removing their disabilities and placing them on a footing of civil equality came up for consideration before the British administrators. In 1856 the Government of Bombay had to consider the case of a Mahār boy, who was refused admission to the Government School at Dharwar. The principle involved in the case occupied the attention of the Government for about two years. Finally in 1858 it was announced in a press-note that "although the Governor-in-Council does not contemplate the introduction of low-caste pupils into schools, the expenses of which are shared with Government by local contributors and patrons who object to such a measure, he reserves to himself the full right of refusing the support of Government to any partially aided school in which the benefits of education are withheld from any class of persons on account of caste or race, and further resolves that all schools maintained at the sole cost of Government shall be open to all classes of its subjects without distinction".[13] In a press-note of 1915 we still find the complaint that contact with Western civilization and English education had not successfully combated the old ideas about untouchability. It further refers to the "familiar sight of Mahār and other depressed class boys in village schools where the boys are often not allowed to enter the schoolroom but are accommodated outside the room on the verandah". In 1923 the Government issued a resolution that no grants would be paid to any aided educational institution which refused admission to the children of the Depressed Classes. By this time the practice of segregating the Depressed Class boys was fast disappearing especially in the Central Division of the presidency. In many Local Board and Municipal Schools Depressed Class pupils are now allowed to sit in their classes like boys and girls of the caste Hindus.

While the Bombay Government was thus enforcing the right of the Depressed Classes to equal treatment, the Madras Government had on its Statute-book so late as the end of 1923 a law empowering village Magistrates to punish the offenders of the lower castes by imprisonment in the stocks though the Government had definitely pledged itself in 1914 to discontinue this inhuman practice.[14] In 1925 a Bill was introduced in the Madras Legislative Council to put under statute the principle of a resolution passed in the previous session of the Council throwing open all public roads, streets, or pathways, giving access to any public office, well, tank, or place of public resort, to all classes of people including the Depressed.[15]

In the Reformed Constitution the Depressed Classes got special representation in local and Legislative bodies by nomination.

The majority of the castes which were under various disabilities, excluding the Depressed Classes, were non-Brahmin. The uniform laws of the British did not recognize any of these disabilities as lawful. Yet the services were mainly manned by Brahmin and allied castes, who were the first to profit by English education. Their traditional attitude towards caste naturally influenced their dealings with the non-Brahmin classes. This situation gradually awakened some of the non-Brahmin leaders and sympathetic officers of the Government demand special treatment to those half-submerged classes. As a response, Chatfield, the Director of Public Instruction in Bombay, allowed in 1878 some concessions in the matter of fees in primary schools to the boys of some of these castes. Later on were instituted scholarships in secondary schools and colleges for boys from some of them.

The early non-Brahmin leaders had urged upon the Government the necessity of special representation for their members both in the administrative bodies as well as in the services. For a pretty long time this appeal remained unheeded. The cry was, however, taken up by the late Maharaja of Kolhapur,[16] and a strong case for it was made by him at the time when Mr. Montague came to India to consult the people and the Government of India as regards the future form of Government. In the Reformed Constitution framed by Montague and Lord Chelmsford special representation through mixed electorates was conceded to the non-Brahmins. Under these provisions the whole Hindu populace in the Bombay Presidency was divided into three sections: (*a*) Brahmins and allied castes; (*b*) the intermediate classes formed by Marathas and others, and; (*c*) the backward classes including the so-called untouchables.[17] This classification, with the addition of other Indians like the Parsis in the appropriate section, was also followed in recruiting the various services.

A Resolution of the Government of Bombay Finance Department, dated 17th September, 1923, expressly prohibited recruitment to the lower services from the advanced class of Brahmins and others till a certain proportion of the posts was held by members of the intermediate and backward classes.[18] It is because of this avowed intention of the Government to see certain castes represented in the services of the Province that heads of Government Institutions, while inviting applications for vacancies under their charge require the applicant to state his caste and sub-caste.[19]

British administrators, following the popular practice, used caste names as a convenient mode of description of persons. The Police Reports while giving details about offenders also mention their caste. The Railway risk-note, that every sender of parcels has to fill in and sign, had, at least till recently, an entry for the caste of the sender.[20] This cannot be regarded as intended to give or elicit information as regards the person's occupation. There is a separate entry provided to describe one's profession. Perhaps the caste-entry has been inserted to enable the officers concerned to form a rough estimate of the moral character of the person.

The unique institution of caste did not fail to arouse intellectual curiosity among the more intelligent of the Britishers in India, officials as well as non-officials, and our understanding of the institution is largely helped by their work. Some of the early officials like Elliot, Dalton, Sherring and Nesfield evinced their interest in the subject by collecting information and publishing it with their comments. Later officials, however, adopted the easier method of utilizing the decennial census for collecting and presenting the information and indulging in the theories of the origins of caste.[21] This procedure reached its culmination in the Census of 1901 under the guidance of Sir Herbert Risley of ethnographic fame. With a view to helping "us towards presenting an intelligible picture of the social grouping of that large proportion of the people of India which is organized, admittedly or tacitly, on the basis of caste" the Census Commissioner changed the classification of 1891 into one based on "social precedence as recognized by the native public opinion at the present day and manifesting itself in the facts that particular castes are supposed to be the modern representatives of one or other of the castes of the theoretical Hindu system". And this procedure Risley chose in spite of his clear admission that even in this caste-ridden society a person, when questioned about his caste, may offer a bewildering variety of replies: "He may give the name of a sect, of a sub-caste, of an exogamous sect or section, of a hypergamous group; he may mention some titular designation which sounds finer than the name of his caste; he may describe himself by his occupation or by the province or tract of country from which he comes."[22]

Various ambitious castes quickly perceived the chances of raising their status. They invited conferences of their members, and formed councils to take steps to see that their status was recorded in the way they thought was honourable to them. Other castes that could not but resent this 'stealthy' procedure to advance, equally eagerly began to controvert their claims. Thus a campaign of mutual recrimination was set on foot. "The leaders of all but the highest castes frankly looked upon the Census as an opportunity for pressing and perhaps obtaining some recognition of social claims which were denied by persons of castes higher than their own."[23] In 1911 the Census-reporter for Madras wrote the following: "It has been pointed out to me by an Indian gentleman that the last few years, and especially the occasion of the present census, have witnessed an extraordinary revival of the caste spirit in certain aspects. For numerous caste 'Sabhās' have sprung up, each keen to assert the dignity of the social group which it represents."[24]

It is difficult to see any valid public reason for this elaborate treatment of caste in the Census Report. The Government have never avowed their intention of helping every caste to retain its numbers and prosperity. Nor have they at any time helped a particular caste because it registered numerical decline or economic dislocation. Not even the declared policy of the Provincial Governments to provide special representation either by election or nomination to certain classes of people necessitates an enumeration of the people by their castes. For this representation is not dependent on numbers. It is not proportional. All that the particular officers of the Government have to do is to determine in the light of their experience whether a particular person is one who can legitimately claim to belong to one of the three large groups of the population, devised for political purposes. And a Court of Law in any disputed case will settle the point by reference to the usual practice of the people. The conclusion is unavoidable that the intellectual curiosity of some of the early officials is mostly responsible for the treatment of caste given to it in the Census, which has become progressively elaborate in each successive Census since 1872. The total result has been a livening up of the caste-spirit.

In the old regime one caste used to petition the sovereign to restrain another caste from carrying a procession through a particular street or from using a particular mark. Such cases are on record in the *Diaries* of the Peshwas. The British Government in India by their declared policy effectively discouraged such interference and thus removed some of the occasions for a demonstration of the bitter caste-spirit. On the other hand, the desire of the Census officials to give an intelligible picture of caste by means of nice grading of contemporary groups has provided a good rallying point for the old caste-spirit.

The one undisputed consequence of the promulgation of a uniform law and of certain administrative measures has been the removal of almost all the legal inequality in the treatment of different caste—particularly the so-called low castes. Only in the case of the Depressed castes has the Government not proceeded to the logical end. One of the disabilities that these castes, which are proud to call themselves Hindus, and which the higher castes eagerly claim as of their fold in a controversy about political representation of the Hindus, is that they are denied access to Hindu temples. They are required to stop outside the temple proper in the compound and satisfy themselves that they have had a glimpse of the idol of God. A devout Hindu feels very strongly that his homage and prayer to God must be paid in full sight of the idol of God. Hindu religion is not an established church. There are temples for the idols of God maintained by private individuals or by public trusts. The latter sometimes receive grants from the State. The famous temple of Parvati at Poona is such a one. The Depressed Classes want to visit the temple as other caste-Hindus do. The trustees refuse to allow them the right. The Government of Bombay, who make a substantial grant towards the maintenance of the temple, have not yet* though fit to intervene as a matter of public policy. I fail to see how the Government, that has accepted the principle that whichever institution is maintained either wholly or partially with the help of public money must impose no bar on any person merely because of his caste or creed, can contemplate with unconcern the distressing plight of the Depressed Classes for a practical demonstration of their elementary rights. It is clearly the duty of the Government, still sadly undischarged, to declare that the problem of access to the Hindu temples that receive any support out of the public money, must be solved on a basis agreed to by the representatives of all the classes of the Hindus, and that failing such an agreement, grants of money from public funds should be stopped.

The British Government, we have seen, did not recognize caste as a unit empowered to administer justice. Caste was thus shorn of one of its important functions as a community. Individual members might, therefore, be expected to feel less of the old feeling of solidarity for their caste-group. But nothing of the kind is observed to have taken place.[25] First, though a caste could not administer justice, the Government would not set aside the customs of a caste in matters of civil law unless they were opposed to public policy. Caste thus retained its cultural integrity. Secondly, many other aspects of the British Administration, some of which like the Census have been dealt with above, provided

* Written in 1930.

more than sufficient incentive for the consolidation of the caste-group. Mr. Middleton, one of the two Superintendents of Census Operations of 1921, makes eloquent remarks about the effects of the British Administration on caste in the Punjab. He observes: 'I had intended pointing out that there is a very wide revolt against the classification of occupational castes: that these castes have been largely manufactured and almost entirely preserved as separate castes by the British Government. Our land records and official documents have added iron bonds to the old rigidity of caste. Caste in itself was rigid among the higher castes, but malleable amongst the lower. We pigeon-holed every one by caste, and if we could not find a true caste for them, labelled them with the name of an hereditary occupation. We deplore the caste-system and its effects on social and economic problems, but we are largely responsible for the system which we deplore. Left to themselves such castes as Sonār and Lohār would rapidly disappear and no one would suffer. . . . Government's passion for labels and pigeon-holes has led to a crystallization of the caste system, which, except amongst the aristocratic castes, was really very fluid under indigenous rule. . . . If the Government would ignore caste it would gradually be replaced by something very different amongst the lower castes."[26] The situation in the Punjab cannot be taken as typical of other provinces. It is well known that the Punjab was not much influenced by rigid caste-system. Yet the process of pigeon-holing and thus stereotyping has undoubtedly counteracted whatever good results might have ensued from the dethronement of caste as a unit of the administration of justice.[27] The total effect has been, at the least, to keep caste-solidarity quite intact.[28]

The relations of an individual member to a group in which he is born, and to which he is bound by ties, traditional, sentimental, and cultural, in a society where almost everyone belongs to one of such groups, and none can hope to have any respectable status without his group, are such that they are not susceptible to change as a result of legal enactment, administrative rules, or judicial decisions. Though caste has ceased to be a unit administering justice, yet it has not lost its hold on its individual members, who still continue to be controlled by the opinion of the caste. The picture of the control of an individual's activities by his caste, given in 1925 by an eminent social worker of Gujarat, convinces one, by its close similarity with my description of caste of about the middle of the nineteenth century, that as regards at least this aspect of caste, there has been almost no change during the course of three-quarters of a century. She observes: "On our side of the country, I mean in Gujarat, the greatest hindrance to all social reforms is the caste. If I want to educate my girl, the caste would step in and say you should not do it. If I wish to postpone my children's marriage till they are sufficiently grown up, the caste would raise its hand and forbid me. If a widow chooses to marry again and settle respectably in her home the caste would threaten to ostracize her. If a young man wishes to go to Europe for bettering his own or the country's prospects, the caste would, though, perhaps nowadays give him a hearty send-off, yet close its doors on him when he returns. If a respectable man of the so-considered Untouchable class is invited to a house, the caste would deliver its judgment against that householder and condemn him as unfit for any intercourse."[29]

It must have become clear by now that the activities of the British Government have gone very little towards the solution of the problem of caste. Most of these activities, as must be evident, were dictated by prudence of administration and not by a desire to reduce the rigidity of caste, whose disadvantages were so patent to them. The most important step they have taken is the recent regulation in some of the Provinces that a definite percentage of posts in the various services shall be filled from the members of the non-Brahmin or the intermediate castes, provided they have the minimum qualifications. This was originally the demand of the leaders of the non-Brahmin movement. And it is the most obvious remedy against caste-domination. But the obvious is not necessarily the wisest. I contend that the restriction on the numbers of the able members of the Brahmin and the allied castes, imposed by this resolution of the Government, penalizes some able persons simply because they happen to belong to particular castes. When in the case of certain services recruited by means of competitive examinations, some vacancies are offered to candidates who have failed to attain a particular rank in the examination, on the ground that they belong to certain castes, which must be represented in the higher services of the country, it clearly implies that even the accepted standard of qualifications and efficiency is abandoned. The result has been the pampering of caste even at the cost of efficiency and justice. The Government of Bombay, in their memorandum submitted to the Indian Statutory Commission, 1928 (p. 94), complain that the District School Boards, where the non-Brahmins have had a majority, "have almost in every case attempted to oust the Brahmins regardless of all consideration of efficiency." Yet this action is only a logical development of the attitude of the Government which nursed, rather than ignored, the spirit of caste.

On the whole, the British rulers of India, who throughout professed to be the trustees of the welfare of the country, never seem to have given much thought to the problem of caste, in so far it affects the nationhood of India. Nor did they show willingness to take a bold step rendering caste innocuous. Their measures generally have been promulgated piecemeal and with due regard to the safety of British domination.

It may be argued that, if the British masters of India did not take any comprehensive steps to minimize the evil effects of caste which they openly deplored, it must be said to their credit that they did not at least consciously foster the institution. But in the face of the utterances of some responsible British officers, after the Rising of 1857 was quelled, it is not possible to endorse this view. The Rising opened the eyes of the administrators of the country as well as of the students of British Indian history to the potentialities of caste. It was almost the unanimous opinion of persons connected with the Government of India that the deep causes of the Rising were to be found in the fact that the Bengal Army was composed largely of the higher castes, viz. the Brahmins and the Rajputs. The special Commission presided over by Lord Peel, which was appointed to suggest a reorganization of the Indian Army, took evidence from many high officials who were sometime or other closely connected with India. Lord Elphinstone opined that it was desirable that men of different castes should be enlisted in the Army, while Major-General H. T. Tucker went further and insisted on the necessity of keeping the country under British domination through the policy of dividing and separating into distinct bodies the nationalities and castes recruited to the Army. Such being the general tenor of the main bulk of evidence the Commission recommended that "The Native Indian army should be composed of different nationalities and castes and as a general rule mixed promiscuously through each regiment". Lord Ellenborough advised the same, but clearly pointed out that the recommendation was based solely on the ground of British interests and not on the consideration of efficiency of the Army. He lamented the fact that if the suggested procedure were adopted "we must abandon the hope of ever again seeing a native army composed like that we have lost. It was an army which, under a General that it loved and trusted, would have marched victorious to the Dardanelles."[30] Ever since then the Indian Army has been studiously purged of the higher castes. The lesson of the Rising, viz. that the safety of the British domination in India was very closely connected with keeping the Indian people divided on the lines of caste, was driven home to the British rulers. Some officials like Sir Lepel Griffin thought that caste was useful in preventing rebellion,[31] while James Kerr, the Principal of the Hindu College at Calcutta, wrote the following in

1865: "It may be doubted if the existence of caste is on the whole unfavourable to the permanence of our rule. It may even be considered favourable to it, provided we act with prudence and forbearance. Its spirit is opposed to national union."[32] The maxim of 'divide and rule' began to be preached by historians and journalists alike.[33] Because the Rising was largely the work of soldiers of the high castes of Brahmins and Rajputs, there was a clamour in England that the high-caste sepoys should be exterminated.[34] Suspicion of high castes therefore dates from the Rising. The valuable lesson so dearly purchased was not going to be lost. It being repeated in the form of the general principle of 'divide and rule' could not have failed to influence the policy and conduct of later officials. It is well to remember in this connection that even the Roman Church, in its desire to propagate its faith, was prepared to accommodate caste in its practical programme, though it was opposed to the humanitarian principles of the Church. Pope Gregory XV published a bull sanctioning caste regulations in the Christian Churches of India.[35]

The British brought with them a casteless culture and a literature full of thoughts on individual liberty. With the introduction of English education many of the intelligent minds of the country came in closer contact with the religion of the rulers and with some outstanding personalities amongst them. As a result some Indians like Raja Ram Mohan Roy and Devendranath Tagore started movements, which aimed at liberalizing religion and practising the brotherhood of man. The Brahmo Samaj had not only monotheism to preach but also to establish a brotherhood wherein man shall not be divided from man because of caste. The Bombay Prarthana Samaj, inspired by the ideals of Brahmo Samaj in Bengal, has also thrown caste overboard as far as its tenets go. While this movement of repudiating caste was being fostered, other capable Hindu minds thought of remodelling Hindu society after the pristine ideals supposed to be enshrined in the *Vedas*. Swami Dayanand preached that the four-fold division of the Hindu people should be substituted for the manifold ramifications of contemporary caste. The one important innovation that this school of thought carried out in its programme of reconstruction was that even the fourth class of the Hindu society, viz. the Shudras, could study the *Vedas*.[36] Viewing both these movements as an outsider one cannot but be impressed by the manifest success of the Arya Samaj movement of Swami Dayananda. Speaking of the Prarthana Samaj of Bombay, it will be very hard to point out examples from among its high-caste leaders, who, when they had to arrange for the marriages of their sons or daughters, made some effort to practise the ideal they preached. Nay, some of the eminent leaders of the Samaj while openly denouncing caste, busied themselves with the affairs of the caste-groups in which they were born. The situation demonstrates the tenacious reality of caste, which was long ago stated in the apt Tamil proverb: "Even an ascetic is not free from love for his caste". The greater popularity of the Arya Samaj, compared with that of the Prarthana Samaj, is due to the following reasons: First, the Arya Samaj tried to revive the ancient purity of the Vedic society and thus appealed to the traditional sentiment of the people; secondly, the sincerity of the members of the Arya Samaj was much better demonstrated in actual practice; and thirdly, its chief centre of activity was transferred to the Punjab, where caste has been flexible.

Movements against caste of a more militant nature were not slow to arise. In 1873 Jotirao Phooley of Poona, though a man of Māli caste and of comparatively little education, startec an association of members called the Satyashodhak Samaj with the purpose of asserting the worth of man irrespective of caste. The breadth of his vision and the extent of his reforming activities led him to proclaim in his books and to carry out in his practice a revolt against the tyranny of the caste-system. He exhorted the non-Brahmin castes not to engage any Brahmin priest to conduct their marriage ritual, which he tried to reduce to a very simple procedure. He had perceived the necessity of educating the class of people to whom his appeal was directed, and had started primary schools both for boys and girls of the non-Brahmin castes as early as 1848. The catholicity of his mind is further proved by the fact that Phooley started in 1851, a primary school for the so-called untouchables in Poona, the very centre of orthodoxy, where, only fifty years before that, persons of these castes could not even move about during the best part of the day.

Phooley's was a revolt against caste in so far as caste denied ordinary human rights to all the members of Hindu society, and not merely a non-Brahmin movement to cast off the domination of the Brahmins. In his writings he demanded representation for all classes of the Hindus in all the local bodies, the services, and the institutions.[37] The movement did not receive any support from the Brahmins in general. Only stray individuals like Ranade showed sympathy with it. Even among the non-Brahmins the progress of Phooley's ideas was slow. It was the late Maharaja of Kolhapur who infused new life into the agitation, so much so that Montague and Chelmsford, in their Indian political reforms, had to grant the demands.[38]

It would be interesting to know the ideas of the late Maharaja of Kolhapur, who did so much for the recognition of the non-Brahmin movement. On the eve of the announcement of the Indian reforms he said: "If castes remain as they are Home Rule in the sense it is meant will result in nothing but a kind of oligarchy. This of course does not mean, I may tell once more, that I am against Home Rule. Surely we want it. Under the present circumstances, however, we must have the protection and guidance of the British Government until the evil of caste-system becomes ineffective. To prevent Home Rule from culminating in oligarchy, we must have communal representation at least for ten years. It will teach us what our rights are. Once we know them, communal representation can be dispensed with."[39]

The purpose for which this staunch advocate of the non-Brahmin movement urged communal representation is by now more than achieved. An analysis of the membership of the various local bodies in the presidencies of Bombay and Madras clearly proves that the non-Brahmins know their rights and are generally keen to conduct a strong campaign against any measure which they feel unjust to them. A number of motions tabled and questions asked in the Bombay Legislative Council tell the same story.[40] The activity of a Madras association of non-Brahmins and handicraftsmen further illustrates this. One Brahmin member of the Government of Madras during Lord Pentland's tenure issued an order that the Viswakarmans—handicraftsmen—must not suffix the word 'Achary' to their names but that they must continue to use the traditional word 'Asary'. The said association memorialized to the Governor, as the word 'Asary' carried some odium in the eyes of the people, protesting against the order, which they described as a stab in the dark. Not being able to move the Governor to cancel the order they sent a petition to the Secretary of State.[41]

Rao Bahadur A. B. Latthe, the biographer of the late Maharaja of Kolhapur, evidently realizing that the case for special representation cannot be sanctioned on the plea urged by his late hero, seeks other grounds—grounds that one knowing Indian conditions is sure to declare as likely to continue for at least a few generations—to support a worse form of special representation. He observes, "Unless, among the Hindus, caste disappears altogether, there is little chance of avoiding political expedients, like communal electorates though their harmful results are obvious."[42]

There are other leaders of the non-Brahmins who are at pains to proclaim that their movement, including their insistence on strict reservation of posts in the various services, is not inspired by any anti-Brahmin feeling. Others again assert that the large class of taxpayers represented by the non-Brahmin classes must have an adequate share of state support in the form of reserved posts.

The logic of these arguments is transparent, and opposed to the accepted criteria of nationality and the guiding principles of social justice. Nevertheless, only a microscopic minority, even of the small number that recognizes the evils of these demands, propounds that communalism must be abandoned. The Chairman of the Reception Committee of the meeting of the Madras non-Brahmin party in 1924 made a strong appeal "to abandon the communal policy pursued hitherto and transform the party into an organization representing the forces working for reform along constitutional lines into which everyone without distinction of caste, religion, or colour would have free admission".[43] The party did not accept this wholesome principle of development until late in 1930.

What are the interests which the leaders of the non-Brahmin movement wish to safeguard by means of special representation? If there are any such interests, are they identical for all the castes that are officially included in the category of non-Brahmins? These are questions which it is not at all easy for the protagonists of the movement to answer. The economic interests of the artisans, the tenant-farmers, land-lords, and mill-workers are not identical. All these are very well represented in the non-Brahmin group. Nor has there been any attempt, to my knowledge, on the part of the Brahmins during recent times to penalize these classes of people simply because of caste-feelings. If any such legislation were introduced the British element in the Government of the country could effectively checkmate it.

The non-Brahmin castes can be regarded as one group only in social matters because the attitude of the Brahmins as regards food and social intercourse, and religious instruction and ministration towards them, has been uniform. There has been enough awakening in the country for the Brahmins not to try the dangerous path of imposing legal restrictions in these matters. Even the Tamil Nadu Congress Committee decided in 1925 that "the gradation of merit based on birth should not be observed in Indian social life."[44] Whatever liberalizing of the Brahmin attitude in this respect has taken place during the last forty years is mainly due to education and social reform campaign and not to the very recent reserved or communal representation.

Reserved representation is thus not necessary. Nay, it is harmful in so far as it tends to perpetuate the distinction based on birth. Co-operation in the satisfaction of the needs of common social life through the machinery of Government is one of the potent factors that have dissolved tribal bonds and created nation-communities. This co-operation may be based on both territorial contiguity and affinity of interests. Special representation for some castes, which have, as shown above, interests that are neither common to them, nor necessarily conflicting with the interests of other castes, means the negation of such co-operation. In countries where the nation-community is strongly built up on the basis of the feeling of the unity no such principle is recognized for the representation of the different interests, even when they can be parcelled out into groups with conflicting interests. Thus we have not heard of 'labour' claiming special representation in the British Parliament. Where it is a question of engendering a feeling of unity the people must be made to co-operate irrespective of their caste. It is only by such activity that the feeling of nation-community can be created. To harp on the caste-differences and to allow special representation is to set at naught the fundamental condition for the rise of community feeling.

Certain types of non-Brahmin leaders find[45] it easy to secure a seat on the legislature or a local body through the door of reserved representation, and that is the main reason, perhaps, why they are so strong in claiming it. But they fail to see that their example would be soon followed by many of the large castes that comprise at present the non-Brahmin category and their chances of an easy seat would be very much diminished. That this is not mere imagination will be clear to anyone who has followed the history of the demand for special representation in Indian political life. Ere long we shall witness the situation of many different castes that are individually large enough, each clamouring for special representation.[46] National life will thus be reduced to an absurdity. As it is, the non-Brahmins in the Bombay Presidency, wherever they could have their way, have shown unmistakable tendency to be anti-Brahmin and to harass their Brahmin employees in the matter of transfers, etc.[47] Perhaps, in the name of justice and efficiency, the time has come when the interests of the Brahmins have to be protected against the majority party. All points considered, special representation is unnecessary and harmful.

It has been mentioned above that the other demand of the non-Brahmins, which is already granted, is reservation of posts in the various services. This feature has latterly been so far insisted upon by the party that a journalist of long standing recently described it as "immediately and on the surface a movement to secure a larger share of offices in the administration".[48] This principle is also liable, like representation, to be reduced to absurdity by separate demands by individual castes, officially forming the non-Brahmin group. There are clear indications of this development in the nearest future. Not long after the declaration of this policy by the Madras Government it was faced with this situation. "The hundreds of small communities into which Indian society is divided were not slow to take advantage of the opportunity which was so conveniently afforded them, and began to clamour for special representation in the Legislature, local bodies, the public services and even educational institutions. The Government, in which also the non-Brahmin element was very influential, tried to satisfy the ever-increasing demand for the plums of office, but naturally could not succeed. It created jealousies and enmities which have now reacted with disastrous effect on the party."[49]

The ground on which reservation of posts can be supported are two. First, that the Brahmins and other castes, which have a very strong majority in the personnel of the services, can and do harass the populace simply because they are non-Brahmins. Second, that in the selection for fresh vacancies the dominant castes make it impossible for the non-Brahmins to get the posts. The former allegation is sometimes made, but our experience does not lead us to believe that such harassment exists on an appreciable scale. Even if it did exist, there is enough general awakening to bring the offenders to book. Caste feeling being what it is it is very likely that strong bias in favour of one's caste-fellows leads many to prefer them or to use influence in their favour to the detriment of the non-Brahmins or other castes. If proper precaution can be taken against such a contingency, there would be no scope for the vicious principle of the reservation of posts. Such precaution, it appears to me, can be effectively taken if all the recruitment to all the public services is made on the results of competitive examinations held by a board consisting of persons well-known for their liberal and casteless views.

The problem of the depressed classes, in so far as it is the result of the caste system, deserves special treatment. Among these classes are castes that follow the skilled occupations of tanning, shoe-making, and working in bamboo and cane. These are considered so low by the other Hindus that, as pointed out before, they were not allowed to approach other castes within a measurable distance. They have thus been segregated most effectively for centuries. Their ideas of cleanliness have lagged very far behind those of caste-Hindus. Education has never been a luxury enjoyed by them. Utterly despised by the higher sections of society they have had no incentive to imitate them. Those who feel that the inhuman treatment of these very useful classes of society is wrong realize that a change in it depends as much upon reform in the habits of these classes as upon a change in the attitude of the caste-Hindus. To alter the habits of these people education, both through teaching and propaganda, is essential. Some aspects of these habits also depend on the economic position of these classes. To better the economic position of the depressed classes is thus necessary in order to bring about a real change in their social status.

In the Maratha region since the time of Jotirao Phooley, all reformers who have felt the injustice of the situation have begun their campaign with provision for the education of the members of the depressed classes.

Individual workers like V. R. Shinde and A. V. Thakkar have done much not only to rouse the feeling of the caste-Hindus against the unjust doctrine of untouchability but also to prepare the depressed classes for better treatment by spreading education amongst them. The problem of the removal of untouchability is now made a national one through the efforts of Mahatma Gandhi. I have already dealt with the liberalizing consequences of certain administrative aspects of the British rule. The campaign has, in no small measure, benefited by the efforts made by Christian and Muhammadan missionaries to convert the depressed classes to their faiths. The more reasonable section of the high-caste Hindus have sensed a real danger to their faith in allowing their doctrine of untouchability to drive away into the folds of other faiths members of the untouchable castes, members who have been quite good and devout Hindus.

The result of this many-sided attack is to be seen in the change of viewpoint of many a member of the higher castes. Incidents like the following one from Bengal are more and more to be witnessed. "Kulin Brahmins of Nabadwip, Shantipur, Krishnagar, Kustia and other places accepted and drank water from the hands of Nāmashudras, washermen, boatmen, dāis, and other untouchables and drank the water amidst scenes of great enthusiasm. Young Brahmins and old Bhattāchāryas, Mukherjis, Bānerjis, Chatterjis, Maitras, all took part in the interesting function."[50] In their determined effort to pass through the roads of Vaikam in Travancore in 1924, which were, in the caste regime prohibited to the untouchables, these latter were helped by many a high-caste Hindu. While the trustees of Hindu temples, taking shelter behind certain decisions of the Privy Council of doubtful applicability, have closed the temple doors to the untouchables, individual owners of private temples have allowed free access for all classes of Hindus to the temples under their management. This is not to say that there is no organized effort to combat the spread of the doctrine of anti-untouchability. In the beginning of 1925 a number of merchants of Bombay, among whom were included some of the leading public men, convened a meeting of orthodox Hindus. Almost every speaker denounced what they called the heresies of Gandhi in respect of untouchability, and declared that the Hindu religion was in danger at his hands.[51] It is more or less clear that the conflict will last for some time to come, and it is the duty of those who have no belief in untouchability to preach its abolition and to demonstrate their belief through their own conduct.

About the time the non-Brahmin movement had begun to gather force some of the untouchable castes of Madras had begun to call themselves Ādi-Dravidas. With the upsurge of self-evaluation they must have begun to make some of the shows which were socially inhibited. In 1921 at Vadakkalur in Trichinopoly district their marriage procession was attacked by castemen, probably because some one of the insignias prohibited to them was flaunted. In the night, the Ādi-Dravidas burnt a number of houses of the local castemen. In 1925 some of the Scheduled Caste converts to Arya Samaj attempted to enter the Brahmin 'agraharam' of Kalpathi in Palghat, and there resulted general fighting. In 1927 the Telugu high caste of Kapus was prevented by the Mālās from conducting a procession of theirs to the accompaniment of particular music and dance, the same being offensive to the latter.[52] In 1930 the Kallans, who according to a Tamil saying 'a Kallan becomes a Maravan' are lower than Maravans, formulated some rules to be observed by the Ādi-Dravidas, and on the latter's refusal to observe them resorted to violence to force them to conform to them.[53]

The growth of city life with its migratory population has given rise to hotels and restaurants. The exigencies of office work have forced city people to put aside their old ideas of purity. Caste-Hindus have to eat articles of food prepared by Christians, Musalmans, or Persians, because Hindu restaurants have not been easily or equally accessible during office hours. In Hindu eating-houses, they have to take their meals in the company of people of almost any caste—as the hotel-keeper cannot manage to reserve accommodation for members of different castes. What was originally done under pressure of necessity has become a matter of routine with many in their city life. This freedom from caste-restrictions about food, though seen in the city, is a mere garb that is usually cast aside by city people when they go to their villages. The force of custom and sentiment is so great that it has led the people to create a dual standard of life rather than break with their village folk. Especially is this true of all formal occasions. While this slow and enforced change was taking place special dinners whereat persons sit in a row irrespective of caste have, from time to time, been successfully arranged by some associations. Conscious effort and the force of flux have effected an altogether healthy and appreciable modification in the people's attitude in the matter of supposed pollution imparted through food and drink by certain classes of people. Whereas in Poona a handful of people like M. G. Ranade and others were subjected to social tyranny and ultimately forced to undergo expiatory rites in 1891–2 for having taken tea at a Christian missionary's place, today* no one even takes notice of the Brahmins dining at the Government House.

In those parts of India, where the untouchables were really unapproachable, certain exigencies of modern life have forced high-caste Hindus to change their attitude and practice to some extent. "In towns, where private scavenging and sweeping are enforced, the scavengers and sweepers have not only to go near the houses but have sometimes to enter into them for scavenging. This has done away with distance pollution".[54]

There is much more freedom in the matter of choice of occupation today than under the old regime. First, new occupations, which require abilities similar to those displayed in older occupation, have arisen out of the new requirements. Many of those occupations, like those of draftsmanship and cabinet-making, have come to be looked upon with greater esteem and are better remunerated than their older prototypes. Draftsmanship is partially allied to clerkship (in so far as it involves desk-work in an office) and largely to the ancient designer's avocation. Recruits to this profession, therefore, hail both from the higher castes of Brahmins and others as well as from the lower castes, such as higher artisans. Such occupations as tailoring and shoemaking have appreciated in public esteem partly because of the new machinery making them easy and less tedious, and largely because the new technique and craftsmanship is associated with the new rulers. They are, therefore, taken up by more and more members of very high castes. Secondly, dislocation of the old economic order and provision of facilities for training in arts and crafts have led to an extensive shifting of the old lines of division between occupations. The total result is that at present** many members of the Brahmin caste are seen engaged in almost any of the occupations, excepting those of casual labourer, sweeper, and scavenger. Many members of the various artisan castes are teachers, shopkeepers, bank clerks, shop assistants, and architects.

In the textile mills of Bombay not a few members of even the untouchable castes have found work quite different from what they were used to under the regime of caste. Whatever restrictions caste

---

* 1930.

** 1930.

imposed on the choice of occupation largely ceased to guide individuals, and it is ignorance and lack of enterprise that kept the occupational un-freedom of caste, even to the extent that it is observed, and not the old ideas of what was considered to be one's traditional or hereditary occupation.

The endogamous nature of caste remained almost the same with this difference that whereas formerly marriage outside one's caste was not to be even thought of, many educated young men and women were prepared to break through the bonds of caste if mutual love or attraction demanded it. In Bombay I have known many examples, mostly members of younger generation, who had managed their own matrimonial affairs, the parties to which belong to two different castes. A large majority of such marriages, known as intercaste or mixed marriages, is formed by couples where the female partner belongs to a caste lower than that of the male partner. Yet the opposite variety, where the male partner belongs to a lower caste, is not altogether rare. As for the older generation, it may be said without exaggeration that, in spite of the talk about social reform, it has made very little advance in its ideas on the subject of intermarriage. When, therefore, elderly persons arrange the marriages of their wards they hardly ever think of going beyond their caste—even though it be a section of a large group—from which to select a bride or a bridegroom. If they venture to ignore the limits of the narrowest division—if for example a Chitpāvan Brahmin selects a girl from the Karhādā Brahmin caste for his son, in the Maratha country—he is looked up to as a reformer. It would be hard to point out examples of marriages between members of outright separate castes arranged for their wards by the elderly guardians. It is the recklessness and enthusiasm of youth alone that is prepared to transgress the bounds of castes for the purpose of marriage.

When the city of Bombay began to attract large numbers of people from rural areas, the immigrants, with their traditions of caste, began to congregate, as far as possible according to their castes, though the village affinity influencing the place of residence, modified this tendency. The Brahmin castes of the Maratha country are mostly vegetarians. while the other castes are usually non-vegetarians. The Brahmins had the additional motives of escaping bad odours given out by fish and flesh when they are being dressed, to try to live together in buildings where only Brahmins dwelt. This tendency for every large caste to live in isolation from other castes has been steadily growing. It will be observed that this desire is only the old caste practice of reserving special parts of the village for the different castes moulded to suit the changed conditions of city life. The inclination of the people was encouraged and aggravated by private charity expressing itself through the channels of caste. With the quickening of caste-consciousness and the fostering of caste-patriotism, philanthropic persons have been building houses and chawls to be rented only to their caste-members at moderate rents. Charity, intending to further the educational interests of a caste, has found expression also in providing free hostels to the student members of the caste. As a result, in those areas of Bombay which are largely inhabited by the middle classes, we find today whole chawls which are occupied by members of one or two castes with close affinity, whole buildings rented at moderate or even nominal rents only to the members of a particular caste, and hostels giving free accommodation to the students of a particular caste. Buildings meant for members of a particular caste generally bear prominent boards blatantly announcing the fact of their reservation and where it is a case of individual endowment also the name of the philanthropic donor. Even the colleges and the University are infested with endowments from which scholarships are to be paid to students of certain specified castes.

The introduction of co-operative schemes of amelioration have afforded another opportunity for caste-solidarity to manifest itself. Co-operative housing more than any other aspect of co-operative undertaking, has appealed to the caste-spirit, though credit societies of individual castes, like that of the Reddis, are not altogether unknown. In fact it would be true to remark that only those co-operative housing societies have succeeded most which have restricted their membership to their caste-fellows. Even in business this tendency to restrict the holding of shares to the members of a particular caste is sometimes apparent. Recently, the Brahmins of Madras started a fund called the 'Triplicane Fund', shares in which could be held only by Brahmins. Those responsible for starting it included gentlemen of "culture, education, and learning". "Such being the case, we regret that one of the rules of the Fund is so narrowly conceived as to exclude all that are not Brahmins from the right of holding shares. It is just this type of exclusiveness that furnishes interested parties like the 'ministerialists' their best nutrient. Those who decry the excesses of communalism should themselves first set the example of a healthy, wholesome, non-communal outlook in the practical affairs of life".[55]

One feature of Hindu society during this century has been the marked tendency for every caste to form its own association comprising all members of the caste speaking the same language.[56] In the old regime the caste-panchayat or council was usually restricted to the confines of the village or the town. Barely, if at all, did the jurisdiction of the council, in the case of the majority of the castes, extend beyond these limits. "In the large majority of cases, the caste-consciousness is limited by the bounds of the village and its organizations do not extend beyond the village area".[57] The functions of these new organizations are: (1) to further the general interests of the caste and particularly to guard its social status in the hierarchy from actual or potential attacks of other castes: (2) to start funds to provide studentships for the needy and deserving students of the caste, usually at the secondary and college stage of education, and sometimes even to help them to proceed to foreign countries for higher academic qualification; (3) to help poor people of the caste; (4) and sometimes to try to regulate certain customs of the caste by resolutions passed at the annual meeting of the members of the caste. All these objects, excepting perhaps that of providing studentships, were used to be achieved, in a great or a small measure, by an arrangement not always permanent. Sometimes an *ad hoc* committee would take up the work and carry it out. I have already referred to the stubborn opposition of the Kammalans of Madras to the supreme position of the Brahmins in the hierarchy. The Kāyasth Prabhus of Poona and many other castes of the Maratha country protested from time to time to the court of the Peshwa against certain restrictions which other castes professed to enforce upon them to stamp their status as low. Surely some elderly persons of the particular caste must have volunteered to put its case before the proper tribunal. Relief of the poor was not usually a duty undertaken by a caste. When a caste decided to apply some of its funds to charitable purposes, it handed over the money to the local priest to be used by him for benevolent purposes. The ruling ideals of the time led people to distribute charity in particular channels. The ideal was rather to build temples and rest-houses, dig wells and tanks, and to endow free feeding at the temples for a certain number of Brahmins and at the public feeding houses for travellers and others in need. All this direction of charity was most often preached and accepted without reference to caste. Only the artisan castes, which had strong guild-like organizations, had some standing provision for helping the indigent among its members.[58] Occasionally a caste would relieve its own poor by feeding them through the headman. The funds for this purpose were available from the residue of the fines imposed on the defaulting members of the caste.[59]

We have noticed above that the Brahmins of South India assembled the Brahmins of four quarters and decided to put a stop to the practice of taking money for a bride prevailing among them. The oil-mongers of Kanchi proposed to bind themselves by certain conditions about donations to temples and to observe them as 'jātidharma', i.e. duty which every member owed to his caste.

The community aspect of caste has thus been made more comprehensive, extensive, and permanent. More and more of an individual's interests are being catered for by caste, and the needy who are helped by their caste-funds naturally owe much to their caste and later in life look upon it with feelings of gratitude and pride. They feel it their proud duty to strengthen the caste-organization, remembering their obligations to it. Thus a vicious circle has been created. The feeling of caste-solidarity is now so strong that it is truly described as caste-patriotism

From the discussion of the non-Brahmin and depressed class movements it will be evident that the old hierarchy of caste is no longer acquiesced in. Many are the castes that employ priests of their own caste. Some of the castes, the goldsmiths of the Maratha country, for example, have already started asserting their dignity by refusing to take food at the hands of castes, other than the Brahmin, which according to their old practice do not reciprocate that courtesy. In this process it is the lower caste that starts the movement in order to raise its own status. To add to this the old profession of a teacher, and the more or less new profession of a Government clerk, are coveted by many more castes than was the practice in the old regime. There is a veritable scramble for these petty jobs. Conflict of claims and oppositions has thus replaced the old harmony of demand and acceptance. The contract in the old and new situation is vividly brought out in the description of village conditions in a part of the Madras Presidency existing more than a century ago and those subsisting ten years ago. A report on the state of the village in 1808 contains the following: "Every village with its twelve 'ayagandeas', as they are denominated, is a petty commonwealth, with the 'mocuddim', 'potail', 'kapoo', 'ready', or chief inhabitant, at the head of it: and India is a great assemblage of such commonwealths. While the village remains entire, they care not to what power it is transferred".[60] The *District Gazetteer of* Tinnevelly, on the other hand, had to record in 1917 the following: "With all the inducements to cooperation it can scarcely be said that the average Tinnevelly village possesses the strength born of unity. General Panchayats are practically unknown, disputes are too readily taken to the lawcourts instead of being settled in the village, and the best efforts of the revenue and irrigation officers and of the police are often hampered by deep-seated faction. It is among the individual castes that the spirit of cohesion is most clearly seen. This often takes the practical form of a 'Mahimai', or general fund, levied by each community for its own use. . . . The objects of expenditure are usually the support of temples, mosques, or churches owned by the contributors; occasionally the money is diverted to petitions or litigation in which the caste as a whole is interested."[61] Caste-solidarity has taken the place of village-community.

To sum up, social and religious privileges and disabilities born of caste are no longer[62] recognised in law and only partially in custom. Only the depressed classes are labouring under certain customary and semi-legal disabilities. Caste no longer rigidly determines as individual's occupation, but continues to prescribe almost in its old rigour the circle into which one has to marry. One has still to depend very largely on one's caste for help at critical periods of one's life, like marriage and death. One's closest companions and friends are mainly delimited by the circle of one's caste. The difference between the old regime and contemporary society lies in this that whereas under the ancient organization the facts mentioned above were almost universally true, today there is a section of society—the modernly educated persons—small yet important, which has risen above all these restrictions. They are bound to serve as beacon lights to the wavering members of society. Attitudes of exclusiveness and distrust, enshrined in the old vernacular proverbs, between caste and caste, still persevere even in the minds of the educated. Caste-associations are very common and command the services of even the most highly educated persons to further their object of helping the members of their castes.

As long as endogamy is prescribed and practised, wider self-interest dictates that one should help the aggrandisement of the members of one's caste. For, the better the economic prospects for the youths of the caste the greater the chances of getting well-to-do husbands for one's daughters. The rule of endogamy is in a way the fundamental factor of contemporary caste.

Caste has thus become the centre of an individual's altruistic impulse and philanthropic activities. The existence of definite organization has rallied round the caste the feelings of consciousness of kind. In the desire to help one's fellows many forget the principles of social justice, and are led to do, consciously or otherwise, injustice to the members of other castes. Unfortunately many leaders in civic life are associated with the movement of amelioration of their respective castes. The mental undercurrents of those are to be led breathe distrust of such leaders. The conduct of these leaders in the matter of the marriages of their wards usually in their own caste—strengthens this lack of confidence felt by the populace, and acts as a buttress against the attacks on caste-endogamy. Hardly any caste accepts its accredited status or concedes the precedence of another caste, though it may demand such precedence of a caste supposed to be lower than it in the old hierarchy.

Economic conditions have led many castes to clamour for petty jobs in the clerical line. This factor enhances the feeling of caste-animosity. Even the apex of the ancient scheme, the priesthood of the Brahmin, which has been the great bond of social solidarity in this finely divided society, is being loosened by caste after caste. At about the end of the British rule in India, caste-society presented the spectacle of self-centred groups more or less in conflict with one another.

References

1. Kikani, p. iii. 2. Kikani, p. 7. 3. Kikani, p. iii. 4. Kikani, p. 132. 5. Ibid., p. xii. cf. Gledhill, pp. 209–10. 6. Mayne, pp. 779–82. 7. Mandlik, p. 430. 8. *The Times of India* (Bombay), 30th June 1928. 9. Kikani, p. vi; cf. D. F. Mulla, pp. 49–63.

10. Latthe, vol. ii. p. 373. 11. Mayne, pp. 108–9. 12. *The Legislative Assembly Debates*, vol. iii, pp. 3899–926. 13. The *Bombay Chronicle*, 31st March, 1924. N.B.: John Wilson wrote in 1877: "Few, if any, of the Antyaja are found in Government schools. This is to be ascribed not only to the Brahmanical fear of contamination and the general caste Government educational authorities as has been the case in some instances of the agents of the missionary bodies" (*Indian Caste*, vol. ii, p. 45. 14. *Forward* (Calcutta). 7th November, 1923. 15. *Bombay Chronicle*, 1st May, 1925. 16. *Memorandum submitted by the Government of Bombay to the Indian Statutory Commission*, 1928. (1929), p. 228. 17. Ibid., p. 44. 18. This resolution was modified by a later one, dated 5th February, 1925, wherein the absolute; restriction on the recruitment from the advanced classes was removed. 19. See notices by the Dean of the Grant Medical College and the Principal of the Gujarat College in *The Times of India*, 26th April 1926.

20. G.I.P. Railway Risk-note. Form "B" B.I.P.—176-9-24-30000. 21. See Kitts, p. 1. 22. *India Census*, 1901, pp. 537–8. 23. *Bengal Census*, 1921, p. 346. 24. *Madras Census*, 1911, p. 178. 25. During the recent (1928–30) Civil Disobedience movement the influence of caste was clearly visible in Gujarat. 26. *Punjab Census*, 1921, pp. 434–4. The last remark of Mr. Middleton appears to me to be an overstatement even in the case of the Punjab, where caste has been more fluid than elsewhere in India. 27. N.B.: I am glad to note that as a result of the agitation carried on by the Jat–Pat-Torak Mandal of Lahore the Government of India made some concession in the matter of the filling in of the column for caste at the Census of 1931 in the case of persons who do not conform to the practices of their caste. 28. Compare J. Murdoch, *Caste* (1887), pp. 38–42, and also the quotation from Sherring therein; and Rev. John Morrison, *New Ideas in India* (1906), p. 33. 29. Lady Vidyagauri Ramanbhai as reported in the *Indian Social Reformer* (Bombay), 5th September, 1925.

30. *Report of the Peel Commission on the Organization of the Indian Army*, 1859, p. 14, and Appendix, pp. 6, 10, 147. 31. Vide Murdoch, *Caste*, p. 43. 32. Kerr, p. 361, footnote. 33. L. J. Trotter, *History of India under Queen Victoria*, vol. ii, (1886), p. 91, and *The Times of India*, 3rd July, 1897 (leading article). 34. Edward Sullivan, *Letters on India*, (1858), pp. 124–5. 35. *Encyclopaedia Britannica*, 11th Ed., vol. v, p. 468 (a). 36. See the account of the Arya Samaj given by Pandit Harikishan Kaul in the *Punjab Census Report*, 1911, pp. 133–6. 37. Phule, pp. 25, 33, 59, 63; Latthe, I, pp. 322–24. 38. This demand for representation in the services was first made in a petition addressed by the artisan castes of Madras to the Board of Revenue in 1840. "All classes of men, to the destruction of Brahmanical monopoly, should be appointed to public offices without distinction. John Wilson, *Indian Caste*, vol. ii, p. 89, footnote. 39. Latthe, vol. ii, p. 494.

40. *Memorandum submitted by the Government of Bombay to the Indian Statutory Commission*, 1928, pp. 527–9. 41. *The Times of India* (Bombay), 25th October, 1924. 42. *The Indian Social Reformer* (Bombay), 3rd January, 1925. 43. *The Indian Daily Mail* (Bombay), 14th October, 1924. 44. *The Bombay Chronicle*, 2nd May, 1925. 45. N.B.: This was written in about 1930. 46. Between the time this was written and it appeared in print the Marwaris of Calcutta put forward a plea for special representation. 47. *Memorandum submitted by the Government of Bombay to the Indian Statutory Commission*, 1928, p. 229. 48. *Indian Social Reformer*, 11th February, 1928. 49. *The Indian Daily Mail* (Bombay), 14th October, 1924.

50. *Forward* (Calcutta), 6th March, 1924. 51. *The Times of India*, 5th January, 1925. 52. *Madras Memorandum to the Statutory Commission*, pp. 596–98. 53. *Census Report, India*, 1931, p. 486. 54. *Travancore Census*, 1921, p. 106. 55. *The Indian Social Reformer* (Bombay), 16th October, 1926. 56. Perhaps the earliest of such organizations is the one started by a Bihar caste in 1891 (*Memorandum for the Indian Statutory Commission*, Bihar & Orissa, p. 87). By 1928 such Sabhas existed for most of the principal castes of Bihar. 57. Matthai, p. 65. 58. Ibid., pp. 65, 68–9. Even the artisan castes sometimes depended on special collections for a specific purpose. The guilds of artisans in Broach, for example, when they required funds, collected them by subscriptions among the members of the caste. (*Imperial Gazetteer of India, Provincial Series, Bombay Presidency*, vol. i, p. 312) 59. Mookerji, p. 186.

60. The Fifth Report from the Select Committee on the Affairs of the East India Company, vol. ii, (ed. 1883), p. 575. 61. *Madras District Gazetteers: Tinnevelly*. vol. i, 1917, p. 104. 62. N.B.: Written in 1930.

11

The Scheduled Castes

Time and again the reader has come across the expression untouchable classes, depressed classes, the names of certain groups like Chandāla, and in the last chapter the term Scheduled Castes too. As is clear from the last reference the term 'Scheduled Castes' is the expression standardised in the Constitution of the Republic of India. Contrary to usual practice the Constitution does not contain a definition of the term Scheduled Castes. Article 341 of the Constitution empowers the President, after consulting the head of the particular State, to notify by an order "the castes, races or tribes or parts of or groups within castes, races or tribes which shall for the purposes of this Constitution be deemed to be Scheduled Castes in relation to that State". And the second clause of the Article empowers Parliament to pass a law to include in or exclude from the list so notified by the President "any caste, race or tribe or part of or group within any caste, race or tribe". I may define the Scheduled Castes therefore as those groups which are named in the Scheduled Castes Order in force for the time being.

The expression thus standardised in the Constitution was first coined by the Simon Commission and embodied in the Government of India Act, 1935, in Section 309. The main Commission, its Education Committee and the Franchise Commission studied the cases of what till then were called either the untouchables, the depressed classes or the backward classes. Though Mahatma Gandhi had, through his weekly *The Harijan* and his Harijan Sevak Sangh and other organisations, his propaganda and his fasts, tried to designate these classes as *Harijans*, the framers of the Constitution, the largest bulk of whom were staunch followers and devotees of Gandhi, surprisingly adopted the term coined by the Simon Commission.

The Scheduled Castes, formerly known as depressed classes, and forming the fifth order of the four-fold society of Hindu theory of caste, have, in the Republican Constitution, been provided with not only special privileges in the matter of recruitment to services but also with special representation in the legislative bodies. It is but proper that their history and present position should, in a book like this, be given separate treatment to enable the readers to get a connected view of the situation.

Ideas of purity, whether occupational or ceremonial, which are found to have been a factor in the genesis of caste, are the very soul of the idea and practice of untouchability. The fact that in the sacrificial creation of mankind in Hindu cosmology, the last order mentioned as having been created from the feet of the Creator is that of the Shudra and that there was no other class of human beings created thereafter adds flesh and blood to the ideas of ceremonial and occupational purity to engender the theory and practice of untouchability.

Outside this indirect support for or suggestion of all classes of men not comprised under the four orders, Brahmin, Kshatriya, Vaishya and Shudra, being unsanctified owing to their lack of association with the body of the Creator, ideas of ceremonial purity were rife enough even in the times of the *Brāhmanas*, i.e. the works of the later Vedic age, for certain restrictions to be placed on the use of and intercourse with the Shudras in the performance of sacrifices. It is expressly stated in the *Panchavimsha Brāhmana* that a person consecrated for the performance of a sacrifice should not address a Shudra, that a Shudra should not be allowed to be present in the hall where a sacrifice was being offered and that the milk to be used for a fire-oblation should not have been milked by a Shudra.[1] The *Aitareya Brāhmana*,[2] in warning a Kshatriya to avoid certain mistakes in the sacrificial ritual, which, if committed, would lead to dire consequences, informs the reader that meticulous adherence to the details of ritual had already become an accepted dogma.

Already in the *Taittiriya Āranyaka* we come across full-fledged rules of abstinence and avoidance to be observed not only in connection with special vows and rituals but also with the seasonal study period. It is stated that for the performance of a certain ritual the performer must not have eaten meat for a whole year, nor must he have had sexual intercourse, nor must he drink from a clay-vessel. But the most significant taboo or prohibition is that the leavings of the performer's drink—and I should presume food too—should not have been drunk or eaten by his son. For it is declared that it, viz. such leavings, is lustre itself. Here is an idea very akin to the primitive idea of *mana*, involved in the concept of the remnants or leavings of one's food or drink. This reference to leavings or remnants of food and drink is not solitary. In the *Chhāndogyopanishad*[3] there is an argument about the partaking of such leavings. A Brahmin by name Ushasti Chākrāyana being in distress begged some food of an elephant-owner who was eating beans. The latter pointing out to the beans he had before him in his dish told him that he had no stock of them besides those. Ushasti asked for some of those laid out in the dish, whereupon the elephant-owner gave him some. And whether out of mischievous ideas or out of usual courtesy—the context suggests the former—he offered him also water from his jug out of which he himself had drunk. Ushasti declined the drink as having been the remnant, 'uchchhishta', and hence polluted. The elephant-owner promptly asked Ushasti whether the beans were not such unacceptable remnants. Ushasti replied that he had taken the beans because without them in his condition he could not have lived and added that he had declined the drink because he would not die without it. Thus ordinarily leavings or remnants of another's food or drink were not to be taken, being considered polluting.

Ideas of ceremonial purity as centred round food and drink, thus, early tabooed the giving and partaking of these between one individual and another, whether without relationship or with the closest of relationship. Milk and by implication food required for a sacrifice was so sacrosanct that it could not be brought by a Shudra without polluting it and thus rendering it unfit for sanctified use. The remnant of sanctified or sacrificial food too, it appears, had come to be regarded as requiring special protection against defilement by its being used by some classes of persons. At least we know quite definitely that giving of the remnants of sacrificial food to a low person was unusual and could be justified only in exceptional cases. In the *Chhāndogyopanishad* it is stated that if one who has realised the true nature of 'Brahman' offers the remnants of the food used for the Agnihotra sacrifice even to a Chandāla it is offered as an oblation in that sacrificial fire.[4] *Per contra*, such food being offered to a Chandāla is an abomination. It is necessary to remember that earlier in the same work[5] it is stated, almost in so many words, that the breed of the Chandāla is a degraded one and is ranked with that of the dog and the pig.

Before 800 B.C. we thus find the idea of ceremonial purity almost full-fledged and even operative in relation to not only the despised and degraded group of people called Chandālas but also the fourth order of society, the Shudras.

The *Dharmasutra* writers[6] declare the Chandālas to be the progeny of the most hated of the reverse order of mixed unions, that of a Brahmin female with a Shudra male. Kautilya, the practical administrator who provides for a number of these so-called mixed castes, agrees with the Dharma-writers in the view that of the mixed castes those that arise out of the unions in the inverse order bespeak violation of Dharma, yet looks upon all of them as mixed castes. He exhorts that they should marry among themselves and should follow the customs and avocations as far as possible of their ancestors. He has no objection if they treat themselves as Shudras; but he, too, regards the Chandālas so low that he advises all other mixed castes to avoid being with the Chandālas. It is interesting to note, however, that he accommodates the sons born of miscegenation in his law of inheritance.[7]

The treatment of Chandālas who, as we know, were an ethnic group already referred to in Vedic literature, and one or two similar groups may be further scanned in order to shed light on the origin and the problem of the scheduled castes in general. There was a group separately recognised by Vasishtha, which was called Antyāvasāyin, which he declared was the progeny of a Vaishya female by a Shudra male. According to Manu, however, the Antyāvasāyin was of much more depraved origin, being the progeny of a Chandāla male and a Nishāda female. His work was confined to the cremation ground, and according to one commentator he was to be identified with the Chandāla. It is not easy to explain away the absence of the listing of this group by other Dharma-writers and by Kautilya the administrator. Both Baudhāyana and Vasishtha mention a degraded caste called Svapāka. Baudhāyana once declares the group to have risen from the union of an Ambashtha male with a Brahmin female, while at another place he attributes it to the union of an Ugra male with a Kshattri female. Manu makes Svapāka the progeny of Kshattri male and an Ugra female, i.e. he gives a derivation which is just the opposite of Baudhāyana's second derivation. He also lists two other groups, one Sopāka and the other Pāndusopāka, whom he derives from a Chandāla father and Kukkusa and Vaideha mother respectively. He prescribes Sopāka the vocation of the hangman and Pāndusopāka that of a cane-worker. It is to be noted that though both Baudhāyana and Manu speak of Svapāka as the group, yet Manu in describing its particular vocation calls it Svapacha.[8] The practical administrator Kautilya speaks of the group as Svapāka and derives it from the union of an Ugra male and a Kshattri female.[9] This derivation agrees with Baudhāyana's second derivation and is just the opposite of that of Manu.

Patanjali, the great grammarian who lived about 150 B.C. and who is generally considered to be a meticulous observer of contemporary usage, has given us his grammatical explanation for the female of the Svapacha group being called a Svapachā and not Svapachi.[10] What exactly were the avocations and status of a Svapachā in Patanjali's time we do not know. But we have the valuable information that Patanjali did not illustrate his remarks about certain grammatical formations based on certain social disabilities with the help of the illustration of Svapachās. In that illustration he speaks of Mritapas in combination with Chandālas. We also know that the practical administrator Kautilya, who rigorously excluded the Chandālas from all social contacts, did not prescribe similar treatment to the Svapachas. But Manu[11] is very explicit and insistent that the Svapachas shall be grouped with Chandālas and treated as their absolute equals. He prescribes them residence outside the village, and the use of shrouds of corpses as their clothing, broken pots for meals, iron for ornaments and dogs and donkeys for their wealth. They were to be the hangmen who were to be prohibited entry into villages and towns during day-time, were to have been stamped with some marks and were to serve as the undertakers for unclaimed corpses.

As stated above Patanjali of an earlier age than Manu, writing as a student observing society and not laying down its norms, grouped together Chandālas and Mritapas as a variety of Shudras. And it is not impossible that this manner of looking upon the Chandālas and the Mritapas may be as old as Pānini's time, that is, 500 B.C. We learr that both the Chandālas and the Mritapas resided within the limits of towns and villages of the Aryas as, it would appear, other Shudras like carpenters, blacksmiths, washermen, and weavers did. The social distinction on the score of status between such groups as carpenters, blacksmiths, washermen, weavers, etc. on the one hand, and the Chandālas and the Mritapas, on the other, lay not in the fact of touchability or untouchability but only in the distinction made in the use of the meal-vessels of these people. Patanjali assures us by implication that whereas the food-vessels used by such groups as carpenters, blacksmiths, washermen and weavers could be used by other groups after cleansing them in a particular manner, the food-vessels of Chandālas and Mritapas could not be so used by others, because no known method of cleansing pots was regarded as adequate to purify them. Chandālas and Mritapas were technically 'apapātras'.

As stated in an earlier chapter Patanjali's remarks lend support to the inference that there were other groups than Chāndālas and Mritapas who had to live outside the limits of Āryas villages and towns.

It is noteworthy that the technical term 'apapātra' used by Patanjali to characterize Chandālas and Mritapas was used by *Dharmasutra*-writers like Baudhāyana but without specifying the groups. Baudhāyana[12] exhorted Brahmins not to recite the Veda within hearing or sight of Shudras or 'apapātras'. Āpastamba (*Dharmasutra*, II, 17, 20) enjoined that they should not be permitted to see the performance of a funeral sacrifice. From the context it may be inferred that 'apapātras' meant the same people to whom the term was applied by Patanjali and even earlier by Pānini.

We may conclude that the classes of people called Chandālas, Svapachas and Mritapas had slowly but surely deteriorated in their social position between the time of Pānini and that of Manu. In the former age they lived within the limits of the village in which other orders and castes lived. In the age of Manu (X, 51–2) they were not only excluded from the village but were assigned duties and perquisites which clearly show that they were looked upon as vile specimens of humanity.

The Buddhist birth-stories called Jātakas, written in Pali, may be taken to reflect mainly the conditions prevailing east of Allahabad about the second century B.C. We read in them of Chandālas as the lowest caste, though here and there in enumeration of castes another group, the later Vedic Pukkusa, is mentioned after Chandālas as lower than it. The references to Chandālas are specific and almost invariably show them as a despised group, to see members of which is to see evil, to avert which one must at least wash one's eyes. They are described as occupying sites outside regular villages and towns whether in the west near Taxila or in the centre near Ujjain. They could be detected by their special dialect. Sweeping was their hereditary occupation.[13]

The causes that led to the degradation of these communities are not known. We can only surmise that in addition to the ideas of ceremonial purity, which necessarily led to the despise of the occupations of these people there was perhaps the baneful influence of the belief that they were the result of miscegenation with Brahmin females.

A word needs to be said about the identification of Mritapa of Patanjali, Svapacha of Baudhāyana, Manu and Kautilya, and the Dom. Alberuni,[14] writing in about A.D. 1020, grouped together Dom and Chandāla as two of the groups "not reckoned among any caste or guild. They are occupied with dirty work, like the cleansing of the villages and other services. They are considered as one sole class, and distinguished only by their occupations." Hemachandra, the grammarian, writing about a century later, in his *Deshināmamālā*[15] tells us that Dumba [Dom or Dumba] was a Deshi word for

Svapacha. He vouchsafes us the additional information that the Chandālas carried a stick in their hands to warn people to avoid their touch, which received a specific Deshi name, viz. 'jhajjhari'. Kalhana, the Brahmin historian of Kashmir, in his *Rājatarangini*,[16] whose writing was completed in A.D. 1150 has narrated how king Chakravarman fell on evil ways, being caught in the whirlwind of passion for two daughters of a Domba musician, Hansi and Nāgalatā by name, who were themselves clever musicians and dancers. Alternatively he speaks of the Domba and the two women as Svapākas. The king was so maddened with passion that he crowned Hansi as the chief queen. Kalhana describes, in a manner which bespeaks his wrung heart, how the ministers and others reconciled themselves not only to working with Svapāki queen and her Svapacha dear ones but also went to the length of eating the leavings of her food. Kalhana's reaction as a moralising historian is characteristic. He remarks, "In the realm at that time surely powerful deities did not reside, how else could a Svapāka woman (Svapāka) have entered their temples!" Nevertheless it is worthwhile noting the different reaction of the same irate Brahmin historian, who was terribly upset by the doings of King Chakravarman, when describing one of the most laudable kings of Kashmir, viz. Yassaskara, who came to the throne about sixteen years after Chakravarman. After narrating how his administration seemed to usher in the dawn of the Golden Age ('Krita Yuga') he almost ascribes his later fall to his not having got rid of those servants of his, who, in the reign of Chakravarman, had partaken of the leavings of food of the Dombas. His grievance appears to be that though versed in the Vedas and accustomed to the use of earth and water for purification the King did not realise that he was being polluted by his association with persons who had partaken of Domba's food-remnants. He has not told us anywhere if the temple which the Domba queen used to visit had been purified by any rite. Yet he makes up for this lack by informing his readers that fire destroyed the great houses and purified the land (VI, 192). We may conclude that the people of Kashmir, in the time of Kalhana, were not much scandalised by either the touch of Dombas or Svapachas, or even by the acceptance of the food of the aristocratic ones among them. And if they tolerated the visits of the Domba queen to their temples we may conclude that in their view the royal status of a person removed all traditional and hereditary disabilities from him. It is in keeping with this attitude that one finds here and there mentioned the Svapāka soldier and his exploits in archery (V, 218). Still more illuminating is the statement about the doings of Shridev, a village Chandāla, who accompanying the villagers of Suskaletra to the battle between Jayapida and the usurper Jajja (about A.D. 750) killed the latter with a stone from his sling (IV, 473–477). It is no wonder that in a society like that, Chandālas were employed as night watchmen (VI, 77).

Further corroboration of the anomalous position and the ambivalent attitude of Kashmirian society towards Chandālas is afforded by the life and career of a great engineer who lived in the reign of Avantivarman (A.D. 857–884). After the reign of Jayapida, there was a great famine in Kashmir. But Avantivarman, after a long time, was able to restore normalcy through the fortunate circumstance of having in his service a great engineer by name Suyya, who trained the course of a river, put up dams and irrigated a large tract of the country which not only relieved the famine but brought plenty to the Kashmirians (V, 71–102). Suyya's parentage as given by Kalhana is the most interesting part of the story. Suyya was so-called because he was the adopted son of a Chandāla woman named Suyyā. Suyyā while sweeping the streets one day found an earthen pot with a lid on it. Opening the lid she was struck by the sight of a fine baby comfortably sucking its own fingers. Suyyā felt the impulse of a mother towards it. What Suyyā actually did may or may not be what has been described by Kalhana the Brahmin. He assures us that Suyyā arranged the baby's nurture with a Shudra wet-nurse. Though the Brahmin historian is very particular in stating that she did not pollute the infant by her touch, yet, under the circumstances narrated by the historian himself, one is almost certain that Suyyā must have handled the baby. Was it merely because Suyyā was paying the fees to the Shudra wet-nurse for the baby's upkeep that Suyya came to be known after Suyyā and did so much to commemorate her memory in his days of triumph? While trying to answer the query, it is necessary to remember that Suyya not only constructed a bridge and named it after her, but also granted a village to Brahmins and named it Suyyā-kundalā in memory of her. We may conclude that the Kashmirians of the ninth century A.D. were quite willing to give scope to the abilities of a person of unknown parentage and of known Shudra and Chandāla fosterage. That a bridge could be named after a Chandāli, and a village named after her could be accepted as a gift by Brahmins speak of the ambivalent attitude towards these groups postulated above as current in earlier ages. However, not only Chandalas and Doms but Charmakārs, or Chamārs, too, are described as untouchables, 'asprishya' (IV, 55, 65, 76; V, 74; VI, 192; VII, 309, 314).

In Hindusthan proper, however, about a century and a half before Kalhana's time, Alberuni (Vol. I, pp. 101–2), a foreign student of our life and civilization, has left a record of a much different situation. But even that situation as will be manifest is at least slightly different from the one of utter degradation posited by Manu. First, one notes that all the four orders are described not only as living together in the same towns and villages but as also "mixed together in the same housings and lodgings". According to Alberuni's information and findings there were two other classes of people, who were "not reckoned among any caste." The first group noticed by him was formed by people following certain crafts, eight in number, who were grouped together as 'Antyajas'. Within this group, which as a whole, forming eight guilds, had to live near but outside the villages and the towns of the four castes, there were two sub-divisions. Jugglers, basket and shield-makers, sailors, fishermen, and hunters of wild animals and birds, could freely intermarry though they belonged to separate guilds. But none of their members would condescend to have anything to do with the fuller, the shoemaker, and the weaver [the Dhed?]. These latter three, forming the second sub-division of the Antyajas, it appears, would either marry among themselves, or at least had close mutuality.

The sixth class of people, Antyajas being the fifth, had, according to Alberuni, four named groups among them, of which two, viz. Doma (Domba) and Chandāla, are the two groups about which we have known so much from Patanjali, Hemachandra and Kalhana. They were occupied with "dirty work like the cleansing of the villages and other services." They were considered, "as one sole class, and distinguished only by their occupation." The Dom's other occupation was that of the player on the lute and of the singer.

Chandālas as a group have been known from Bengal. In the Census of 1901, at which caste-names and caste-precedence were scrutinized and registered rather minutely, the Chandālas of Bengal, who were otherwise known as Nāmashudras, numbered over 2 million, being the largest caste of East Bengal. Its status was low in social scale, being considered to be a clean untouchable group. It had eight main functional divisions which neither ate nor intermarried among themselves. The agricultural section stood out pre-eminent and the boating division followed. The caste or rather the group was not served by community barbers but by their own castemen working in that capacity. The Brahmins that served it were classed as a degraded Brahmin group.[17] From the Census of 1921 onwards the group has been recorded as Nāmashudra and in the Census of 1931 they numbered 2.1 million. In the Census of 1951 we have the Dom, an unclean untouchable group, alternatively called Chandāla. Yet the Nāmashudra is one of the Scheduled Castes of the Government of India Order. The caste numbered 320 thousand in 1951, in West Bengal. They are now mostly occupied in cultivation and boat-plying. Some of them are carpenters, traders and shopkeepers. "A considerable number now follow the various so-called learned professions." Yet their social position as a caste is very low.[18]

The Chanāl caste of Simla Hills in the Punjab appears to bear similarity of name with the Chandālas but was concerned with skinning of dead animals and leather-working. No other group or caste has been known to have the name of the Chandāla.

The Doms, one of whose occupations has been singing, dancing and playing on instruments in the Punjab, have been carrying on as village sweepers and as workers in cane. But in the Sub-Himalayan districts of Kumaon and Garhwal, Dom lives by agriculture and village handicrafts. In Bengal he forms an immigrant caste introduced there for the specific purpose of the filthiest of work. In Bihar and part of U.P. he is divided into two sections: one, the settled one, being a village worker, mat-weaver and basket-maker "with a little scavenging thrown in"; the other section, a more or less nomadic one, provides gangs, "said to be expert and artistic burglars and thieves". South of the Narmada in the Andhra Pradesh they are weavers of coarse cloth and in the Deccan "acrobats, dancers and bad characters generally". The hill community of the Doms according to Baines "is divided into four groups, field labourers, weavers, and metal workers; cane-workers and the lower artisans; exorcists, porters and leather-workers; and, finally, musicians, mendicants, and tailors". In the Punjab there is another group, slightly differing in name, called Dum, and otherwise known as Mirāsi, who are vocationally minstrels and genealogists, some Jāt families employing them for this purpose. They have also musical pretensions, and their women give dance performances before females. Almost all of them are Muslims. In Bengal there was a section which carried on fishing. In Andhra Pradesh they are found in small numbers under the name of Dombār or Dommāra, which is also the name of a caste in Maharashtra noted for similar attainments.[19]

In 1901 the Doms under all appellations totalled over 850 thousand, being in significantly large numbers only in Bengal and the U.P. In the former they numbered over 350 thousand and in the latter province over 240 thousand. In both regions they were grouped among the unclean untouchables as almost the lowest amongst castes. That they are commonly looked upon as the lowest group in Bengal is evidenced by the fact that the old name of the most despised caste, Chandāla, has been latterly reserved for them. Yet the position of the caste in the Hindu caste hierarchy is by no means so certain. For Baines, a careful ethnographer, could make only the following qualified remark about it: "Here, then, is found a caste which, if not at the bottom of the social scale, is, at least, not far from it."[20]

The Doms ate all manner of unclean food. For them no Brahmin could be found to administer to their religious needs; neither would the common barber nor the common washerman work for them. In 1951 their number in West Bengal was 110 thousand.

The Dom was only one of the castes traditionally concerned with scavenging. The other castes were the Chuhrā in the Punjab, the Bhangi Mehtar in Rajasthan and Bombay, the Bhuinmāli and Hari in Bengal and the Haddi in Orissa. In the South, partly the Mālā in Andhra Pradesh and partly the Paraiyan in Tamilnad carried on scavenging. While the Mālā chiefly was a leather-worker, the Paraiyan, was a field-labourer. Leaving out the Mālā and the Paraiyan, the precise numbers of which castes engaged in scavenging cannot be ascertained, and confining one's attention to those castes which were wholly engaged in scavenging, one finds that in 1901 the latter castes, including the Dom, had together more than 3.6 million members. The largest single caste, ignoring again the Paraiyan and the Mālā, was the Chuhrā of the Punjab, having been over 1.3 million strong.

The Marathi Mahār, the Telugu Mālā and the Tamil Paraiyan, though because of their village menial status are grouped together as field-labourers, conveyed pollution without touch, either at a specific distance or by their shadow, and were classed as impure untouchables. In 1901, they numbered 2.56, 1.86 and 2.26 million respectively. Drumming and playing on pipe-music is one of their side-occupations satisfying one of the needs of village life. No boundary dispute in a village could be finally settled without the help of these castes in their respective regions. More often than not, disposing of the dead cattle of the village was also their duty.

In the current list of Scheduled Castes, Chanāl or Chandāla figures in the States of Madras, Orissa, Punjab and Haryana; and Nāmashudra in Assam and West Bengal. The Dom appears in the States of Bihar, Madras, Orissa, Rajasthan, Uttar Pradesh and West Bengal. The very wide though discontinuous distribution of Chandāla and Dom, two groups which undoubtedly appear to have been ethnic in origin, creates a presumption in favour of the theory that some of the untouchable groups must have originated in the conquest of the natives by the incoming Aryans.

By far the largest group appearing under a single name, though widely distributed, being represented over the whole of the Indo-Aryan area and sporadically even in Madras, is the Chamār or the Chāmbhār, whose name proclaims him to be a worker in leather. We know definitely that under more or less the same name the Chamār's craft flourished in the Vedic age but are not quite sure that it was entirely free from the stigma of despise. Manu[21] speaks of two groups or castes concerned with leather working, both of them being very mixed in origin. Their names are the unfamiliar and non-current Kārāvara and Dhigvana. The former is described in occupational terms as Charmakāra, 'cutter of hide', the origin of the current terms, Chamāra and Chāmbhāra, for the leather-working caste in the Indo-Aryan regions. The Dhigvana's occupation, that of working in leather and trading in leather products, is represented in recent and contemporary society in the above-mentioned regions by the Mochi or Muchi. From the context in Manu's text it is clear that though the groups must have been despised first because of their supposed mixed origin, and second, because of their work in dirty, filthy and impure commodity, yet they were not required to live outside villages or towns.

The Chamār has been one of the village menials in the traditional village economy, entitled to his customary share at the harvest. Though his chief contribution to the life of the village was through his hide and leather working yet he played no mean part in it, as a field-labourer. It was the largest single group going under one name next only to the Brahmin. The Chamār numbered over 11.2 million in 1901, when the Brahmin registered 14.9 million. The largest contingent of Chamārs came from U.P., forming about 52.6 per cent of the total. Mochi or Muchi is more or less an urban caste and not always so designated and separated from the Chamār. But wherever separated it is accorded a higher status. In 1901 only a million persons were registered under this name. The superior status enjoyed by this caste can be clearly seen from the fact that in the Scheduled Castes and Scheduled Tribes Order (Amendment) Act, 1956, the Mochis of Gujarat division had been dropped out of the list of the Scheduled Castes of Bombay State.

The Chamār caste, even in early mediaeval times showed peculiarity, marking it off from the other untouchable classes. Kalhana has proudly narrated (*Rājatarangini*, IV, 58–76) the tale of a 'charmakrit', leather-worker, otherwise called 'padukrit', shoemaker, who lived in the capital city of Kashmir in the reign of King Chandrāpida (A.D. 682). The king had commissioned his officers to build a temple and they had chosen a particular site for it; but when they began to lay out the plan they found that the hut of a Chamār which was coming in the way had to be removed. They argued with him but failed to get him to agree to their proposal for anything. The Chamār boldly sought and got the audience of the king and after delivering a homily on the sanctity of and sentiment for one's home, however tiny, he made the generous gesture of yielding to the king's request and handed over his hut. Risley[22] has told us that in Bengal the Chamārs all trace their descent from Rāidās, a well-known saint and a disciple of the more famous Brahmin saint Rāmānanda. Rāidās must have lived about the end of the fourteenth century. While many Chamārs in U.P. and perhaps Bihar were embracing Rāidāsism, a person who is described as 'mochi', a member of a section of Chamārs, is recorded to have built a temple of Vishnu at Raipur in about A.D. 1415.[23]

A large majority of Bengali Chamārs profess the creed of the Shri-Nārāyana sect and those westwards the Satnāmi sect. The latter was started by a Rajput named Jagjiwan Dās of Bara Banki district in U.P. who died in A.D. 1761. Jagjiwan Dās had prohibited the use of meat, lentils, 'brinjal' (the egg-fruit vegetable) and intoxicating drink. Between A.D. 1820 and 1830 one Ghāsi Dās, a native of Bilaspur district, further reformed the movement by abolishing idol-worship. He exhorted his followers also to stop using cows for cultivation work, ploughing after mid-day, and also taking food to the fields to be consumed there during rest, a sort of a self-respect and social upgrading movement.[24]

Risley tells us that the Chamārs of Bihar are more orthodox in matters of religion than their eastern brethren, some of them having "advanced so far in the direction as to employ Maithil Brahmins for the worship of the regular Hindu gods." The aptitude, and attitude, of the Chamārs and the reformist work of these pioneers must be said to have impressed upon the Chamārs their Hindu loyalty. This fact alone can explain the apparently curious phenomenon that, in spite of egalitarian and communist propaganda the Chamārs of Jaunpur described by B. S. Cohn are moving "directly towards the main stream of the great tradition of orthodox Hinduism."[25]

Among the alternative names assumed by this caste group figure not only Rāmdāsia, Satnāmi and Rāidāsi but also Rohit, Rohidās, Rabidās, Ruidās, Rāmnāmi and Rishi. Though the Chamār is counted among the unclean untouchables because of the fact that the flesh of dead animals or beef or both entered in his diet yet in some parts of the country he used to be served by some kind of a Brahmin.

Hide and leather working has been the traditional occupation of the Mādiga and the Chakkiliyan in the South Together their members numbered over 1.1 million in 1901 A section of the Mālā also carried on this occupation. It is worthwhile noting that in the Vedas the root 'mla' meant 'to tan'.

Above the impure untouchables were the pure untouchables, who had abjured beef and such other anathematic diet and who polluted only by their touch. In the U.P., the Pāsi, who numbered over 1.2 million in 1901, the Kori, who numbered about a million, were the largest single units among the twenty-five or so castes which were listed under this category. In Bihar among the seventeen castes of this group the numerically most important were the Dosādh, over 1.2 million, and the Musāhāra, over 600 thousand. The largest bulk of the castes of this group, numerically speaking, came from Bengal, where among the twenty-five such castes, the Rājbansi Koch, the Nāmashudra already referred to, and the Bāgdi were the largest, having over 2.4 million, over 2 million and over a million members respectively. In West Bengal the Census of 1961 showed the Rājbansis, the Bāgdi and the Nāmashudra as numbering twelve, eleven and seven hundred thousand respectively.

In Madras, the principal castes of this group were the Pallan, the Shānān and the Thiyan, numbering over 800 thousand, over 600 thousand and nearly 600 thousand respectively.

These ten castes were the largest single units each with a million or more members among the two hundred or so castes that were classed as clean untouchables. In 1901 these clean untouchables together numbered about 20 million, and the ten castes specifically mentioned above formed more than 50 per cent of the total.

I shall leave out the Nāmashudra about which caste I have already given some particulars. Of the others, the Rājbansi Koch were grouped by Baines under the category of dominant land-holders. In West Bengal according to the Census of 1961, the Rājbansis numbered somewhat over 700 thousand only and are described as included among the castes "that get the appellation of 'jalia'," among the others figuring Bāgdis, Bauris, Kaivartas. Many of the Rājbansi Koch, though described as an aboriginal cultivating caste, have been putting on the sacred thread to claim Kshatriya status.[26]

The Bihari Musāhāra, the Bengali Bāgdi and the Tamil Pallan, Baines classed as field-labourers. The Musāhāra as his name indicates eats field-rats but the Bengali Bāgdi is believed to be more particular about his diet. The Pallan must be distinguished from the Palli. The latter are classed as Shudras who habitually employ Brahmins and whose touch only slightly pollutes, while the former are grouped with castes which pollute without touch and at a distance.

The Bihari Dosādhs, described as watchmen, are so situated because of their former soldierly tradition and present propensity towards crimes against property. And as not all of them can maintain themselves by this activity a fairly large section is engaged in porterage and daylabour. Baines[27] informs us that the Dosādhs furnished many recruits to the Muslim armies of Bengal and not a few of them fought on the side of Clive in the battle of Plassey.

Some artisan castes have been relegated to the class of pure untouchables in the caste-system. I have here selected the most interesting case of such castes, the one which is perhaps the largest in numbers. It is the Kori of U.P. and Bihar which is described by Baines as the weaver caste of Northern India. The weaver has not been one of the regular officials or menials of the village-community. He has been generally placed above workers in leather and such other impure materials, the Bengali Tānti and perhaps the Maharashtrian Koshti enjoying even higher status. The Kori in particular seem to have connection with the leather-working caste as the names of their sub-sections show.[28]

The remaining three castes, the Pāsi, the Thiyan and the Shānān, are some of the toddy-tapping castes of the country. The Pāsi, the largest among them, have their concentration in U.P. but are also met with in Bihar. Their traditional occupation is believed to be toddy-tapping, the name having been derived from the word 'pāsa' meaning 'a noose', 'a loop', the rope-belt which the members use as foot-rest while climbing up the palms. The same occupation was carried on on the south-western coast by the Thiyan, the 'southerner', and by the Shānān in the extreme south and the south-east. The name Shānān appears to be a comparatively recent innovation. Anyway in the region in which the Shānārs are found, an inscription of the 11th century A.D. mentions the Idiga and the Iluvan as the toddy-tapping castes. The word Shānān or Shānār is tried to be derived from either the Sanskrit 'shoundika' or from a Tamil word meaning 'the learned', 'the noble'.[29]

The Shānān have resented for nearly a century the low status accorded to them. In 1874 they appear to have first attempted militant assertion of their dislike of the status assigned to them by attempting to enter the Minākshi temple at Madura, entry to temples having been prohibited to them and to the other castes of their status.[30]

Such are the principal castes that made up the group of untouchables and unapproachables. In 1901 the whole group totalled 53.2 million and formed 27.4 per cent of the Hindus of the then India. After 1911 till 1914 half a dozen estimates of the persons belonging to the untouchable or exterior or excluded castes were made and are presented in the report of the Franchise or the Lothian Commission which worked in connection with the Simon Commission and its report, leading to the Government of India Act, 1935. They vary widely from one another and as they were made with an eye on the political representation of these people I have left them out. The Census of 1951 has provided us its total enumeration of all the persons belonging to those castes specified in the relevant Constitution Order as Scheduled Castes. They numbered 51.3 million and formed 16.9 per cent of the Hindu population of India—Bharat. In 1961 the Scheduled Castes population numbered 64.5 million and formed 14.69 per cent of the total population of the country.

As pointed out in an earlier chapter it was perhaps Jotiba Phooley of Poona who was the pioneer in modern times of the movement calculated to improve the condition of and to secure social equality to the erstwhile untouchable and unapproachable classes. V. R. Shinde, the twentieth century torchbearer of Phooley spirit, has stated[31] that the Bengali Brahmin Shashipada Bandyopadhyaya started his uplift work among the labourers of Baranagar, among whom untouchables seem to have figured, in 1865. But definite mention of Bandyopadhyaya's relations with the Chandālas occurs in Shinde's account of the progressive Brahmin's work in 1870. He, we are informed, used to attend the religious discourses current among one sect of the Chandālas. In later years he used to dine with them and nurse their children.

The Maharashtrian Brahmin-scholar, R. G. Bhandarkar, appears to have gone a step further, though perhaps fifteen to twenty years later. In his presidential address to the Ninth Indian Social Conference held in 1895 he makes an incidental reference to the touching references made by a Mahār religious preacher, 'kirtankāra', to the treatment accorded to the untouchables and the great work of the saints, particularly of the Brahmin Eknāth, in their cause, in his discourse which was given in the house of R. G. Bhandarkar. Bhandarkar invited the Mahār religious preacher to deliver a religious discourse at his house before 1890 and opined that the Mahārs had good deal of natural intelligence and were capable of being highly educated.[32]

The next landmark in the ameliorative movement is the starting of the Depressed Classes Mission in Bombay by V. R. Shinde and his work for that society. He toured over the whole country addressing meetings in towns, exhorting people to help the untouchables to rise socially and educationally, and making notes of the actual conditions of their life. I had the good fortune to be present at some of his appealing lectures at Junagad in Saurashtra in the year 1910–11.

From 1924, and perhaps also earlier, Mahatma Gandhi took up the cause and made it a plank in his political platform. The great endeavour of eradicating this feature of the social life of India which the national Government has embarked upon during the last ten or twelve years stems from his teaching.

But before Gandhi's advent on the Indian political horizon, something was being done by the then government of the country. In an earlier chapter, I have stated the principal steps taken since 1858. It is seen that some really effective measures began to be taken only after the Reforms of 1918. A complete account of such steps is both impracticable and unnecessary. Some representative data will be laid out to enable readers to form a relative estimate of the measures taken before the achievement of Independence. In 1901, U.P. with 10 million untouchables, and Madras with 9.4 million stood second and third respectively among the provinces in the matter of number of untouchables. The then Bengal with 10.9 million untouchables led all. In 1951 West Bengal with 4.7 million Scheduled caste people stood fourth in the list, Bihar with 5.1 million taking the third place. U.P. with its 11.5 million Scheduled caste people and Madras with its 8.5 million towered over all the others. The surprising fact revealed by the Census of 1961 is that in Madras (Tamilnad) the 79 castes listed as Scheduled according to the President's Order showed an almost 25 per cent decrease in their population and registered only 6.07 million (*Madras*, VA i; pp. 10, 17) members. In West Bengal, on the other hand, the 63 Scheduled Castes numbered 6.9 million souls.

Some facts about educational conditions of these castes in the last two States before the Government of India Act, 1935 will be found enlightening. The memorandum submitted to the Indian Statutory Commission by the Government of the United Provinces states[33] that special efforts to encourage the education of the depressed classes were made "in the latter part of the quinquennium 1916–17 to 1921–22". The size of the special efforts can be judged from the fact that in 1927 the sum set apart for the-purpose was Rupees one and a half lakhs. In detailing the educational progress of these classes the memorandum has to begin with the primary education at which stage alone a fair number of pupils of these castes could be met with. As regards the state of further education the memorandum states that whereas in 1921–22 there were 392 and 7 pupils respectively at the middle and high school stages and none either at the collegiate stage or in normal schools and teacher's training classes, in 1926–27 there were 1,359 and 41 at the first two stages and 11 at the intermediate, 4 at the post-intermediate and 29 in normal schools and teacher's training classes. These figures and the information conveyed by them the authors of the memorandum prefaced with the words: "Even in higher education these classes have been making head-way". The memorandum submitted by Madras Government[34] records, besides the progress of these classes at the primary stage of education, the number of their pupils reading in secondary schools. Whereas in 1921–22 there were 1,217 of them, in 1926–27 they were 2,647. The Madras Government had also opened two hostels at its own cost to lodge and board students of these classes desirous of taking higher education and to support them in the educational institutions. It brought pressure to bear on the managers of institutions and the local public to admit pupils of these classes into schools not specially intended for them. As a result, the number of such pupils rose from 4,630 in 1920–21 to 16,486 in 1926–27.

I have stated some of the provisions of the Constitution in this behalf. In accordance with one of them the President of India appointed L. M. Shrikant as the Commissioner for Scheduled Castes and Scheduled Tribes towards the end of 1950. He issued his first report, that for 1951, in 1952 and has been issuing an annual report since then, giving the organizational set-up and other matters connected with his duties as well as a full account of the money grants and expenditure and the nature of activities financed by them and the organizations handling them. He was assisted in his onerous responsibilities by six assistant commissioners, one at the headquarters and five at different regional centres. His report for the year 1954, Appendix XII (p. 366), gives the distribution of funds amongst Scheduled Castes and other backward classes students pursuing post-matriculation education from 1944–45 to 1953–54. According to that statement in 1945–46 Rs. 2,21,000 in round numbers were allocated—and I take it spent too—to the post-matriculate students of the Scheduled Castes, while in 1953–54 the sum for them was Rs. 26,86,000, a phenomenal increase! In 1959–60 (Ninth Report, App. XVII), the total expenditure on this head rose to more than 1,43,84,000. Appendix XIII gives the total number of these scholars in 1954–55 to be 10,392. In 1963–64 the expenditure on the post-matriculate scholarships account came to Rs. 2.93 crores (29.3 million), the number of scholars being 60,157 (Appendix VII, *Thirteenth Report* of the Commissioner of Scheduled Castes and Scheduled Tribes).

The result of the national endeavour is already reflected in the live registers of the employment exchanges. On the last day of 1954, there were 3,670 technicians, 747 teachers, 15 doctors and 6 engineers among the 59.637 seekers of employment from the Scheduled Castes (Appendix XI). On 31st December 1959, there were 6,191 technicians, 2,852 teachers, 4 doctors and 5 engineers among the 1,71,295 persons registered for employment. In 1963 as many as 461 thousand applicants were registered and 60,954 were placed in employment (*Thirteenth Report* p. 174).*

---

* Further break-up of the figures is not available.

Besides the amount spent on scholarships, the Union Government spends a huge sum on projects and activities designed to remove untouchability and to effect the welfare of the Scheduled Castes. The total expenditure incurred for this purpose in 1952–53 was Rs. 28.5 million and that in 1954–55 Rs. 37.3 million, the increase of about 31 per cent in two years testifying to the grand scale of the national endeavour. In 1963–64 the expenditure having amounted to Rs. 69.4 millions showed an increase of 86 per cent (*Eighth Report*, p. 29).

As stated in an earlier chapter, State legislatures passed certain legislative measures for the removal or rather for counteracting the disabilities of untouchability. That activity went on after Independence with great regularity and zeal. The crowning glory of it is the Untouchability (Offences) Act, 1955, or Act No. XXII of 1955, being the first direct step taken by the Central Government against untouchability. Under it enforcement of religious disabilities such as non-access to places of worship, etc., or of social disabilities like non-access to shops, watering places, etc., or abetment of such is a cognisable offence punishable with imprisonment for up to six months and/or with fine of up to Rs. 500 and cancellation or suspension of licences and public grants.

It prescribes punishment also for any indirect support of untouchability such as social boycott or excommunication of persons who refuse to practise untouchability. The Act provides for a severe onslaught on any clandestine practice of untouchability in its Section 12. It lays down that where any of the forbidden practices, such as those mentioned above, is committed in respect of a member of a Scheduled Caste it shall be presumed that the act was committed on the ground of "untouchability", unless it is proved to the contrary.

During the seven years, 1956 to 1962, as many as 3,596 offences under this Act were reported to the Police, 3,106 or 86.4 per cent of which were proceeded with; and out of these 2,097 were disposed of, resulting in only 600 acquittals from among them (*Eighth Report*, p. 22).

The legislative, administrative and executive part of the nation has thus implemented the national pledge made in the Constitution that Untouchability is hereby abolished and has given a thundering proof of its serious purpose. But readers of this book need not be told that the legislative measures against untouchability can at best produce a few dents in the solid wall, whose demolition requires the operation of an active sentiment of the people at large. To illuminate the subject it is then necessary to know how the people at large have been behaving.

When the untouchables of a village in Hamirpur district in U.P., on the orders of their caste panchayat, declined to do the scavenging for the village, the other menials and officials of the village community retaliated by refusing their customary services to the untouchables and brought them round to revoke their decision. In the village of Kakori near Lucknow when the barbers refused to shave the untouchables the latter threatened to down brooms. The caste Hindus of Top, a village eighteen miles from Kolhapur on the Poona-Bangalore road, resented the action of Government in granting land for cultivation to the local Harijan Co-operative Farming Society and when the grass raised in the land was getting ready they entered the fields and destroyed several cart-loads of it. The festivities of the colourful event of Dasara in Mysore in 1953 had to be curtailed owing to a dispute between caste Hindu wrestlers and the State Minister for Law on the score of allowing wrestlers of Scheduled Castes to enter the same arena where the caste Hindu wrestlers were to show their skill and prowess. The latter would not agree to the Minister's permission to Scheduled Caste wrestlers and the Scheduled Castes would not give up their newly won right.[35]

In Agadgaon, a village in Ahmednagar district, as a consequence of some altercation between a member of the Scheduled Castes and two caste Hindus, evidently on the score of appropriately respectful behaviour of the former towards the latter, in 1955 caste Hindus raided the houses of the members of the Scheduled Castes, seriously injuring thirty of their men and women. When the Bambhis, the hide-cutting caste of Rajasthan, of Mathania, a village near Jodhpur, refused their customary service of removing the dead cattle of the village, caste Hindus organised a social boycott. At Barabanki in U.P. the scavengers sensing the new potentialities decided to have a shave by the village-barbers. The latter hesitated and the former downed their brooms in the barbers' quarters but to no purpose. We are told that the attempts at rapprochement of the district authorities did not bear fruit. The Mālās of Nelapatla village in Khammam taluka of Hyderabad refused to allow a bridegroom of the Mādigas, another Scheduled Caste, to proceed on horseback. There was a serious clash in which even spears were used.

When Kaloo Ram, a Brahmin of Halia Kheri, a village in Bhopal and a former sarpanch of the place, participated in an inter-caste dinner, both his castemen and the barbers of the place boycotted him; and the panchayat ordered him to pay Rs. 100 for arranging a caste dinner after his purification. Chhita Lala, a Scheduled Caste member when attending the meeting of the village council of Sampla in Baroda, of which he was a member, sat facing the caste Hindu members; but the latter felt so insulted at his "insolent" behaviour that they harassed him till he left the village.

When in March 1956 some members of the Scheduled Castes began to draw water from a public well in Jeel village in Nagaur district of Jodhpur some Jāts attacked them and beat them off. When the police arrested five of the alleged assailants, about a thousand Jāts raided the Collector's office at Nagaur. There had to be a lathi charge to disperse the crowd. Five constables and thirty Jāts were injured in the fracas. In May in the village of Umbhrai, about forty-two miles from Thana, when there was acute shortage of water two social workers who went there to persuade the caste Hindus to allow the members of the Scheduled Castes to draw water from the village well had to return injured in the fight that took place at the well. At Kulasekaranatham, a hamlet about twenty-five miles from Tirunelveli, landlords attacked their Scheduled Caste tenants when the latter attempted to plough certain fields over which they claimed cultivation rights, and later burned twenty-seven houses and thirty hay-ricks belonging to the Scheduled Castes. Shri Atmaram, the Patel of Ranitarai in Balod Tahsil of Raipur district and a Scheduled Caste member, got it proclaimed by the beating of drum that practice of untouchability was an offence under the Act referred to above. The caste Hindus of the place resented his action so much that they harassed him and forced him to leave the village with his family.[36]

For a fortnight between May 21 and June 9 in 1957 over a wide area of 100 to 150 square miles round about Jagatsingpur the Orissa Scheduled Castes of Doms and Pāns were being harassed in various ways including burning of their huts and beating them up. It was a systematic and planned affair, "courts" being held and notices being given in advance. Murder of a whole family of four persons in Santhalpur on June 3 was reported to the State Assembly by the Home Minister.[37] An earlier instance of vendetta against the Pāns is recorded by F. G. Bailey[38] which report I record here for the interesting and instructive development it led to. In 1948 the Pāns of Boad attempted to enter the Kondmals temple just outside the Bisipara village. The other 'clean' castes of the village under the leadership of the 'Warrior' caste objected and placed armed men round the temple, threatening to kill any Pān who dared to cross over into the temple. The police called to help the Pāns could not do anything and the Pāns decided to drop the idea never to repeat it. They went on worshipping at the temple through the mediacy of Brahmins for some time. Later they built their own temple dedicated to the same deity that is the presiding deity of the Kondmals temple. And there "rites parallel to those carried on in the main temple are performed by one of their own men, a schoolmaster".

Bailey assures us that the step has not excited division nor has the propriety or impropriety of the new temple been much discussed. The schoolmaster who officiates as the priest at the new temple "is regarded by the Warriors as a modest, learned and decent man".

At Borsal near Burhanpur in Madhya Pradesh in a quarrel that ensued on refusal of a shopkeeper to sell 'bidies' (leaf cigarettes) to a Scheduled Caste person a child was killed and 16 persons injured and property worth Rs. 1,000 was damaged.[39]

On the 22nd February 1959 in Sardar Vallabhbhai Patel's own district, the chosen district of Mahatma Gandhi, i.e. Kaira, occurred an incident which more than anything else brings out the extraordinarily difficult nature of the problem that faces the country in this matter. As part of the programme of the campaign for the removal of untouchability the local Congress leader, a prominent Brahmin lady, proposed a dip in the holy pond at Lasundra by the local members of the Scheduled Castes, a bold move indeed but too much of a frontal attack. The lady, perhaps with laudable object of publicizing the event, got together a crowd of 300 members of the Scheduled Castes and formed a procession with herself, the Collector of the district and his Deputy and some members of the Legislative Assembly of Bombay at the head and started for the destination, the holy pond. On the way a crowd of caste Hindus armed with all kinds of weapons—there were a number of armed women in the crowd—blocked the way so effectively that the leaders of the procession quietly persuaded the processionists to disperse. The leading lady and some of her Congress colleagues announced their intention "to go on a three day fast of atonement" and the incident evidently was closed.[40]

On the night of August 29, 1960 a frenzied mob of Leva Kunbis of the village of Salve in Erandol taluka shouting slogans demanding the extermination of the Pārdhi community massacred eight people of that community. One of the accused was a former Block Development Officer.[41]

In September 1962 in the village of Jhandi near Patiala a quarrel ensued between Jāt landowners and some Scheduled caste persons who, on the advice of the 'sārpanch', had begun cultivation work on a plot of the village common land. One Jāt and two Scheduled Caste persons were killed.[42]

At mid-day on September 4, 1962 at Kacchotia in Rajgarh district, Madhya Pradesh, a mob of 100 to 125 caste Hindus attacked some Scheduled caste people working in their field and killed four of them and caused hurt to some others. It was a case of vendetta for two attempts of some Scheduled caste people to force entry into the village temple.[43]

In Etawah district, U.P., the two Scheduled caste students who had secured admission to the Government College hostel were greeted with brickbats and cat calls when they entered the hostel in August 1963. Later, the students were dragged out by the inmates of the hostel and beaten.[44]

In Shirasgaon, a village thirtyfive miles from Aurangabad in Maharashtra, four Scheduled caste ladies were stripped naked and after being paraded through the streets were mercilessly beaten. The village with a population of 600 had only three families of the Scheduled castes. The action was supposed to be a vendetta for an alleged criminal assault on a caste Hindu girl by the husband of one of the ladies. Needless to say the whole population must have connived at the brutally barbarous action and also that the Scheduled caste families left the village in post-haste.[45] Later in the year, in July the entire population of Scheduled castes of a village in Sangrur district in the Punjab having had the misfortune of being suspected to have not voted in favour of the sarpanch in the panchayat elections was "virtually" hounded out of the village. It was, it would appear, eventually readmitted at the intervention of the then Union Home Minister, G. L. Nanda.[46] Still later in the year two districts in Maharashtra, Akola and Buldana, recorded attacks, murders, and arson against Scheduled caste people. However, for a change, caste Hindus were the worse for it in the Buldana district fracas, the Scheduled castes of the locality there being numerous and energized by their conversion to Buddhism.[47]

In 1966 Kolhapur district very near the cultural centre of Maharashtra recorded a vendetta on the Scheduled castes for an altogether new type of grievance. It is reported that they refused to supply firewood for the Holi-fire of the village and were visited with the consequence of having to see their houses set on fire.[48]

While these gruesome events reveal the persistence of the occasional but darkest feature of the situation of the Scheduled castes, daily and routine life of the village registers fair amount of segregation and contemptuous treatment offered by the people at large. Panchayat members of these castes are "not permitted to sit on cots or carpets along with their colleagues",[49] a situation which is poignantly similar to that registered in some seventeenth century records hailing from Tamilnad which I have mentioned in the first chapter on the authority of John Matthai!

The noble Constitution of India which has outlawed untouchability has also provided for certain strategic vantage ground being placed at the disposal of these erstwhile untouchable classes. But they are of such a nature and are so bound with somewhat similar positions of some other classes that they are best considered together in one context, that of the endeavour of securing a casteless society. And that is the subject matter of the last chapter.

References

1. A. B. Keith, *Vedic Index*, "Shudra"; *Shatapatha Brāhmana*, XIV, 1, 1; Eggeling's trans., V, p. 446. *Panchavimsa Brāhmana*, VI, 1, 11. 2. *Loc. cit.*, V, 8, 13. 3. I, 10, 1–5. 4. V, 24, 1–5. 5. V, 10, 7. 6. *Baudhāyana,* I, 8; *Gautama*, IV, 16–18, 28; *Vasishtha*, XVIII; cf. *Manu*, X, 47, 7. 7. *Kautilya* in Shama sastri's trans., pp. 209–10; R. P. Kangle's trans., pp. 244–49. 8 *Vasishtha*, XVIII, 3; XXVI, 13; *Baudhāyana*, 1, 8, 9, 11; *Manu* X, 19, 37–39, 51. 9. Shamasastri's trans., p. 210; Kangle's trans., p. 248.

10. Panini, III, I, 134. 11. Op.cit., X, 51–6. 12. I, 21, 15. 13. Amba Uddālaka, Kunāliya, Khandahāla, Chittasambhuta and Mātanga Jatakas. 14. Sachau's trans., vol. I, pp. 101–2. 15. 2nd ed., pp. 152, 161–2. 16. *Rājatarangini*, R. S. Pandit's trans, pp. 183–8, Text, IV, 473–77; V, 71–120, 128; VI. 69. 17. *India Census*, 1901, vol. I. p. 542. 18. *The Tribes and Castes of Bengal*, 1953, pp. 72, 75; Dutt, N. K., II, 146–56. 19. Baines, pp. 63, 84–5, 106, 108.

20. Ibid., p. 84. 21. X, 36, 49. 22. *Tribes and Castes*, I. p. 176. 23. *Ep. Ind.*, II, p. 229. 24. Risley, *Tribes and Castes*, I, p. 178; Russell and Hiralal, I, pp. 307–09. 25. Risley, loc. cit., p. 179; McKim Marriott, p. 75. 26. *Bengal Census Rep*., 1921. pp. 358, 366. 27., Op. cit., p. 82. 28. Baines, p. 63. 29. Vide "asprishyata" in *Jnānakosha* (in Marathi) by S. V. Ketkar.

30. *Madras Government Memorandum to the Indian Statutory Commission*, pp. 596–98. 31. V. R. Shinde, *Asprishyatecha Prashna* (The Problem of Untouchability) (In Marathi), pp. 56–90, 215. 32. R. G. Bhandarkar's Collected Works, vol. II, p. 491. 33. Pp. 397–98. 34. Pp. 559–60. 35. *The Times of India*, 27-7-53; 13-8-53; 7-10-53. 36. *The Times of India*, 13-1-55, 22-4-55; 29-3-55; 12-5-55; 18-5-55; 19-5-55; 11-11-55. 37. *The Times of India*, 2-3-56; 2-5-56; 20-5-56; 3-7-56. 38. *The Times of India*. 19-6-57. 39. Bailey, I, pp. 215–22.

40. *The Times of India*, 28, 29-4-58. 41. *The Times of India*, 24-2-59. 42. *The Times of India*, 4-1-61. 43. *The Times of India*, 21-9-62. 44. *The Times of India*, 20-5-63. 45. *The Times of India*, 31-8-63. 46. *The Times of India*, 4-1-64. 47. *The Times of India*, 28-7-64. 48. *The Times of India*, 4-12-64. Current Topics. 49. *The Times of India*, 12-3-66. Current Topics.

50. *The Times of India*, 12-9-66, the leading article 'Mockery'.

12

Caste and Politics: General

In the first edition of this book published in 1932, there were two chapters, the last two, together making up more than a fifth of the book. They were headed 'Caste, Recent and Contemporary' and 'Conclusions'. In the present edition the material is divided between chapters ten, thirteen and fourteen. As the book happened to be in an international series and was published by Messrs Kegan Paul & Co., it had the chance of receiving a review in *Man* (1932, p. 268), the monthly Journal of the Royal Anthropological Institute of Great Britain. The reviewer, after pointing out defects which did not exist in the book, and paying the book some almost left-handed praise, concluded his script with the remark: "The last two chapters have rather a political or semi-political, trend, and so need not be discussed here."

Almost a year later the only Indian Anthropological journal, *Man in India* (1933, p. 65), carried an unsigned review of the book. The Indian reviewer with more praise for the book gave what appears to me to be a shorter shift to the two chapters mentioned above. He stated that they dealt with "somewhat controversial questions of the present and the future of caste in India", and as such "need not be dwelt upon in the review".

I wrote to the editor of *Man*, Sir John L. Myres, a letter mildly protesting against the reviewer's cavalier fashion treatment of the last two chapters. He published an explanatory note in *Man* mentioning some of the points I had made against the reviewer's statement. As regards my main contention, that pertaining to the last two chapters, his note reads: "He (Ghurye) regrets that the reviewer refrained from comment on the last two chapters of the bock dealing with the 'changes that have come about in the institution of caste as a result of the conditions created by contact with European culture and political domination by the British', on the ground of their 'political and semi-political trends'. This, however, under the constitution of the Institute, was inevitable."

F. G. Pratt was the only one of the many reviewers that handled this book who appreciated the two chapters. He said in his review published in *International Affairs* (November, 1932): "In the two closing chapters of this book Mr. Ghurye describes the modern forms of this ancient institution which still maintains its hold. . . . Legislative and administrative policy in relation to caste is not the least of the many great problems which future Governments of India will have to face."

Even the highly appreciative reviewer of the book concluded his script in the *Literary Supplement of The Times* London (November, 1932) prefacing his final laudatory remark with "Politics apart".

---

* The substance of this and the following chapter was made public through the observations which I made, while inaugurating the Conference of Indian Sociologists held in Bombay on the 14th of October 1967, making a plea for the cultivation of a branch of Sociology to be styled 'Political Sociology'.

Study of political developments in social institutions was thus out of bounds for social anthropologists in the early thirties. I think the first breakthrough from this stifling cordon was registered, ironically enough, by a British anthropologist and that, too, from the University of Cambridge, whose Department of Anthropology was presided over and directed, for more than two decades, by retired British Civil Servants of British India. It tickled me to note that the particular piece of work was published in the pages of the big brother of the monthly *Man, the Journal of the Royal Anthropological Institute*, when a retired British Indian Civil servant was its President! Perhaps the constitutional embargo of the Institute had vanished with the British Empire in 1947!

Kathleen Gough investigated the changing kinship usages among the Nāyars of Malabar in the setting not only of economic but of political changes, between 1947 and 1949, and published the results in 1952. My interest in kinship systems and terminologies has been rather old and I have been following it up from time to time. About the time Gough's paper appeared in the Journal I was preparing the manuscript of my book *Family and Kin in Indo-European Culture*. Only a year before Gough's investigation had started, I had published a rather longish paper entitled *Kinship Usages as Reflected in Indo-Aryan Literature*. And Politics, whether resulting from or conditioning social systems, had led me to expound the political developments in the caste system that were taking place during more than half a century before 1930. I therefore avidly read through Gough's paper. I am sorry to record that I was disappointed. There I found assertions about political events and economic factors having caused changes, the changes themselves being not clearly recorded. And I was struck by Gough's nonchalance at Ignoring and even misunderstanding the Nambudiri Brahmin's social organization, the changes that were coming about in it and its intertwining with Kshatriya and Nāyar life. If she had given these factors their due consideration she would have seen that economic and cultural factors were common to both communities and that the special political factor present in the Nayār community could not alone be credited with whatever change in kinship pattern that had occurred!

M. S. A. Rao, one of my research students, had already written his thesis on *Social Change in Malabar* and I knew that his careful study of kinship terminology of Malabar would contradict some statements that Gough had made about kinship terminology. Rao published the work in 1957. The Malayalam kinship terminology which he has given there, even after noting Gough's work, does not fully support Gough's contention.

Gough took ten years more to enlighten her readers more fully on the subject of her enquiry through her papers contributed to a seminar on matriliny published in 1961 as *Matrilineal Kinship* (pp. 317–23, 344, 372, 383) edited by David M. Schneider and herself. There she explains the political aspect which affected the Nāyars in about A.D. 1800. And that was the disbanding of the Nāyar militia by the British. She also states that among the Nambudiris only the eldest son was ordinarily allowed to marry within the caste.

Rao's above-mentioned work (pp. 189–90) shows that the social malaise of the traditional Malabar society had begun about A.D. 1743. The Cochin ruler's restrictions coming later hastened the breakdown. The unrest among the Nambudiris, too, must have counted for a bit. The strain of keeping away the younger males of the caste from the Nambudiri females combined with the problem of the ageing spinsters did count for something, for some atmosphere of needed change!

In 1954, H. N. Stevenson, in the midst of his endeavour establishing the proposition that status in the Indian caste-system was ritual ranking, suddenly felt interested in tracing "the connection between the introduction of voting systems (municipal and otherwise) by the British in India and the emergence of caste *sabhās* as political organisms." Making the point in a footnote (J.R.A.I:, p. 49, 1) he graciously referred to my work stating that I had therein noted that "the creation of *sabhās* has not lessened jāti differences". At the bottom of the previous page of Stevenson's essay, in the 3rd footnote, he quoted, the well-known opinion of Mahatma Gandhi about *varnadharma* as distinct from current caste and supporting the former even in modern conditions. As his comment on the Mahatma's view Stevenson made the following remark: "This statement appears to postulate a sort of hereditary trades-unionism freed from the caste restrictions of pollution, endogamy, and commensality", and casually added in brackets, "See also the views of Ghurye, 1932 and Radhakrishnan, 1947, (183–5)."

The last casual mention does me injustice. It suggests as if my view was very much like that of Mahatma Gandhi. And as no page reference is provided by Stevenson, readers have no ready reference to check up my views.

My view of Mahatma Gandhi's *varnadharma* was very critical and was expounded in two or three pages (182–184) ending with a reference to A. J. Toynbee's criticism of Plato's fourfold ideal society. And it is in that connection that, on page 183–84, the page which Stevenson mentions as his authority for my view that "the creation of *sabhās* has not lessened jāti-differences", I observed: "Altogether it appears to us that a return to the fourfold division of society is impracticable. . . . And, as pointed out in the last chapter caste-consciousness becomes more definite and virile. We have seen that even among the castes which are grouped together for political purposes, the common purpose of fighting other castes has not proved strong enough to induce individual castes, comprised in the group, to ignore their claims at the time of the distribution of the spoils of office."

As for Stevenson's desire to know whether the Sabhās came to be organised first at the introduction of elected local self-government by the British I may point out that as far as caste consciousness in matters of election is concerned I had already pointed out that in Bombay Province at least it became manifest in the elections of second half of the third decade of the twentieth century. Stevenson's call did not, or even has not, produced much earlier evidence so far. In the 1955 collection of village studies, *Village India* edited by McKim Marriott, the essay on Madhopur Chamārs by B. S. Cohn (p. 66) contains the information that in the twentieth century only a nominated village panchāyat for local self-government was introduced in Madhopur, a village in Jaunpur District. It was only "in the twenties" of the century that elections for the District Board came to be held (p. 69); for though these Boards were introduced in the eighties of the nineteenth century their composition was so limited and circumscribed that open and free elections cannot be posited in their case."

If Stevenson wanted to know the beginnings of political consciousness on caste lines he could have known it from my book under reference as at least dating back to about eighteen seventies as far as Government jobs were concerned. The kind of caste sabhās Stevenson has in view came to be formed much later for political purposes. They are caste-alliances and not caste 'sabhās'. Caste sabhās, i.e. combined association of a number of sub-castes of one caste began to be formed in Maharashtra at least in the eighties of the last century and became common by the end of the first decade of the twentieth century. The Deccan Sabha, a politico-economic association started by Justice M. G. Ranade and the Satyashodhak Samaj founded by Jotiba Phooley were the inspirers of these *sabhās*. Kshātraikya Sabha, i.e. the Association for the unification of all Kshatriyas, was started by Vanamali, in whose honour there is a public hall at Dadar in Bombay, in A.D. 1885. The object of these 'sabhās' was to reunite the sub-castes of a caste and carry on propaganda for the acquisition of higher social status than was generally accorded to the caste. Their further ramifications into entire community-like organizations was fully dealt with by me in the chapter entitled 'The Future of Caste' and is now elaborated in the chapter headed 'A Casteless Society or a Plural Society?'

The political development of caste i.e. the alliances of certain castes against certain others to gain political power, as has been contended by me since the first edition of the book in 1932, is in large measure, the consequence of the British handling of the caste situation with a parochial viewpoint!

Gough's second, more extended and more pronounced venture into Political Sociology is her study of Kumbapettai, a village in Tanjore district. In parts at least it appears to have more Politics in it than pure Political Sociology. In her 1955 contribution, entitled 'The Social Structure of a Tanjore Village', in Marriott's *Village India* she essayed a political analysis of the caste structure of the village. I found it interesting in itself and also because it proves to be a further step on the road that I had taken almost a quarter of a century before. This village having Brahmins as the dominant caste, where the Brahmins still hold two-thirds of the total land, and where "rights of land management might not be sold at all to persons of other castes", I think stands alone among the many villages that have been surveyed up and down the country. Even among the four Tanjore villages that have received the solicitous attentions of the 1961 Census, there is none which has a considerable number of Brahmin families in it. And Tanjore District as Gough informs her readers had about 200 thousand Brahmins in 1951, having administrative rights in about nine hundred villages (I, 37). The Brahmins formed about one-fifteenth of the total population of the district.

Gough added to our knowledge of the socio-political situation in the village by two more contributions. In 1956 she published, in *American Anthropologist*, her second contribution in the form of a paper entitled 'Brahmin Kinship in a Tamil Village'. In 1960 appeared her third and the largest contribution on the subject in *Aspects of Caste, Cambridge Papers in Social Anthropology*. No. 2, edited by E. R. Leach, Reader in Social Anthropology in the University of Cambridge. This marks the second stage of the break-through, a Cambridge Social Anthropologist having indulged in the handling of Political Sociology in a Classical University's publication in Social Anthropology! Caste in a Tanjore Village', as the contribution is headed, carries the political analysis in terms of caste to its logical end.

Gough's naming of her paper in the *American Anthropologist* as Brahmin Kinship makes it the first castewise specification of kinship. If it should prove to be a reality it must be counted as a valuable discovery in the field of kinship and an important element in Political Sociology.

Only three years before Gough's paper in the *American Anthropologist* Irawati Karve had published her book *Organization of Kin in India* (1953). Her lists of kin nomenclature showed no signs of any castewise difference. And she had assured her readers that she had collected her kin terms, including of course the Tamil ones, from many castes. Gough tells us clearly that the Brahmin kin terms are in some items different from those of the lower castes and lists the whole terminology, putting the headings of Brahmin and Low Castes to the two columns which carry the terms separately (*American Anthropologist*, 1956). It is clear, however, from her discussion that the kin nomenclature current among the Vellālas is likely to be more after the pattern of that of the Brahmins than that of the Pallans, who are the low castes of Gough's Kumbapettai. And it is my surmise, on reading between the lines, that there might be a bridge covering the gulf between the Brahmin-Vellāla kin-nomenclature and the Pallan Paraiyan (?) one, provided by kin terms current among the intermediate groups, like the Pallis, the Idaiyans, the Kammalans!

The most significant terms providing the supposed contrast are some of those relatives who are known as affinal in other kin-terminologies. I shall here pick out only four terms, in order not to encumber the discussion with too much detail, which might appear too technical for students of caste, and present them in tabular form.

It is seen that the differences in the lists of the investigators are great. The state of the last three terms as reported by Gough is favourable to her double thesis. First it differentiates the Brahmin from the Low Caste in the first term; second, the last term, i.e. its absence, helps the argument regarding the patrilineal lineage group being not very strong. The second term, which is quite clearly a Sanskrit loan word 'nanāndri' suitably modified, in so far as it is used by both the groups for a woman's brother's wife and not for husband's sister, emphasizes the same fact of weakness or shallowness of the patrilineal lineage group. In so far as Morgan's list of 1870 gives the Tamil term for Husband's Brother's Wife though in the slightly variant form "Orakatti", Gough's list must very definitely be described as faulty or defective. That Gough should not have noted the difference is surprising, especially as she is so conversant with changes that have been taking place during the last eighty years or so. To make matters still worse, in a slightly variant form a term for husband's brother's wife is attested in a Tamil folksong, and that, too, current among the non-Brahmins. The term is "oppadiyal" [Srinivas, (2), II, 67].

	Terms			
Investigator	*Korundan or Koluntan*	*Kolunti or Koluntai*	*Natanar or Nattanar*	*Orpadi*
Karve	Husband; Husband's Younger Brother; Younger Sister's Husband.	Father's Sister's Daughter; Mother's Brother's Daughter; Younger Brother's Wife.	Husband's Sister; Son's wife's mother; Daughter's Husband's Mother.	Husband's Brother's Wife.
Gough	Husband's Younger Brother (Brahmin & Low Caste, the latter with a slight verbal difference making it 'Korundanar'); Husband's Elder Brother.	Wife's Younger Sister (low caste only, the form being 'Korundiyar')	Brother's wife (woman speaking) (Brahmin & Low caste)	Not found

In the case of Karve, the two middle terms as discovered by her are supportive of her particular thesis about kin and organization of kin among Dravidian-speaking peoples, that age is the fundamental principle of distinction in nomenclature and of organization of kin. The second term also upholds her contention that in Dravidian kin terminologies there is no such thing as affinal kinship or terms for purely affinal kin.

Karve published the second edition of her above-mentioned book in 1965. Not only has she repeated her earlier assurance about the terms in the lists having been obtained from many castes but also has she totally ignored the work of Gough and consequently her Tamil kinship terms!

M. S. A. Rao (op. cit., pp. 129–30) has attested the term in the form of 'nattun' in both the senses, husband's sister and brother's wife (W.S.), in Malayalam. For Tamil M. N. Srinivas (*Some Tamil Folk-Songs*, 1944) gives these two senses to the term 'nattina', as husband's sister in one folk-song (I, 71) and as brother's wife (W.S.) in another (II, 67).

In view of Karve's halting statement about the Tamil kinship term 'maittunan' for wife's brother, that it "seems to be derived from the Sanskrit word mithuna or maithuna", it may be pointed out that the term "maithuna" is used to denote wife's brother in *Parāshara Grihya Sutra* (III, 9, 13) and has thus venerable Sanskritic antiquity; for the work cannot be dated later than 500 B.C. It is therefore a direct loan word in Tamil.*

Gough confined her study to changes since A.D. 1800 about which time it appears the village was founded by Brahmins who had received grants of land there. Being a late formation, post-Muslim, it is known as a *mirāsi* village (III, 20) and not as an '*agrahāra*' as it would have been in the pre-Muslim period.

Political Sociology, i.e. political analysis in terms of the caste system of the critical period of seventy years from 1790 to 1860, when fifteen new castes came into the village, naturally depicts a different picture of the village from the one that stands out in the later years.

It appears to me that the later period from 1860 to 1965 (Gough II) or 1960, is clearly divisible into two: (1) one from 1860 to about 1930 and the other from 1930 to date. About 1930 all over Tamil Nadu the Justice Party and its activities, the inner urges of a number of non-Brahmin castes and the progress of Brahmin emigration from Tamil Nadu has become established phenomena. Their consequences in terms of Political Sociology became manifest in the next thirty years. They were further aggravated by the new political set-up of the country and the progress of Communist propaganda and organization of Chinese origin. The political sociology of this intermediate period which I ventured to adumbrate in 1932 was of course only a broad outline. If it could have been supplemented or even supplanted by a detailed one from Tamil Nadu it would have proved very illuminating in more ways than one. But Gough, for reasons best known to her, has denied us this illuminating knowledge. Even from the point of view of a full understanding of the situation of the latest period which she has so lucidly, almost vividly, presented the characterization of the political sociology of the middle period is a desidaratum.

Gough's statement about the non-Brahmin castes and her listing of the same (III, 16–18) incline one to expect a five-fold classification of the total population. But actually one finds a three-fold grouping made and used throughout as frame of reference in the analysis of political life of the community. The three-fold classification of Brahmins, non-Brahmins and ādi-Drāvidas is clearly reminiscent of the three-fold classification used by the British steel-frame since about 1925. And it was this classification that, I had pointed out, constituted the political channelling of caste effected by the British, in the chapter entitled "Caste, Recent and Contemporary", forming the penultimate chapter of my book *Caste and Race in India* (1932).

The new catalytic elements during the last thirty years or so have been two: First, the Communists have successfully won over large numbers of the working people suffering under age-long disabilities and energised them for militant action; second, varied legislation about land, improving the position of many tenants and liberating the semi-serfs, has not only emancipated them, as they should have been, but also has emboldened them to ask for more, questioning the rights of anyone as superior. Faith appears to have declined. The experiences of the activity of the Independence movement,

* This unsatisfactorily ambiguous situation as regards both castewise differences in Dravidian Kin-terminology and affinal relatives irrespective of them, *vis-a-vis* Indo-Aryan kin-terminologies, prompted me to place before the Conference of Indian Sociologists, which I inaugurated in Bombay on 14th October 1967, my suggestion that the Indian Sociological Society should organize an authoritative survey of Indian kin-terminologies and publish them in an appropriate form in 1970 as a fitting mark of homage to Lewis Morgan whose indefatigable industry and exemplary zeal gave to the world, in 1870, its first conspectus of kin-terminologies of the human family including those of India.

particularly of the August 1942 campaign, further had shown the way for their new political orientation and activity direction.

Overtly at least there has emerged a tendency in some parts of the country for only two caste-groups to be pitted against one another: "Kamma and Reddi" in Andhra Pradesh, "Okkaliga and Lingāyat" in Mysore (*Indian Journal of Public Administration*, 1962, p. 627):

The scene in Madhopur of Jaunpur District, U.P., depicted by Bernard Cohn in 1955 (McKim Marriott, *Village India*, 53–76) shows the evolving society to be bi-segmental and not tri-segmental.

Cohn (ibid, pp. 69–72) informs us that in the Provincial elections of 1937 Nuniyas or Noniyas, salt-workers, and Chamārs, leather-workers, the so-called untouchables, joined hands and gave what was perhaps the first indication on that side of the country of "the growing solidarity of lower castes in opposition to the Thākurs, the Rājput landlords of the place, the traditional dispensers of local justice and the erstwhile masters of the lower castes, of the village." In the panchāyat elections of post-Independence 1948, the lower castes, now known as the Praja party, acquired the leadership of an Ahir, a Brahmin, a Kandu (grain parcher), and a Teli (oil-presser). The Rājput Thākurs sensing the situation totally non-co-operated, declining even to exercise their right of vote. The party got elected to power but failed to carry on administration. The Thākurs are believed to have resorted to bribery of the poorer members of the party in power side by side with the institution of legal proceedings against their low caste tenants who were members of the party. Between these two mill-stones the Praja party was being ground to powder. To hasten the complete pulverization of the party the Thākurs are believed to have got murdered one of the leaders of the party. As the finale of this political orientation Cohn observes: "Today, political solidarity among the lower castes of Madhopur has vanished, and there is much discouragement."

The sympathetic student of Indian Village community, one of the glorious group of British Civil Servants of India, B. H. Baden-Powell, had sounded seventy years ago, a warning which may be reproduced for enlightenment. Baden-Powell wrote (*The Indian Village Community*, 1896, pp. 442–3):

"It must be remembered, in schemes for local government by village agency that while there is a natural tendency on the part of modern administrators to resort to the idea of democratic and elective council, popular election in India (at any rate in rural districts) is still a very tender plant; and it is rare to find an election which means anything but the most unblushing sale of votes or the exercise of personal influences. The fact is that in India, in spite of all modern and more superficial aspirations, there is a strong underlying current of aristocratic feeling; and to ensure the success of village councils, and the like, it is essential that well-chosen and educated chiefs or presidents, of really respected family as well as of local influence, should be induced to become associated with them."

In Bijnor District, U.P., according to Selig S. Harrison (pp. 269–70) in 1953 there was cleavage and rivalry between the Jāts and the Chauhān Rājputs, and also between the Chamārs of the Rāidāsi Sabhā and the Shoshit Sangh ("League of the Exploited") which was a league of such lower caste-groups as gardeners and potters. The actual electional situation out of this quadrangular disposition of caste-forces as described by Harrison again proves Baden-Powell's warning to be correct and presents a marked contrast to the political development of caste in Tamil Nadu. As such it needs to be quoted. Says Harrison: "The Chauhāns will not follow behind a dominant Jāt faction [the Jāt leader having sponsored the Communist party, the Rājputs naturally turned to the Congress], and the untouchables [Chamārs], too, will keep their votes intact for sale to the highest bidder rather than enter into an inevitably subordinate relationship to any caste Hindu peasant faction. *Here, in the militant solidarity of the untouchables, the Communists face an almost insoluble problem* [?]"*:

Further east in Azamgarh District from the village Pakri Buzurg was reported a cleavage between the Kshatriyas, Rājputs, and Mallahs, the boatmen-fishermen. The former with some other castes support the Indian Congress and the latter with some other castes are affiliated with the Communist party (*Census of India*, 1961, U.P., Part VI, 22, pp. 4, 55–56). The bisectional scene thus appears to be more common, though in the process of crystallization caste by itself is not the sole agent.

Westward, in Rajasthan, there was keen rivalry and even cleavage between the Rājputs and the Jāts, where we are told "There has been a traditional animosity between the two communities because of the fact that the Rājputs are landlords and the Jāt tenants". The Swatantra Party, the Party which largely represents the wealthier classes, landlords and others, was believed to be dominated by Rājputs in Rajasthan (*Times of India*, 7-5-1961). On the village level, in the Panchayati Raj elections, the toughest struggle was alleged in Jodhpur Division, to be between the Rājputs and Jāts. In Jaipur Division, where one of the two parties was for opposing the alleged "Jāt-oppression"; the other pleaded for a combined Jāt-Ahir-Gujar-Mina combination construably against the Rājputs (Harish Chandra Mathur in *Indian Journal of Public Administration*, 1962, p. 613). In Gujarat, "Pātidars may be with one party and Baraiyas with another" (Ibid, p. 627, Myron Weiner).

South-west, in Kerala as far as the Hindu society is concerned the political scene presented is that of a bisectional society, the two largest and important castes of Nāyars and Izhavās having well-organized separate associations of their members. (K. C. John in the *Times of India*, 24-1-1968).

In Bihar three castes appear to divide the loyalties and make the socio-political scene a trisectional one. We have the Bhumihār, Kāyastha and Rājput pulling on three sides. In Orissa, F. G. Bailey's investigation suggests a different state of affairs. The castes have not been so organized as the Nair Service Society in Kerala (Bailey, 3, 92, 134). Thus neither the Brahmins nor the Karans, writer class, show associations similar to that of the Nāyars. Further they appear to be divided *inter se* among the two or three leading political parties not as groups but as individuals, so that no party claims the allegiance of a whole caste group from among these two and one or two other castes.

To resume the story of the acceptance of the study of the political impact on social institutions as a respectable branch of the Anthropological and Sociological studies, I may mention that in 1957, Professor M. N. Srinivas chose the study of the political development of caste since my study of it till 1952 for his presidential address to the Anthropological Section of the Indian Science Congress, and published it the same year in *The Journal of Asian Studies*.

And then there came F. G. Bailey's Orissan trilogy. Bailey's progress from the exploration of the economic frontiers of caste in his first book through that of the political frontiers of it in his second contribution to his march into the domain of almost pure political science in his third book, *Politics and Social Change*, published in 1963 is an eloquent testimony to the fascinating nature of the study of the impact of Politics on social institutions, and to the fact of this study, which I had started in 1932, having come of age!

Bailey's study of three villages and of the political activity and relations within them gives a clear indication that though "struggles and conflicts may still take place within the village between caste-groups [a 'caste-group' consisting of members of the same caste living in the village]", the political

* Italics mine.

allegiances and alliances are not confined within the village (Bailey, F. G., *Tribe, Caste and Nation*, 1960 pp. 260–1.) This physical or territorial extension of the boundaries of caste allegiance or alliance is not, however, the old regional solidarity of caste for social and perhaps also for economic ends but represents the newer trend of political aggrandisement.

However, the data and the conclusions which Bailey, after further study of the caste-situation in Orissa, has recorded in his book *Politics and Social Change*, do not harmonize with this view. It is clear that his 'warriors', Brahmins, and 'writers', and 'cultivators' are not organized on the above-noted pattern. And though his 'Oilmen' were organized and thirsting for plums of political power, they could not be said to have been mobilized for political action at the election stage; nor it is clear that they had voted as a group for the 'Oilman' who succeeded to be a member of Government (pp. 91–2, 127–28, 132, 133, 134).

Bailey, in his discussion of caste and its role, has brought in the notion of "Plural Society" (*Tribe, Caste and Nation*, 257). He informs his readers that the caste system is sometimes "praised as a remarkably mature and intelligent solution to the problems of living in a plural society", and in his footnote refers to J. S. Furnivall's book, *Colonial Policy and Practice*, published in 1948, and to Abbe Dubois' work *Hindu Manners and Customs*, written about 1828. The Abbe does not mention 'plural society' and he could not have done so because the notion was born about nineteen-thirties and in English garb was first given to the world by J. S. Furnivall in 1938 in his book, *Netherlands India*. And what Furnivall has said about caste and plural society at page 308 of *Colonial Policy and Practice*, i.e. the specific reference provided by Bailey as the authority for his statement quoted above is this: "Perhaps the only plural society inherently stable is the Hindu society in India. Here there are separate groups or classes, partly racial, with distinct economic functions. But in India caste has a religious sanction, and in a plural society the only common deity is Mammon. In general, the plural society is built on caste without the cement of a religious sanction."

Bailey could have seen that Furnivall's certification for caste was actuated by the religious sanction which supported it and thus stamped it as a permanent condition. He could have also seen that the characterization of plural society made by Furnivall only two pages earlier makes the description of Hindu society as a plural society untenable. Furnivall says: "The plural society arises where economic forces are exempt from control by social will." In the caste society in operative force, i.e. before the imposition of British rule on India, economic forces were rigidly circumscribed by the traditional division of occupations. Further, Furnivall expatiating on the political aspect of a plural society (p. 306) mentions three distinguishing characteristics, viz. (i) 'The society as a whole comprises separate racial sections'; (ii) 'each section is an aggregate of individuals rather than a corporate or organic whole'; and (iii) 'as individuals their social life is incomplete'. Even India as a whole, much less the Hindu society or the caste-system as a whole, does not answer the first test of Furnivall's categorization. For Furnivall himself tells his readers that India has "a comparatively homogeneous population"; and quoting from the Indian Statutory Commission's report the statement—mark that it refers to the period of fifteen years after the British implementation of Diarchy in 1921—'the violent sectional antagonism between Hindus and Mohammedans, or Brahmins and non-Brahmins has certainly impaired the efficiency of local bodies', unreservedly refers to "other tropical dependencies, *with a more strongly plural character*" (450; Italics mine).

If Bailey had consulted Furnivall's book, *Netherlands India* published almost a decade before his book mentioned by Bailey, to get clarification of Furnivall's notion of a plural society, which in the book referred to by him envisages at least two types of it, he would have found that the notion was not only nebulous but in its earlier and clearer characterization did not fit any but the so-called "more strongly plural" societies. Plural society, says Furnivall in *Netherlands India* (pp. 446–47), is "a society comprising two or more elements or social orders which live side by side, yet without mingling, in one political unit." He counted among his species of plural society not only South Africa and Canada but also Ireland and even the United States of America.

Even in Furnivall's *Colonial Policy and Practice*, Bailey could have found that Furnivall did not laud caste as the saviour of India from the anarchy of a plural society under Colonial government, nor did he even consider. India as wholly saved from that anarchy. Says Furnivall (9): ". . . if India is *in some measure* exempt from the 'atomization' of society that is found elsewhere in the tropics, the explanation may be in the fact that the impact of the West has been less violent, and that caste has afforded a considerable measure of protection." (Italics mine).

The notion of Plural society, has proved to be very alluring and self-propagating. Once a thinker is caught in its mesh he tends to move in it without, conscious thought. And Bailey is no exception, though he uses the expression segmentary society as contrasted with organic society in his third work, the most political of his trilogy. He says about Orissa, as he evidently had not said before in his two works, after studying it for about six years, that it is "not a unity. It is not yet single complex society, but an aggregate of many simple societies, imperfectly linked into what may be a cultural and linguistic whole, but is hardly yet a social whole. . . .

"The distinction [between 'simple' and 'complex'] resembles that between segmentary and organic types of society" (F. G. Bailey: *Politics and Social Change, Orissa in 1959*, 1963, p. 219, Italics mine).

I should modify Bailey's models and say that Orissan, rather Indian, was a pluralist national society as opposed to monolithic nationalist societies, whose pluralistic aspect had yet to adapt itself to the new setup. In this sense, I think that the model proposed by Despers against the plural model may be more appropriate. He calls it the 'reticulated model'—a society with over-lapping and diagonally running groupings, which are quite often superimposed upon one another (*American Anthropologist*, 1964)*.

---

* For a detailed discussion of the concept of "Plural Society" see my *Social Tensions in India*, 1968.

13

Caste and Politics in Tamil Nadu

In Tamil Nadu (Madras) there has been noticed a pattern of public activity by a political party and a section of the people during the last fifteen years which was partially at least noted by me in the third and the fourth editions of the book, i.e. in 1957 and in 1961. Though the later activity has been even more violent and perturbing I would have passed by it with the usual notice in this edition, too; but the action of the late lamented Mr. Annadurai, the Chief Minister of Tamil Nadu, as the head of the State, implementing the programmes of the Political party that was mainly concerned in the disturbing patterns of public activity referred to above, as reported in the newspapers about April or May 1967, has led me to enquire into the antecedents, both political, social and cultural of Tamil Nadu, and to deal with the contrast the caste-system of Tamil Nadu, bears to that of Uttar Pradesh in the hope of showing up the total complex and pattern of the activity in its proper perspective.

Mr. Annadurai, who is the author of the story "Chandramohan"[1] an attack on Shivaji, the extraordinary leader of Hinduism in the latter part of the seventeenth century, is reported to have translated the national motto, which is inscribed below the National Emblem, into Tamil, and has got it inscribed or written in Tamil script. The National Motto, 'Satyameva Jayate', a sentence taken from an old *Upanishad*, is in Sanskrit language and is written in the Devanagari script. The associations of the motto thus transport, or are expected to transport, Indians to their glorious past of two thousand five hundred years ago. Annadurai's action has destroyed the national motto as a national symbol which it has been such for the last seventeen years.

Nagaland which has declared English as its State language will certainly translate it into English and have it inscribed in Roman script. Even if one or more of the other linguistic States do not follow suit, enough damage to the motto as an evocative symbol would have been done. Tamil Indians in other parts of India than Tamil Nadu will fail to recognise the motto. The large amount of Union-published literature and that published by other States, though it would be carrying the emblem and the motto, will fail to evoke the kind of reaction to the motto that is desired to be evoked by it as a national symbol. Altogether the overt act of translating the motto and changing its script must be construed to indicate a mental act of secession from the Union or at least a sharp turn away from the Union!

Realization of this probability brings to one's mind the historical fact that between 300 B.C. and A.D. 600, either Tamilnad or a very large part of it was not a part of the Indian dominion as a whole, ruled over from wherever it might have been. Even the great monarch Ashoka, who had succeeded in extending the North-West Frontier of India to Afghanistan, had to let alone the Southern peoples as outside his dominion. He mentions (II Rock Edict; XIII Rock Edict) the Chodās, Padas, Satyaputa and Keralaputra as beyond the southern boundary of his empire. The first two people are easily recognizable as the ancestors of the later famous dynasties, the Cholas and the Pāndyas. Satyaputa is somehow attempted to be fitted into the later Cheras. May it not be that Satyaputa was the earlier version of later Setupathis of Ramnad? However that may be, the southernmost portion, perhaps the districts of Tanjore, Madura, Ramanathapuram and Tirunelveli (Tinnevelly), had managed to keep out of the Indian Empire of the great monarch Ashoka.

Actual contexts of references are positive proof of the status of these peoples and countries. The Second Rock Edict of Ashoka in its Girnar version,[2] after referring to 'conquered territory', mentions "neighbours". And among them figure the Cholas, the Pāndyas, Satyaputa, Keralaputra and Antiyoka the Yavana king. The thirteenth Rock Edict in its Shahbazgarhi version first speaks of neighbouring countries upto six hundred 'yojanas' around, and begins with Antiyoka, the Yavana king, and ends with Alikasandara, and then speaks of Chola-Pāndyas as of the South. Against this it mentions, further, people who are of the kingdom, i.e. Ashoka's subjects among whom figure Āndhra-Pulindas.[3] After Ashoka, Khāravela, the Kalinga monarch, about 150 B.C., has recorded his having exacted a tribute of pearls and jewels from a Pāndya king.[4] Later, the great Gupta monarch, Samudragupta (C.A.D. 330–75), records his conquest and subsequent release of all the kings of the South (Dakshināpatha). But in the actual list of kings and places we have one located in Nellore District, a king of Kanchi and one of Vengi [?] (Sircar, pp. 256–7). There is no mention of Cholas, Pāndyas or Cheras.[5]

The national poet, Kalidasa, who must have lived about that time, however, was mightily impressed by the traditions and performance of Pāndya kings. He mentions them in two contexts in his semi-epic of dynastic glory of Ikshvākus.[6] In the first context we are informed that an Ikshvāku king had actually conquered the Pāndyas and carried his successful arms upto the mouths of the river Tāmraparni. In that connection Kalidasa mentions the river Kaveri, which I believe is the earliest reference to that prosperity-producing river of the South in Sanskrit literature. In the second context, Kalidasa brings in the Pāndya king to the self-choice marriage of the famous Vidarbha princess Indumati, specifying his city as Uraga. This is again the earliest and perhaps also the solitary reference to the famous early mediaeval and late ancient city or town of Uraiyur in Tiruchirapalli (Trichinopoly) district. What is intensely intriguing is that Kalidasa not only makes Agastya, the patron saint of Tamilnad, that Pāndya king's chief chaplain but asserts that Ravana, the enemy of Rama of the *Rāmāyana*, had to effect a treaty with him to secure his domain from the Pāndya king's molestation on the occasion of Ravana's march against Indra. Kalidasa may or may not have had in his mind the tradition, later recorded in a Tirunelvelli epigraph of the third decade of thirteenth century A.D.,[7] that the Pāndya kings had in their possession a garland which they had secured from Indra, the great monarch of the Gods (*Ep. Ind.*, XII, pp. 39, 41, 51 and footnote 1). But he does emphasize the fact of the Pāndya king attending the self-choice marriage and contending for the hand of Indumati of the Vidarbhas, having a long garland over his shoulders!

During the most glorious period of 'native' rule over this land, then, the peoples and kings of Tamilnad had managed to keep themselves almost segregated, excepting for the Pāndyas of the extreme south. And unlike the contemporary descendants of the Rājputs of the North the descendants of these Pāndyas have to be sought in contemporary Tamilnad in its nook and corner!

The pattern of public activity of the last fifteen years in Tamilnad, which clearly stamps it as anti-Brahmin, anti-Sanskrit, anti-North and even anti-Brahmanic-Hinduism, cannot fail to remind a serious student of Indian history, political and social, of its curious precursor of nearly nine centuries ago. K. A. Nilakanth Sastri has drawn our attention to an inscription of about the end of the eleventh century A.D. of the reign of the Chola monarch Kulottunga I, which has recorded the effects of a clash between the 'Right hand' and 'Left hand' castes. It resulted "in the burning of the village, Rājamahendrachaturvedimangalam, Pāpanasham taluq of Tanjore District, the destruction of its sacred places and the looting of the temple treasury by robbers."[8]

The existence of this faction, the 'Right hand' castes and the 'Left hand' castes, has been noted as a peculiarity of the caste system of Tamilnad by most modern observers and students at least since the beginning of the nineteenth century.[9]

In extension of what I have said about this faction earlier in the book I should now add what Sastri has so kindly made readily available to us regarding its nature in the last quarter of the twelfth century. He has quoted (*The Cholas*, p. 551) what he calls "a curious" inscription of the reign of the Chola monarch Kulottunga III (A.D. 1178–1216).

According to the record, the *Idangai*, i.e. the 'Left Hand' castes claimed themselves to have been created from the *agnikunda* (fire-pit) for protecting the sacrifice of Kashyapa. One emperor named Arindama is believed to have imported a large colony of Brahmins from Antarvedi, the sacred region lying between the two rivers the Ganga (Ganges) and the Yamuna (Jumna). And it is maintained that 'Left Hand' castes came with the Brahmin colonists "as the bearers of their slippers and their umbrellas".

One of the many later conflicts between these factions—they appear to have been almost always for maintaining certain rights of social prestige—occurred in the beginning of the nineteenth century. Gustav Oppert, writing in the eighties of the last century,[10] took great trouble to acquire some authentic information about these castes from a long judgment dated the 25th June 1809, delivered by the then District Magistrate of Chingleput.

It is known from it that all the castes involved in the schism had "more or less distinctive flags of their own". It vouchsafes the further interesting information that the 'Right Hand' faction had sixty castes in it and the 'Left Hand' ones, i.e. those who, in the Chola inscription of the twelfth century referred to above, are represented as the supporters and helpers of the Brahmin colonists from the North, had only six. A. C. Burnell had, a few years earlier, told us that the factious distinction was primarily between the landlords and their serfs, the Vellālans and the Pallans being the leaders on the one hand and "the Brahmins, artizans and other interlopers" forming the opposition on the other.[11]

Brahmins thus appear to have been associated with 'Left Hand' section in the last quarter of the twelfth century and also at the beginning of the last quarter of the nineteenth century. But Schoebel, in his *History of the Origin and Development of Indian Castes*, a work in French published in 1884, obligingly referred to by J. H. Hutton,[12] asserts that Brahmins who were spoken of as 'Mahājanam' "are often regarded as belonging to neither division". And Hutton assures us that "Later immigrants into south India, such as Muslims, Marwāris, and Gujarātis, are like Brahmins, generally regarded as outside this dual system entirely".[13]

Tamilian allergy or opposition to Brahmins thus appears to have been in evidence from at least the thirteenth century. It is now appropriate to see how the matter stood in the matter of language, thought, and tradition about and before the fourteenth century. A brief review of the literary and religious history of the period before the fourteenth century will enable us to appraise the situation.

It is commonly agreed that the Brahmanic culture of the North with its Sanskrit language must have been carried by small bands of Brahmins from the North as typified in the Brahmanic story of Agastya[14] (Chitrav: *vide* Agastya) and the Buddhist story of Bāvari (*Suttanipāta*). In Tamilnad it must have arrived some three to four centuries before the Christian era. The oldest Tamil literature, and that is the oldest among all the Indian languages except Sanskrit and Prakrits, the Sangam literature, is acknowledged to reflect full influence of Brahmanic culture in the region.[15] As Nirmala Ramachandran, a Bharata-Natya artiste, believing and preaching though she is the view that the dance-form 'Bharata Natya' was the traditional Tamil dance "later perfected by the early Aryans", observes: ". . . by the time of the Silappadikaram, that is the second century A.D., Aryanization had already started which had its effect in influencing all phases of life including the arts and literature."

But the very fact that such literature of high perfection and emotional appeal as some works of the Sangam age should have been produced in the vernacular Tamil is a feature of the culture-spread in Tamilnad which is peculiar to the region and sets it off from the other regions in the matter of the spread of the Brahmanic culture of the North.

There is another equally significant factor in this early cultural amalgamation which must be noted carefully. And that is that this early literature was not designed to vernacularize the Northern cultural tradition enshrined in the Sanskrit language. It does not appear that any of the Sanskrit works of the Northern Brahmanic culture were rendered into Tamil in that age. But most elements of the incoming Indo-Aryan culture were assimilated and appear in the vernacular literature of the age as if they were the concepts, beliefs and emotions of the Tamilians of Tamilnad. So to say, Tamil version of the Northern Brahmanic tradition was already formed in the Sangam age, and total cultural amalgam was in the process of formation. There was thus given to the Brahmin prospectors rather a short period to accumulate prestige for themselves through the possession and use of Sanskrit lore of theirs, unhampered or unrivalled by the vernacular tradition.

To add to the difficulties in the way of Brahminization of Tamilnad through the sole channel of Sanskrit lore, the already developed Tamil language came to be soon handled by some Tamilians who in the perspective of time must appear to have been inspired personages.

It is noteworthy that among the Tamil poets of the Sangam age Brahmins formed "about one-tenth of the total number".[16] And we are told by Nilakanta Sastri,[17] that the famous Tamil work, entitled *Kural*, is, as poetry, "a work that transcends the limitations of time and place", and that though based on Sanskrit sources, it introduces new and significantly deeper thoughts and ideas than are met with in the Sanskrit original. It is ascribed to the pre-seventh or pre-eighth century epoch. The author of the work was Tiruvalluvar or Tiru Valluva Nāyanār. He came from the caste, Valluvans, who have been the priests of the Paraiyans and the Pallans, the two most important Tamilian castes of untouchables.[18] J. N. Farquhar,[19] almost half a century ago, wrote: "No work holds a higher place among the classics of the south than the sacred *Kural*, a poem consisting of 2,660 short couplets, dealing with virtue, wealth and pleasure."

From about the sixth century A.D. devotional upheaval, native to the soil of Tamilnad, began to make its appearance in the form of the Shaiva saints known as Nāyanārs and the Vaishnava hymners known as Alvārs. Such devotional poetry as the Tamil saints or poet-philosophers, whether Shaiva or Vaishnava, poured during two or more centuries upto the end of the ninth century, was not known in any part of Indo-Aryan India before the thirteenth century A.D.

The Tamil hymns of the three most prominent of the sixty-three Shaiva saints were collected together, in the tenth or the eleventh century, by a Brahmin named Nambi Andar Nambi; and the collection has ever been known as the *Devaram* or *Tevaram*. Of the sixty-three canonized saints "many were Vellālas"; and Appar (A.D. 580–630), one of the great triad Appar, Sambandar and Sundarar, was a Vellāla.[20] It was, again, an extraordinary Vellāla, by name Sekkilar, who wrote the most famous and elaborate hagiographical work known as *Periya Purānam* in the twelfth century A.D.

The work is described by K. A. Nilakanta Sastri as "the ocean in which all the streams of Shaivite legend mingle in the Tamil country" and which "has influenced the lives and thoughts of the Tamil Shaiva population almost incessantly from the date of its composition,"[21] having been treated as the fifth Veda. Sekkilar to my mind foreshadowed the later social history or the contemporary social scene in Tamilnad. He was the chief minister of Kulottunga II of the Chola dynasty. The first formulation of the Tamil Shaiva Siddhānta, too, was the work of a pious Vellāla, Meykandadeva, who lived in the thirteenth century.[22]

Long before the Vellālas had begun to participate in the Tamilian literary and devotional upsurge, a Paraiya woman had carried off the honours. Karaikkal Ammai, the Paraiya lady, who must have lived about A.D. 550, is described by Nilakanta Sastri as "perhaps the earliest author whose works have entered the Shaiva canon". She is also credited with having originated the genre of literature known as Prabandham in Tamil. (Sastri, *History of South India*, pp. 368, 423.)

The Vaishnava counterpart of *Devāram* known as *Nālāyira Divyaprabandham* or simply as *Divyaprabandham*, "four thousand Sacred hymns", goes actually under the authorship of Nāthamuni, the Alvār philosopher, who was the grandfather of the preceptor of the great philosopher Rāmānujāchāryas , and is known to have lived between A.D. 824 and 924. The earliest of these Tamil hymns were composed by a saint who is dated as "not later than the fifth or the sixth century A.D.".[23] Though Nāthamuni used both Tamil and Sanskrit as the vehicle of his religio-philosophical thought, Yamunāchāryas the preceptor of Rāmānujāchāryas, turned more to Sanskrit. The great Rāmānujāchāryas formulated his philosophy of qualified monism in Sanskrit, on the basis of the Tamil teachings of the Vaishnava saints, a long succession of whom did the preaching for over four centuries before him. It should be noted that one of the most famous of these Alvārs, Tirumangai, who must have lived not later than the eighth century A.D., was a low caste man who wanted to marry a higher caste woman, as Nilakanta Sastri informs us.[24] Jagadisa Iyyar[25] tells us that he is always represented in sculpture with a sword in hand, a rather remarkable feature in emotional and devotional Vaishnavism. He states that Tirumangai was Commander-in-Chief of the Chola army! His contribution to the *Nalayiraprabandham* is the largest of all the Alvārs.[26]

This brief statement regarding the early growth of Tamil literature, purely literary, religio-philosophical or secular, is enough to give one an idea of the force and volume of the upsurge. It must have started within three or four centuries of the first arrival of Brahmins or others carrying Indo-Aryan cultural heritage in Sanskrit language, prospecting for solitude or even spread of their ideas, and lured by the beauty and propriety of the Kaveri-watered lands studded with enticing mountains.

In the next phase, Indo-Aryan heritage was vernacularized through translations and perhaps adaptations. An inscription of the early tenth century mentions among the achievements of the early Pāndya kings the translation of the *Mahābhārata* in Tamil.[27]

The activity mentioned at the beginning as disquieting, it appears to me, is the next phase. It is symptomatic of inward alienation and militant Tamilism. Preparation of a non- or anti-Vālmiki version of the *Rāmāyana*, in supersession of *Kamban Rāmāyana*, effacing the picture of Rāvana as the Dravidian of the South, has been declared to be "the most important among cultural activities of debunking and reconstruction of classic cultural epics".[28]

It is in keeping with this upsurge that the journal entitled *Tamil Culture* started its publication in 1952. And interpretation of the activity outlined above as the third and the militant phase of Tamilism is corroborated by the conversion of this journal into an organ of Tamil International Academy in

1955. Strange coincidence only but noteworthy in the context is the cessation of the publication of the journal entitled *Indian Culture* at about the start of the journal *Tamil Culture*, after a useful career of more than twenty-five years!

In Tamilnad the incoming batches of Brahmins—one such brought in about the end of the thirteenth century is mentioned in an inscription already referred to—had only a brief period when they could impress themselves and establish Indo-Aryan prestige through their Sanskritic lore. Both devotional and heroic literature in Tamil had rendered Sanskrit literature in the field first superfluous and then disliked as unintelligible and non-conforming to the medium of local patriotism and of native usage. The anti-Brahmanic and anti-Indo-Aryan trend inherent in this upsurge can be inferred from the fact that a number of the most important of not only the religio-philosophers but also the emotion-rousing devotees and litterateurs were Vellālas and even Paraiyans.

The aftermath of Rāmānuja's literary activity through Sanskrit perhaps influenced a slight modification in this Tamilian upsurge and though his Life written by Pinbalgia Perumal Jiyar in the thirteenth century was in Tamil, the treatise *Arthapanchaka* giving "an excellent summary of Shri-Vaishnava doctrine" of Rāmānuja by "the head of the school of Srirangam" in the fourteenth was in "Sanskritized Tamil". It is noteworthy that the head was one Pillai Lokāchāryas , who must have been a Vellāla as his title indicates.[29]

A Tamil inscription from Tinnevelly of the second decade of the thirteenth century recording a grant made by King Māravarman Sundara-Pāndya I transports us into an atmosphere which foreshadows the coming event of the eclipse of Sanskritic lore including supersession of the Vedas. In the preliminary eulogistic account of the family and the particular king we read: ". . . Virtue increasing abundantly on the earth surrounded by the expansive ocean; the righteous sceptre swaying (in all directions) driving away the black Kali (age); the wide earth becoming cool under the shade of (his) single parasol; the three kinds of Tamil (*iyal, isai* and *nāgam*) glowing in order; the four kinds of the Vedas being learnt (by students) and growing simultaneously; the five kinds of sacrifices being performed in accordance with (established) practice; the six kinds of faiths (Bhairava, Bāma, Kālāmukha, Mavirada [?] and Shaiva) being finely expounded, the seven kinds of music (*padal*) spreading along with *iyal* . . ." was crowned to widen the path of Manu who was brought into existence by Brahma residing on the dew-settled lotus flower"[30] (*Ep. Ind.* XII, pp. 40–2, 50–51).

Contrasting markedly with this upsurge of Tamil stands the behaviour-pattern of the two northern Dravidian areas, Andhra Pradesh and Mysore (Karnataka). Even so late as the 15th and the 16th centuries the local or regional languages, viz. Telugu and Kannada, when they are used in inscriptions, are specified in an apologetic tone as 'deshabhāshā', the language of the region. Thus a Guntur district record of Reddis, dated A.D. 1413, which is written partly in Sanskrit and partly in Telugu registers at the end in Sanskrit: "The boundary signs of this village are (now) being written in regional language (deshabhāshā)."

A grant of the 16th century made by a Vijayanagar king written in "nandinagari" script and Kannada prose, similarly ends with the statement "the boundaries of this *āgrahara* are given in the language of the century."[31]

It may be pointed out further that, whether South India, or rather Tamilnad, had or had not in Muruga,[32] identified with Subrahmanya or Skanda or Kārtikeya, another special deity like Ayanār, one Nakkira Deva, "a writer of eminence" believed to have lived before the middle of the sixth century A.D., had already composed a poem in his honour which was entitled *Tirumuruhattuppadai*.[33] The *Skandapurāna* was translated into Tamil verse, giving 'the famous' *Kanda Purānam*, by Kanchi-Appar of Conjeevaram in the twelfth century, while Arunagirināthar composed a series of lyrics in Tamil on the god Subrahmanya entitled *Tiru-pugal*.[34]

It is noteworthy that though the deity is commonly referred to as Skanda, Kumāra, Kārtikeya or Mahāsena in his earlier career in North India, and was taken up by the Ikshvāku dynasty of the South as its tutelary deity under the title of Swami Mahāsena,[35] he is mentioned as Subrahmanya, Shanmukham, Murugan, Velāyudhan or Velāndi in Tamilnad after his eclipse in North India. This itself suggests an opposition between Tamilnad and North India. The names Swami Mahāsena and Brahmanyadeva appear in a North India Gupta inscription of the first quarter of the fifth century A.D.,[36] the latter name appearing for the first and also the last time in North Indian records. It may not be a mere accident that the great Shaiva saint Appar, a Vellāla by caste as already pointed out, in his hymns speaks of Shiva as the father of the Kadamba youth, i.e. Subrahmanya.[37]

I have dealt with the importance of the deity in South India at length in my *Gods and Men* (pp. 82–89). Here I shall mention only one feature of this complex most relevant to the topic in hand. The special worship associated with this deity in Tamilnad is what is known as the "Kāvadi" and it is most favoured among the Pallis and the Kallans. As will be later noticed the Kaikolans associate their origin with Skanda as their tradition makes them the descendants of one of the helpers of Skanda in his battle with Padmāsura. It is again the Tamilian myth-making that has improvised the demon that Skanda is believed to have fought with and killed. In the Kaikolan account he is Padmāsura—in the standard tradition of North India so beautifully presented by Kalidasa in his *Kumārasambhava*, the demon is named Tarakāsura. In another Tamilian account which presents him as the God "held in great veneration, particularly by the Kuravas" vouchsafed by K. K. Pillay[38] the demon is Suran.

Subrahmanya's sixth is a regular festival both in Andhra Pradesh and Tamilnad. But Subrahmanya is the snakegod in Andhra Pradesh and women on his sixth offer silver hoods at his temple for children. The festival in Tamilnad appears to be a much grander affair.[39] We are informed that in one village of South Arcot District it lasts for ten days, whereas that of Mariammā lasts for three days and that of Ayanār for only one day.[40] This justifies the observation of M. N. Srinivas, made by him almost a quarter of a century ago, that "Subrahmanya is one of the most popular, if not the most popular, deity of the Tamilians",[41] commenting on the folk-songs either singing his praise or having special references to him and his worship. M. N. Srinivas had made some investigation into festivals observed by Tamilians during his tenure as a Research Assistant in the Department of Sociology, Bombay University, the folk-songs mentioned elsewhere in this book being one part of that work. From the notes of the investigation I have I find that "a good many non-Brahmins observe a fast once a month on the day when the constellation *Krittiky* prevails, in honour of Subrahmanya" and that "throughout the *Kartiky* month mudlamps are lit in the house in the evening".

The worship of Murugan or Velan, according to Nilakanta Sastri, may go back to the early ages. He thinks that in the pre-historic finds from Adichanallur the presence of iron banner bases and representations of fowls in bronze and iron tridents are evidence enough for his assertion. Further he suggests the date of these finds, from typological parallels in Syria and Cyprus [?] to be about 1200 B.C.[42] I am not at all satisfied with this reasoning and have kept the question open as in my above statement. I am convinced, however, that Murugan was an old deity of Tamilians and had some features facilitating his identity with Subrahmanya. I think the identification of the two was established fairly early when the early Tamil upsurge was at its height.

I have mentioned above the flattering reference to Subrahmanya, Shiva being described as the father of the Kadamba youth, by the saint Appar. Jagadisa Iyyar[43] tells us that Arunagiri, the author of the renowned songs called *"Tirupugal"*, had Subrahmanya as his patron deity and that representations of both of them are sculptured on the east of the Tiruvannamalai (Chingleput District) temple. He has quoted a long extract from an inscription translated in an Archeological Survey Report, which is a fairly early testimony to the extraordinary glorification of Subrahmanya in Tamil Nadu and as such deserves to be studied in detail. But, not to crowd this work and the argument, I shall quote here only one statement occurring in it which is most significant for our present purposes. It runs: "... the moon (Subrahmanya) born in the *Yaga* (sacrifice) which Nārada bred up (kindled) and who came to burn Tiripurakodu, he who taught Agastya the pure classic Tamil, the *Āgamas* and the truth of the six letters."[44]

In the above context the Tamilian saying "a Brahmin's Tamil and a Vellāla's Sanskrit are equally bad"[45] is eloquent testimony of the linguistic chasm following the fissure of caste. We get the proposition; Brahmin equals Sanskrit and Vellāla equal Tamil, and the conclusion that Brahmin is the opponent of Vellāla. Therefore Brahmin and the North from which he came are anti-Tamilnad!

Thus we find all the elements in embryo which I emphasized early in this analysis of the recent pattern of public behaviour in Tamilnad. The Indo-Aryan Agastya is displaced to the second place as a teacher of the people of Tamilnad; for he received his instruction from Subrahmanya, a form of the Tamilian deity Murugan. Pure Classic Tamil is the important language of culture and replaces the Indo-Aryan Sanskrit. Thirdly, the Āgamas, some of which are in Tamil, are enthroned as the source of Tamilian Shaivism, disowning thereby any debt to North Indian thought on the subject. Fourthly, by recording the fact of a six-lettered 'mantra', adorational formula, as specific to Subrahmanya, the deity is placed in the same rank as Shiva and Vishnu, the only two Supreme godheads in the Hindu pantheon that had and have such specific formulae!

In my *Gods and Men*,[46] I have traced the decline of Skanda worship and influence in Northern India and the growth of the Skandaswami cult in South India and established the fact that the two processes were more or less a close sequence. Thus Skanda-cult typifies the opposition between the North and the South. And if Muruga should prove to be not only an early Tamil deity but also almost pre-historic the episode would stand out as the first triumph of Tamilian resurgence!

Religious ministration, whether the highly emotive one of temple-worship* or the ritual one of priestly service at various domestic rites, has been divided. The Brahmin with his Vedic ritual and Sanskrit formulae has not been able to have his way for a long enough period in Tamilnad to establish his supreme position as the all-India elite and thereby to orient firmly the Tamilian to the Indo-Aryan North.

It appears that it was the Chola King Rājarāja I (A.D. 985–1014) who instituted the recital of the *Tevaram*, the Tamil hymns of the great Shaiva saints of Tamilnad, as an essential part of the temple worship.[47] And it was the greatest monarch Rājendra Chola I (A.D. 1012–44) who provided for the recitation of *Tiruvāymozhi*, the Vaishnava counterpart. Iyyar[48] points out that these two Tamil devotional works acquired the sanctity of the *Vedas* in the eyes of the Tamilians.

Rājendra Chola established a choir of fifty persons at his great temple at Tanjore for daily singing, to the accompaniment of musical instruments, the Tamil hymns of the *Tiruppadiyam*. The daily wage of these reciters sanctioned was double that of each of the four Brahmins employed in another temple in A.D. 1038 to recite *Stotras* and *Vedas*. The daily wage paid to the reciters of the Vaishnava hymns of the *Tiruvāymozhi* in another temple was identical with that of the reciters of Tamil Shaiva

* For the temple ritual and its impressive and consequent emotive nature see my *Religious Consciousness*, 1965.

hymns in the Tanjore temple. The wage of a Brahmin appointed to expound the Shivadharma in A.D. 1054 was only seventy-five *kalams* of paddy a year and was the same as that of a junior accountant of the Tanjore temple. The officiating priest, *nambi*, of a temple got two *kurmis* per day and sixteen *kalams* of paddy a year. The daily wage of a member of the above mentioned Tanjore choir was three *kurmis* of paddy per day. The relative valuation of the services of a Brahmin in the early part of Rājendra Chola's reign, when the native Tamil upsurge gathered momentum, may further be judged from the fact that the wage of a Brahmin cook in A.D. 1018 was the same as that of a wood-cutter.[49]

The valuation of the services of Vedic Brahmins as worshippers in terms of money was evidently not known to or was ignored by J. N. Farquhar,[50] when, more than forty-five years ago, he wrote, regarding the introduction of the *Tevaram* or *Devaram* "set to Dravidian music", that "sung by a special choir, quite distinct from the priestly ministrants, they gave the worship a fresh interest and splendour without disturbing the ancient Sanskrit liturgy". For though the ancient Sanskrit liturgy was not disturbed and a fresh interest in splendour to temple worship was added it has to be concluded, both from the relative number of ministrants employed and from their relative wages, that the devotional Tamil hymnal worship had come to be valued more than the Vedic ritual, which was intended to be relegated to the background, if not to the scrap-heap. This view finds further support in the inscription in a Vaishnava temple wherein it is stated that a Brahmin knowing the Vedas was appointed at that temple only in case a man conversant with the Vaishnava system of temple worship (*Koyilnambu*) was not available.[51] In recent and contemporary practice we are informed that in Shaiva temples Brahmins recite the Vedic hymns or verses while others called Pandarams recite the Thevaram.[52]

In the *Times of India* issue of 18th May, 1953 the informative Madras Newsletter of its news-serviceman, detailing some aspects of the pattern of public activity mentioned above, began with the statement: "Protagonists of Tamil have acquired 'forceful allies' in the heads of religious 'mutts' who jumped into the language fray last week with a vengeance. The priests have now given a 'holy' twist to the two-month old controversy which was until recently restricted to a war of words on chaste *versus* corrupt Tamil". The religious heads, as the writer expressed it, "have come forward to deliver the 'gods' from the unintelligible Sanskrit 'rigmarole' that is being showered on them, i.e. the name of *archana* (recitals during *pujā*). The head of one of these mutts, Kunrakudi, "held *these adamant Aryan sanatanists* responsible for the iconoclasm and irreligiousness in Tamilnad". He further asserted that if the *pujaris* [worshipping priests] were to cast off their superiority complex and to 'conduct' *archanas* [liturgical ritual of worship] *in a language understandable to the average devotee*, there would be no anti-God demonstration in the State. . . ." Upon this the head of the highly respected *Ahobila mutt* authoritatively pronounced his decision in favour of the *pujaris* and *archakas* and denounced the contention of the head of the 'mutt' who had castigated them for continuing with the Sanskrit texts for worship. The *archakas* themselves then met in a conference and "protested vehemently against the interference of *Kunrakudi, Adigalar* [head] in temple affair" and declared his propaganda to be 'vicious' and 'sectarian'.[53] And the storm passed over for the time at least!

Above I have mentioned one "widely popular poet" of the Sangam age by name Tiruvalluvan and have ascertained his caste as Valluvan. These Valluvans, who, it is arguable from Tiruvalluvan's achievement and also from the common belief that they were the priests of the Pallava dynasty of Kanchi, were highly intelligent and clever in ritualistic performance from early times, have been the priests of the Paraiyans and Pallans, the two largest of the untouchable castes of Tamilnad. And Sir Athelstane Baines[54] told us more than half a century ago that "it is conjectured that the sacerdotal functions of this caste were superseded by those of the Brahman, when the latter found his way into the Dravidian region". He drew almost a marked contrast between the South and other parts of India when he observed that "the impure castes, and, in the Dravidian country, a good many of the lower agricultural castes, employ their own caste-fellows for priestly duties outside the temple, *whilst a few castes, officiate for not only their own but for other castes of similar or slightly superior rank*".* Baines' "few castes" include Vellālas, the backbone caste of Tamilnad, the second largest one in numbers but the leading one in point of organised endeavour to oust the Brahmin from his spiritual supremacy.

It is noteworthy that out of the five 'maths', religious training institutions and ascetie centres, in Tanjore District, all except the one Brahmin 'math', that of Shankarāchāryas's Kāmakotti centre at Kumbhakonam, are owned, and run and manned by Shudras. The remaining four and at least one in Tinnevelly would appear to be those of the Vellālas. The four Tanjore 'maths' between them had an income of not less than three lakhs of rupees a year and owned not less than 33,000 acres of land, besides having control over the properties and management of not less than thirty-five temples in Tamilnad. The principal 'math', that of Dharmapuram, was founded about 350 years ago. As a matter of fact its foundation may be much earlier as it is known that a daughter institution started by this centre at Benares was in existence there in A.D. 1580. The priests officiating at the temples under the control of these 'maths', of course Vellālas or Pandārams, are appointed from among those that are admitted to the instruction given at the 'math' of Dharmapuram, and therefore owe allegiance to and carry the message of the Vellāla version of Hindu religion and moral and metaphysical philosophy. All the priests officiating at Vellāla ceremonies as well as those of many lower castes are subordinate to the pontiffs of these 'maths'.

I should note here in particular one temple under the Vellālan control to emphasize the possibility or probability of cleavage. The temple in question is the one at Tiruvadamarudur, about six miles from Kumbakonam. It is also significantly known as Madyārjunam. At the annual festival in January, known as the 'Pushyam', an unusually large number of Paraiyan pilgrims visit it. "There is a figure called *Chola Brahmahatti* at the eastern gate. And the story current about the figure is highly instructive as it directly embodies the discomfiture and impotence of the Brahmin. It is said that a Chola king murdered a Brahmin and the sin personified as *Bṛahmahatti*, 'hatyā' meaning slaughter, stood waiting for him to come out of the temple in order that the murder could be avenged. It is believed that inside the temple Shiva himself apprised the king of his predicament and advised him to go out by the back door. The king having acted on the salutary advice of Shiva, the *Brahmahatti*, has remained there waiting ever since.[55]

The intensity of the Vellālan upsurge in the cause of overthrowing Brahmin supremacy in the matter of religion can be gauged from the contrasts presented by the great Kāmakotti 'math' of Shankarāchāryas at Kumbakonam, which tradition relates was founded by Shankarāchāryas himself originally at Canjeevaram (Iyyar, p. 333). The Kumbakonam 'math' which appoints the managers of only three temples had an income of only Rs. 14,000.[56]

The Tamilian upsurge had tended to overtop the religious importance of the North. In the midst of such equations as Kanchi = new Varanasi, we find some claims of superiority like the assertion about Tiruvadi in Tanjore district. There is a saying about Tiruvadi that "it is holier than Benares by one-sixteenth". And a story is told how a Brahmin on his journey to Varanasi undertaken to consign

* Italics mine.

the charred bones of his father to the Ganga there discovered that Tiruvadi was holier than Varanasi. On his discovery the Brahmin is said to have thrown the bones into the Cavery at Tiruvadi.[57]

The opposition to North-orientation, hostility towards Sanskrit language, enmity towards Brahmins and more than indifference towards certain Hindu dieties of the Brahmanic pentad, known in Tamil as Ainjandideva (P. V. Jagadisa Iyyar, p. 314) is seen not to be a new phenomenon but an element in the social heritage of Tamil Nadu. It may not prove to be a passing fancy as the complex has shown itself to have been present in Tamilnad a thousand years ago, very probably making itself apparent within five or six centuries of the coming in, in very small numbers, of Brahmins from North India, carrying their Indo-Aryan culture in Sanskrit language.

An analysis of the Tamilnad caste system combined with our peep into the socio-cultural history taken above will help us to adjudge whether the above-mentioned appraisal of the Tamil Nadu pattern of public activity of the last fifteen years is an imaginary fear or a reasonable probability.

The largest single caste of Tamilnad was in 1901, the Pallis, who numbered about 2.6 million. They figure among field-labourers in Sir Athelstane Baines' (p. 148) classification. They are known, and perhaps they like to be known, as Padaiyachis, i.e. foot soldiers. And they have proclaimed themselves to be Vanniyans, i.e. Kshatriyas of the Fire Race (Agnikula). In 1903 the caste representatives from thirty-four villages in South Arcot bound themselves in writing not to have two wives at a time, nor to allow a woman to remarry during the lifetime of her first husband.[58] Gough[59] describes them as tenant cultivators in Kumbapettai, a village in Tanjore District. In 1901, eighty per cent of them were concentrated in the five districts of South Arcot, Salem, North Arcot, Chingleput and Tanjore, in the descending order of their percentage concentration, 28.5 per cent being in South Arcot and 9 per cent in Tanjore. According to Baines, "they were once a dominant tribe under the Pallavās, but were reduced to predial servitude when the Vellālans entered their country". Their assumption of the sacred thread brings them into collision with both priest and peasant.[60] In Vellore many Pallis adopt the title of Mudaliyār[61] which is the specific title of the highest section of Vellālas.

The Vellālas, the supposed masters of the Pallis, are classed as peasants in Baines' scheme. They were the second largest caste with about 2.4 million members. Baines is of the opinion that being widely spread out they could not be called a caste.[62] I do not agree; for if the Ahirs, let alone the Rājputs, of U.P. or Bihar can be called caste—the Ahirs of U.P. numbered in 1901 about 3.8 million—I do not know any reason that can go against Vellālas being called a caste. The utmost that should be admitted is that of the main four geographical divisions, the Konga division, settled round Coimbatore, is probably a separate caste, as they sport a different name, viz., Kavandan. Over 900 subdivisions, i.e. sub-castes according to Baines,[63] were entered at the Census enumeration which were after scrutiny reduced. It has to be pointed out that the title Kavandan was formerly borne by the Pallis too,[64] a circumstance which must add support to the above mentioned admission. The *Salem District Gazetteer* (139) registered only ten main, mostly territorial divisions, of the Vellālas in that district. It further added that the Konga Vellālas, one of these ten divisions, had eight subgroups, all territorial. Gustav Oppert[65] assured us that like the Paraiyans the Vellālas were divided into eighteen "classes". Perhaps the actual sub-castes, the endogamous units, are not more than 150 ($18 \times 8 = 144$). But even if we grant 400 sub-castes, a Vellāla sub-caste would be about 6,000 persons strong. With only 150 sub-castes, a sub-caste unit, on an average, would be 16,000 strong.

According to H. R. Pate, the author of the *District Gazetteer of Tinnevelly* (pp. 137–39) the Vellālas have three main divisions: (1) the Tonda mandala section, which sporting the title of Mudaliyārs is known as Mudaliyārs, who consider themselves the highest class of Vellālas; (2) the Karaikattār or

Pāndya Vellālas bear the title of Pillais; and (3) the Pillaimār Vellālas, who are further divided into two sections, which neither intermarry nor interdine with each other. The Tondamandalam division, Baines informs us, settled in the region of the old Pallava kingdom in the eighth century A.D. and that it is "strictly Brahmanistic in customs and religion". W. Francis in his *Madras Census Report of 1901*, however, records four main divisions. The fourth division is the Konga Vellālas of the Kongu country which comprises the districts of Coimbatore and Salem. They are known as Kavandans and are not infrequently spoken of as distinct caste, as stated above. The third division of Pate's account, the Pillaimār, appears properly in its territorial designation of Soliyā (Sozhiā) or of the Chola country in Francis' account. It is concentrated in Tanjore and Trichinopoly districts.[66]

The Vellālas regularly marry their girls only after puberty, though they rank in the social hierarchy immediately after Brahmins. Many of them perform daily 'puja' in their own houses, wear 'Rudrāksha' beads, and as Pate assures us, "study the *Devaram*" [Tamil hymns of great Nāyanārs or Shaiva saints composed before the eighth century A.D.].

As far back as 1866 the Collector's office of Tinnevelly was full of Vellālas and the then new incumbent of the office, Mr. Puckle, "applied for their transfer to other districts in favour of Brāhmans". Pate further observes that the Vellālas of Tinnevelly town looked upon the Brahmins of the place as "recent interlopers" and that they competed with Brahmins not only for elections to local bodies, like municipal councils, college committees and boards of temple management but also in matters of religion.

Vellālas do not take food at the hands of Padaiyachis who regard themselves as Kshatriyas, nor the food offered by a merchant who passes for a Vaishya.[67]

A well-known Tamil proverb declares that Kallans, Maravans and others gradually turn into Vellālas. "The group is thus swelled by outsiders adopting its titles and claiming to belong to it."[68]

Regarding marriage regulation and the extent of the endogamous unit in practice, H. R. Pate observes[69] about one of the three divisions mentioned above: "In practice, however, things are very different. The *marai* system in regard to brides is the same in this caste as in most others, that is, a man should marry the daughter either of his paternal aunt or of his maternal uncle". When and where the rule is impossible to be carried out it can be disregarded but the freedom thus granted is not absolute; for "in practice the circle of families from which a choice may be made is always limited. It is a defined circle and continues from generation to generation. The origin of these exclusive societies is extremely hard to trace. The families of the two parties may live in the same place or far from one another; sometimes the bond is community of occupation, sometimes it can only be a common place of origin or perhaps even a common ancestor. Whether these distinctions are increasing in number it is difficult to say; all that can be said is that they represent in effect an infinity of endogamous subdivisions. One reason for the limitation of choice and for distrusting the formation of connections with strange families is to be found, no doubt, in the fact that members of many other castes like Shānāns and even sometimes Paraiyans assume the name of Pillai and attempt to pass themselves off in society as Vellālans."

The Paraiyans, the untouchable caste of Tamilnad, whom the other and much smaller untouchable caste, Pallans, despise for their beef-eating but who look down upon the latter, numbered about 2.2 million. Their position in the social hierarchy of castes is defined by the circumstance that they polluted a Brahmin if they entered his street or went near him, and polluted all Shudra castes if they entered their houses or touched them. They were of course not allowed inside the temples.[70] They on their part, however, would not permit a Brahmin to tread in their part of the village. They even went further and declined to take food from Kammalans, Vanniyans (Pallis), and Nagarattu Chettis.[71]

Their caste, having only four endogamous divisions among them, is described as "well-organized". At the wedding the bride and the bridegroom "tuck their cloths behind after drawing the ends between the legs in the Brahman-fashion" and the groom wears the sacred thread.[72] Their special priests, the Valluvans, well-known as masters of astrology, serve them and the Pallans too, uttering Sanskrit texts at the wedding rites.[73]

However low they might have been ranked, they have a special privilege which appeared to raise them above all once a year at least. Gustav Oppert (55, f.n.) has quoted a passage from Bishop Caldwell's *Comparative Grammar of the Dravidian Languages* which testifies to this as a practice still current in the third quarter of the 19th century. At the annual festival of "Egattal, the only mother,—a form of Kali, and the tutelary deity of the Black Town of Madras—" when the *tali* was to be tied round the neck of the goddess on behalf of the entire community, it was a Paraiyan who was always chosen for the rite as the bride-groom of the goddess.

The social oppression which the Paraiyans and the next caste of Pallans suffered had not drawn them together nearer each other. And this being so in spite of the fact that their priests were the Valluvans testifies to the mutual hatred of these castes, the most efficient inbuilt mechanism of the caste-system guarding its activities and life.

The name Paraiyan, Baines[74] tells us, does not occur in the eleventh century Tamil Dictionary where we have only Pulayan. An inscription of the eleventh century is "probably the earliest in which the name Paraiyan is used." The sub-castes of the Paraiyan "which are very numerous indicate the practice of most of the more reputable handicrafts." "In the earliest records" their congeners figure as Eyinan who though "excluded from the villages" were "credited with the possession of hill forts and considerable power on the lines of the Dasyu of the *Sukta* period."

Pallans, the next caste in size and one of the untouchables, who, unlike the other and bigger untouchable caste, the Paraiyans, claim close affiliation with Brahmanic stocks, priding themselves as superior both to the Paraiyans and the smaller caste of the Chakkilians, numbered 825 thousand. Like the Kallans they assert that they are of the lineage of Indra; and one section of theirs is known as Devendra Pallans.[75] "They are perennially at feud with the Paraiyans."[76] In Tinnevelly and Madura District there were 233 thousand and 220 thousand of them respectively. These two and the districts of Tanjore and Trichinopoly together accounted for 87.4 per cent of the Pallans. More than half of the Pallans are found in the districts where the Maravans are in their greater concentration, and the Shānārs in high concentration! Small chance for the Pallans in these districts to secure the kind of just triumph, that they could score according to K. Gough's finding, in Kumbapettai.[77] It is noteworthy that in Tinnevelly where the Pallans had their greatest concentration, 233 thousand, the Paraiyans numbered only 94 thousand. Tanjore, the district in which Paraiyans had their third largest quota, 310 thousand, had 159 thousand Pallans. In Salem there were 185 thousand Paraiyans as against only 32 thousand Pallans. Thus the only district in which the Pallans could have the fullest satisfaction of lording it over their supposed inferiors in point of untouchability, having, as will be seen from the figures given later, the inveterate opponents, Maravans and Shānārs, in strong numbers, the former claiming allegiance of the Pallans to themselves, could not provide solace to the social soul of the Pallans!

Idaiyans or Konars as they are otherwise, and now more frequently, known, the traditional shepherds and cattle-breeders of Tamilnad, were the fifth largest caste, claiming no less than 695 thousand members. They have been claiming themselves to be Yādavas of the Krishna legend of the North; and it seems, latterly they have come to be known as Yadhavas.[78]

They have an imposing 'math', monastic institution, at Palni.[79]

Shānāns, or Nādars as they are now more commonly described, are the traditional toddy-tappers of Tamilnad. They numbered a little over 600 thousand. Eighty per cent of them were accounted for by the five districts, Tinnevelly, Madura, Tanjore, Coimbatore and Salem. This spread appears peculiar but must be explained by the nature of the traditional occupation, though it is rather strange that the coastal districts of South Arcot and Chingleput should neither of them have even 35 thousand Shānārs, that being the lowest number found in any of the five districts, viz. Tanjore. Toddy-tapping and selling toddy as such or in the form of liquors enables some of them to amass wealth; and they have, for almost more than a century, been putting forward a claim for their Rājput origin.[80] Since 1891 they have been returning themselves as Kshatriyas.[81] Baines, who informs us that in the inscriptions of the tenth century the toddy-tapping caste is named as Iluvan and not Shānān, vouchsafes the further interesting detail that under the Kadamba dynasty of Mysore many members of the caste were employed in the army and were afterwards settled as "a semi-military peasantry" on the land. He states the general position of the caste in Tamil society to be that of "the lower field-labourers just above that of the menial class." "In former years" he further observes, "it appears that the Shānān, like the weavers, were prohibited from living within the village site."[82] F. W. Francis, writing in the *Census Report of Madras, 1901* (p. 128), indirectly upholds Baines' observations. He says about the Sivakasi riots of 1895–1899: "How strongly even the lower ranks of society still feel upon points of caste etiquette is sufficiently shown by the fact that the claim of the Shānārs to a measure of equality in the temple with those above them in social precedence was recently sufficient *to get a whole district by the ears*." (Italics mine)

Five subdivisions, all of which are pronounced to be territorial in origin, are recorded. One of them the Malnad or Karukkumattaiyan is by far the most numerous and is conceded to be the highest. The fifth division, Pulukka Shānān, is formed by the domestic servants of the caste and in many places is not permitted to feed with members of the other sections. Between the other four groups commensality is permitted but not intermarriages.

In villages where both those who have taken to agriculture and those who still follow the traditional occupation of toddy-tapping occur, each section lives by itself, and an agriculturist seldom marries a girl from the tapping family unless lured to it by a substantial dowry.

"Almost every settlement of Shānāns has its own, Amman temple" under their control. The important Amman temple Koranganni in Tiruchendur taluka, "to which thousands of all classes congregate on feast days", is the property of the Shānāns. Here and there, they own and control Shiva temples too. Perhaps they themselves act as the 'pujāris'. Their barbers are "repositories of the ritual with whose aid they conduct their marriages. Brāhmans are rarely called in."[83]

The investigator of the 1961 Census, carrying out the scheduled survey of the village Pudukulam in Tirunelveli (Tinnevelly) District, whose population composition gives us 34.4 per cent of the total as Christian Nādārs, 8.2 per cent as Hindu Nādārs and 16.9 per cent as Maravans (pp. 6, 13), has made an observation which highlights a feature of the caste system of Tamilnad, and, though not quite unique, is yet a particularly remarkable trait of it. As the observation is made by a patriotic Indian and that, too, after about fifteen years of Independence, after almost three Five Year Plans involving Social Welfare and Community Development, it acquires sociological significance on the background of continuity. He says: "The cleavage between the different castes is much more marked in the Nādār-Maravar relationship. Throughout the history of South India Maravars and Nādars have hated each other with an intensity which cannot be seen anywhere else."

The Shānārs we are told have befriended the Paraiyans and Pallans (ibid., p. 103). The Shānārs numbered 294 thousand in Tinnevelly district in 1901; the Paraiyans 94 thousand and the Pallans 233 thousand. Thus the combined strength of the three allies was about 621 thousand. Against this the Maravans, a much smaller caste than the Shānārs, could show only 211 thousand, and neither of the two castes, Agamudaiyan and Kallan, which together with the Maravans are known as the Thevar, the triple community, had significantly large numbers in the district of Tinnevelly.[84]

The Maravans come immediately after Vellālans in the caste hierarchy we are told in the *Tinnevelly District Gazetteer* (p. 134), a statement which must be taken with a little caution and some reservation. For as a recent investigator has attested the correctness and continuance of the Tamil saying about the hiearchical situation obtaining among the four castes, Kallan, Maravan, Agamudaiyan and Vellāla, the Agamudaiyan is interposed between the Maravan and the Vellāla. The saying is thus rendered in English by the investigator (*Kunnalur*, Thanjavur Dist., p. 13): "A Kallan can become a Maravan by respectability, and by economic status he may develop into an Agamudaiyan and by slow degrees he will become a Vellāla."

As a matter of fact it is a distinctive feature of the caste system of Tamilnad that a purely agricultural caste—readers should bear in mind the fact that Sir Athelstane Baines has classed the Vellālas as peasants and not as dominant landlords—should be looked up to as a higher-status-group by castes which are described as military and dominant and whose history and present connections both stamp them as military and royal or ruling!

Gustav Oppert (p. 49) noted, more than seventy-five years ago, that the Maravans in Madura and Tinnevelly Districts claimed to be Rājputs and pointed out that their chief, the Setupati of Ramnad, was "one of the oldest most respected princes in Southern India". The great contribution of the Setupatis in the creation of the Rameshvaram temple-complex is well-known. Baines (p. 48), who speaks of the Setupati of Ramnad as a Zamindar, expands our knowledge of the martial nature of the caste. He says that the Maravans furnished strong body of militia and "for generations lorded it over the rest of the population".

Six divisions are known. The seventh is formed by the Pulukka Maravans or Parivaram. Though the divisions are strictly speaking described as endogamous yet intermarriage between any two has been known. One of the divisions has two subdivisions, their distinguishing mark being that the women of one wear a big 'tali' and those of the other a small one. Though strictly speaking the divisions are endogamous, intermarriage is not unknown. Zamindars of the two sections are known to have intermarried. They wear sacred ashes though they profess to be Vaishnavites.[85] Tirumanjar or Kalla Alvār is said to have been a member of this caste.[86]

The riots against Shānārs mentioned in the quotation from F. W. Francis were not the first attested ones. The earliest violent clash between the Maravars and Shānārs occurred in 1874; and the occasion was an attempt on the part of the Shānārs, in defiance of the social ban, to enter the Meenakshi temple at Madura. The Shānārs' attempt failed.[87] Later they attempted by means of a crimnal complaint to assert their right to enter the great Shaivite temple of Meenakshi. The case failed. Two years later a similar attempt at Tirutangal in the Srivilliputtur taluk, too, proved unsuccessful. In 1885 there arose in a village in the Sattur taluka trouble over an attempt made by the local Shānāns to take a procession through the streets of other castes in opposition to the wishes of the village folk. In 1895 a similar dispute smouldering for some time in many villages of Tinnevelly burst out into a riot at Kalugumalai. The landlord of Ettaiyapuram, a trustee of the local temple, had obtained an injunction restraining the Shānāns from taking processions in the streets in which the car-processions of the temple idol used to take place. The Shānāns in retaliation resolved to plan a countering of the move and *en masse* got converted to Roman Catholic Christianity. At their instance, it would appear, the converting Mission bought an old shop in one of the car streets and just before the day arrived on which the Hindus were, in the course of their festival, to drag their car trough the street, a *pandal* was rigged up across the road in front of the new chapel, which evidently was a modification of the old shop hastily put up. When the car reached the spot processionists saw that the *pandal* was such an obstruction that there was no alternative but to pull it down. In the meantime seventy Shānāns stationing themselves in the vantage spots of their houses "began throwing stones on the crowd". The Brahmin manager of the temple estate who went upto the defiant Shānāns to reason with them was immediately stabbed to death by one of the Shānāns. A general riot ensued in which seven Shānāns and two of the Brahmin manager's men were killed. "The infuriated crowd set fire to the thatch roof of the chapel and burnt and looted the Shānān quarters." A special police force was thereupon stationed at the village.

The special police stationed at Kalugumalai in 1895 was withdrawn in January or February in 1899 and it was in March of the year that what is described as "the most serious Shānān disturbance" or as "the memorable outbreak of 1899" took place in Ramnad district.

The events of 1895 at Kalugumalai, evidently, had roused the Shānāns of Sivakasi in the Sattur taluka where many wealthy Shānāns resided. They made a petition to the Tinnevelly Temple Committee that a Shānān may be appointed a trustee and a member of the managing body of the local Shiva temple. Their request having been rejected, some Shānāns attempted to force their way into the temple which resulted in a disturbance. Some temple property was burnt during its continuance.

The Shānāns were tried and acquitted by a Magistrate. They repeated a forceful entry into the temple. Again they were tried and acquitted. Thereupon the temple was shut by the trustees. And the Shānāns appear to have scored a partial victory.

During this turmoil a Maravan landlord of Ramnad had sought the intervention of a court about forty miles distant from Sivakasi. The proceedings were marked by bitterness of feelings on both sides, creating much bad blood between the Shānāns and the rest of the Hindus.

On the 26th April 1899 the Shānāns of Sivakasi took the initiative which could not but lead to riots. They set upon the local Maravans and burnt fifty-five houses of theirs. The local Maravan, joined by their caste-fellows from Madura and *a number of Pallans conducted a systematic campaign of arson and pillage against Shānān villages in Ramnad District.* (Italics mine.)

On the 6th June a united attack was made by over five thousand Maravans on Sivakasi Shānāns, killing sixteen of them. It was followed by an attack on the Christian Shānāns of Tenkasi taluka. Military reached the district on the 7th June and by the 16th June peace and order were re-established. Nineteen Hundred and fifty-eight persons were arrested. Special police were stationed, "the cost of which was met by fines levied on the inhabitants of defined areas."

"The hostility [to Shānāns] was shared by practically the whole Hindu community; the feeling of Vellālans being positively as bitter as any."

The riots evidently let off the steam, for though the cases in the Courts went against Shānāns they kept unmoved and quiet.[88]

In 1902 the Shānāns started, in the Nanguneri taluk of Tinnevelly district, a movement prohibiting their women from carying headloads, or from wearing beads or leaden bracelets and from going to the market. This bold move of self-respect, imitating the etiquette of higher castes, strengthened the dispute that the people had with Shānārs respecting their contribution to the village fund; and the Maravars of Periyatalai took up the cudgel against them leading to a brief riot.[89] It would appear the Shānārs had won the first round in social upgrading!

The feud cropped up some years later at the same place in 1918. The immediate cause, however, was purely personal, being the beating of a Maravan by a Shānān in the market and the outrage committed by a Shānān on a Maravan woman. Unknown numbers of both Shānārs and Maravars were killed and two policemen lost their lives and nine were injured.[90]

The longstanding Maravan-Shānār feud, mostly socioeconomic in origin, took a political turn in 1957 and resulted in one of the worst caste-riots of all time. The arson, murder and police-fire casualties were so great that the *Times of India* wrote two leading articles on the happenings, one on the 23rd September headed "Reign of Terror", and the other on the 3rd October 1957 headed "Social Tensions". The latter calling for 'a high power' inquiry ended with the sentence: ". . . . public inquiry into the riots should help Government and public leaders to devise ways and means of eliminating the divisive factors and forging closer the bonds of unity." Inspite of this warning and of public clamour for an inquiry, the Indian Government treated the incident as closed with a tour by one of its members over the large disturbed areas of Ramnad district!

The first clashes, the preliminary skirmishes, occurred between July 4 and September 10, and the full-blooded riots, in which, according to the statement of the Madras Home Minister, 2,830 houses were burnt down and 25 persons were killed, seem to have started from the 12th September. The reign of arson, murder, firing and maiming lasted till about the end of the month. The Home Minister of Madras is reported to have stated on the 26th September that there was only "uneasy peace" at the time. In a report appearing in the issue of the *Times of India*, 6th October, 130 villages were said to have had nearly 3,000 houses of the members of the Scheduled Castes burnt down. In an earlier report, 50 villages were said to have been razed to the ground. With the statement made on the 26th October by the Home Minister of Madras the curtain may be said to have been drawn on the whole tragic episode, none being the wiser for all the harrowing and disgraceful suffering.

The genesis of this holocaust is very instructive as revealing the explosive nature of the caste situation lending itself an easy field for exploitation for political purposes. Unholy alliance of caste and politics will surely jeopardise not only the peace but even the security of the country. The Maravans expected and claimed the support of the Scheduled Castes in their political ambitions. The Scheduled Castes, thankful to the Congress for their special rights and facilities, helped the Congress. But this intransigence of the Scheduled Castes was, it is suggested, not purely in-directed but was fostered from outside, not so much by the Congress but, as the *Times of India* News Service put it, by another and higher caste group, which, in the terminology of the post-Reform period formed a component of the Intermediate classes.[91]

Kallans, who, according to the Tamil saying noted above, tend to turn Maravans in their social climbing, are a larger community and numbered 495 thousand in 1901. The Agamudaiyans, the highest of the group of the Thevars, numbered only 319 thousand while the Maravans were 339 thousand.

The legend current among the Maravans at least somehow connects the three castes with the life of Rama. It makes the three castes descendants of three brothers who are believed to have given some help to Rama in his enterprise of crossing over to Ceylon. The youngest brother, who was the ancestor of the Maravans, having been promised by Rama that he would not forget his help, came to be known as Maravan, the first part of the word meaning something like "unforgotten". The eldest brother was the ancestor of the Kallans, who came to be so called, i.e. 'concealers', because he did not reveal to Rama the secret. The second brother behaved arrogantly towards Rama and his descendants therefore have come to be called Agamudaiyans or Ahamudaiyans, "the arrogant ones." The thevars are otherwise known as Mukulather.[92]

The Kallans, perhaps not denying this legend, have an altogether different story to tell about their origin. It makes them the progeny resulting from Indra's illicit intercourse under false pretenses with Ahalya, the wife of sage Gautama. Tradition current among Agamudaiyans more or less agrees with this.[93] Their deity, too, is special. It is Karuppan whose worship-priesthood is also recruited from among the Kallans or the Kusavans (potters) (*Dist. Gaz., Tanjore*, p. 85: *Madura*, p. 85). At least three endogamous sections have been known among them, which appear to be territorial. They are: (1) Terkunād (South country) Kallans of Tanjore; (2) the Kilnād (east country) or Mulurnād Kallans of Milur taluk and (3) the Melnād (west country) or Piramalnad Kallans (*Madura, Dist. Gaz*., p. 93). In Madura the Kallans are "divided" into ten divisions which are said to be endogamous units but Thurston's personal information vouchsafes the practice of endogamy only among four of them, viz. Melnādu, Sirudinādu, Mella-Kottainādu, Puramalainādu. The other nādus are: (1) Vellurnādu, (2) Pakaneri, (3) Konam-kottainādu, (4) Kandadevi, (5) Tennilainādu, and (6) Palayanādu.[94]

The Raja of Pudukottai is their acknowledged head, whom they refer to as Tondamān "in memory of their former colonization of the Tondamandalam or the Pallava country."[95] Their social importance was evident at the bull-games which used to be held at Dindigul in Madura District. The games were described in 1874 by J. Walhouse[96] as "very solemn celebrations", at which Kallans alone could "officiate as priests and consult the presiding deity." On the occasion they used to *hold quite a Saturnalia of lordship and arrogance over the Brahmans*.

This lordship of Kallans later appeared in a not honourable way, leading as it did to exactions and in 1896 the ryots of Dindigul struck against it. The wide-spread movement which was thus inaugurated came to be known as the 'anti-Kallar agitation'. Its origin lay in the seduction of an Idāiyan woman and her daughters by a Kallan whom he kept as his mistresses. An Idāiyan leader incensed at the incident turned the resentment of the people against the exactions of the Kallans into a movement to drive them out of Dindigul taluka. Thousands of villagers attending the meetings convened in furtherance took solemn oaths to do without the traditional Kallan watchmen, whom they boycotted to the extent of refusing them any food or drink. They established a fund to compensate those villagers whose cattle were stolen—for the Kallans were great cattle-lifters—or houses were burnt, and provided every village with a horn which was to be blown in case any thieving party was suspected to be operating there. Further every one hearing the sound of the horn was enjoined to run to the rescue. The exhortations and injunctions were fortified by laying down a scale of fines to be paid by those who failed to act up to them. The movement appeared to succeed; but the Kallans, showing fight, serious riots occurred in 1896 and 1897 in which several lives were lost and villages were burm. Anti-Kallar movement organisers having overstepped the limits of law in some cases were prosecuted which encouraged the Kallans. Taking advantage of the factions in the villages the Kallans managed to recapture their positions.[97]

At least two other castes of Tamilnad deserve mention in the context of the peculiarities of its caste system, before I can pass on to the all-India elite, and the one common Indian caste, the Brahmin. They are the Kaikolans, the weavers, and the Kammālans, the artizan-caste-quintet.

The Kaikolans, the weavers of Tamilnad, though slightly larger in number than the Maravans, having 347 thousand members in 1901, did not have any territorial concentration to speak of. In no district did they number hundred thousand; and in only two districts they numbered 50 thousand or more. In Coimbatore district, so famous for its 'sāris', they were 64 thousand of them, and in North Arcot 55 thousand. They are said to be divided into 72 nādus or desams whose significance is hard to understand; for we are informed that all of them except one intermarry. They have a "Mahāsabha' at Kanchi to which all other caste organizations are supposed to be subordinate.

The Kaikolans are called Sengundar ('red-dagger')[98] because of a legend current amongst Tamilians. Once Shiva was very much enraged against demons harassing the earth and six fire-sparks issued out of his eyes, which frightened Parvati. Parvati hastily retiring to her chamber dropped nine "beads" from her anklets. Shiva converted them into as many females, "to each of whom was born a hero with full-grown moustaches and a dagger". Subrahmanya at the head of these heroes destroyed the demons. One of the nine heroes was Virabahu; and the Kaikolans or Sengundar are said to be his descendants. Another version has it that when Shiva ordered Subrahmanya to march against the demon Padmasura who was troubling the people Parvati requested Shiva not to send the boy by himself. Shiva agreed on condition that Parvati would withdraw her previously pronounced curse that the nine females mentioned above who were impregnated by Shiva will bring forth no child. The females, damsels or maidens, gave birth to nine heroes with red daggers in their hands. Subrahmanya had a special precious dagger, and "the word Kaikol is said to refer" to it. The Kaikolans were the descendants of the nine heroes accompanying Subrahmanya in his successful expedition against Padmasura.[99] Thurston's version of the tradition of origin, though only slightly different, deserves to be noticed for the relevance it has to inter-caste relations in Tamilnad. He says that "the word Kaikolan is the Tamil equivalent of the Sanskrit Virabahu, a mythological hero, from whom both the Kaikolans and a section of the Paraiyans claim descent."[100]

The following "subdivisions" of the Kaikolans are recorded by E. Thurston (III, p. 336): (1) Sozhiā; (2) Rattu; (3) Siru-tāli ('small marriage badge'); Peru-tāli ('big mariage badge'). "The women of the Siru and Peru-tāli divisions wear a small and large tāli respectively." Thurston states further that the community is divided into seventy-two nādus. These seventy-two 'nādus' or 'desams' are grouped into two units, one of forty-two and the other of twenty-eight(?). The former unit is called "mel" (western) and the latter "kil" (eastern). The grouping, however, has no significance for marriage; for seventy-one of the nādus intermarriage is permitted. Only one nādu, because of its legendary refusal to participate in the sacrifice of the first-born, got "isolated from the rest of the community".

Each one of the seventy-one nādus is further divided into "kilaigrāmams" ('branch villages'), "perur" ('big') and "sittur" ('little') grāmams".

One section of theirs, the Senguntha Mudaliārs, strange as it appears, provides recruits to the Devadāsi class. In spite of this they have raised themselves in the social scale during the course of seven decades. In the classification of the Census of 1891 they were placed below such castes as Vellālas, Reddis, etc.; but by 1961, according to the findings of the village survey investigator, they were "on par with these Non-Brahmin communities."[101] The upward march is accompanied by a vigilant watch over any attempts by a lower caste to demonstrate approach to equality with them. The Senguntha Mudaliārs (Kaikolans) of the village Ayyangārakulam in Chingleput District, we are told, do not permit the small caste of Nāttārs (50,000 in 1901) to carry their dead to the burial ground through their locality, thus forcing them to make a long detour.[102] The Nāttārs, whose traditional occupation was fishing, have succeeded in exchanging it for the much more respectable one of silk-weaving. But so far it has only stiffened the attitude of the Mudaliārs!

The Kammālans, the peculiar artisan caste of Tamiland, numbered 497 thousand and thus almost equalled the Kallans. In Madura district they numbered 101 thousand, in Tinnevelly 83 thousand, while in Tanjore they were 62 thousand and in South Arcot only 48 thousand.

The Kammālans, also known as Panchala, have three territorial endogamous groups, viz. Pāndya, Cholā or Soziā and Kongā. The first group is principally found in the southern districts of Tinnevelly and Madura, the Soziās in Trichinopoly, Tanjore, Chingleput and South and North Arcot, while the

Kongās are concentrated chiefly in the western districts of Coimbatore and Salem. Some of them, as for example the Tattāns (goldsmith) of Pāndya group, are further subdivided on territorial basis.

The "five occupational sections" are: (1) Tattān (goldsmith); (2) Kanan (brass-smith); (3) Tacchan (carpenter); (4) Kal-Tacchan (stone-mason) and (5) Kollan or Karuman (blacksmith).

They "regard themselves as the real Brahmins and as the descendants of the divine artificer *Vishvakarmā*, call themselves Vishva Brahmins. They assume the title of *Āchāryas*, wear the holy thread, and claim the right to perform religious ceremonies among themselves, especially at marriages."[103]

They are known, in a Suit of A.D. 1881, to have proclaimed themselves to be Deva Brahman as opposed to the Brahmins whom they represented as being Go-Brahman Oppert, p. 59. f. n.). John Fryer, who visited India in 1690, appears to refer to this attitude of the Kammālans.[104] An inscription of the twelfth or eleventh century, however, mentions the grant of certain social rights to them, which evidently were not enjoyed by them previously, indicating that their social position was low.[105] The caste is highly organised, its organization being "one of its most interesting features". Each of the five divisions (functional or occupational) has at its head a headman (Natamaikkaran) and chief executive officer (Kāryasthan). Over them all is the leader known as Anjuveettu Natamaikkaran or Anjujati Natamaikkaran. His election is made by drawing lots in the temple of the caste goddess Kamākshi Amman from among the five representatives of the five sections, the procedure involving nomination of special members as a first step. The Anjuveettu Natamaikkaran is theoretically invested with full powers over the caste, and all members thereof are expected to obey his orders. He is the final adjudicator of civil and matrimonial causes.[106]

Lastly the all-India caste of Brahmins, the one caste, which whatever its components and however varied its occupational spread in the different linguistic regions of the country, has the same designation, i.e. Brahmin. The Tamil Brahmins numbered, in 1901, only 415,931. Their number was thus not much different from that of the Telugu Brahmins but much less than that of Brahmins in many regions of Indo-Aryan speech. They formed only 2.9 per cent of the then total Hindu Tamil population. As against this proportion of the Tamil Brahmins in Tamil population, the U.P. Brahmins of the twelve superior sections alone, numbering about 4.7 million, formed 11.5 per cent of the Uttar Pradesh Hindu population in 1901. The Gujarat Brahmins who numbered, in 1891, 569 thousand formed about 5.7 per cent of the Gujarati Hindu population. The Bengali Brahmins numbering about 1.45 million formed, in 1931, about 6.5 per cent of the Bengal Hindus.[107]

The Brahmins of Tamilnad who formed such a small percentage of the total Hindu Tamil population were further very unevenly distributed over the Tamil districts. Tanjore district with nearly 120 thousand of them claimed 29 per cent of the total Brahmins of Tamilnad. In 1951 they numbered about 200 thousand in the district and yet formed only about 6.7 per cent of the total population of Tanjore district. The next district of their concentration was Tirunelvelli (Tinnevelly) which claimed, in 1901, only 51 thousand of them, Madura following with 37 thousand and Trichinopoly coming next with 31 thousand.

Tanjore district is not only the central one but also the core, nay almost the soul, of Tamilnad. The number of other caste people and their relative concentration is a matter of much consequence for the Brahmanization and North-orientation of the culture of the Tamilian peoples. At least eight other castes had a hundred thousand or over of their members living in the district in 1901. They are in the descending order of their numbers: (1) Paraiyans; (2) Pallis; (3) Vellālans; (4) Kallans; (5) Pallans; (6) Ambalakkārans; (7) Valaiyans and (8) Agamudaiyans. These nine castes together accounted for nearly 71 per cent of the total population of Tanjore district. Paraiyans numbering 310 thousand had a concentration of 14.4 per cent; and the Agamudaiyans, having the lowest number among these castes in this district, i.e. just 101 thousand, were in the concentration of nearly 31 per cent. Kallans, who represent in Tamilian society the lowest section of the triadic group called the Thevars, of whom the Agamudaiyans form the highest section, numbering 188 and showing a concentration of over 37 per cent, may be added to the number of the Agamudaiyan, while considering the cultural and political aspects of caste and the conditions for the infiltration of Brahmanic influence and north-orientation.

Pallans, the agrastic serf-like servants of Brahmins in the olden dispensation,[108] in the three districts of Tanjore, Madura and Tinnevelly totalled 610 thousand, accounting for more than 72 per cent of their total population in Tamilnad. Brahmins, on the other hand, numbering in Tinnevelly 51 thousand and in Madura 37 thousand, totalled in the three districts together just over 200 thousand. Kammālans, the caste which even as early as the fourteenth century had declined to accept the Brahmins as the apex of the caste-society and had proclaimed itself to be the equal of the Brahmins and was thus consciously opposed to them, totalled in the three districts almost 250 thousand. What is more they outnumbered the Brahmins in Madura district by 170 per cent and in Tinnevelly district by 63 per cent, though in Tanjore they were only 62 thousand strong. Vellālans, the less vocal but more competent and persistent competitors and opponents of Brahmins and of North-Indian orientation, the backbone of Tamilnad, had almost 180 thousand of their members in Tinnevelly, i.e. in a majority of 270 per cent over the Brahmins. While assessing the situation in respect of acculturation one must bear in mind the wide-spread and well-organized temple-monastic centres founded and maintained by the Vellālas in many districts. In Madura the Vellālas, numbering 276 thousand, could put the Brahmins hopelessly out of the picture for they outnumbered the latter by more than six hundred per cent!

The Pallis or Padaiyachis or Vanniyans, as they like to name themselves, who with their tradition of Agnikula Kshatriyahood and a fairly large contingent, 235 thousand, though only in fifth rank concentration, in Tanjore, perhaps bear testimony both to the acculturation process and to its frustration. With all their talk of the Vellālas having dispossessed them of their lands and their supposed Kshatriyahood, they have been more tenants than farmers. Ambalakkārans, the fishermen, are the caste of Tanjore. For it is so to say their home, where live nearly 80 per cent of their total of 163 thousand members. And they have succeeded in raising their status by adopting many of the items of the Brahmanic way of living.[109]

The Valaiyans, of whom 137 thousand in Tanjore district, forming 44.5 per cent of their total membership in Tamilnad, with their highly local and non-Indo-Aryan heritage could not but add to the difficulty of the task set to the Brahmins. With full 45 per cent of their members, again, in the adjoining district of Madura, their interests, economic, political and cultural, could not fail to render the society rather impervious to Indo-Aryan influence and orientation.

The study of caste-geography further reveals the interesting and somewhat intriguing picture of the northern districts having been left a clean field for the non-Brahmin and local castes by the immigrant and/or the locally accepted Brahmins! In the districts of South Arcot, Chingleput and North Arcot together the Brahmins numbered not more than 76 thousand. And they were less than 15 per cent of their total strength in Tamilnad! It appears as if the Brahmins had treated these districts as out of bounds for them! The truth of the matter is that they were drafted either from the North or from the local stock to Tanjore by kings to take care of the large number of temples there. Kathleen Gough[110] has kindly provided us the supporting information that the Brahmins "own the land and have administrative rights in about 900 out of a total of 2611 villages" of the district.

South Arcot may be said to be *par excellence* the district of the Pallis or Padaiyachis, who nurse a grievance against Vellālas, that the latter ousted them from their lands and reduced them and also the Paraiyans to agricultural servitude. The Pallis numbering 728 thousand and the Paraiyans 566 thousand, the two together totalled nearly 1.3 million out of the total population of 2.35 million. Only two other of the important castes had a population of a hundred thousand each in this district.

They were the Vellālas, who numbered 146 thousand, and the Idaiyans or Konans, shepherds, who counted 104 thousand. In North Arcot, the Pallis numbered 357 thousand, the Paraiyans 193 thousand and the Vellālas 165 thousand. The Paraiyans led in Chingleput district with 321 thousand of their members, followed not far by the Pallis with 262 thousand of theirs. The third largest quota was that of the Vellālas who numbered only 92 thousand. In the three districts together the Brahmins could muster only 76 thousand in a population of 6.87 million. Thus the Brahmins formed not even 1.2 per cent of the total population of these three northern districts!

Of the three western districts, Salem, Coimbatore and Tiruchirapally (Trichinopoly), Salem contained Pallis in very strong concentration, 516 thousand of them or 20 per cent of their total population being there. But a strong contingent of Vellālas, numbering 395 thousand, could or would counter-balance their significance. Further the presence of not an insignificant number of Paraiyans, 185 thousand, could tip the balance in favour of the Vellālas. The Brahmins numbering only 16 thousand could hardly count for anything, either cultural or political. And the adjoining district on the south side, Coimbatore, was essentially a Vellāla one, there being 690 thousand of them, representing their highest concentration among all the districts. And what is important, no other caste was represented in the district in any strength, either a hundred thousand or above. There were 79 thousand Shānārs or Nādars and 64 thousand Kaikkolans, weavers. In this population a mere 19 thousand Brahmins could be easily submerged. In the total population of the two districts amounting to over 4.4 million a mere 35 thousand Brahmins as against the strong ferment of the Vellāla contingent could achieve very little!

Tiruchirapally is singularly devoid of concentration of any of the principal castes we have been discussing. The three castes that have a population of more than a hundred thousand each in this district are, the Pallis, the Pallans and the Vellālas. Their numbers were 148, 109 and 102 thousand respectively. The Brahmins numbered 31 thousand. Proportionately to their total number in Tamilnad the Brahmins were not badly represented, the district showing them in a concentration which is the fourth in rank and not much less than that in Madura. It is, however, the home of the Nattaman caste which numbering totally 150 thousand has 60 thousand of its members there.

Turning to Tanjore district which is the cultural centre of Tamilnad, I should further examine the representative nature of it from the viewpoint of caste-geography. In the *Madras Census Report* of 1901 not less than 63 separate Tamil castes are listed for district-wise distribution. Of these only 20 castes had a strength of a hundred thousand or more members each. The total number of Tamil Hindus in Tamilnad was about 14.2 million and the 20 castes together totalled about 13.4 million, i.e. over 94 per cent of the total Tamilian Hindus. In Tanjore district the nine castes, which had each a hundred thousand or more members in that district, had as their members 15.9 million, the total inhabitants of the district numbering 22.45 millions. They thus accounted for almost 71 per cent of the total population of the district.

Only three of these nine castes were represented in the district in their highest concentration. And they were Brahmins, Ambalakkārans and Valaiyans. It must be particularly marked that the great Chetti caste, such a liberal benefactor of the temple institutions in Madura, in which it had 82 thousand or 28 per cent of its members, was represented in Tanjore district by only 24 thousand persons. Tanjore district which is culturally said to be the microcosm of Tamilnad[111] turns out to be its hub from the viewpoint of caste-geography.

It is no wonder that under the circumstances of history briefly narrated above and the implications of the numbers and distribution of castes and their members that W Francis, writing more than sixty years ago, noted that the influence of the Brahmins on the religious and social life of the people at large is small. Large sections of the society regard it as in no way necessary that their marriages or their funerals should be ministered by any kind of professional priest. If any non-relative is ever needed in any rite it is the social leader in the caste that discharges the function of the officiating priest.[112]

General implications of the caste-system and caste-geography may now be made more explicit. And that is best done by comparing and contrasting the caste-system and caste-geography of Uttar Pradesh, the region which alone can claim to be the home of the origin of the system.

To begin with, one notices the vastness of the region, called Uttar Pradesh today, the United Provinces of Agra and Oudh of yesterday. It has 50 districts as against 12 of Tamilnad. Its Hindu population in 1901 amounted to something over 40 million, while that of Tamilnad was only 14.6 million. The separate castes listed for district-wise distribution, in the Census Report of 1901, in Tamilnad were 63 or 64 as against not less than 180 in Uttar Pradesh. Castes, which had each a membership of one hundred thousand or more, numbered only about 20 in Tamilnad as against 46 or so in Uttar Pradesh, those having three hundred thousand or more members each being 29.

The twenty Tamil castes with one hundred thousand or more members each together accounted for a larger percentage, viz. 91, of the Tamil Hindus. These 29 castes which had each 300 thousand or more members totalled 33 million and formed 81 per cent of the total Hindus of U.P.

The Chamār, unlike the Paraiyans of Tamilnad, was the biggest caste. Unlike Tamilnad caste-scene that in U.P. presented the Brahmins as the second largest caste, the Brahmins formed a little less than eighty per cent of the Chamārs. They formed 11.57 per cent of the total Hindus of U.P., while the Chamārs accounted for 14.47 per cent of them.

In Tamilnad the two main 'untouchable' castes taken together formed the largest single group but this grouping together is purely a theoretical and an arithmetical entity never so far realized in actual life. Even in Tanjore district where the spread of communist egalitarian militance is said to be rife[113] we are informed by K. Gough that "bitter competition for work and caste rank existed between the Devendra Pallans, Tekkathi Pallans and Paraiyans".

The Paraiyans by themselves formed 14.7 per cent of the Tamil Hindus no doubt, but they were outclassed in point of percentage by both the Pallis and the Vellālans, the former being 17.5 per cent and the latter 16.3 per cent of the Tamil Hindus.

In the U.P. caste system the third largest caste that of Ahirs, claiming themselves to be Yādavas, or Yādava Rajputs, the descendants of the house of Lord Krishna, and cherishing a long tradition of having ruled over various parts of the country from about the second century B.C., though cattle-breeders and agriculturists now with a fair grasp on the military profession, have not been opposed to Brahmins or Brahmanic culture. The next caste in size is the Rājputs, well-known for their royal traditions and respect for Brahmins and Brahmanic learning and institutions. As a matter of fact with their genealogies traced back to the Sun and Moon they may be said to be the solid basis of Brahmanic culture, and its defenders at all odds. These two ethnic groups formed 9.39 and 8.36 per cent respectively of the U.P. Hindus. The three castes, Brahmins and their supporters in the olden traditional regime, Rājputs and Ahirs, formed nearly 30 per cent of the total Hindus.

Another group, the Jāts, though much smaller in numbers, being about one-fifth of the Ahirs, and having much stronger and almost current tradition of a ruling stock though it began only in the fifteenth century, is ranked above Ahirs as non-Shudras and as just below the Baniās, who speak of themselves, and are not infrequently acknowledged, as Vaishyas. It is of western and Punjab affiliation and is confined to the western districts of U.P. It is found to have a hundred thousand and more of its members in three districts: They are the important central Indo-Gangetic districts of Aligarh, Meerut and Mathura. They generally claim themselves to be Rājputs and in the Meerut district all of their 92 classes are identical in name with those of Rājputs.[114]

The Baniās, the traders and merchants, well-known to be markedly religious or rather superstitious and inclined to pay homage and substance to Brahmins and to stand by their side in religio-social plans, claim more than 1.3 million members. Though all of them are very much divided on caste and religion lines, it is quite clear that this conservative element of Hindu society is very much of a Brahmanic asset, when it has not turned Jains, in the acculturation process. The very fact that it is shown alternatively as Vaishya, the third caste in the traditional 'varna'-grouping, emphasizes its role favourably for Brahmanic acculturation.

The Chamārs occur in the concentration of a hundred thousand or over members in 28 of the districts, while the Brahmins do so in 23, 18 of them being common to both. Gorakhpur which is the district with the highest concentration of Chamārs, viz. 6 per cent of their State total, is also the district of Brahmins' highest concentrations, there being nearly 5.7 per cent of their total number in U.P. in that district.

Traditions or legends about origins of different castes, too, is a point that impinges upon one's attention. We have seen that some castes in Tamilnad trace their origin to divine or semi-divine source, the divinities or semi-divinities being of the Puranic or Vedic pantheon. None of them so far as is known have condescended to own morganatic or straight origin from any of the higher castes. In U.P. not only various castes have posited Rājput origin for themselves and claimed Kshatriyahood as the agriculturists Kurmis, about 2 million, have done but some have even thought the higher caste connection so covetable as not to mind even if it can be asserted to be only a left-handed or illicit one. Thus the Ahirs have a Nandbans division, which, claiming Rajput origin, asserts, it would appear without detriment to their social pride, that they are descended from a Raja of Chitor by a *dolā* marriage with an Ahir princess.[115] The Lodhā, a good agricultural caste numbering about 1.1 million which is described as "a quiet, well-behaved and industrious part of the population", have Kācchwāha as one of their two main sections, which "professes to be the offspring of the union, between a Kācchawāha Rājput and a woman of inferior caste".[116] Similarly the Kachhi, a specialised agricultural caste equally hardworking, has Kāchhawāha as one of its two sub-castes, which it derives from a Kāchhwāha Thakur, i.e. Rājput, and a slave girl".[117]

Lastly I may emphasize the close connection between the temporal and the spiritual authority that must have loomed large for the villagers of U.P. in the fact that if Rājput has been a Thākur to him for the last seven or eight centuries, the Brahmin too figured in the eleventh and twelfth centuries as a Thākur, Brahmins being mentioned in records with the prefix of Thākur (Thakkura).[118]

Reference

1. L. I. Rudolph in the *Journal of Asian Studies*, 1960–61, p. 288. 2. Sircar, p. 19. 3. Sircar, p. 39. 4. Sircar, p. 213. 5. Sircar, p. 257. 6. *Raghuvamsa*: IV, 44–50 and VI, 59–65. 7. *Ep. Ind.* XXII, pp. 39, 41, 51 and footnote 1. 8. *The Cholas*, p. 551. 9. Baines, pp. 18, 58.

10. p. 63, footnote. 11. *Ind. Ant.*, 1873, p. 274. 12. *Caste in India*, 3rd ed., p. 67. 13. Ibid., p. 69. 14. Chitrao: *viḍe* Agastya. 15. R. K. Pillay in *Tamil Culture*, 1966, p. 16. 16. Ibid., pp. 169, 178–9. 17. *The Cholas*, pp. 66–76. 18. Gustav Oppert, *op. cit.*, p. 66; Thurston, III, 303. 19. J. N. Farquhar, p. 121.

20. Narayana Ayyar, *Origin and History of Shaivism in South India*. 1936, pp. 122–23. 21. *The Cholas*, 1955, pp. 12, 51, 66–76, 574–75, 674–76. *History of South India*, 1966, pp. 151, 379, 423; P. V. Jagadisa Iyyar, *South Indian Temples*, pp. 212–17. 22. Nilakanta Sastri, *History of South India*, p. 435; cf. J. N. Farquhar, *Outline of the Religious Literature of*

India, 1920, pp. 257–58. 23. Nilakanta Sastri, pp. 355, 368–72, 426; Iyyar. p. 461 footnote. 24. *History of South India*, pp. 426–7. 25. Jagadisa Iyyar, p. 461, footnote. 26. Nilakanta Sastri, *History of South India*, pp. 372, 427. 27. Sastri, ibid., p. 116. 28. L. I. Rudolph in the *Journal of Asian Studies*, 1960–61, pp. 288–89. 29. Farquhar, p. 246.

30. Farquhar, p. 255. 31. *Ep. Ind.*, XI, p. 325; XIX, 131–34. 32. K. K. Pillay in *Tamil Culture*, 1966, p. 166. 33. Farquhar, pp. 147–48. 34. Farquhar, pp. 257, 347. 35. Sircar, pp. 215–222. 36. Sircar, p. 279. 37. Narayana Ayyar, p. 381. 38. K. K. Pillay: *Tamil Culture*, 1966, p. 166. 39. Iyyar, p. 475. 39. *A. P. Census* 1961, VI, No. 16, *Pasarlapudilanka*, East Godavari district.

40. *Madras Census* 1961, VI, No. 9, pp. 112–13. 41. *Op. cit.*, I, 55; II, 77. 42. Sastri, *History of South India*, pp. 57–8. 43. *Op. cit.*, p. 191. 44. Iyyar, pp. 191, 475. 45. Risley, *People of India*, p. 305. 46. Pp. 50–69. 47. Iyyar, p. 217 where a whole passage from the *Annual Report of the Madras Epigraphieal Department* for the year 1908–09 is quoted. 48. Pp. 21–22. 49. Sastri, *The Cholas*, pp. 557–59.

50. J. N. Farquhar, p. 256. 51. Iyyar, p. 89. 52. Thurston, I, p. 330 53. Cf. *Social Tensions in India* for this. 54. Baines, pp. 90–91. 55. *Dist. Gaz. Tinnevelly*. pp. 137–41; *Dist. Gaz. Tanjore*, pp. 72, 218, 222–23, 229–30, 232. 56. *Dist. Gaz. Tanjore*, p. 218. 57. *Dist. Gaz. Tanjore*, p. 276. 58. *Dist. Gaz. South Arcot*, pp. 103–4; *Salem*, 142; *Trichinopoly*, 111; *Tanjore*, 83; Gustav Oppert, 99. 59. Gough, (I), 37.

60. Dr. Baines, pp. 74–5. 61. Oppert, 99 footnote. 62. P. 54. 63. Baines, pp. 54–5. 64. *Tanjore*, 83. 65. Oppert. p. 57. 66. Thurston, VII, pp. 373–74. 67. Thurston, VII, 369. 68. *Tanjore Dist. Gaz.*, 82. 69. *Tinnevelly*, pp. 139–40.

70. *Tanjore Dist. Gaz.*, 89. 71. *Salem*. 202. 72. *South Arcot*, 104–5. 73. *South Arcot*, 105; Gustav Oppert, 68. 74. Baines, pp. 74–6. 75. *Tanjore*, 90; 1961 Census Village Survey Monographs: *Pudukulam*, (Tiruneveli Dist.), 8; *Gohsarpatti*, (Ramanathapuram Dist.), 8. 76. *Salem*, 189; *Golwarpatti*, 8. 77. Marriott's *Village India*, p. 47; Leach, *Aspects of Caste*, p. 59. 78. Baines, p. 103; *Pudukulam, Tirunelveli Dist.*, p. 5. 79. *Madura Dist. Gaz.*

80. *Madras Census Report*, 1871, pp. 103–5. 81. *Tinnevelly Dist. Gaz.*, p. 125. 82. P. 71. 83. Tinnevelly *Dist. Gaz.*, pp. 129–31. 84. *Madras*, 1961, *Village Survey Monographs: Golwarpatti*, p. 10.; *Thadagam*, p. 14; *Vilangulam*, p. 4. 85. *Tinnevelly Dist. Gaz.*, pp. 133–4. 86. *Tinnevelly Dist. Gaz.*, pp. 134, 403. 87. *Madras Government Memorandum to the Statutory Commission*, pp. 596–98. 88. Dist. Gaz., *Tinnevelly*, pp. 126–28. 89. *Dist. Gaz., Tinnevelly*, p. 126.

90. *Madras Government Memorandum to the Statutory Commission*, pp. 596–98. 91. *The Times of India*, 28/29–4–58. 92. *Dist. Gaz., Trichinopoly*, p. 120; *Madras Village Monograph*, 26; *Golwarpatti* (Ramanathapuram), p. 10. 93. E. Thurston, I, p. 7. 94. E. Thurston, III, p. 71. 95. Baines, p. 47. 96. *Indian Antiquary*, III, p. 91. Italics mine. 97. *Madura Dist. Gaz.*, p. 92. 98. Thurston, III, pp. 31–2; *Madras Census Report*, 1891. 99. Thurston, III, pp. 31–2; *Madras Census* 1961, Part IV, No. 1, *Ayyangarkulam*, p. 7.

100. *Tribes and Castes of Madras Presidency*, III, p. 31. 101. *Madras Census* 1961, Part VI, *Thiruvelleri*, Tiruchirapalli District, p. 14. 102. *Ayyangarkulam*, p. 87. 103. Thurston, III, pp. 107, 113; Oppert, 58. 104. *Madras Census Report*, 1871, p. 157 and footnote. 105. *South Indian Inscriptions*, III, p. 47 106. Thurston, III, pp. 108–9. 107. N. K. Dutt (2), pp. 1–2. 108. K. Gough, I. pp. 41, 44–5; II, pp. 33, 42. 109. Baines, p. 81.

110. K. Gough, I, pp. 37. 111. K. Gough, I, pp. 38–39. 112. *Madura Dist. Gazetteer*, p. 84. 113. K. Gough, II, pp. 47, 51; III, pp. 58–59; *Times of India*, 28-8-67. 114. *Meerut Dist. Gaz.*, p. 89. 115. *Manipuri Dist.* Gaz., p. 88. 116. *Etawah Dist* Gaz., p. 72. 117. *Manipuri Dist.* Gaz., p. 89. 118. *Cawnpore Dist. Gaz., Farrukhabad Dist. Gaz., Ep. Ind.* IV, pp. 111–2, pp. 170–71; *Ind. Ant.*, XIX, p. 535; *Ep. Ind.*, XIX, pp. 291–94.

14

A Casteless Society or a Plural Society?

Max Weber, the German sociologist, hailed for his brilliant interpretation of the relation between capitalism and Protestant ethic, wrote in 1916–17 about Indian caste: "All caste relations have been shaken and the stratum of intellectuals bred by the English are here, as elsewhere, bearers of specific nationalism. They will greatly strengthen this slow and irresistible process."[1] Readers of this book will realize the limited correctness of the appraisal and note the exaggeration in the sanguine optimism about the future of caste.

The practice of caste changed no doubt and a section of the Hindus not only acquiesced in that change but actively helped it. The orthodox Hindus did not like the modifications that had come about owing to changed circumstances. They actually deprecated them, and if they had the power they would fain reinstate the old situation. The progressive elements, on the other hand, not only welcomed the changes but proposed further modifications. Among these there were at least three, more or less clearly distinguishable, schools of thought. There were those who believed that the best way to bring about the desired end was to hark back to the imagined pure state of Hindu society which was characterized by the existence of only the four traditional castes, viz. Brahmin, Kshatriya, Vaishya, and Shudra. The greatest exponent of this point of view was Mahatma Gandhi, who expressed it only three or four years after Weber expressed his, without of course any knowledge of Weber's views on caste.[2]

There were others who would go ahead rather than look back on the past in the vain hope of reinstating it under totally different conditions. But they thought that the only way in which abolition of caste can be achieved as a concrete fact is, in the first place, to amalgamate the various sub-castes of a present-day caste, which have much cultural unity and economic similarity. Then the castes which are approximately on a footing of equality would be consolidated, and the procedure may be followed till society becomes casteless. They contended that this process being slow would afford sufficient time for education and the formation of informed opinion, with the necessary adjunct of the requisite mental adjustment of those classes which are not yet prepared for a wholesale change in their agelong customs.

The third point of view considered caste to be so degrading in some of its aspects and so anti-national in others that it would abolish it altogether without any hesitation or delay.

Mahatma Gandhi did not give us a complete programme by means of which he proposed to reinstate the four-fold orders. It is not quite clear whether persons would be assigned to one or the other of these classes on the ground of their birth in a particular caste or on the strength of the occupation they now follow. Yet as he laid great stress on birth and heredity and subscribed to the view "once born a Brahmin always a Brahmin", he would no doubt rather rearrange the other castes into their proper groups on the basis of birth. If this procedure were sought to be put into operation I do not hesitate to state that there would be great strife among the various castes. The Kshatriya, Vaishya and Shudra classes have not remained as distinct and intact as the Brahmins. There is much difference of opinion as to which of the castes should be included in one or the other of the above three classes. Even if an amicable settlement on this point were possible, what about the untouchable classes? Gandhi was vehemently opposed to untouchability, and he would naturally propose some respectable status for these classes. Where are they to be provided for? Wherever it may be proposed to include them, there is bound to be a tremendous protest from that class. The criterion of birth in a caste for the purposes of the proposed four-fold classification is thus found to be quite unsatisfactory. If the actual occupation of an individual is to be the test of his status, how are the modern occupations to be accommodated in this old scheme of four-fold humanity? Even if we successfully adjust the claims of all persons and classify them properly, it is an open question if marriage between the classes is to be permitted or prohibited, or if any social restrictions in the matter of food, etc., are still to continue. Altogether it appears to me that a return to the four-fold division of society is impracticable, and even if accomplished would serve no more useful purpose than that of reminding us of our past heritage.

To propose to abolish caste by slow consolidation of the smaller groups into larger ones is to miss the real problem. The method has been tried in old Bombay Presidency for the last forty years and more with disastrous results. The sub-castes that join together to create a super-organization retain their internal feelings of exclusiveness in fair vigour. The new organization takes up a rather militant attitude against other castes, especially those which are popularly regarded as immediately higher or lower than the caste which it represents. And as already pointed out, caste-consciousness becomes more definite and virile. We have seen that, even among the castes which were grouped together for political purposes, the common aim of fighting other castes had not proved strong enough to induce individual castes, comprised in the group, to ignore their claims at the time of the distribution of the spoils of office.

As I envisage the situation and as the analysis of caste under British rule must make it clear, the problem of caste arises mainly out of caste-patriotism. It is the spirit of caste-patriotism* which engenders opposition to other castes, and creates an unhealthy atmosphere for the full growth of national consciousness. It is this caste-patriotism that we have to fight against and totally uproot. If the procedure advocated by the protagonists of the second viewpoint were to prove successful, I believe the problem of diminishing caste-patriotism will be ever so much more difficult. It would lead to half a dozen large groups being solidly organized for pushing the interests of each even at the cost of the others. Acute conflict will be the consequence.†

Apropos of this it would be instructive to note what two distinguished British intellectuals wrote concerning caste and caste-like fissures in a society, almost about the same time that Max Weber in Germany and Mahatma Gandhi in India were expressing their views. Arnold Toynbee, the 'universal historian', in his criticism of Plato's ideal social organization written for the 10th volume of *The Encyclopaedia of Religion and Ethics* (p. 552b), emphasized the utter impracticability of the four-fold division of society. James Bryce, the philosophic historian, jurist, and statesman-diplomat, went deeper when he wrote in his *Modern Democracies*:[3] "Social structure is an important factor. Where men are divided by language, or by religion, or caste distinctions grounded on race or on

---

* Latterly this phenomena is being referred to as 'casteism'.

† Readers may please note that this was written in 1932.

occupation, there are grounds for mutual distrust and animosity which make it hard for them to act together or for each section to recognize equal rights in the other. Homogeneity, though it may not avert class wars, helps each class of the community to understand the mind of the others, and creates a general opinion in a nation."

My comments on Mahatma Gandhi's views were written in about 1931. The upsurge of Indian nationality had just gathered phenomenal force. Yet the various representations made by caste organizations, before the Government of India Act of 1935 emerged from the anvil of the British Parliament, clamoured for all kinds of special attention to vociferous caste-groups. Buildings for members of one's caste were being built, co-operative banks run by specific castes were multiplying, community-centres based on caste were being built up, maternity homes and general hospitals intended for the use of members of specific castes were being founded in the midst of the new setup created by the sweeping success of the Indian National Congress at the polls in 1936–37. In the political sphere only the Scheduled Castes, the erstwhile untouchables, had figured as a separate caste entity. In Bombay, in addition, the Marathas had managed to get some special treatment in the Constitution. The various non-Brahmin groups of the earlier era had vanished into the womb of the all-embracing Congress. Socialistic and communistic ideas of social equality and classless society were preached ever so vehemently. The World War II came in 1939. Soon thereafter the Congress intensified the national struggle.

Freedom dawned on India on the 15th August 1947. The nationalist upsurge of more than sixty years became incarnate as the nation—state of India (Bhārat).

B. R. Ambedkar, the leader of the Scheduled Castes, who was adamant against accepting change in the special representation of these castes in 1932 for which Mahatma Gandhi had to undertake a fast unto death, not only acquiesced in their special representation only for ten years but also became the sponsor of the Constitution in 1949. A. B. Latthe who was one of the leaders of non-Brahmin movement, and who in 1925 insisted on communal electorates till such time as caste disappears, was prepared to forego such special representation during the progress of the Indian Round Table Conferences in London. Pondering over the Coyajee report on Kolhapur riots of 1948 he remarked: "As an humble friend of the non-Brahmin movement of thirty years ago, I still think the movement was, essentially justified but later on it degenerated into naked communalism of several non-Brahmin communities which ultimately broke it up. . . . The vicarious punishment of all Brahmins for the sins of a few among them is foolish and hatred of one community against another is suicidal to democracy. The days of caste oligarchies have gone and cannot and ought not to be revived. Those in the State who encourage narrow communal pride . . . are the worst enemies of the people and the State."[4] These were portents auguring well for the emergence of a casteless society. But did they really represent the social trends? Were they not merely the political veneer masking the rough fissures of caste sentiment?

The Democratic Republican Constitution of India was promulgated on the 26th January 1950. Its very preamble solemnly asserts that the People of India have constituted themselves into a Sovereign Democratic Republic, which, as stated in Article 1 of the Constitution, is named "India, that is Bharat", to secure to all its citizens Justice, Liberty and Equality and to promote Fraternity. Justice is specifically described to be of three types, not only political but economic and social as well. Equality is of not only opportunity but also of status. Justice and Equality, as thus defined, between them, cut the very roots of caste. Citizens of India—Bhārat avowed that the purpose of their political association is to guarantee to every citizen not only equality of opportunity, but absence of unequal treatment in social and economic matters. The guarantee of equality of status must be taken to refer to equality of legal status, which is the standard meaning of status. The fourth objective of the Nation, Fraternity, is to be, as I understand it, only a consequence of the actual achievement of the first three objectives.

The implementation of the ideals is further elaborated in the section on Directive Principles of State Policy. Article 38 states: "The State shall strive to promote the welfare of the people by securing and protecting as effectively as it may a social order in which justice, social, economic and political, shall inform all the institutions of the national life."

Of the Articles laying down the Fundamental Rights in the Constitution there are three in which caste, along with race, language, religion and some other categories, figures and are thus relevant to our purpose. Article 15 reads: "(1) The State shall not discriminate against any citizen on grounds only of religion, race, caste, sex, place of birth or any of them. (2) No citizen shall, on grounds only of religion, race, caste, sex, place of birth or any of them, be subject to any disability, liability, restriction or condition with regard to—(*a*) access to shops, public restaurants, hotels and places of public entertainment; or (*b*) the use of wells, tanks, bathing ghats, roads and places of public resort maintained wholly or partly out of State funds or dedicated to the use of the general public."

While Article 15 forbids discrimination against any citizen, particularly in matter of access, Article 16 guarantees to him equality of opportunity relating to employment or appointment. It reads: "(1) There shall be equality of opportunity for all citizens in matters relating to employment or appointment to any office under the State. (2) No citizen shall, on grounds only of religion, race, caste, sex, descent, place of birth, residence or any of them, be ineligible for, or discriminated against in respect of, any employment or office under the State." Of the three provisos to this important Article, one, the 4th, is significant for our purpose, as it is the one which speaks of category of citizens, well-known during the later days of the British rule in India. It was, as pointed out in Chapter X even in 1932, almost a creation of British administration. Ostensibly it was created to mete out social justice but its ready and effective use against the rise of Indian unity against British rule in India was the unconscious source. Clause (4) of Article 16 reads: "Nothing in this article shall prevent the State from making any provision for the reservation of appointments or posts in favour of *any backward class of citizens* which, in the opinion of the State, is note adequately represented in the services under the State."* This is a permissive provision intended to enable the government to implement effectively the objectives of social justice laid down in the Preamble generally and in Article 38 specifically.

However, the mode of securing social justice and equality of opportunity permitted by Article 16(4), that of 'adequate' representation of citizens in the services of the State, is only one item of the three-pronged approach to the problem, contemplated and proposed in the Constitution of 1950. The primary unit of this three-itemed approach is the representation of certain classes of citizens in the legislatures of the country. Part XVI of the Constitution containing Articles 330 to 342 was designed to provide for this item, as well as the third one of the three-fold approach to the securing of social justice and equality of opportunity. It is significantly entitled "Special Provisions Relating to Certain Classes".

There are four categories of these classes that are mentioned and attempted to be provided for through these "special provisions". Of these I shall leave out the Anglo-Indians, whose case is

---

* Italics mine. Note that the expression is in the singular number.

quite clearly a hangover from the past and strictly limited in time and therefore evanescent. The Scheduled Tribes may similarly be left out as our present purpose is with caste-system proper and as the provisions for the Tribes are much more varied both in nature and extent and as regards the prescribing and implementing authority.

The Scheduled Castes—they were to be and are specified in a 'public notification' by the President of the Union under Article 341—had reserved seats, nearly proportionate to their number, both in the House of the People or the Lok Sabha of the Union and the Legislative Assemblies, or Vidhan Sabhas, of the States, under Articles 330 and 332, for ten years. The reserved representation of the Scheduled Castes was to cease after 1960 and was thus intended to be a temporary feature.

Under Article 335 they are assured of their "claims" being taken into consideration "consistently with the maintenance of efficiency of administration, in the making of appointments to services and posts in connection with the affairs of the Union or of a State." Thus Article 335 may be said to have guaranteed a certain proportion of Government service posts to the Scheduled Castes. And this special treatment—we may speak of it as reservation of posts—was and is to be permanent, subject only to the consideration of efficiency of administration! Descheduling would of course end it altogether; but it is easier said than done.

The securing of fair or adequate representation of the Scheduled Castes and of "any backward class of citizens" is considered so imperative in the Constitution that Article 320(4) introduces an exception to and a restriction on the functions and powers of the Public Service Commission in the matter of the carrying out of the obligation of the State under Articles 16(4) and 335. Clause (4) of Article 320 says: "Nothing in clause (3) [of Article 320] shall require a Public Service Commission to be consulted as respects the manner in which any provision referred to in Clause (4) of Article 16 may be made or as respects the manner in which effect may be given to the provision of Article 335."

The third item of the scheme for implementation of the ideal of equality of opportunity and of social justice is formed by special measures for the removal of difficulties and for the provision of facilities and services to the "backward classes". These classes are not defined but are specified as "socially and educationally backward". Article 340 under clause (1) empowers the President, it may be said to ask or require him, to appoint a Commission "to investigate the conditions of socially and educationally backward classes within the territories of India and the difficulties under which they labour and to make recommendations as to the steps that should be taken by the Union or any State to remove such difficulties and to improve their condition and as to grants that should be made for the purpose by the Union or any State and the conditions subject to which such grants should be made." Clause (2) of the Article requires the Commission to do the job and "present to the President a report setting out the facts as found by them and making such recommendations as they think proper." Clause (3), the last one, of the Article requires the President to "cause a copy of the report so presented together with a memorandum explaining the action taken thereon to be laid before each House of Parliament."

These provisions taken together ought to make it clear to anyone that the Constitution intended that both the Scheduled Castes and the "backward classes" were to be afforded special treatment for the overcoming of their social and economic difficulties to enable them to realize and experience the active condition of social justice laid down in Article 38, in the manner and to the extent that were to be prescribed by the Union Government on the basis, or rather on the consideration, of the report of the Backward Class Commission enjoined to be appointed by the President.

It is unfortunate that the terminology of the above Articles and clauses speaking of "backward classes" is not quite uniform, and that to make the matters worse there is Article 46. It says: "The

State shall promote with special care the educational and economic interests of the weaker sections of the people, and in particular, of the Scheduled Castes and the Scheduled Tribes, and shall protect them from social injustice and all forms of exploitation." We have here a category of citizens or "people" which is designated "the weaker sections", and what is significant is that the Scheduled Castes and the Scheduled Tribes are two of its components. We may logically conclude, in view of the reference to "educational and economic interests" and to "protection from social injustice", that the "backward classes" spoken of in Article 340, whoever they may be, are the third component of the category "weaker sections of the people."

It may be said that at the worst there is only ambiguity. The outright empowering of the State, i.e. the Union Government and everyone of the State Governments, "not only to promote the educational and economic interests" of "the weaker sections of the people" but also to do so "with special care" appears to take the matter of the determination of the manner and extent of special facilities to be afforded to the "socially and educationally backward classes within the territories of India" straightway out of the hands of the Union Government or of the President and his Backward Class Commission

And here I have to bring to the reader's notice the gravest of defects in the wording of the Articles in the Constitution dealing with the topic under discussion. The substantive Article 340 empowering the President to appoint a Backward Class Commission to take counsel, authoritative and well-considered, leaves out the report of the Commission at a loose end with only the requirement that there shall be a memorandum laid on the tables of the Houses of Parliament "explaining the action taken thereon". It does not specifically ask the President to specify the "backward classes" in an "Order". This is enjoined in Article 338 and therefore in an indirect or subsidiary way. The correct interpretation of the articles in question may not make a President's "order" specifying "backward classes" other than the Scheduled Castes and the Scheduled Tribes a condition precedent to the implementation of "the steps" and "the grants" part of Article 340 and also of clause (4) of Article 16. The memorandum explaining the action taken "on the report by the President and the Union Government mentioned in Article 340(3) should have to be deemed adequate for the purpose.

However, for purposes of the competent functioning of the Special Officer, enjoined to be appointed by Article 338, President's Order specifying the Backward Classes is a necessary precedent. Even the "steps that should be taken by the Union or any State" to remove difficulties of these classes as contemplated in Article 340(1) have to be specified to enable the Officer to discharge his function of supervising, and through supervision of advising, the stages of the progress towards the achievement of the goal of the national endeavour of securing equality of opportunity and of establishing climate of social justice.

That the category of "backward classes" is a statutory one and was intended to be detailed in President's Order is made plausible by the use of that expression in a Constitutional provision for the appointment of Ministers. According to a proviso in Article 164, in the States of Bihar, Orissa and Madhya Pradesh there "shall be a Minister in charge of tribal welfare who may in addition be in charge of the welfare of the Scheduled Castes and backward classes or any other work."

In view of the fact that Article 46 is one of the Directive Principles of State Policy and not a substantive right or function like Article 340 the directive of Article 46 is to be put into effect in the light of and under the guidance provided by Article 340 except as respects the Scheduled Castes and the Scheduled Tribes. That this may be the correct view of the relative interdependence of the articles in question is rendered plausible by the inclusion of the "backward classes" of Article 340 among the classes coming under the purview of the Special Officer for the supervision of the operation of the "safeguards" for the Scheduled Castes and the Scheduled Tribes specified and enjoined in Article 338. It reads: "(1) There shall be a Special Officer for the Scheduled Castes and Scheduled Tribes to be appointed by the President. . . . (3) In this Article, references to the Scheduled Castes and the Scheduled Tribes shall be construed as including references to such other backward classes as the President may, on receipt of the report of a Commission appointed under clause (1) of Article 340, by order specify and also to the Anglo-Indian community."

The Scheduled Castes and the Scheduled Tribes are specifically mentioned in Article 46 as the beneficiaries of the State function of promoting with special care the economic and educational interests of "the weaker sections of the people." They are, therefore, entitled to special facilities and economic help, whatever may be the ways of special facilities that may be provided under Article 340.

It is significant that Article 275 provides for the funds to be made available from the Consolidated Fund of India only in the case of the Scheduled Tribes. Its clause (1) has this: "Such sums as Parliament may by law provide shall be charged on the Consolidated Fund of India in each year as grants-in-aid of the revenues of such States as Parliament may determine. . . . Provided that there shall be paid out of the Consolidated Fund of India as grants-in-aid of the revenues of a State such capital and recurring sums as may be necessary to enable that State to meet the costs of such schemes of development as may be undertaken by the State with the approval of the Government of India for the purpose of promoting the welfare of the Scheduled Tribes in that State etc." Thus in the matter of receiving grants from the Government of India for the implementation of the directive regarding the securing of social justice through affording special economic aids the provisions of Article 340 remain paramount whether to the Backward Classes or to the Scheduled Castes.

The States were and are competent to spend for welfare of all "weaker sections of the people" and of the Scheduled Castes any sums out of their resources for any schemes they prepare for the purpose. And the expression "weaker sections of the people" is such that, without listing any group or groups, all the people likely to be included in the category "Backward Classes" may be subsumed under it. But the President and the Union Government cannot ask the States to spend specific amounts on the welfare of Backward Classes without listing them and specifying the ameliorative activities or programmes to be undertaken. When this is done the States cannot ask for grants-in-aid or subsidies in that behalf as they can do as respects the Scheduled Tribes.

To a student of Indian society as to any politician who has judiciously and without preconception tried to understand the social climate that had come to settle down during the last stages of the British rule in India, the need to ponder over the rather inharmonious provisions mentioned above in a Constitution that was to usher in a casteless society should have been clear. The Congress party, the one political party that, for fifteen years since the promulgation of the Republican Constitution had undisputed and unassailable power to do what could be rationally expected to bring in a casteless society, however, was not mentally prepared for such a programme. I need not dilate on the causes of this situation in view of what I have said above about Mahatma Gandhi's views on caste. I shall present here a few salient features of the social horizon of the Congress Party in power.

In August 1950, the Government of India appointed a committee of which Shri R. R. Diwakar, sometime Governor of Bihar, was the chairman, "to inquire into the question of abolition of caste and communal distinctions in Governmental activities in accordance with the Constitution." It seems the report remained confidential. One of its recommendations was that the State Governments should consider the desirability of the omission of the mention of caste in all forms and records.[5] Some proof of implementation of the pious recommendations of the Diwakar Committee was forthcoming in 1956 in the non-official legislation called the Indian Registration Amendment Bill which was piloted through the two Houses of Parliament by S. C. Samanta and P. T. Leuva. It renders unnecessary the recording of caste and sub-caste of parties mentioned in a deed for registration. During the course of the debate one member, belonging to the Praja Socialist Party, suggested a wider measure making it impossible for all suffixes or prefixes signifying caste to appear anywhere. The reply of H. V. Pataskar, the Minister for Legal Affairs, is worth noting as it brings out the complexity of the situation and provides justification for my statement on backward classes made above. He is reported to have said that "such legislation at the present moment would create a difficulty since the Constitution gave a special position to backward classes and scheduled castes and tribes" and to have added that "the question could be taken up after the Law Commission had submitted its report."[6] This difficulty was first put forth by the Parliamentary Secretary to the Education Minister to oppose the consideration of F. B. Dabhi's Bill "to withdraw official recognition to caste distinction amongst Hindus."[7] The ambivalent attitude of the Government of the day is clearly reflected in the manner in which Pataskar opposed the amendment to a clause in the Representation of the People (Amendment) Bill in the Rajya Sabha. Jaspat Roy Kapoor, a member of the Congress Party, moved a clause requiring a candidate for election to declare at the time of his nomination that he was not a member of any political organization bearing a caste or communal name or restricting its membership to one caste, community or religion. P. Subbaroyan, the well-known ex-minister of Madras State vigorously supported the amendment which was, however, lost.

There is some evidence to attribute this attitude of the major political party, which is the Government of the country, to socio-political reality within it and to political expediency. In 1952, on one occasion Jawaharlal Nehru stated his conviction that caste-loyalty of the Bihar Ministry had militated against efficiency and integrity in the affairs of the State, and declared as the President of the Congress that persons thinking and acting on caste-basis should be expelled from the party. Within two months of the declaration, in a post-election statement of thanksgiving the chief of the Congress party in Bihar averred that to be proud of one's own caste, birth and blood in the limited sphere was not bad, but that it became bad or rather worse when it crossed the limit! The late Sardar Vallabhbhai Patel, when criticised for accepting a purse from his caste in his own village, is reported to have replied that by being Indian he had not ceased to be a Pātidār. The Congress leaders of Saurashtra are reported to have utilized caste loyalties and animosities when U. N. Dhebar, past President of the Congress, was the chief of the party. The use of this factor in the Andhra election of 1955 was so blatant that *The Times of India*, latterly a pro-Congress paper, came out with a leading article contrasting this behaviour, of the Congress High Command with its prompt action in appointing a committee after the Avadi session of the organization to suggest measures for the elimination of caste-basis.[9]

Even more than the inharmonious nature of the various Articles in behalf of the ideal of social justice, the absence of time-limit or/and of provision for declassing or delisting of Backward Classes, once specified as such, renders the complex of articles intended to implement the endeavour to establish full social justice of a caste-less society a stabilizer of caste. They thus create conditions of social atomization. This is the condition of what J. S. Furnivall, while characterizing the Indonesian society under Dutch Colonial Government, designed a "plural society".* There is much to detract from the use of the term as respects the caste-society of pre-British days but much to recommend it to designate the condition that bids fair to establish itself under the current implementation and operation of the complex of the articles of the Constitution discussed above.

The progress of the implementation of the inharmonious provisions has gone the way of progressive atomization. In September 1950 (*Report*† *of the Commission for the Scheduled Castes and Scheduled Tribes*, 1951, pp. 29–31, 120–122) the Ministry of Home Affairs issued a resolution regarding the continuance of the reservation of posts and services for the Scheduled Castes and the Scheduled Tribes and the Anglo-Indians in certain percentage. The percentages of reservations were to continue as they were current on the 14th August 1947 till the population figures of the Census of 1951 were available. The order was "applicable to all services under the control of the Government of India."

In 1951 the Government of India stepped on the road to social atomization by getting the first amendment to the Constitution passed, and thus adding to it the charter for discrimination in education and economic matters on behalf of a section of the people, mentioned in Article 340 as "socially and educationally backward classes" but neither defined nor enumerated anywhere. The amendment gave us clause (4) of Article 15 which reads: "Nothing in this Article or in clause (2) of Article 29 shall prevent the State from making any special provision for the advancement of any socially and educationally backward classes [class?] of citizens or for the Scheduled Castes and the Scheduled Tribes." In April 1951 the Government issued a circular letter (*Report*, 1951, p. 55) making it clear to the State Governments that "it was not the intention of the Government that any privileges or concessions to which any Backward Classes were previously entitled should be taken away from them merely because they did not happen to be included in the Scheduled Castes and Tribes. The State Governments were, therefore, requested to continue to follow the administrative practices in the matter of concessions to Backward Classes, which were in force in the States before the issue of the President's Orders unless they were inconsistent with any other provision of the Constitution." This circular, over and above sanctioning the old practice regarding special treatment to certain groups of people and castes, abrogated the moral authority and the legal power accruing to the Government of India under Articles 340, 341 and 342 of the Constitution!

The Government of India itself had begun awarding scholarships to students of Backward Classes since 1949–50 in which year 349 scholars belonging to these classes received about 250 thousand rupees by way of scholarships (*Report*, ibid., p. 56). The list of Backward Classes recognised by Government of India for its scholarships in 1951–52 (ibid., Appendix XIX), contained, leaving out Muslims and Christian sections of castes, the names of over 990 different castes or sub-castes!

The Report of the Backward Classes Welfare Board of Bombay State for the year 1953 contains a list of Backward Classes specified for the State besides its Scheduled Castes and Scheduled Tribes. They numbered more than 125 different castes. In Madras under its Educational Rules, in July 1953 "greater facilities for education of the children and dependants of persons belonging to certain occupational communities, viz., the barber, fishermen, dhoby (washerman), and potter communities, who reside and practise their hereditary occupations in the rural areas" were announced.[10] It appears from the context that the castes enumerated were few and the conditions not entirely based on caste-qualification but occupational-cum-rural residence one.

* See my book *Social Tensions in India* for a full discussion of this concept.

† Referred to as *Report*.

It was only in 1953, two years after having taken a decision and having effected a Constitutional channel for the proliferation of backward classes, that the President appointed the Backward Class Commission under Article 340. The terms of reference framed by Government for the Commission show quite clearly that Government had envisaged the potentialities of the Commission's work for throwing caste into the background, although providing for the welfare and advancement of the backward classes and weaker sections of the nation.

The time-factor, unless the latter part of the Commission's function (numbered b ii) can be understood to include a condition about time-limit, however, it would appear, had escaped the Government's vision. This is the more surprising in view of the explicit limit set in the Constitution for the reservation of seats in the Legislatures. Art. 334 before its amendment in 1959 stated that the reservation of seats for the Scheduled Castes and even the Scheduled Tribes shall cease on the expiration of the period of ten years from the commencement of the Constitution.

The Commission was asked to "(a) determine the criteria to be adopted in considering whether any sections of the people in the territory of India (in addition to the Scheduled Castes and Scheduled Tribes specified by notifications issued under Articles 341 and 342 of the Constitution) should be treated as socially and educationally backward classes; and, in accordance with such criteria, prepare a list of such classes setting out also their approximate numbers and their territorial distribution;" (*b*) "investigate the conditions of all such socially and educationally backward classes and the difficulties under which they labour"; and (*c*) "*make recommendations* (i) as *to the steps that should be taken by the Union or any State* to remove such difficulties or to improve their condition and (ii) as to the grants that should be made for the purpose by the Union or any State and the conditions subject to which such grants should be made; (*d*) "investigate such other matters as the President may hereafter refer to them"; and (*e*) "present to the President a report setting out the facts as found by them and making such recommendations as they think proper."

The Commission presented its draft report sometime in 1955. In about July or August of that year I received a copy of the draft from a high official of the Union Government along with a letter asking me to submit a critical appraisal of it within a very short time. I prepared a fairly longish note on it, giving *inter alia* my evaluation of the caste situation and advising against caste being made the basis of social welfare and social advancement programmes, and sent it to the official. He on his part acknowledging the receipt of the note expressed his appreciation of the views. It appears the policy-making authority, too, liked the views expressed by me. For about three or four weeks after my receipt of the official's acknowledgment, the same official wrote to me a letter stating that Government would like to publicize some portions of my note and asked me, if I had any objection to such publicity in my own name, whether the views could be set out without reference to me. I immediately replied stating that the Government may use my note in the way it liked best and that I did not reserve any choice to me in the matter.

It is well known that the Government did not accept and implement the report of the Backward Class Commission. In the memorandum accompanying the document placed on the table of the Houses of Parliament in 1956 the Government stated that the criteria of the Commission could not be accepted. They requested the State Governments to hold *ad hoc* surveys for determining the precise criteria and also numbers that would come within the category of such classes (*Sixth Report*, p. 8). It is clear the Government of India by then had forgotten about the steps for advancement and also the grants to be made for the purpose. If we do not find any reference to time-limit or its possibility or need we need not wonder!

The replies of the State Governments, we are told, were "not found useful" and the Government of India "had to request the Office of the Registrar General of India to conduct *ad hoc* surveys with a view to determine the criteria." In 1957–58 the Registrar General was stated to have submitted his final report of the surveys conducted and we were told that "it will soon be possible for the Government of India to arrive at some definite decision as regards the preparation of the list of backward classes other than Scheduled Castes and Scheduled Tribes, who, in their opinion are socially and educationally backward and deserve governmental help for their progress." (*Seventh Report*, pp. 8–9).

In actual fact, however, even as late as 1963–64 or 1965 there was no such list forthcoming. The *Thirteenth Report of the Commissioner for Scheduled Castes and Scheduled Tribes*, published in 1965, does not contain such a list; nor is there any indication of the existence of such a one. The fact that in the part of his report, a very insignificant part comprising not more than 4 out of the 185 pages or so of the whole, which is devoted to the Backward Classes we came across only two broad categories: (*a*) denotified communities and (*b*) the nomadic and the semi-nomadic Tribes and other backward classes, and the annual report of the Union Department of Social Security for 1964–65 confirm the inference. The reporter of the *Times of India*,[11] writing from New Delhi as on 28th March 1965, tells the readers of the paper that the Planning Commission had tentatively provided Rs. 205 crores in the Fourth Plan for various schemes for the welfare of the Backward Classes as against Rs. 114 crores of the Third Plan. And the "Backward Classes" contemplated to be served are declared to have been (*a*) the 65 [?] million Scheduled Castes; (*b*) the 30 [?] million Scheduled Tribes; and (*c*) the denotified communities and nomadic tribes "whose annual income is below a specified minimum." The last category was to receive "a generous measure of assistance, particularly educational facilities!"

It was perhaps because the Government of India was expecting to receive definitive guidance in the matter of fixing the criteria of backwardness in terms of Article 340 from the Registrar General whom it had asked to carry out *ad hoc* surveys and whose report was said to have been ready in one of the Reports of the Commissioner for Scheduled Castes and Scheduled Tribes that the then Home Minister, Gobind Ballabh Pant, assured the Lok Sabha on 11th August 1960 that "The Government was giving thought to the question of revising the criteria for determining the backwardness of people for purposes of providing assistance."[12] (*Times of India*, 12-8-60).

Pant went further and said that "he appreciated the view that economic criteria would be desirable rather than caste." Not stopping there at the door of desirability he asserted that "State Governments maintained their own lists of Backward Classes on the basis of caste" adding that "*the Centre and Parliament, however, had decided that caste should not be recognised for any official or Government purposes*."* All the same he did not feel any awkwardness in putting in an apology for the States' view and practice being based on caste! He is reported as having said "But the States found it difficult to disturb their lists or to change them substantially as they felt that some of those who were now enjoying certain benefits perhaps feared that they might be deprived of them." And this is to be held up as ideal of loyalty to the Constitution which entrusted the authority and the power to determine everything including even the kind of 'benefits' to be bestowed on the groups which were to be listed as Backward Classes to the President and the Government of India! The Constitution had evidently decided to open a new page in the matter of securing social justice and not to go over those which were written in British Colonial ink.

The performance of G. B. Pant was in actual fact worse than that, if, short of treason, any performance can be worse than disloyalty or even inattention to the Constitution. For he himself

---

* Italics mine.

had authorized the States to go their own way, directly asking them, as stated above, to prepare their own lists and programmes. The memorandum accompanying the Report of the Backward Class Commission laid on the tables of the Houses of Parliament as presented to us, the lay public, by the Commissioner for Scheduled Castes and Scheduled Tribes, mentioned above, did not include even a directive that before implementing their lists and schemes, the States should submit them to the Centre with full particulars including those of money-grants and their sources. Yet when Pant made his apologies in the Lok Sabha he coolly told Ramnathan Chettiar that "the Mysore Government had declared all communities except one as backward and the State High Court had held this step as wrong" and that "the State Government had since appointed a committee to reconsider the position."

With this development of the cavalier-fashion implementation by the Central Government of the rather inharmonious complex of provisions for securing equality of opportunity and full social justice to the Scheduled Castes and the Backward Classes, I should have expected the leaders like G. B. Pant to realize that a radical overhaul of the Constitutional provisions was called for, if the ideal of a casteless society and an integrated nation was to be achieved. But unfortunately it did not happen so; and here is India in 1968 heading towards the dangerous rocks of a "plural society".

Mysore, the storm centre of Backward Class ideology, was the State to figure first in the Lok Sabha in this connection. The new committee stated by Pant to have been Chairman of the Committee, R. Nagangowda, a former is the one known as the Nagangowda Committee after the minister and a Congress member of the State Assembly appointed by Mysore State for determining freshly the criteria of backwardness within the purview of Article 340 then. In the final report the Committee, we are told (*Times of India*, 13-6-61, *continuing "Battle for Privileges"*), did not basically depart from the stand "that *backward classes should be listed only on the basis of caste and community*".* It went beyond the Constitution and proposed that the Backward Classes should be divided into two groups; (i) "backward classes", and (ii) "more backward classes". (*Times of India*, 1966–61; 20-9-61: 'Backward Classes' by B. Shiva Rao). One of the statements of the socially and educationally backward classes in the Report for purposes of Article 15(4) of the Constitution gives 79 communities as backward and 135 others as 'more backward'. B. Shiva Rao, bewildered and pained at the way some castes were left out and some were shifted this way and that way, quite rationally and properly ended his informative communication with an exhortation which I think should have and could have been attended to by the Congress and which if acted upon could have saved the situation somewhat. His statement is another way of saying what I have said above and what in effect would have been in fact the import of my note on the Report of the Backward Class Commission sent to the authorities. Shiva Rao says: "It should be within the competence of the Congress High Command, if it really intends to root out casteism, to lay down a firm and clear policy and insist upon uncompromisingly on its pursuit by all Congress Ministries."

The Mysore Government order dated July 31, 1961 based on the report of Nagangowda Committee listed 81 communities, as belonging to socially and educationally backward classes and 135 as "more backward". The order had "classed 90 per cent of the people in the State as backward, leaving only 10 per cent of them as advanced!"[13]

It must be borne in mind that there is no such category as "more backward" in the Constitution. It is clear from this categorization by the Nagangowda Committee that that Committee had scant respect for the Constitution. That the Government of Mysore should have followed suit in their official

---

* Italics mine.

order only under-scores the observation I made above regarding the abrogation by the Government of India of the moral authority and legal power conferred on it in this behalf by Article 340 of the Constitution!

The Government order in its application to the reservation of seats in the Medical and Engineering Colleges of the State caused such hardships to the deserving people of the State that one Balaji and 23 students aggrieved by its operation went in suit against it. The Supreme Court finally struck down the order; and the Mysore Government was brought to its senses to this extent that it set about formulating "a new criterion for reservation" (*Times of India*, 3-8-62; 1-2-64: Leading article entitled 'Caste and Merit').

The learned editor of the *Times of India*, pricked by the decision of the Supreme Court in the later case of *Chitralekha* v. *Mysore State*, penned a very thoughtful and forthright leading article in its issue of February 1, 1964. *Inter alia* he had to take into consideration the effect of the judgment of the Supreme Court in the case of *Balaji* v. *Mysore State*. He rightly pointed out that the judgment was definitive on the negative side but had left the positive side wholly open; for "it does not say to what extent it [caste] might be a relevant factor in ascertaining and determining the social backwardness of any group of persons". The editor shrewdly pointed out that consequently *"in practice the State Governments might make caste the dominant test in categorising backward classes while claiming that they have not done so."* (Italics mine.)

In 1965 came out the *Report of the Kerala Commission on Reservation of Seats in Educational Institutions* which was presided over by a High Court Judge. After all the endeavour of finding neutral criteria for ascertaining backwardness as envisaged in Article 340, the Commission's five groups of Backward Classes openly declared its total failure of the endeavour to circumvent religion or caste. The five groups with their total number of persons in each are: (1) Ezhavās, 3.6 million; (2) Muslims, 2.9 million; (3) Latin Catholics, and (4) Other Backward Christians, together 9 hundred thousand; (5) Other Backward Hindus, the 91 castes or sub-castes listed under the category numbering 1.6 million. The Scheduled Castes people numbered 1.4 million and the Scheduled Tribes only 2 hundred thousand. Thus the total of the people entitled to special treatment, setting at naught the anti-discriminatory provisions of the Constitution, numbering 10.6 million formed 62.7 per cent of the total population of Kerala.

The two Hindu groups that were left out as advanced were Nāyars or Nāirs, who totalled nearly 2.6 million and Brahmins having the insignificant number of 254 thousand, i.e. only one-tenth of the Nāirs. The third advanced group was that of Christians, other than those listed as backward, numbering about 2.7 million.

The work and the final recommendations of the Kerala Commission deserve praise and uphold one of the features of my viewpoint, viz. the need for and the propriety of Constitutional time-limit for any concession, facility or assistance that may be included in the programme of amelioration and welfare of the so-called Backward Classes and even the Scheduled Castes. The Commission recommended that for purposes of the discriminatory reservation of seats in educational institutions under Article 15(4) only the five listed groups, with 91 listed castes of the fifth group treated as one body [?], should be entitled to it and that their percentage shares shall be in order: 9, 8, 2, 1, and 5. It further (*Report*, p. 78) recommended that the reservation of seats should be laid down for five years in post-graduate courses and ten years in others!

Towards the end of the year, on 25th November, R. M. Hajarnavis, the then Minister of State for Law and Social Security, told the Lok Sabha that "following the judgment of the Supreme Court, the Central Government had accepted economic factors and not caste as the basis for determining the backwardness of people." He further affirmed that eight States—only three, Andhra Pradesh, West Bengal and Assam, are mentioned by name in the news item[14]—had accepted the economic criterion for determining backwardness. The elite public naturally felt happy over the news, not collating actual data or putting such practices as those of the Mysore State in the context of recommendations of a highly judicious Commission on this matter made for Kerala, by the side of Hajarnavis' assertion. How could then they show a healthy scepticism about it? And the editor of the *Times of India* came out with a leading article entitled 'New approach', in the issue of the paper for 30th November 1965, proclaiming in its title delight felt at the happy tidings. Forgetting his own comment made almost two years before in his leading article of 1st February 1964, he said: "The Supreme Court, going by the spirit of the Directive Principles of the Constitution, rightly held last year that, although caste might be a relevant circumstance in ascertaining the social backwardness of a class of citizens, it could not be the sole dominant test." He had, in his earlier article, which referred to an earlier judgment of the Supreme Court, remarked that "it does not say to what extent it [caste] might be a relevant consideration." And he goes on to observe: "The Government has not been slow in acting on this admirable judgment. Mr. Hajarnavis has told the Lok Sabha that not only the Centre but as many as eight States—the editor too kssps the names to himself, if he knew them—have decided that in future they will determine whether a particular group of people is backward or not on the basis of its economic condition and not its caste. It is not too much to hope that other States will not take long to fall in line with this decision."

We know from what is written above that in actual fact a judicial committee presided over by a High Court judge, after good deal of deliberation, had made recommendations in this behalf which basically were centred on caste and religion, economic factor coming in only subsidiarily.

We know, too, that a much greater authority and a powerful leader in the Congress, G. B. Pant had informed the same august body, which was being regaled with the ostensibly happy tidings by Hajarnavis, five years before, that "not only the Central Government but also Parliament had decided that Caste shall not be mentioned or considered for any Governmental or official purpose". Further we were told, at least through the Current Topics column of the *Times of India* (7-6-61), that about the end of May 1961, the Chief Ministers of the States meeting in New Delhi had "agreed that *there should be no reservation of Government posts* [for Backward Classes] *and that so far as educational concessions are concerned economic backwardness and not caste or community should be the criterion.*"*

Under these circumstances I wonder how the so-called acceptance by eight [?] States of economic status in supersession of caste at the end of 1965 can be regarded as evidence of Government not having been "slow"!

In Maharashtra we have good evidence of caste making progress in getting itself recognised by Government for purposes of ascertaining backwardness. In 1953, as noted above, there were 125

* Italics mine.

castes listed as Backward but by 1967 as many as 160 castes were enumerated in detail as "Other Backward Classes, the list being alphabetically arranged."*

Two months after the report of the case *Ashok* v. *Dean, Medical College, Nagpur*, the issue of *the Times of India* as of 2nd October carried the news that Maharashtra Government had enlarged the list to 178 castes, or "classes" to use the term used by the Minister who made the announcement, evidently as a cloak for the unconstitutional-looking word "castes"! This is the kind of relegation of caste to the background that is going on owing to the Government of India having abrogated the moral authority and the legal power conferred on it in the Constitution by Article 340!

We do not know the basis on which the Ministry of Education of the Government of India distributes its largess, post-matric scholarships. As noted above there was a list of over 990 castes which were classed as Backward by the Ministry. But by 1955 the list was ignored as not valid. (*Fifth Report*, p. 123). Yet we are told (ibid. pp. 116–17) in 1955–56 that as many as 35,281 Backward Class students had applied for the award of inland scholarships available with the Ministry of Education and that only 11,439 of them were selected for the award! In the same year the number of Scheduled Caste students applying for inland scholarships was 17,216, all of whom received the award. In 1963–64. whereas the Backward Class students receiving post-matric scholarships of the Government of India numbered 17,540 and registered an increase of about 53 per cent only, the number of such scholarships to the Scheduled Castes students having been 60,157 had risen by 214 per cent!

The process of proliferation and entrenchment of caste under the specious plea of social justice and upgrade-levelling up of the so-called Backward Classes and of the Scheduled Castes protected Statutorily, though only for a limited period, was thus going on merrily, while the public was being assured of the intention and the determination of the Governments of the Union and of the States to kill caste by ignoring it in all spheres including the Constitutional. The great leader, the staunchest protagonist of secularism and an ardent critic of caste-patriotism or casteism, Jawaharlal Nehru, on his part, behaved in an ambivalent manner on the very first occasion when a severely cold and chastising front was urgently called for.

We were informed in February 1961—mark the time which fairly synchronizes with the time of G. B. Pant's declaration in the Lok Sabha and of the supposed decision of the Chief Ministers of States that only economic status and neither caste nor community should and would form the basis for the distribution of educational and economic concessions on the score of backwardness—that Nehru inaugurated in Hyderabad the All-India Legislators' Convention of Scheduled Castes and Tribes, the first of its kind, it appears. We learn that out of the 784 Legislators of the Scheduled Castes and the Scheduled Tribes, 250 were present on the occasion. Nehru's dislike of and opposition to caste was, however, too strong not to urge him to snub the organisers and the constituents of the Convention.

Jawaharlal Nehru is reported to have said on the occasion of the Convention of the Scheduled Castes and Scheduled Tribes Legislators (*Times of India*, 6-2-61) that he did not like conferences of sects and castes and all that. This was in effect a caste conference [with due deference to Nehru I should point out that it was worse than a one-caste conference. It was a conference of a group of castes, which, though *inter se* socially opposed to one another and insistent on social segregation

---

* *Ashok* v. *Dean, Medical College, Nagpur, The Bombay Law Reporter*, August 1967. My attention was drawn to this case by my daughter, Mrs. Kumud Desai.

inter se, had come together to secure a large size of the national cake by reservation, which may be leisurely divided and distributed among themselves] which he did not like because it only emphasised the existing barriers of caste which 'we want to abolish'.

Nehru's weighty and pregnant words, fortunately for us, are quoted in the news-despatch and I need make no apology for quoting them. Nehru said: "But this business of legislators of Scheduled Castes and Tribes from all parts of the country coming together seems to me rather odd. We are interested in raising the level of these castes and tribes. The question is how to do it. We must be clear as to what we are aiming at." With apologies to the late leader I may point out that this was just what was asked to be done by the Constitution-makers under the powers and protection of Article 340. And it was almost exactly the point I had in view when in the note on the draft report of the Backward Class Commission I had advised the dropping of caste basis for considering backwardness.

Nehru, we are informed, countered the demand for reservations of jobs on the ground that such reservation might be alright in regard to other than responsible positions. He declared: "Therefore I am not prepared to accept that appointments should be made on consideration of caste and not of merit and ability." Further he is reported as having accepted "the limited reservation of posts only for a certain period." Otherwise reservations "were prone to create vested interests." As regards reservation of seats for the Scheduled Castes in the country's Legislatures and the ten-year extension accorded to it by an amendment Nehru said: "I hope all of you will bear in mind that there should be no further extension." I must say, though painfully, that in this hope Nehru was more of a sanguine optimist than the realist that he showed himself to be when he talked of the genesis of vested interests. It is hardly likely that Nehru should not have poignantly realised that he, the Government and the Congress Party which he led had already started the process of creating "vested interests" in the matter of reservation of seats in the Legislatures when they carried through an amendment of the Constitution to extend it to 1970.

The very Convention of the Scheduled Castes Legislators was evidence of the fact of a vested interest which was determined to attempt its perpetuation. The process started a decade earlier when in 1950 was founded in New Delhi, the All-India Backward Classes Federation. (*Fifth Report*, p. 162). The Legislators' Convention mentioned above demanded "a high power Commission to assess the benefits conferred on the Scheduled Castes and Tribes by the existing constitutional safeguards." (*Times of India*, 8-2-61: *Caste Barriers*). The All-India Federation of Scheduled Castes, Scheduled Tribes and other Backward Classes in March 1964 presented a memorandum to Nehru which *inter alia* demanded the creation of separate Ministries at the Centre and in the States to look after the interests of Scheduled Castes, Scheduled Tribes and backward classes (*Times of India*, 28-3-64). In April next year, S. M. Siddiah introduced a Bill seeking to appoint a commission to report on the welfare of the Scheduled Castes (*Times of India*, 16-4-65).

In the course of a thoughtful leading article, evoked by the claim made in the Lok Sabha to have 22.5 per cent of the Government posts reserved for recruitment from among the Scheduled Caste members, the editor of the *Indian Express*, in its issue of 26th August 1966, emphasized the view-point here adumbrated regarding the Government of India's implementation of the special treatment provisions of the Constitution and the ambivalent attitude of leaders like Jawaharlal Nehru. He wrote: "The strong opposition to the recent move for de-scheduling some of the Scheduled Castes who have achieved a measure of economic progress shows *how continued enjoyment of concessions can* *create a vested interest even in backwardness*.* The list of 'backward' classes has grown instead of becoming smaller as a result of the economic improvement made by some of them. If the economic yardstick is not to be applied in determining which communities should be included among the Scheduled Castes, then the Scheduled Castes will remain permanently Scheduled. . . ."

The resolutions passed or the statements made at the annual Convention of the All-India Backward Classes Federation held at Hyderabad in September 1967 are further evidence of the fact that special treatment which was intended to be a special privilege of restricted duration is being tried to be turned into a birthright of a permanent nature. They also reveal that the specially treated groups took special interest in fixing the list of backward classes on the basis of caste in preference to that of economic status.

We are informed that "the Convention stated that the confidence of the backward classes in the ruling party has been 'rudely shaken' because of the delay in considering the report of the Backward Classes Commission." The Convention called on the Government to consider the report and provide facilities, preferential treatment and other amenities for removing the social and educational backwardness of the backward classes. The Convention "regretted that, though the Commission, under the chairmanship of Kakasaheb Kalelkar, had prepared a comprehensive list of 'other backward classes' in each State, and the report was placed before Parliament, 'it was neither discussed nor any move initiated to give considered thought to the problems faced by more than 60 per cent of the people' [?]".

The editor of the *Times of India* penned a leading article in the issue of the paper for 12th September 1967 to applaud what he calls "New Approach" suggested by Vice-President V. V. Giri in his inaugural address. However, the main conclusion of it turned into a statement of the limitations of the approach. For as soon as the editor's pen began to probe into the so-called backward people and their doings to evaluate Girl's proposal it had to record things unfavourable to the implementation of the proposal. The editor had to write: "If there is something radically wrong with welfare programmes it is not because the benefits conferred have been unreal but because they have gone to the more advanced and politically well-organised communities who are least in need of any special assistance. *Backwardness in this context has become a privilege to be fought for and retained to consolidate political power*."†

The upshot of all this development is the emergence of a vested interest; and I am almost certain that before 1970 another amendment of the Constitution will prolong the life of reservation of seats in the Legislatures for the members of the Scheduled Castes and Scheduled Tribes by at least a decade. Thus the "reservation" would be fully "major". A whole generation having enjoyed it, the year 1980 would be found to be more likely to usher in its permanence than abolition, unless very firm and well-considered action is taken from now on. Already it is rather late for such action and there is no time to lose, if we desire to avoid growing into a "plural society".

I have mentioned above that at a meeting of the Chief Ministers in Delhi it was resolved not to reserve jobs or posts for Backward Classes. On the other hand, there is the power conferred on States by the proviso to Article 16 laid down in clause (4). And what is significant is that, it is the only place where 'adequate' representation in the services is mentioned. Article 335 laying down representation in the services for the Scheduled Castes, on the other hand, sounds emphasisless or colourless. For it says that their claims shall be considered. It does not say that there shall be adequate representation

---

* Italics mine.

† Italic, mine.

of the Scheduled Castes in the Services. There is further the proviso in it that the claims are to be adjusted only "consistently with the maintenance of efficiency of administration".

Whatever the criterion adopted for the determination of backwardness there are bound to be in every State—and it appears to me that under the existing provisions caste and/or community will have to be taken into consideration for purposes of Article 16(4)—a number of castes or sub-castes included in the list of Backward Classes, as is the case in the recommendations of the Kerala Commission already mentioned, none or only insignificant number of the members of which figure in the services of the State or States or of the Union. It cannot be argued by the Government of any State in which such a situation exists as respects a particular caste, sub-caste or community that it can go on thinking or taking for granted that the representation is not inadequate. It is thus clear to me that either the Constitutional provision of Article 16(4) is or has to be set at naught or that States have been by some method managing to represent such classes in the services. If the caste or the community not having any or very few of its members in the services of the State is fairly large and therefore has managed or can manage to send a few members to the State Assembly, we may rest assured that no State Government would dare to resist its claim to get some posts, whether its members are adequately qualified for them or not. What is actually happening is, however, not capable of being revealed as the Commissioner for the Scheduled Castes and Scheduled Tribes, who is empowered to report on Backward Classes too, cannot and has not, done so owing to there having been no Presidential Order naming and enumerating the groups to be designated as Backward Classes!

The Government of India was quick in acting in pursuance of Article 335—as a matter of fact it had acted in this wise even before the promulgation of the Constitution or even before its formulation. It issued a Gazette notification dated 13-9-1950 fixing the percentages of posts reserved for the Scheduled Castes without any reference to or indication of a time limit for its continuance. What is still more surprising, intriguing and dismaying is that the notification stated that the percentage reservation was to be in force "pending the determination of the figures of population at the Census of 1951"! This statement made in August 1950 i.e. within nine months of the promulgation of the Constitution was not modified when in 1952 the Government of India issued some Supplementary Instructions as respects the notification, nor even in its amendment issued in May 1955. This reference to population figures has naturally created the expectations and nurtured the aspirations of the leaders of the Scheduled Castes of a higher percentage reservation of posts and has culminated in the demand for 22.5 per cent of the posts to be reserved for the Scheduled Castes, which I have mentioned above as having been made on the floor of the Lok Sabha in August 1966.

The percentage of open competition posts—all this relates to the appointments and jobs in the services under the Union Government—reserved for recruitment from among the members of the Scheduled Castes was fixed at 12.5 and that of other posts at 16.66, i.e. one-sixth of the total such posts, and was raised to 17.5 per cent evidently in accommodation to the population figures of 1951 Census (*Times of India*, 30-8-63: "Carry Over of Job Reservation Void"). Need one wonder or marvel at the rapid growth of India's population?

Soon it was discovered that "sufficient number of qualified [i.e. having the minimum qualifications with the maximum age limits extended by three years] candidates were not forthcoming"; and the Government of India issued the above-mentioned instructions in 1952 and their amendment in 1955. The result of these two steps was to establish firmly the notion that the percentage-reservation was not merely the upper limit of such intake of members of the Scheduled Castes in the Union services but that it was 'a finite and must quota.' For the Government order thus modified required the unfilled portion of the reserved quota percentage to be carried forward to the subsequent years to be added to the annual quota for recruitment.

The wording of the amended order is such that a little pondering over it with the help of a little arithmetic should present one with the ludicrous and un-Constitutional situation that if the order was adhered to and worked out logically during the decade 1950–1960, in the latter year of the decade*, or at the latest in 1965, there would have been no open competition post available for recruitment for any citizen of India other than the members of the Scheduled Castes! This sounds so preposterous that in the interests of easy comprehension and acceptance of my statement I quote the actual wording of the order (*Commentary on the Constitution of India* by Durga Das Basu, 4th ed., vol. 5, p. 154): "If a sufficient number of candidates considered suitable by the recruiting authorities, are not available from the communities for whom reservations are made in a particular year, the unfilled vacancies should be treated as unreserved and filled by the best available candidates. The number of reserved vancancies thus treated as unreserved will be added as an additional quota to the number that would be reserved in the following year in the normal course; and to the extent to which approved candidates are not available in that year against this additional quota, a corresponding addition should be made to the number of reserved vacancies in the second following year." Actually in 1963 the reservation accounted for 65 per cent of the posts (*Times of India*, 30-8-63). And the Supreme Court struck it down in the case known as *Devadasan* v. *Union of India*.

The Supreme Court appears to have struck down the rule "inasmuch as it resulted in making the reservation of the Scheduled Castes and Tribes unreasonable and excessive" and "as violative of the equality guaranteed by Articles 14 and 16(1)" (Ibid).

Mr. Justice J. R. Mudholkar delivering the judgment striking down the rule observed: "Each year of recruitment will have to be considered by itself and the reservation for backward communities should not be so excessive as to create a monopoly or to disturb unduly the legitimate claims of other communities." It was a majority judgment, Mr. Justice K. Subba Rao, dissenting. (*Times of India*, 30-8-63).

It is clear that what is struck down is not the rule as such but its unrestrained application. Thus if the percentage reserved does not exceed, for example 45, then I do not think that the judgment of the Supreme Court will prevent its implementation.

It appears to me that the rule in effect also would contravene the provision about "the maintenance of efficiency of administration" of Article 335 itself. For it would or could introduce a very large number of minimally qualified candidates in important cadres at a single recruitment instead of a steady and limited supply of such, working in a large group of maximally qualified servants of the State and thus enabling the whole machinery of administrative cadres to get accustomed to the minimally qualified members.

The reaction to the decision in high quarters gives clear indication that reservation—percentage has already become a vested interest. Jagjivan Ram, who was then out of the Union Ministry and was therefore mentioned as the "former Union Minister of Transport and Communication", is reported to have said that "the total percentage of employees belonging to these castes [Scheduled Castes and Scheduled Tribes] is still much less than *what is due on the basis of population*."† Jagjivan Ram was addressing a seminar on employment of Scheduled Castes and Scheduled Tribes held under the auspices of the Planning Commission at the end of January 1964. One of the recommendations

* This is computed on the basis of average percentages of intake of the Scheduled Castes candidates between 1948 and 1960 as presented by D. N. Rao in the *Indian Journal of Public Administration*, 1963, pp. 92–4.
† Italics mine.

made by the seminar, we are told, "the most important" one as the *Times of India* 'news serviceman' put it, was "the establishment of a central executive authority vested with necessary powers to nominate Scheduled Castes and Scheduled Tribes candidates against vacancies reserved for them." This step taken, the separation of the Scheduled Castes and Scheduled Tribes from the rest of the Indian society would be so complete that a further definite step on the path of the development of "plural society" can be said to have been taken!

Sixteen months* later, i.e. on 31-5-1965, I find a very thoughtful leading article by the editor of the *Times of India* in my file of cuttings, the immediate occasion being the scheme of "a network of centres to be opened to coach" candidates of "the backward classes" under the aegis of the Department of Social Security (now Social Welfare?) of the Union Government which had already two such centres running. The editor observed: "Any scheme under which candidates from the Scheduled Castes and Scheduled Tribes are coached for UPSC and other competitive examinations in institutions established exclusively for the purpose would perpetuate the very discrimination it is hoped to abolish. Already the principle of reservation is being used by interested parties as a lever to create a special class within the backward classes. Some Scheduled Caste leaders have demanded that candidates from the community should be directly 'nominated' to Government service. *There is also the equally preposterous demand that reservation should operate at every stage in a Scheduled Caste official's progress from recruitment to retirement.*"†

In a leading article of the *Indian Express* (21-8-66) its editor, writing fifteen months after the above-quoted observations, ended with the significant and astounding revelation that "influential sections among Harijans [Scheduled Castes of the Constitution?] are interested in perpetuating social distinction for their own narrow purposes."

A little over a year after this, the Administrative Reforms Commission's study team is said to have "spelled out the extent of the deterioration" in the quality of recruitment to non-technical all-India services, which, in general terms, was common knowledge for sometime before. It is said to have pointed out that "the percentage of first division entrants has dropped from 42 in 1950–55 to 25 in 1960–65 and of third class men risen from 4 to 19 in the same period." (*Times of India*, 24-10-67: "Public Services").

To a fair-minded person and to any patriotic Indian it must become clear that the proviso of the maintenance of the standard of efficiency of administration of Article 335 requiring the Government to take the claims of the Scheduled Castes to be represented in the services and posts has been set at naught. My contention that the rule, said to be struck down by the Supreme Court, contravenes the spirit of Article 335 is fully borne out.

However, it is clear to me that all the development briefly outlined above, which in its own way is quite clearly tending the Indian Society towards becoming a "plural society" rather than a casteless society, which was the ideal set out by the Constituent Assembly and has to be the goal of the Government and the people, has not affected the Government in the right manner. Evidence of this statement is afforded by the officials' committees appointed by the Union Government to expedite a larger intake of Scheduled Castes members in its services. The editor of the *Times of India* penned a leading article to criticize the recommendations of one of the most recent of such committees in the issue of the paper of 22nd February 1968. He declared that the proposals sought "*to create a vested interest in backwardness itself.*"‡

* I should not be taken to suggest that the learned editor did not write on the subject, and against the trend in between.

† Italics mine.

‡ Italics mine.

The story of the creation and implementation of special provisions for the Scheduled Castes and Backward Classes does not leave any doubt in my mind that before long we will have an amendment to the Constitution to extend the legislative representation of the Scheduled Castes at least by ten years.

We will thus have a few caste and sub-caste groups turned into political parties in miniature and vested interests for preserving their special spoil of the social cake of the Government jobs. From there accretion of other economic and political interests would not fail to begin and thus to solidify them as exclusivist and separatist communities.

It is well known that even in high quarters caste is a passport not only to acquaintance but also to special consideration. Here I may draw the reader's attention to a feature of Hindu social life which is calculated to strengthen caste sentiment. The ramification of ties of kinship with its consequent socially approved and morally binding rights and duties is very wide. It happens sometimes that a large number of people can claim some relationship within the approved ambit, which in practice may mean a good portion of the entire caste. The natural clientele of a man coming from an old family and rising to the top tends to be large. The vicious circle of kin-feeling is thus wide; and caste-feeling appears as only a slight extension of kin-feeling.

As specimens of the behaviour of political leaders—readers may kindly bear in mind the fact that charges have been made repeatedly and in many quarters that political parties and particularly the leading party, the Indian National Congress, has been utilizing caste patriotism—albeit dexterously and indirectly in their election campaigns—I may mention the following events.

Some of the leaders have taken a rational step in the matter of the blatant proclamation and easy identification of one's caste. In many cases one's caste is recorded in one's surname. For there are many castes in which the name of the caste or sub-caste group itself is used as the surname. Progressive individuals have realized the antisocial potentialities of this practice and some of them, though very few, have recently come forward to adjust their names. The reaction to such individual action so far known testifies to the vitality of caste-feeling. When Manickavelu Naicker, the then Revenue Minister of Madras, announced in April 1955 that he would no longer use Naicker which is a caste-name as his surname, the caste-group, which now describes itself as the Vanniakula Kshatriyas, passed resolutions accusing him of showing disrespect to the entire community. He is said to have received threatening letters. The outcome is still not known. When a month later, the North Indian Shriman Narayan Agarwal, the General Secretary of the Congress, dropped his caste surname and described himself as Shriman Narayan only, the reaction took the desirable form of inducing the General Secretary of the U.P. Pradesh Congress to drop his caste name.[15] The ex-Congress President, Kamaraj, has made himself known as such without his caste appellation of Nadar.

As against this activity, which may, after all, be only indicative of social expediency and worldly wisdom protecting the high-status leaders, we have the recent behaviour of one of the long continued and important members of the Government of India, B. R. Bhagat, which bespeaks nurture of caste patriotism. Bhagat was reported in *the Bombay Samachar* of Bombay (27-6-67) to have been present along with all the other Members of Parliament who are his caste-men, Yādavs, at the All-India Yādav Mahasabha meeting held at Delhi. This was quite clearly one of a series which as M. S. A. Rao's painstaking research (*The Economic Weekly*, August 1964) shows began in 1963. These meetings have since then been passing a resolution calling upon the Government to form a separate Yadav regiment in the Army. The particular meeting was inaugurated by the Defence Minister, Swaran Singh. The distressing fact is that such high officials, should bless such meetings and indirectly and partially commit themselves to the views and proposals. More poignantly dangerous still is the fact that the lever in the matter of the Yadav Mahasabha agitation is the existence of a fairly large number of men and officers of the Yādav (Ahir) caste in the Army!

In one field of integrative activity, much wider in scope and more potent in effect than the older ones, has caste registered another triumph. For sometime past, as was inevitable with the formation of caste-societies and the holding of caste conferences, caste-journals had made their sporadic appearance. *The Lohānā Hitechchu*, a Gujarati weekly issued by the committee of the Lohānā caste in Bombay, appears to have been the earliest regular journal started by a caste for the benefit and propaganda of its members, having been published first in 1914. It has continued its publication ever since. The consciousness of this caste about itself can be judged by the fact that in its annual conference of 1955 it is reported to have collected rupees 500 thousand for the purposes of caste benefit. The highly educated caste, known as Kanara Saraswat, came next with its English monthly of that name started by the Kanara Saraswat Association in 1919. Two years later the *Gujarati Samsta Lād Mitra* began its bi-monthly career in Baroda. The Marathi *Prabhu Tarun* of the Pāthāre Prabhu caste of Bombay City and the Gujarati *Pātidār* issued by the *Pātidār* caste from Anand, both of them monthlies, came next in 1923. The Gujarati *Anavil Pokar* issued by the Anavil Bandhu Printing Press of Surat followed next in 1926 to awaken the landlordly Brahmin caste of South Gujarat. Twelve other journals were started by other castes before 1948. This type of caste-activity took a spurt since 1948, i.e. after the achievement of independence. Since 1948 upto the date of the publication of *Nefor Guide to Indian Publications* in 1956, twenty-five caste journals had been whipping up the sentiment of caste solidarity among the members of their respective castes.

It is interesting to note that of the forty-two caste journals listed in the publication, referred to above, only one belonged to a Bengali caste. Seven of them were conducted by castes of Maharashtra and the remaining thirty-four by Gujarati castes.

K. M. Kapadia's[16] inquiry among secondary school teachers reveals that a much larger percentage of Gujarati teachers report such activity as known to them than the Maharashtrian ones. The growth and abundance of this zealous activity in combination with club and social programmes reported by the above-mentioned investigator in Gujarat, where the Congress is believed to have the strongest hold, offers material for serious thought to the political leaders of the country! I must, however, warn the reader that I am not convinced that there were no caste magazines, journals or annuals, either in Bihar, U.P., Andhra Pradesha or Madras.*

The caste-centred or caste-based periodicals quite definitely increased in number in the period elapsed since the above was written. *The Press in 1965* which work takes the place of the earlier *Nefor Guide*, though a huge publication, is far from a complete and a correct record. I find for example that the *Sociological Bulletin* which was published in Bombay quite regularly from 1952 to 1966 as a six-monthly periodical does not find a mention in it. When I find that quite a few of the caste-centred periodicals noted above have dropped out of *The Press in 1965* I cannot take it that they have ceased publication. I have, therefore, to warn the reader that the caste-scene as represented in this Government publication is much of an understatement and that the actuality is much worse than one may be led to believe from its perusal.

The 'monthlies' it appears to me, are the less likely to be missed and are also the more stable approaches and communication media. Moreover their number is such as to be manageable for me for

---

* All this was written before 1960.

computation. The purpose being to project the caste-scene in an indicatory way, the comprehensive and exhaustive approach being beyond my individual effort, I have selected three areas, Gujarati, Hindi, and Marathi. The Hindi area is represented by three States, Madhya Pradesh, Rajasthan and Uttar Pradesh; the Gujarati by Gujarat and Maharashtra. In each area only monthlies in the Regional or State language are considered, being counted the most representative for caste-category.

The total number of Gujarati 'monthlies' in Gujarat and Maharashtra listed in the publication is 297; and 27 of them or 9 per cent are caste-based. Sixteen out of the 27 caste-centred Gujarati 'monthlies' are post-1948; to be more specific began their existence in 1950 and after. Thus 59 per cent of the Gujarati caste-based 'monthlies' are of post-Republican era. Only 9 out of the total of 185 Marathi monthlies i.e. 5 per cent, are caste-based. Even among these the proportion of those 'born' after 1948 is not much different, being 56 per cent. The first of these post-1948 'monthlies' began its existence in 1952.

In the Hindi area, i.e. in the three States, Madhya Pradesh, Rajasthan and Uttar Pradesh, together there are 434 Hindi 'monthlies'. Of these 51 are caste-based. For two of these the source of information is silent as to their year of start. Out of the 49 Hindi caste-based 'monthlies', 34 are post-1948. Thus the percentage of post-1948 journals to the total caste-based Hindi monthlies of known beginning is much higher, being 69.4, than is the case with either Marathi or Gujarati caste-based monthlies.

The earliest of such journals dates back to 1902, in which year the Haihaiya Kshatriya Mahasabha—note the hoary-antiquity-claiming designation of the caste, dating its origin back to about the beginning of the second millenium B.C.—of Uttar Pradesh began its journal.

Of the 85 caste-based monthlies from these three linguistic areas listed in the Government publication, *The Press in 1965*, 39 were started after 1956 to whip up caste-patriotism. This enterprise of turning a caste into a total community and of atomizing the Hindu society is thus a vigorous growth of post-Independence era, promising to surpass the accelerated rate of not only economic but of population growth as well!

Monthlies are not the only unit of the media of communicative integration. Perhaps the annuals, the special reports like that of Chitrāpur Sāraswat community, detailing the achievements of its shining lights, and the various jubilee issues, whether silver, golden or diamond ones, carry out this task even more effectively. But unfortunately it is not possible to assess their volume and extent from the available sources.

Group integration through mutualities of various kinds, particularly economic, purely social and helpful on critical occasions, is stronger than through any other medium and what is more, it tends to become a habit with the individual members of the group. This aspect of the recent process of caste being turned into an entire community is also emphasized as having been in evidence during the British rule! A measure of the increase and proliferation of this feature of community formation can be had from the trusts registered with the Charity Commissioner or similar official of the sixteen States of the Union.

I have examined the list of such trusts and trust-units published by the Charity Commissioner of Maharashtra State, then of course Bombay, in 1954* under the title *Directory of Public Trusts,*

* Prof. D. N. Marshall, Librarian of the University of Bombay, kindly addressed a registered letter to the Charity Commissioner asking if any later edition was available, and if a research worker could get access to the recent records if no later edition was available. Unfortunately he did not receive any reply. He had also addressed a registered letter to the Charity Commissioner, Madras, but it came back undelivered, an official of that designation not being known there!

for Greater Bombay and Bombay Suburban District. I have counted not less than 1,700 of these units to be caste-centred. The purposes of these numerous units vary from that of affording shelter to the needy members of the caste through arranging annual dinners or get-togethers and seasonal or occasional festival celebrations to maintaining marriage halls which may be open to others than caste-members and buildings to be rented only to caste-members. A fairly large number of them offer scholarships to poor students of the caste, some run schools, others again maintain maternity-homes for caste-members and a few run hostels for caste-students. The publication unfortunately does not mention the year of the starting of the trust which makes a period-wise break-up impossible.

Not less than 87 castes or sub-castes are represented among the owners of these trusts, at least 33 of which are Brahmin castes or sub-castes. They come from all strata of society and their names, too, are instructive for the caste-situation, showing extreme atomization. Some of them are indicative of the upward-looking tendency of castes too; but none I think among the names is so interesting as that of the Gujarati potter caste. The Kumbhārs, as they are known both in Marathi and Gujarati and even in Hindi with a slight modification, have made themselves known as Prajāpatis* through their trust registered as "Prajāpati Pragati Mandal". The achievements of this caste in this field in Surat district are well brought out in the late Dr. K. M. Kapadia's useful survey of the educational history of Navsari taluka.[17]

Illuminating historical accounts of the community-type-development of caste have recently been made available by the painstaking researches of K. M. Kapadia and Vilas A. Sangave for two linguistic defined areas. Kapadia's account, referred to above in connection with 'Prajāpati' trust of Bombay, gives us a picture of the community-making development in a Gujarati area involving half a dozen castes. He has given us an account of the growth of caste and communal hostels for students that was begun in the Navsari town about 1934. (*Sociological Bulletin*, 1959, pp. 40, 53–54, 57–8).

Vilas Sangave has provided for us even a more illuminating and comprehensive account of the community-making activities of ten Maharashtrian castes of Kolhapur city, a cultural centre of Maharashtra famous for its Ambabai temple and now for its establishment of the Kshatra Jagadguru (High Pontiff of Kshatriyas) and for the priest-training institution known as the Shahu Vaidic School. He has himself emphasized the changes that are worth noting for our purpose and detailed them seriatum. They invite themselves to be offered to the readers of this book in the original and in toto. Sangave notes:

"1. The caste sentiment is being made deep-rooted by organising activities for children, women, students and others. Balak Mandirs [Kindergarten Schools] and Mahila Mandals [Womens' Clubs] are becoming common features of all castes. Formerly such separate associations did not exist.
2. The caste Panchayat is preserved in a modified form by introducing the principle of election in constituting the Panchayat or the Managing Committee of the caste, as the case may be.
3. The systems of caste Panchāyats and caste rules are made more definite by framing written constitution for the caste Panchāyat.
4. The Students' Boarding House is made the central place of caste activities. All social and religious functions of a caste are organised in the boarding of that caste and even meetings of

* It is a Sanskrit word and as such means creator. 'Prajāpati' is the principal or supreme deity in the later Vedic literature.

co-operative societies of that caste are held in the boarding. Thus the contact is maintained between the old and the new generations.

5. The occupational castes are making determined efforts to improve the economic conditions of caste members by establishing co-operative credit and industrial societies.
6. The castes have started by establishing separate housing colonies to bring members closer together in different ways. Even though housing colonies are open to all members irrespective of caste, they are generally meant for the members of the caste sponsoring the scheme.
7. Formerly the Brahmins used to officiate as priests for all castes and thus formed a link between all castes. Now it can be noticed that many castes like Pānchāl Brahmins or Daivadnya Brahmins have a priest of their own caste, or many castes like those of Nhāvis, Dhors and Chāmbhārs call Maratha Priests, or in some cases the members of the caste (e.g., among Vadārs and Māngs) act as priests.
8. Efforts are made by every caste to get facilities from the Government and for this purpose they are prepared to be included in the intermediate or backward classes as the case may be. For example, *Āryas Kshatriyas and Nhāvis tried to get themselves included in other Backward Classes*. Formerly the tendency was to upgrade their position, e.g., barbers wanted to be called as Nāi Brahmins, artisan castes as Vishwakarmā Brahmins.
9. The frequency of all caste members coming together has recently increased. Now all caste members assemble at one place nearly 10 to 12 times in a year for attending social, religious and National Functions and the meetings of cooperative societies. Even social gatherings of all caste members are held.
10. Regular cess is collected from the members and previous permission of Panchāyat or Managing Committee is essential for performing marriage and other ceremonies." (*Sociological Bulletin*, XI, 1961, pp. 36–61)."

For South Indian castes, particularly Tamilian, some indicatory information on the specific topic as was available in the sources at my disposal is presented in the last chapter. It is woefully sketchy and defective and I am glad to add to it more specific information about one caste, the largest one of Tamilnad, the Pallis, who have been proclaiming themselves to be 'Vanhikula', or Fire-descended, Kshatriyas for long. And for this filling up of a gap in our knowledge we are indebted to the American couple, Lloyd I. Rudolph and Sussanne Hoeber Rudolph.[18] They report:

"*The Vanniya Kula Kshatrya* [Kshatriya] *Sangham* of North Arcot District held its 34th annual conference in 1953, and the South Arcot *Sangham* held its tenth in 1954. . . . In 1952, the *Vanniya Kula Kshatriyas* published a volume, the introduction of which gave expression to the sabha's attempt to build a sense of caste patriotism* and solidarity which would make it a more effective force."

Another nineteenth century movement of caste consolidation has been recently brought to my notice by the painstaking and zealous work of M. S. A. Rao, published as a paper in *The Economic Weekly* in August (29), 1964, (pp. 1439–43), entitled *Caste and the Indian Army*. The movement,

---

* I used this expression in 1932 to characterise the sentiment of caste as it had begun to take shape since about 1921 and though I was much criticised and though some of the critics coined the term 'casteism' to denote that sentiment I have continued to use it. I am glad to note that keen-eyed Americans have upheld me by their use of it more than a quarter of a century later.

so well described by Rao, brings into our community-making scene the North Indian caste of regal past, known as Ahirs now proclaiming itself as Yādav. The All-India Yadav Mahasabha owes its origin to the nineteenth century work of one V. K. Khedkar, a member of the Maharashtrian caste, known as Gowli, of Ratnagiri district.

Rao informs us that the Mahasabha was actually started at Allahabad in 1924 and that before its formation "there were in existence many caste associations at the regional level" like the Ahir Kshatriya Mahasabha of U.P. The All-India Yadav Mahasabha "propagates its aims and objectives by holding annual conferences in several parts of India, and by running a monthly journal called *Yadav* [This is listed as having been started in 1925 in the Government publication *The Press in 1965*] which is being published from Varanasi."

Rao's fruitful curiosity was whetted perhaps by the conference organised by the Mahasabha at Delhi in January 1963, as an aftermath of the Chinese attack on our posts in Ladakh in November 1962. The Delhi conference took a delegation of one hundred members to meet the Defence Minister to press its demand for a Yādav regiment. The Mahasabha did not end its activities in this behalf with the presentation of the case to the Defence Minister. As Rao tells us it "launched a vigorous campaign on two fronts; it is persuading the Government through negotiations on the one hand, and is seeking the support of its caste members and of the general public on the other."

On the extension of the field of caste, Rao judiciously remarks: "The agitation of the Sabha for the formation of an Ahir regiment in the Army shows how caste in Independent India is claiming new grounds". The fact that the original book of V. K. Khedkar as revised by his son in 1924 was published in 1959 under the title *The Divine Heritage of the Yadavas* brought to our notice by M. S. A. Rao, is testimony enough to the upsurge of Caste-patriotism in the post-Republican era!

This hardening of castes on an All-India basis or of sub-castes into castes on the linguistic basis for economic, educational and political uplift or aggrandisement is another step on the road to 'plural society' and away from one to a casteless society. The social solvent of this process, intermarriage, on the other hand, is still only on the horizon.

I have emphasized, in the chapter entitled 'Caste during the British Rule', the fact that endogamy has continued to be the outstanding feature of caste and have also spoken of the fresh struts to caste-endogamy provided by the newer developments turning a caste into a community. In this context I may point out a feature or two which appear to be heartening. D. F. Pocock, a British anthropologist, who resided and worked among Pātidārs of Gujarat, has reported about them[19]: "In these days when violations of caste endogamy are on the increase, although the castes in question can do little to affect the lives of the runaway members, who are usually city dwellers, such marriages can be condoned in terms of the caste hierarchy." The Pātidārs of Gujarat, who have hypergamy as a custom but confined to their caste, in ignoring hypergamous unions outside the caste are helping forward the process of social integration through fusion of blood. On the other hand, the highly educated caste of Chitrāpur Sāraswats, members of which are well-placed and generally progressive without inhibition, recently, about 1950, started a social centre of their own for their youth, where recreation of some sort is provided and under whose auspices dramatic and elocution competitions are held and trips and picnics arranged. And caste-youth clubs whose membership is confined to unmarried members of the caste are also coming into existence.

The Hindu Marriage Act of 1955 put caste out of court for a Hindu marriage and introduced a rational system for the social recognition of the union. This registers a great advance in social opinion regarding inter-caste marriage. It is very difficult to assess the actual situation, however.

Impressionistically speaking, one can say that the frequency of inter-caste marriages is slowly rising and bitterness against them is fast decreasing.

How hard the situation regarding inter-caste marriage is in this finely graded, thoroughly stratified, and stably customed Hindu society can best be appreciated if one should be appraised of the fact of mass marriages at periodic mass meeting of a caste so prevalent in many parts of the country. Here I shall give only one illustration, which is both ready to hand and recent and pertains to the highest caste, the Brahmins. In the Current Topics columns of *the Times of India* issue of 10th July 1963 the writer informed the readers of the paper of the annual assemblage of the Maithil Brahmins of Bihar as "a social event in its own way", whereat about 200 thousand persons were present. At the assemblage known as "Saurath Sabha" whose main business is to act as the marriage market, "several thousand marriages were settled" with the help of the hereditary record-keepers called 'Panjikars'. The caption "Wind of Change" given to his script by the columnist should not mislead the reader to think that the change pertained to the spirit of caste. The columnist being impressed by the record-keeper's alacrity in registering the new-age qualifications of bridegrooms much in demand, viz. medical and engineering attainment, gave expression to his impression in the catching, but in the context slightly misleading, caption.

Some attitude indications made possible by the labours of recent investigators may be presented to enable the reader to better assess the situation for himself. B. V. Shah's study[20] of the attitudes of the students of the M.S. University of Baroda provides one such indication.

Shah found that 60.5 per cent of the students of his sample expressed their desire to marry in their own endogamous group i.e. the so-called sub-caste, or better, in the case of Gujarat, sub-sub-caste, and 4.5 per cent were prepared to extend their marital circle to the whole caste. He found that 22.5 per cent were prepared to marry in a caste of similar or higher status and only 12.5 per cent would do so in any caste without reference to its status. This verdict of the College-educated youth is not at all very hopeful for the ushering in of a casteless society in the near future.

An American anthropologist,[21] a year earlier, had given us an analysis of the contents of fifty advertisements appearing in a Sunday edition of the *Hindustan Times*. He found that in 70 per cent of the cases caste was "an important determinant in marital match" and that in the remaining 30 per cent, caste was "not a positive determinant" but was "only relevant". Gould's final verdict was: "This clearly shows the vitality of the rule enjoining caste endogamy."

K. Anand's large sample of one thousand matrimonial advertisements, appearing two years later in *the Hindustan Times* and in *the Tribune*, furnishes more reliable data about the operative force of caste in Northern India. He[22] found that 37 per cent of the female advertisers had mentioned the caste requirements of the partner, being, it appears from the author's way of stating, the same sub-caste, and that 3 per cent had no objection to a spouse from a different sub-caste; and that 13 per cent did not mind caste difference. As 63 per cent of the female advertisers had mentioned their caste, *a priori* we may conclude that 37 per cent of the female advertisers did not mind a spouse of any caste. If that is so then it must be acknowledged to be a great advance towards a casteless society! The male advertisers evidently were less caste-minded, as only 29 per cent of them required their partner to be of the same caste as theirs and 33 per cent had stated that caste-difference was immaterial to them. However, as 65 per cent of the male advertisers had stated their caste, only 35 per cent of them may be adjudged as indifferent to the caste of their spouse, thus making the male advertisers a little more conservative than the female ones! Partial explanation of this apparent contradiction, is provided by the difference in the educational status of the two sexes in the sample. Females who were graduates or still further educated happened to form 67.8 per cent of their total advertisers, while among the males, persons of parallel educational status formed only 45.4 per cent. Females with the educational grade possessed by 67.8 per cent of their sample have little choice regarding marriage and cannot afford to be squeamish in the matter!

In 1937 I stated in my paper (Sociology and Social Work), published in *The Servant of India* that in our social setting one of the three or four specific and new fields of Social Work is that of providing well-supervised and guided clubs and recreation centres for the youth of both sexes. Now that the State has embarked on the paternalistic stage in the field of Education, one of the most important activities towards welfare, one with complex and likely far-reaching consequences, is the starting of such centres alongside of hostels for students. The State will do well to start such centres and hostels to begin with in all big cities and towns which are the headquarters of talukas or districts. Youth in pleasurable activity is most likely to forget such extraneous considerations as caste. The natural tendency should be strengthened by written declarations to be made by the inmates of hostels and the users of clubs that they will not observe any restrictions on the basis of caste and shall endeavour to ignore caste, passively by withholding support from any caste-organization and actively by transcending caste-bias.

One caste of Maharashtra, the Chitrāpur Sāraswats had, as pointed out about, already in 1950 begun to exploit the possibilities of such a centre for preventing marriages outside the caste. Brahmins of Poona joined the company in 1967. The Brahmin Vināmulya Sevā Mandal (the Free Social Service for Brahmins Circle) of Subhashnagar, Poona City, on 16th April 1967 issued the following enticing circular to Brahmin boys and girls: "Come to our premises, get acquainted with each other and try to find your own partner from among the gathering. Though the immediate response was reported to be poor (*Times of India*, 17-6-67) the organization continued its get-togethers every Sunday and in the May-marriage season of 1968 a large number of marriages had come to be credited to them!

The events in Tamilnad in regard to marriage, taken into consideration along with the fact that the priesthood for the Hindu society, which had never been very homogeneous and central, has been still further atomized and disparate, shows up other fissures of a serious nature in the body social, capable of developing it into a 'plural society', properly so called and not merely in the convenient but loose sense of the term.

The non-Brahmin movement in South India, Tamil Nadu (Madras), had managed to give itself the high-sounding and desirable designation of the 'Justice Party'. It got liquidated in the elections of 1936–7. Sphinxlike, however, it burst up in 1945 under the regional but locally supernational designation, Dravida Kazhagam or Dravidian Federation (R. Jayaram in *the Times of India*, 11-2-68). Its leader E. V. Ramaswami Naicker, popularly known as Periyar, tuned it to be more non-Brahmin in attitude than its predecessor, the Justice Party. He insisted that the non-Brahmins of Tamil Nadu should call themselves Dravidians and not 'Non-Brahmins'. Mr. Naicker's anti-Brahmin attitude had taken its shape almost quarter of a century before he had become the head of the Dravida Kazhagam. As a member of the old Justice Party, far back in 1923 he had started an association called *'Suyamariyathai Sangham'* or 'Self-Respect Group'. In the words of R. Jayaram (loc cit.) "its main objective was to root out from 'Dravidians' all superstitious beliefs based on religion and caste" and "to debunk all Brahmanical or Sanskritic beliefs and practices." The group started a weekly journal to propagate its views and through its columns as well as through other newspapers it contributed a series of articles "decrying Hindu ceremonials and rituals". The group did not stop with the highly desirable advocacy of inter-caste marriage but took the highly undesirable and disruptive step of propounding what it called "self-respect marriage" or "reform marriage", in Tamil *Suyamariyāthai* or *seerthirutha*. Its essence consisted in eschewing a priest and his rituals; someone from among the gathering for the wedding "irrespective of caste and creed was to discharge the function of the priest, the rituals consisting in exchange of garlands by the bride and the bridegroom and the tying of the 'tāli' by bridegroom round the neck of the bride". The first 'Self-Respect marriage', as such marriages have come to be known, took place in 1929. According to Jayaram's estimate there were not less than 60,000 of such marriages current till 1968.

The insistence on a marriage union being recognised as perfectly valid without the presence of some priest and also without the accompaniment of some activity indicative of a ritual, it appears, has been current among some of the castes of Tamilnad. It was admitted, for example, in a case before Madras High Court in 1946 that "a ceremony which consists in tying what is called *"Nadu Veettu thāli"* was a customary form of marriage, though not the usual one, among Naickers; and a presumption in favour of validity was drawn.[23] In another case where a Naicker marriage, gone through in 1935, was involved, it is clear from the evidence that the ceremony had consisted in putting a lamp in the centre of the courtyard, a 'purohit' priest "officiating", and the tying of a 'tāli'. Nelson's century old account of the essentials of a Vellāla marriage does not testify to the presence of a priest but is positive on the performance of some ritual. Says Nelson[24]: "A lamp is kept burning on a stool placed near [the place where the bride and bridegroom are seated, it being previously garnished with cowdung]; and a measure of paddy and a rude symbol of *Vighneswara* made of cow-dung in which are struck a couple of blades of the Aruham grass are also placed near them. After both have prostrated themselves before the symbol" the bridegroom tied the golden *tāli* round the bride's neck. At that time "a basin of milk is brought in which have been steeped a few leaves of the *Ficus Religiosa* and the heads of the pair are sprinkled from it by the relatives on both sides."

The validity of a Chetti marriage, taken place in 1934, came to be called in question in a Madras Case[25] which was decided in 1964. The learned judge observed: "It seems to me that the essentials of the custom [about marriage rites among the Nattukottai Chettis] are the lighting of the sacred fire and tying of the thāli [*tāli*]". A 'purohit', priest, was quite clearly present and officiated at the marriage but is not mentioned among the judge's essentials of a Chetti marriage.

A marriage performed under the aegis of the reform-marriage movement, a *Suyamariyathai* marriage, on 14th July 1934 came up for the consideration of its validity in a case for partition of joint family and its property and was decided by Madras High Court in 1954. It was alleged that a widower of the Nattukottai Chetti caste had married a widow of the Reddi caste on the abovementioned date under the auspices of the 'Purohita Maruppa Sangham' or Anti-Purohit Association. The learned judges held the marriage invalid and observed: "It will be a dangerous doctrine to lay down that a community meaning thereby a definite body with the appellation of a sub-caste or caste should have liberty to lay down the requisites of a valid marriage without statutory authority or even without the authority of a long established custom or usage. It is perfectly open to a dissentient sect or community to secede from the sacerdotal authority. But it is not open to such a conglomeration of persons to alter the Hindu law and lay down a law of its own as if they possess legislative authority."[25]

In 1955 came the great landmark of social progress towards a casteless society. The Government of India put on the Statute Book of India, a consolidated law known as the Hindu Marriage Act 1955. It cannot too strongly be impressed upon the minds of the readers that a proposal of the kind had been on the anvil of the country since 1942. Its draft in essentials was prepared by a Select Committee of the Constituent Assembly in 1948 and a Bill based on it was to be passed by the provisional Parliament but unfortunately it did not get passed before the dissolution of that Parliament.[26]

The Special Marriage Act, 1954, required a marriage to be registered for its validity if it were under its provisions and also provided for registration of marriages solemnised in other forms than the one laid down in the Act. Among the conditions of marriage are (1) a certain scheme of prohibited degrees with a provision for recognition of any customary usage; (2) the age of majority of parties to the union and (3) absence of bigamy.[27]

The Hindu Marriage Act of 1955 lays down that for a Hindu marriage to be validly solemnized four conditions must be observed: Among them may be mentioned as generative of social homogeneity: (i) absence of bigamy: (ii) ages of the bride and the bridegroom not being less than 15 and 18 years respectively; (iii) absence of certain degrees and types of relationship with a proviso in favour of customary usage. Section 8 of the Act provided for State-Governments to make rules for the registration of Hindu marriages to facilitate proof of the fact. A Hindu marriage under this Act has been subjected to the common provisions for, (i) restitution of marital rights; (ii) judicial separation; and (iii) divorce, common in the marriage rules of the modern civilized world. For the decision of any issue under these provisions or to secure the rights and benefits under these provisions registration certificate becomes a necessity. Claims on property of various kinds, too, must rest on the validity of a marriage in so far as they are made on the basis of relationship established through it or arising from its consequences.

The Madras High Court having ruled that the *suyamariyathai* marriages were not valid Hindu marriages, one would have thought that they would have been discontinued since 1954; but the large number of such marriages estimated to be current in 1968 makes it certain that they continued to be performed even thereafter. Even the Act of 1955 with its modernised provisions making for conditions that should introduce homogeneity and solidarity in this fundamental social institution for the Hindus did not deter the Dravida Kazagam from encouraging and solemnizing *suyamariyathai* marriages!

The D.M.K. introduced a Bill in the Madras Legislative Assembly in 1960 to validate [or legalize?] (*Times of India*, 11-2-68: R. Jayaram's 'Social Change in Tamilnad'), 'Reform-marriages', which failed to get through. The D.M.K. election manifesto of 1967 stated as one of the objectives of the party to validate. 'Reform-marriages' through appropriate legislation. Accordingly the D.M.K. as soon as it became the Government of Madras (Tamil Nadu) introduced the Hindu Marriage (Madras Amendment) Bill, 1967 in the Assembly and got it passed in November that year. The Bill defines a Self-Respect marriage (reform-marriage of some writers) 'as any marriage between any two Hindus solemnised in the presence of relatives, friends or other persons (*a*) by each party declaring that each takes the other to be his wife or her husband as the case may be; or (*b*) by each party garlanding the other or placing a ring upon any finger of the other, or (*c*) by the tying of the *tāli*'. Without going into further details I may state that this legislation introduces a new form of marriage which sets at naught not only some rudimentary ritual that appears to accompany most forms of marriage solemnisation known to be current among Tamilian respectable though humble castes at least for a century but also the caste headman or an elder of the caste or elderly relatives. Such conditions as of avoidance of certain relationship between the spouses considered to be a part and parcel of the moral code of a people would evidently be difficult of being observed. Restriction of bigamy, an advance in morals and marital happiness, is of course non-existent. The sentiment of Hindu India as a whole is flouted and the right of any successful political party to change the Indian law of marriage for its own State of domination is asserted. Two and conceivably three or four different laws of Hindu marriage, one of them being the Indian law under the Hindu Marriage Act of 1955, may rule side by side in a State in time to come. This step taken by the D.M.K. in Tamil Nadu thus widens the path towards a 'plural society'.

References

1. Gerth and Mills, *From Max Weber*, (1947), p. 397. 2. *Young India* by Mahatma Gandhi, 1919–22, pp. 479–88. 3. Vol. I, p. 28. 4. *Times of India*, 1-11-1948. 5. *Times of India*, 13-8-1950. 6. *Times of India*, 10-3-56; 16-4-55. 7. Ibid., 24-5-56. 8. Ibid., 20-2-52. 9. *Times of India*, 2-9-55; 8-3-55.

10. P. Kodanda Rao in *The Times of India*, July 24, 1953; *Madras Information, Palm Gur Supplement*, July 1953, pp. 2, 15. 11. *Times of India*, 29-3-1965. 12. *Times of India*, 12-8-1960. 13. *Times of India*, 14-9-1962. 14. *Times of India*, 26-11-1965. 15. *Times of India*, 21-4-1955; 18-5-1955. 16. *Sociological Bulletin*, vol. Ill, p. 32. 17. Ibid., 1959, pp. 16–68 (specially 53–6). 18. *Pacific Affairs*, 1960, p. 15. 19. *Ghurye Felicitation Volume*, p. 197.

20. *Social Change and College Students*, 1964, pp. 171–78. 21. Harold A. Gould in *Asian Survey*, 1963, p. 437. 22. *Sociological Bulletin*, 1965, p. 61. 23. Desai, Kumud, p. 76; *A.I.R.* 1946, Madras, 466–8. 24. *Manual of Madura District*, 1868, p. 33. 25. *A.I.R.* 1964, Madras, 126–27. My attention was drawn to this case by my daughter Mrs. Kumud Desai. 26. Desai, Kumud, pp. 53–4. 27. Ibid., pp. 7 and 13.

Appendix A: Punjab

Name of Caste (Number of individuals measured is given in parentheses)		*Cephalic Index*		*Nasal Index*		*Cephalic Length*		*Cephalic Breadth*		*Nasal Length*		*Nasal Breadth*	
		M.	*St. Dev.*	*M.*	*Dev. St.*	*M.*	*St. Dev.*	*M.*	*St. Dev.*	*M.*	*St. Dev.*	*M.*	*St. Dev.*
Arorā	(27)	72.79	3.80	71.60	5.05	–	–	–	–	–	–	–	–
Chuhra	(80)	73.49	2.69	75.29	6.04	186.74	6.15	137.16	4.75	48.06	2.21	36.11	2.45
Gujar	(13)	72.30	2.66	67.37	4.87	–	–	–	–	–	–	–	
Kanet:													
Kulu	(60)	74.11	2.57	74.00	5.98	–	–	–	–	–	–	–	–
Kanet:													
Lahoul	(30)	77.48	2.37	66.45	5.53	–	–	–	–	–	–	–	–
Khatri	(60)	74.15	3.02	73.30	6.89	185.72	6.05	137.50	5.24	48.82	2.76	35.70	2.81
Māchhi	(19)	72.50	1.82	70.29	5.22	–	–	–	–	–	–	–	–
Sikh	(80)	72.76	2.92	69.10	6.06	–	–	–	–	–	–	–	–

M=Mean; St. Dev.=Standard Deviation.

Appendix B: United Provinces of Agra and Oudh

Name of Caste (Number of individuals measured is given in parentheses)		*Cephalic Index*		*Nasal Index*		*Cephalic Length*		*Cephalic Breadth*		*Nasal Length*		*Nasal Breadth*	
		M.	*St. Dev.*	*M.*	*St. Dev.*	*M.*	*St. Dev.*	*M.*	*St. Dev.*	*M.*	*St. Dev.*	*M.*	*St. Dev.*
Bania	(80)	72.02	3.36	80.55	9.28	–	–	–	–	–	–	–	–
Babhan	(26)	73.52	2.25	73.60	7.24	–	–	–	–	–	–	–	–
Bhar	(100)	73.66	3.06	81.97	8.59	–	–	–	–	–	–	–	–
Brahmin	(100)	73.29	3.12	74.88	8.02	187.56	5.58	137.42	4.60	46.57	3.04	34.72	2.70
Chamār	(100)	72.90	2.92	86.52	7.64	185.18	5.79	134.98	4.21	41.02	2.75	35.19	2.20
Chhatri	(100)	73.12	3.12	78.36	7.70	188.35	6.51	137.68	4.60	45.80	3.76	35.65	2.52
Dom	(100)	74.28	3.54	83.60	8.86	183.91	6.63	136.40	4.49	45.44	3.47	37.72	2.65
Kāyasth	(100)	72.48	2.99	78.87	8.22	186.62	5.75	135.42	4.91	44.66	3.19	34.99	2.54
Khatri	(15)	71.98	2.71	79.15	9.29	–	–	–	–	–	–	–	–
Kol	(32)	72.51	2.96	82.39	7.42	–	–	–	–	–	–	–	–
Kurmi	(100)	73.25	3.23	79.46	8.38	184.05	6.21	135.13	4.12	44.02	2.95	34.84	2.56
Lohār	(45)	72.93	3.34	83.45	11.43	–	–	–	–	–	–	–	–
Musāhar	(18)	74.29	2.94	86.17	7.84	–	–	–	–	–	–	–	–
Pāsi	(100)	72.68	3.21	85.92	9.11	185.10	6.89	134.48	3.87	41.26	3.21	35.23	2.28

M = Mean; St. Dev. = Standard Deviation.

Appendix C: Bihar

Name of Caste (Number of individuals measured is given in parentheses)		*Cephalic Index*		*Nasal Index*		*Cephalic Length*		*Cephalic Breadth*		*Nasal Length*		*Nasal Breadth*	
		M.	*St. Dev.*	*M.*	*St. Dev.*	*M.*	*St. Dev.*	*M.*	*St. Dev.*	*M.*	*St. Dev.*	*M.*	*St. Dev.*
Babhan	(59)	76.98	3.66	73.55	7.02	–	–	–	–	–	–	–	–
Bind	(13)	73.68	3.64	82.76	7.68	–	–	–	–	–	–	–	–
Brahmin	(67)	74.91	3.02	73.24	6.35	187.88	6.27	140.81	4.74	49.33	3.53	36.11	2.54
Dom:													
Maghaya	(100)	76.21	3.25	82.58	6.98	186.37	6.29	142.20	4.26	48.04	3.09	39.62	2.42
Chamār	(62)	76.26	4.35	82.93	7.20	184.42	7.28	140.35	5.28	46.08	2.90	38.13	2.52
Kurmi	(71)	75.82	3.50	79.04	6.96	186.97	6.67	141.55	4.54	47.66	3.46	37.45	2.42
Musāhar	(77)	75.79	2.91	89.20	8.86	183.17	5.91	138.69	4.18	45.52	3.01	40.40	2.97

M = Mean; St. Dev. = Standard Deviation.

Appendix D: Bengal

Name of Caste (Number of individuals measured is given in parentheses)		*Cephalic Index*		*Nasal Index*		*Cephalic Length*		*Cephalic Breadth*		*Nasal Length*		*Nasal Breadth*	
		M.	*St. Dev.*	*M.*	*St. Dev.*	*M.*	*St. Dev.*	*M.*	*St. Dev.*	*M.*	*St. Dev.*	*M.*	*St. Dev.*
Brahmin	(100)	78.89	3.63	70.89	6.85	181.76	5.82	143.25	4.54	49.71	4.09	35.09	2.72
Chandāl	(67)	78.11	4.04	74.27	6.83	183.31	6.94	143.18	4.52	49.69	2.69	36.79	2.88
Kāyasth	(100)	78.30	3.82	70.78	6.34	182.47	6.08	142.88	4.95	50.19	3.09	35.39	2.52
Koibart	(100)	77.57	3.85	76.83	6.70	–	–	–	–	–	–	–	–
Muchi	(27)	77.22	3.55	75.30	6.92	182.93	6.76	142	4.45	49.19	2.94	36.89	2.66
Rājbansi	(100)	75.36	3.21	76.86	5.81	186.28	6.85	140.26	5.15	48.96	2.85	37.57	2.52
Sadgop	(48)	77.95	3.23	74.24	7.46	–	–	–	–	–	–	–	–

M = Mean; St. Dev. = Standard Deviation.

Appendix E: Bombay

Name of Caste (Number of individuals measured is given in parentheses)		*Cephalic Index*		*Nasal Index*		*Cephalic Length*		*Cephalic Breadth*		*Nasal Length*		*Cephalic Index*	
		M.	*St. Dev.*	*M.*	*St. Dev.*	*M.*	*St. Dev.*	*M.*	*St. Dev.*	*M.*	*St. Dev.*	*M.*	*St. Dev.*
Bhil: Khandesh	(103)	72.56	3.04	95.80	11.84	182.92	6.11	132.61	4.43	41.12	3.49	39.05	3.14
Chitpāvan Brahmin	(100)	77.41	3.95	76.99	6.60	186.43	7.37	144.25	5.16	49.34	3.26	37.87	2.15
Deshasth Brahmin	(100)	77.09	4.37	79.73	6.14	185.50	6.39	142.94	5.41	48.93	2.91	38.81	2.25
Kātkari	(109)	74.37	2.65	88.46	8.05	178.86	6.20	133.04	3.95	44.04	2.94	38.78	2.49
Kunbi	(100)	77.52	4.36	79.44	5.70	180.10	6.35	139.49	5.55	47.81	2.62	37.95	2.09
Mahār	(100)	77.17	3.55	82.23	6.20	181.40	5.83	140.12	5.15	47.21	2.58	38.73	2.37
Marātha High (Caste)	(100)	76.34	4.11	71.47	6.35	184.62	6.39	140.92	6.52	52.02	3.37	37.01	2.44
Marātha Ghati	(100)	78.33	4.53	80.32	7.47	–	–	–	–	–	–	–	–
Nāgar Brahmin	(100)	79.93	4.33	73.58	7.66	184.51	7.47	147.16	5.97	50.76	3.56	37.18	2.57
Prabhu	(100)	80.00	3.80	76.18	7.13	–	–	–	–	–	–	–	–
Shenvi Brahmin	(100)	79.08	4.06	75.15	7.46	186.22	7.18	147.15	5.29	50.27	3.63	37.62	2.36
Son Koli	(100)	77.62	3.24	76.77	6.96	185.00	5.83	143.45	4.71	49.62	3.15	37.98	2.62
Vāni (Gujarat)	(139)	78.52	3.46	76.30	8.09	–	–	–	–	–	–	–	–

M = Mean; St. Dev. = Standard Deviation.

Appendix F: Madras

Caste		*Language*	*Cephalic Index*		*Nasal Index*	
			M.	*St. Dev.*	*M.*	*St. Dev.*
Kapu	(49)	Telugu	78.08	3.70	–	–
Smārta Brahmin	(60)	Kannada	78.45	4.41	–	–
Coorg	(32)	Kodagu	79.72	3.79	72.12	5.22
Billāva	(50)	Tulu	80.36	4.40	–	–
Sivalli Brahmin	(40)	"	80.44	5.21	–	–
Vakkaliga	(50)	Kannada	81.76	5.03	–	–
Todā	(76)	Todā	73.76	2.22	–	–
Yeruva	(25)	Kannada	73.48	3.06	89.76	5.26
Vellāl	(40)	Tamil	73.92	2.74	–	–
Nāyar	(39)	Malayālam	74.44	2.85	–	–
Pattar Brahmin	(25)	Tamil	74.44	3.31	–	–
Tamil Brahmin	(40)	"	76.55	3.44	–	–

M = Mean; St. Dev. = Standard Deviation.

Appendix G: Differential Index

(Based on six characters: Cephalic index, cephalic length, cephalic breadth, nasal index, nasal length, and nasal breadth)

PUNJAB	
Chuhra and Khatri	.88
UNITED PROVINCES	
Brahmin and Chhatri	.89
" " Kāyasth	1.47
" " Kurmi	1.83
" " Dom	2.56
" " Pāsi	3.17
" " Chamār	3.32
Pāsi and Chamār	.27
Kurmi and Chamār	1.71
BIHAR	
Brahmin and Kurmi	1.75
" " Chamār	2.42
" " Dom	2.95
Chamār and Kurmi	1.45
BENGAL	
Brahmin and Kāyasth	.43
" " Chandāl	1.11
BOMBAY	
Deshasth Brahmin and Son Koli	.95
" " " Chitpāvan Brahmin	1.02
" " " Mahār	1.61
" " " Kunbi	1.73
" " " Shenvi Brahmin	2.10
" " " Nāgar Brahmin	2.59
" " " High Caste Maratha	2.64

GENERAL						
U.P. Kurmi and Bihar Kurmi	..	..	..	..	..	3.49
U.P. Chamār and Bihar Chamār	..	..	..	..	..	4.01
U.P. Brahmin and Punjab Chuhra	..	..	..	..	..	1.02
" " " " Khatri	..	..	..	..	..	1.38
" " " Bihar Brahmin	..	..	..	..	..	2.05
" " " Chitpāvan Brahmin	..	..	..	..	..	3.66
" " " Deshasth Brahmin	..	..	..	..	..	3.94
Bengal Brahmin and Shenvi Brahmin	..	..	..	..	..	2.30
" " " Chitpāvan Brahmin	..	..	..	..	..	2.44
" " " Bihar Brahmin	..	..	..	..	..	2.52
" " " Deshasth Brahmin	..	..	..	..	..	2.96
" " " U.P. Brahmin	..	..	..	..	..	3.89

Bibliography

Abram, A. *Social England in the Fifteenth Century*, 1909.
Adams, G. B. *Civilization during the Middle Ages*, 1910.
Altekar, A. S. *A History of Village Communities in Western India*, 1927.
Apastamba. *Dharmasutra* (Buhler's trans., in SBE, 1879).
Arthashastra by Kautilya. Ed. by R. Shama Sastri, 1919.
———. Translation by R. Sharma Sastri (2nd ed.).
———. Edited and translated by R. P. Kangale.
Ashley, W. G. *An Introduction to Economic History*, Vol. I, Pt. i, 1888.
Attenborough, F. L. *The Laws of the Earliest English Kings*, 1922.
Baden-Powell, B. H. *The Indian Village Community*, 1896.
Bailey, F. G. *Caste and the Economic Frontier*, 1958.
———. *Tribe, Caste and Nation*, 1960.
———. *Politics and Social Change*, 1963.
Baines, Athelstane. *Ethnography* (Castes and Tribes), 1912.
Baliga, B. S. *Tanjore District Handbook*, 1957.
Bashford, J. W. *China, an Interpretation*, 1916.
Baudhayana. *Dharmasutra*, (Buhler's trans, in SBE, 1882).
Bengal Census, 1921. *Census of India*, 1921, *Bengal Report*.
Bevan, E. *History of Egypt, Ptolemaic Dynasty*, 1927.
Bhattacharya, J. *Hindu Castes and Sects*, 1896.
Blunt, E. A. H. *The Caste System of Northern India*, 1931.
Bose, P. N. *History of Hindu Civilization during British Rule*, Vol. II, 1894.
Breasted, J. H. *A History of Egypt*, 1916 ed.
———. *Ancient Times*, 1917.
Briggs, G. W. *The Chamars*, 1920.
Brinkley, Capt. F. *Oriental Series*, 11 Vols., 1902 ff.
———. *Japan*, 3 Vols., *China*, Vol. I, etc., 1902 ff.
Brissaud, J. *A History of French Private Law*, trans. by J. W. Garner, 1912.
———. *A History of French Public Law*, trans. by J. W. Garner, 1915.
Brooks, B. Allard. *A Contribution to the Study of the Moral Practices of Certain Social Groups in Ancient Mesopotamia*, 1920.
Brough, John. *The Early Brahmanical System of Gotra and Pravara*, 1953.
Cambridge History of India. Vol. I, *Ancient India*, edited by E. J. Rapson, 1922.
Chadwick, H. M. *Studies on Anglo-Saxon Institutions*, 1905.
Chamberlain, B. H. *Things Japanese*, 1905.
Chanda, R. *The Indo-Aryan Races*, 1916.
Chapekar, N. G. *Chitpavan* (2nd ed.), 1966.
Collection of Smritis. *Smritinam Samuccaya*, ed. Anandashram Sanskrit Series, No. 48, 1905.
Cox, O. C. *Caste, Class and Race*, 1948.
Croce, B. *My Philosophy*, 1949.
Crooke, W. *The Tribes and Castes of the North-Western Provinces and Oudh*, 4 Vols., 1896.

Crooke, W. *Natives of Northern India*, 1907.
Dasgupta, T. C. *Aspects of Bengali Society*, 1935.
Desai, Mrs. Kumud. *Indian Law of Marriage and Divorce*, 1964.
Desai, H. G. *A Glossary of Castes, Tribes and Races in the Baroda State*, 1912.
Dhalla, M. N. *Zoroastrian Civilization*, 1922.
Dill, Sir Samuel. *Roman Society from Nero to Marcus Aurelius*, 1905.
———. *Roman Society in the Last Century of the Western Empire*, 1910.
Dobree, Bonamy. *English Revolts*, 1937.
Douglas, R. K. *Society in China*, 1894.
Duff, A. M. *Freed Men in the Early Roman Empire*, 1928.
Dutt. N. K. *Origin and Growth of Caste in India*, I (1931), II (1965).
Eliot, Sir Charles. *Hinduism and Buddhism*, 3 Vols., 1921.
Ency. of R. and E. *Encyclopaedia of Religion and Ethics*.
Erman, A. *Life in Ancient Egypt, trans*. by H. M. Tirard, 1894.
Farquhar, J. N. *Outline of the Religious Literature of India*, 1920.
Featherman, A. (IIb), *Social History of the Races of Mankind* (Second Division), Oceano-Melanesians, 1888.
———. (V) *ibid*., (Fifth Division), *Aramaeans*, 1881.
Fick, R. *Social Organization in North-East India in Buddha's Time* (trans. by Maitra), 1920.
Forbes, A. K. *Rasa Mala*, 2 Vols., 1856, ed. by Rawlinson, 1925.
Forbes, James. *Oriental Memoirs*, ed. 1934.
Friedlander, Ludwig. *Roman Life and Manners under the Early Empire* (trans. of the 7th ed.), 1909.
Gangopadhyay, Bella. *Marriage Regulations Among Certain Castes of Bengal*, 1964.
Gautama. *Dharmasutra* (Buhler's Trans, in SBE, 1879).
Geer, R. M. *Rome*, 1940.
Ghurye Felicitation Volume. Edited by K. M. Kapadia, 1954.
Gledhill, Alan. *The Republic of India*, 1951.
Godavari Dist. Gaz. *District Gazetteer of Godavari*, pt. I.
Gough, Kathleen. (1) In McKim Marriott's *Village India*, 1955.
———. (2) In American *Anthropologist*, 1956.
———. (3) In E. R. Leach's *Cambridge Papers in Social Anthropology*, 1962.
Haddon, A. C. *The Wanderings of Peoples*, 1919.
Hamilton, Walter. *A Geographical Description of Hindustan*, 2 Vols., 1820.
Harrison, Selig. *S. India: The Most Dangerous Decades*, 1960.
Hemadri. *Caturvargacintamani* (Bibl. Ind.), 1871 ff.
Hobhouse, L. T. *Morals in Evolution*, ed. 1923.
Hose, C. and McDougall, W. *The Pagan Tribes of Borneo*, 2 Vols., 1912.
Huebner, R. *A History of Germanic Private Law* (trans. 1918).
Hultzsch, E. *South Indian Inscriptions* (ed. and trans. 1890 ff).
India Census, 1921. *Census of India*, 1921, *India Report*.
Irving, B. A. *The Theory and Practice of Caste*, 1853.
Jastrow, Morris (Jr.) *The Civilization of Babylonia and Assyria*, 1915.
Johns, C. H. W. *Babylonian and Assyrian Laws, Contracts and Letters*, 1904.
J.A.S.B. *Journal of the Asiatic Society of Bengal*.
J.B.B.R.A.S. *Journal of the Bombay Branch of the Royal Asiatic Society*.
J. R. A. I. *Journal of the Royal Anthropological Institute*.
Kanakasabhai Pillai, V. *The Tamils Eighteen Hundred Years Ago*, 1904.
Karandikar, S. V. *Hindu Exogamy*, 1920.
Karve, Mrs. I. *Hindu Society, an Interpretation*, 1961.
———. *Kinship Organization in India*, (2nd ed.), 1965.
Keane. A. H. *Man, Past and Present*, 1920.

Kerr, James. *The Domestic Life, Character and Customs of the Natives of India*, 1865.
Ketkar, S. V. *History of Caste in India*, 1909.
Kikani, L. T. *Caste in Court*, 1912.
Kitts, Eustace J. *A Compendium of the Castes and Tribes found in India*, 1885.
Kroeber, A. L. *Anthropology*, 1948.
Lambert, J. Malet. *Two Thousand Years of Guild Life*, 1891.
Latthe, A. B. *Memoirs of His Highness Shri Shahu Chhattrapati, Maharaja of Kolhapur*, 1924.
Latourette, K. S. *The Chinese, Their History and Culture*, 2 Vols., 1934.
Leach, E. R. *Aspects of Caste in South India, Ceylon and Pakistan or Cambridge Papers in Social Anthropology*, 2, 1962.
Leage, R. W. *Roman Private Law*, 1906.
Leffingwell, G. *Social and Private Life at Rome in the Time of Plautus and Terence*, 1918.
Logan, W. *Malabar*, 3 Vols., 1887.
Longford, J. H., *Japan of the Japanese*, 2nd ed., 1915.
Louis. *Ancient Rome at Work*, 1927.
Lowie, R. H. *Primitive Society*, ed. 1949.
Mbh. *Mahabharata* (Kumbhakonam ed.).
MacIver, R. M. *Community,* ed. 1920.
MacIver and Page. *Society*, 1949.
Madras Census, 1871. *Census of India*, 1871, *Madras Report.*
Malcolm, Sir John. *Memoirs of Central India and Malwa*, 1823.
Mandlik, V. N. *Vyavahara Mayukha*, ed. 1880.
Mann, H. H. and Kanitkar, N. V. *Land and Labour in a Deccan Village*, No. 2, 1921.
Manu. *Laws of Manu* (Buhler's trans. in SBE, 1886).
Marriott. McKim. *Village India*, 1955.
Martin, R. M. *The History, Antiquities and Statistics of Eastern India*, 3 vols., 1838.
Maspero, Sir Gaston. *The Dawn of Civilization*, 5th ed., 1910.
Matthai, John. *Village Government in British India*, 1915.
Mayer, A. C. *Caste and Kinship in Central India*, 1960.
Mayne, J. D. *A Treatise on Hindu Law and Usage*, ed., 1914.
McCrindle. *Ancient India.*
Mollendorff, P. G. *The Family Law of the Chinese*, 1896.
Mookerji, Radhakumud. *Local Government in Ancient India*. 1919.
Muir, J. *Original Sanskrit Texts*, Vol. I (2nd ed.), 1872.
Muirhead, J. *Historical Introduction to the Private Law of Rome* (3rd ed.) 1916.
Mulla, D. F. *Jurisdiction of Courts in Matters Relating to Rights and Powers of Castes*, 1901.
Mysore Census, 1901. *Census of India*, 1901, *Mysore Report.*
Narada Smriti. Jolly's trans, in SBE, 1889.
Nesfield, J. C. *Brief View of the Caste System of the North Western Provinces and Oudh*, 1855.
North, C. C. *Social Differentiation*, 1926.
O'Malley, L. S. S. *Indian Caste Customs*, 1932.
Pandian, T. B. *Indian Village Folk*, 1898.
Panjab Census, 1911. *Census of India*, 1911, *Punjab Report.*
Panjab Census, 1921. *Census of India*, 1921, *Punjab Report.*
Parasara. *Parasara Dharma Samhita* (B.S.S.).
Pargiter, F. E. *Ancient Indian Historical Tradition*, 1922.
Patanjali. *Vyakaranamahabhasya* (B.S.S.)
Petrie, Sir W. M. Flinders. *Social Life in Ancient Egypt*, 1923.
Patil, P. S. *Phooley* (Marathi), 1927.
Polock and Maitland. *The History of English Law*, Vol. I (ed. 1911).

Ranade, M. G. In *JBBRAS*, Vol. XX.
Renard, G. F. *Guilds in the Middle Ages* (trans., 1919).
Rickards, R. *India*, 2 Vols., 1892–93.
Risley, Sir H. H. *Tribes and Castes of Bengal, Ethnographic Glossary*, 1891.
———. *The People of India* (2nd ed., 1915).
Rivers, W. H. R. *The History of Melanesian Society*, 2 Vols., 1914.
Rose, H. A. *Glossary of Punjab Tribes and Castes*, 1911.
S. B. E. *Sacred Books of the East*, 1879.
Schaeffer, H. *The Social Legislation of the Primitive Semites*.
Senart, E. *Caste in India* (trans., 1930).
Sherring, M. A. *Hindu Tribes and Castes*, 1872.
Sircar, D. C. *Select Inscriptions*, 1942.
Slater, Gilbert. *Some South Indian Villages*, 1918.
Smith, J. Toulmin. *English Guilds*, 1870.
Smith, W. Robertson. *Kinship and Marriage in Early Arabia* (ed. 1903).
Sombart. *Socialism*, 1898.
Spence, L. *Mexico of the Mexicans*, 1917.
Spencer, Herbert. *Principles of Sociology*, Vol. III (ed. 1897).
Srinivas, M. N. *Marriage and Family in Mysore*, 1942.
Steele, Arthur. *The Law and Custom of Hindu Castes*, 1868.
Subramanian, N. *Sangam Polity*, 1966.
Shudrakamalakara. By Kamalakarabhatta (Nirnayasagar P., ed. 1928).
Shukraniti. Trans, by Benoy Kumar Sarkar, 1914.
Tawney, R. H. *Equality*, 1931.
Thurston, E. *Castes and Tribes of Southern India*, 7 Vols., 1907–9.
Traill, H. D. *Social England*, Vol. I, 1898.
Trevelyan, G. M. *English Social History*, 1944.
Trichinopoly Dist. Gaz. *District Gazetteer of Trichinopoly*, pt. I.
Tucker, T. G. *Life in the Roman World of Nero and St. Paul* (ed. 1924).
U.P. Census, 1901. *Census of India*, 1901, *North-Western Provinces and Oudh Report*.
Vad, G. C. *Selections from the Satara Raja's and the Peshwa's Diaries*.
Vaidya, C. V. *History of Mediaeval Hindu India*, 3 vols., 1921 ff.
Vasishta. *Dharmasutra* (Buhler's trans. in SBE, 1882).
Vedic Index. By A. A. Macdonell and A. B. Keith, 2 Vols., 1912.
Vishnu. *Institutes of Vishnu* (Jolly's trans. in SBE, 1889).
Warde, Fowler. *Social Life at Rome in the Age of Cicero*, ed. 1929.
Werner, E. T. C. *Spencer's Descriptive Sociology*, No. IX, 1910.
——— *China of the Chinese*, 1919.
Westermarck, E. A. *History of Human Marriage*, 5th ed., 3 Vols., 1921.
Wilkinson, Sir J. G. *The Manners and Customs of the Ancient Egyptians*, new ed., 3 Vols., 1878.
Williams, M. W. *Social Scandinavia in the Viking Age*, 1920.
Wilson, John. *Indian Caste*, 2 Vols., 1877.
Woolley, C. Leonard. *The Sumerians*, 1928.
Yajnavalkya. *Yajnavalkyasmriti, with Mitakshara*, ed. by S. S. Setlur, 1912.

INDEX

Abhiras, 33, 40
Aborigines, Aboriginal castes,
Aboriginal tribes, 18, 67, 92
exclusion of, 92
and Shudra, 90
Abdul Fazal, castes in time of, 57
Ādi Dravidas, 182
Administrative Reforms
Commission, on deterioration in the quality of recruitment to all-India service, 231
Agamudaiyan, 70, 201
Āgri, 20
Aheriya, 3
Ahir, 3, 18–20, 22, 57, 91, 183
Aitareya Brahmana, 162
Ajātashatru, philosopher-king, 26
Akbar, castes in time of, 9
Alberuni, 57, 164, 166
Ambedkar, Dr. B. R., 113, 214
Anglo-Saxons, 82, 85, 89
Annadurai, C. N., 187
Anti-Brahmin movement, 188
Anti-priest movement, 240
Antyajas, 51, 166; see Outcaste
'Anuloma', 116–118
'Apapātra', 164
Āpastamba, 42
Arabs, absence of endogamy among, 70, 78
Arora, 18
Arthashastra, 50; see Kautilya
Artisan castes of Madras, struggle for higher social status, 180
non-Brahmin priests of, 7–8
Arya, contrast with Dasa, 28
illicit unions with Shudra, 22, 27–28
contrast with Shudra, 86
invasion of India by, 64
Aryan, people, 24, 27
Arya Samaj, attitude towards caste, 154
reasons for the popularity of, 150
Aryan type, 62, 66
Āryāvarta, 46
Aryo-Dravidian type, 66, 70
Asat-Shudra, 49, 53
Ashrafin, 11
Asprishya Shudra, 5
Ashvapati, philosopher-king, 26
Audich Brahmins, 107
Ayogava, mixed caste, 27

Baden-Powell, B. H., 117
Bailey, F. G., 117
Balaji, admission to professional college, 224
Backward Classes, list specified in Bombay State, 220
greater educational facility given in Madras to, 226
list has grown instead of becoming smaller, 228
coaching candidates for UPSC examinations, 231
Backward Class Commission, 221
appointment of by the President, 217
draft report on, 221, 227
government not implementing the report, 225
Backward Class & reservation of appointments for, 215
special facilities for, 217–218
minister in charge of welfare of, 217; Special Officer for, 217–218
Bagdi, 170
Bahaliya (Baheliya), 3
Baines, Sir A., 108, 197, 201
Balija, 55
Bālistika, 44
Bāna, on Chandāla, 50–52, 65
Pārashava brothers, 53
Baniā, divisions and sub-division of, 19, 123
occupational nature of, 33
territorial sub-castes of, 97
physical affinity of, 91–92
Bansphor, 4, 17
Baoriya, 57
Barai, endogamous sub-divisions of, 18–19
Barber, 5, 14, 44, 139; as match-maker and marriage priest, 14
Barbosa, Duarte, on castes in Malabar, 57
Barhai, seven sub-castes of, 17
Bari, 17
Basor, 4
Basu, B. N., effiorts liberalize marriage law, 144
Battle of Plassey, 170
Bauri, 65, 70
Beals, A. R., 138
Berad, sub-castes of, 21
Bevan, Edwyn, on Romans and Egyptians, 88
Bhadralok, 11
Bhagat, B. R., nurturing caste-patriotism, 237
participating in All-India Yadav Mahasabha meeting, 232
Bhagavadgitā, assurance of Vaishya and Shudra, 33–34
duties and functions of four castes, 34
Bhandāri, 2, 18
Bhandarkar, D. R., 123, 134
Bhandarkar, R. G., 171

Bhangi, 4, 18
Bhātiā, ethnic origin of, 18
Bhattacharya, J. N., 183, 204
Bhil, 18, 20, 51, 57
Bhilala, 51
Bhuiyār, 3
Bisen, 57
Bishnois, sectarian origin of 18
Blacksmith 27, 51, 56, 75
Blunt, E. A., 4, 95–97
Bonnerjea, Bisen, 124–125
Borradaile, H., a Bombay Officer, 143
Brahmanic culture, 22, 36, 92–93, 95, 159
Brahmin Government of Poona, 3; *see* Peshwas
Brahmins, 3–20, 31, 35, 36, 40, 44–50, 54–60, 62, 67–71, 76–81, 83, 84, 86, 88, 89, 92–95, 97, 99–109, 115, etc.
Brahmins, quarters, 50; revolt against the supremacy of, 38, 55, 148, 150–151; saints, 54
 sole receiver of gifts, 8, 25, 30, 41
 supremacy over Kshatriyas, 3, 127, 142, 196
 absence of caste-councils, 142
 exclusive right of priestcraft, 26, 93
 food restrictions for, 10
 in Malabar, 18; marriage among, 10
 occupations of, 94
 privileges of, 128
 as priests, 143
 feeling against, 31; *see also* Anti-Brahmin
Brahmin priests, replacement of, 7, 143
Brahmin Vināmulya Sevā Mandal, 239
Brazil, caste in, 77–78
Brihaspati, 128
Bryce, James, 213
Buchanan, 9
Buddha, assertion of Kshatriya pre-eminence by, 30, 36
 discussion with Ambattha, 37
 previous births of, 37
 attitude towards caste, 145
Burud, 56; *see* cane-worker
Burnell, A. C., 189

Cane-worker, 167
Carpenter, 17, 41–44, 47
Caste and community special deities of, 3
 disabilities of, 6, 173
 endogamy of, 113–114
 food restrictions of, 93
 intermarriage, 9, 12, 76, 80
 in Malabar, 5, 7, 10, 57
 based on nicknames, 96
 based on occupation, 94
 origin of, 51
 privileges of, 31
 in Punjab, 117
 revival of spirit of 146
 revolt against, 38
 based on sect, 109
 social intercourse of, 12, 40
 solidarity of, 40, 50, 93, 183
 based on names of tribes, 111
 based on territory, 101
 community-type-development of, 235
 non-recognition for official purposes, 222
 process of proliferation, on plea of up-grading backward classes, 226
 relegated to the background by the Government of India, 195
Castes, the four traditional, 212
 views of Max Weber, 212–213
 views of Mahatma Gandhi, 154, 161
 return to four-fold division impracticable, 161
 attitude, towards, dual standard in, 155
 its authority set aside by courts, 147
 as basis of discrimination in schools, 81, 220
 in censuses, 146
 power of, 183
 the community aspect of, 158
 control over individual's actions, 196
 dependence on, 12, 14
 exploitation for political purposes, 203
 Phooley's revolt against, 171
 political development of, 184
Caste consciousness, new forms of, 156–157, 179;
 during elections, 179
Caste animosity, 159
Caste associations, 158
Caste charities, 101
Caste Disabilities Removal Act of 1850, 143
Caste-group rivalries, 232
Caste-journals, 233
Castes and linguistic barrier, 100
Castes (low), their access to temples, 180
Caste-names, dropping of, 146
Caste-patriotism, 213
Caste representation in recruitment for jobs, 197
 as an unwise step, 42; *see also* communal representation
Caste Sabhas, 179
Caste Society, features of, 220
Caste societies, formation of and integrative activity, 233
Caste solidarity, manifestation of, 156
Castes of Tamil Nadu; *see* Tamil Nadu
Celts, 89
Ceremonial purity, 239
Chakkiliyan, 6
Chamār, Chāmbhār, 168
Chanals, 168
Chandāl, 168
Chandāla, 165
 origin of, 168
Chandel, 57
Chandragupta, Shudra origin of, 33
Charan, 19
Charudatta, pursuit of Vaishya's occupation by, 53
Chasa, 65
Chatfield, concessions in fees to backward castes by, 145
Chattri, 64, 91
Chelmsford, Lord, 145, 151
Chero, tribe, 3
Cheruman, 65

Chetti, 17
Chhatri, 62, 64, 91
Chief Ministers' view of job reservations for backward classes, 225–226, 228
view of criteria for educational concessions, 25
Chitpāvan Brahmins: Physical affinity with Deshasth Brahmins, 71, 131, 135
green-gray eyes of, 71; *see* Konkanasth Brahmins
Chitrāpur Sāraswats, and caste-youth clubs, 234, 237
Chuhrā, 167
Citizens, category of, a creation of British Administration, 215
Clean Shudras, 7–8
Clubs and recreation centres for the youth of both sexes, author's suggestion for setting up of, 239
Cohn, B. S., 169, 179
Colebrooke, H. T., on diversity of occupations of castes, 9
Communal representation, 151–152
Community, 240
Concessions, continued employment can create a vested interest even in backwardness, 227–232
Confucius, division of people into five classes by, 76
Congress Party, creating "vested interests" through amendment of the constitution, 232
Consolidated Fund of India, funds available to scheduled tribes only, 218
Co-operative housing and caste, 157
Coppersmith, 7
Constituent Assembly and its ideal of casteless society, 231, 241
Constitution of India, objectives of, 230
Convention of the All-India Backward classes Federation, 227–228
emergence of a vested interest as the upshot of, 228
Criteria for determining the backwardness of people, government on revising of, 222
pant views economic criteria desirable rather than caste, 225
Cross cousin marriage, 136

Dabhi, F. B., and bill on removal of caste distinctions amongst Hindus, 38
Daha, 86
Dana-stutis, 47
Dāngi tribe, 18
Darji, 19
Dāsa: contrast with Arya, 86
Dāsapura, 57
Dasharatha, Shudra, wife of, 57
Deshastha Brahmins, devotion to secular pursuits of, 135
territorial derivation of, 90
sub-castes of, 19
physical affinities of, 62
Depressed classes, 6, 145, 153–155
disappearance of segregation in schools, 104
special representation in local and legislative bodies, 161
entry into Hindu temples, 154
mission, 202
and missionaries, 154
problem of, 213
Depressed classes, representation for, 172
Deshināmamālā, 164
Devapi, 26
Dhangar, 21–22
Dharkar, 70
Dharkatta, 57
Dhed, 19
Dhimar, 19, 20, 22
Dhobi, 4, 19
Divide and Rule policy, 150
Diwakar, R. R., heading committee on abolition of caste distinction, 219
Dom, Domb, 70
prominence at the burning ghat, 14
Dombs (Dombas), 165
Dosadh or Dusadh, 70
Draupadi, objection against Karna's low birth by, 46
Dravidian Brahmins, 66
Dravida Kazhagam, or Dravidian Federation, 239
Dravidian languages, 199
Dravidian type, Dravida type, 67
Druids, theory and practice of contagion among, 89
Dube, S. C., 97, 137–138
Dublā, nickname-origin of, 18
Dutt, N. K., 107, 119, 125
Dvija, Dvijati, 90; *see* Twice-born castes
Dyer of clothes, 51

Egypt, Ptolemaic, 87–88
Egyptians and Greeks, 87
Ekajāti, 90
Ekanāth, performance of purificatory rites by, 54
Eliot, Sir Charles, on Buddhist revolt, 48
Ellenborough, Lord, on the recruitment of the Indian army, 149
Elphinstone, Lord, on Indian army, 149
Endogamous nature of caste, 90, 156
Endogamy, 10, 53, 64, 114 and occupations, 125 in Africa, 78
in pre-historic Rome, 194–194
among Anglo-Saxons, 82, 85, 89, 90
as outstanding feature of caste, 237.
Epstein, 137–138
Espanol, 77
Eta, untouchability of, 76–77
Exogamy, 133

Farquhar, J. N., 109, 190, 195
Ferreira, J. V., 120
Fick, R.: on the nature of Buddhist revolt, 48
on the endogamy of castes, 237–238
Fishermen, 78
Food: Kachchā, Pakkā, 4, 5
restrictions of, 5
Forbes, James, on Brahmins of Travancore, 8

Francis, F. W., 198, 200–201, 208
Fryer, John, on the anti-Brahmin attitude of Kammalans, 3
Fundamental Rights, 215
Furnivall, J. S., 185
on "plural society" of Indonesia, 185

Gachupin, 77
Gadariā, 18
Gahapati, 43
Gaharwal, 57
Gait, E. A.
on multiplicity of castes, 11
on prohibition of intermarriage, 11–12
Gamalla, 3
Gandhi, Mahatma, 154, 161, 175, 179, 212–214
views on caste, 212
Gaoli, Gauli, Gavli, 17, 19
Garasiah, 57
Gaudakaranika, 57
Gautama, 43, 45
Giri, V. V., Vice-President, 228
Goa, 101–102, 117
Goāla, 65, 70
Goldsmith, non-Brahmin Priests of, 7
Golla, 65
Gond, tribe, 18
Gondhali, sub-castes of, 19
Gosāi, sectarian origin of, 18
Gotra, 50
Gotra and Marriage, 135
Gough, Kathleen, 178, 207
Gould, Harry, on caste endogamy, 238
Gour, Hari Sing, 144
Govallave (cow-erdsmen), 56
Government of India Act, (1935), 172, 214
Gregory XV, Pope, Bull on caste-regulations, 150
Griffin, Sir Lepel, on the usefulness of caste, 149
Greeks, 74, 87
ceremonial purity among, 164
Group integration and caste being turned into an entire community, 234
Guguli Brahmins, 57
Guha, B. S., 69, 72
Guilds, 81
Gujar, 121
Guptas, Imperial, 53
Gurav, inclusion in the village assembly of, 13
Guriā. 65

Haddon, A.C., 67, 71
Hajarnavis, R. M., 225
Halwāi, 5
Hamilton, Capt. Alexander, on divisions among Baniyās, 57
Hammurabi, Code of, 75
Harijan, The, 161
Hari Rao, P., 110
Harsha, Harshavardhana, 52
Havig Brahmins, pursuit of agriculture by, 9
Hawaiians, three class-divisions among, 78
Hemachandra, 164
Hemādri, 54
Hindu Marriage Act of 1955 (the) and inter-caste marriages, 237
as a land mark of social progress, 241;
conditions in, 242
violation of conditions by Tamil Nadu, 231
Hindu Marriage (Madras Amendment) Bill, 1967, 241
Self-Respect marriage validated, 240
Hinin, untouchability of, 76
Holeya, 4, 6
Home Rule, 151
Hunas, invasion of India by 53
Huns, 67
Hutton, J. H., 96
Hypergamy, 111

Inter-caste (non-varna), 174
as a custom in Gujarat, 97
Ibbetson, Denzil, 112
Idaiyan, 199
Idiga, 3
Ilava (toddy-tapper), 56
Impure castes, 8
Impure work, 52
Independence movement, 182
Indian army, exclusion of higher castes from 236
Indian Mutiny, 9
Indian Statutory Commission, 149
Indo-Aryan culture, 92
Indo-Aryans, 67
Indo-Aryan type, 66
Indus Valley Civilization, 124
Inter-caste marriages, 238
Intermarriage, 116
Iranians, 85
Ireland, Celts in, 79
Irula, 65
Irving, B. A., 9
Iyyar, Jagadisha, 191, 193
Iyer, Anantha Krishna L. K., 135
Izhava (toddy-tapper), 7

Jackson, A. M. T., 96
Jagjivan Ram, on reservation for scheduled castes and scheduled tribes, 230
Jainism: Vaishya followers of, 33, 36
assertion of Kshatriya's so-social supremacy by, 3
Jajali, episode of, 35
Jalabyabahāryas-Shudra, 5
Jalācharaniya-Shudra, 4
Janaka, philosopher-king, 127
Jāt, 121
Jātakas, 44
Jāti, 40
Jehangir, castes in time of, 57
Jnāneswar, 54
Jogi, 18, 20
John, K. C., 184
Joriā, 17
Joyce, T. A., on differential index, 61
Justice Party (of Tamil Nadu), 239
The non-Brahmin in South India, 152–156

Kachchā food, 4, 6
Kahār, 17
Kaibart, 65, 70
Kalelkar, Kakasaheb and Backward Class Convention, 228

Kalhana, 165
Kālidāsa, 188
Kali age, 53
Kallan, 18
Kamba Rāmāyanam, 191
Kambojas, corporation of warriors, occupations of, 43
Kammalans, opposition to Brahmins of, 3; *see also* Artisans of Madras
Kamsala, 3
Kanaujiā Brahmins, military services of, 9
Kānchi equated with Varanasi, 157
Kandu, 183
Kanet, 67
Kanikar, 68
Kanmalar, 57
Kapadia, K. M., 233, 235
Kapoor, Jaspat Roy, a congress member for removal of caste or communal name, 219
Kapu, 65
Karandikar, S. V., 120
Karnatak Smārta Brahmin, nasal index, 65
Karve, D. K., 106
Karve, Irawati, 101
Kāsār, 17
Kashmiris, 60–63
Kassites, migration from Emlam, 74
Kathi, physical affinity of, 69
Katiā, 20
Kātkari, tribe, 21, 68
Kauravas, 46
Kausik, 57
Kautilya, 33; *see also* Arthashastra
Kavasha, low birth of, 26
Kayans, three classes of, 78
Kāyasth, 63
Kāyastha Prabhu, 57; *see also* Prabhu
Keane, H. H., on the close correspondence of nasal, index to social status, 64
Kentish society, three subdivisions of, 79
Kenyaks, three classes of, 78
Kerala Commission on Reservation of Seats in Educational Institutions, 226
  on need for a constitutional time-limit for any concession, 227
Kerr, James, on the usefulness of caste, 87
Ketkar, S. V., 97
Kevattas, 44
Khand, 57
Khandāit, 65
Kharwar, 3
Khāsiā, 57
Khatri, 62
Khedkar, V. K., 237
Khond, tribe, 18
Kin organization among Dravidians, 111–116
Kirkpatrick, W., 113
Kisan, 17
Koch, Kochh, tribe, 65
Kol, tribe, 20
Koli, 19
Komati, 3, 57
Konkanastha Brahmins: exemption from duties of, 8
  devotion to secular pursuits, 9
  endogamy of, 10
  territorial derivation of, 17
  see also Chitpāvan Brahmins
Konkani, 85
Kori, 17
Korwa, 3
Koshti, 17, 19
Krishna, preaching of, 33, 37
Kshatriyas, 7, 18, 20–33, 23–30
  dependence on Brahmins, 23–29
  alleged extinction of, 67
  marriage among, 42–47
  occupation of, 40–43, 65
  and priestcraft, 23–28
Kulinism, 113, 118
Kulwādi, 9
Kumbhār, Kumhār, 11, 18, 20, 36
Kunbi, 14, 19, 63
Kulal, 158
Kurmi, 17, 53, 67
Kurumba (Kuruba), 63
Laet, a class in Anglo-Saxon England, 72–76
Latthe, A. B., non-Brahmin leader, 144
  on Communal electorate, 233
  on Kolhapur riots, 1946, 214
Leather-workers, 21
Leuva, P. T., Piloting the Indian Registration Amendment Bill, 219
Lewis, Oscar, 121, 138
Lingāyat, 7
Linga-Banajiga, 65
Lodha, 210
Lohānā, ethnic origin of, 18
Lohār, 17; inclusion in the village assembly of, 19
Lonari, sub-divisions of, 21
Lothian Commission, 170
Lunia, occupational origin of, 17

MacAlister, Professor, on Celtic class structure, 79
MacIver, R. M., on the distinction between caste and class, 1
Madhava, commentator on Parāshara-Smriti, 53
Mādhyandina Brahmin, 80–88
Madiga, 6, 65
Madyana Pariyana, 83
Maga Brahmins, 55
Mahābhārata, 20–39
Mahār, 2, 6, 8, 55, 68, 89
Maharaja of Kolhapur, advocacy of non-Brahmin cause by, 210–215
Maharashtra, caste making progress for ascertaining backwardness in, 200
  listing of backward castes in, 216
Mahāvira, preachings of, 36
Maithil Brahmins, 169
  mass settling of marriages among, 233
Mālā, 167
Malabar society, social malaise of, 169
Malayalam kinship terminology, 168
Malaiyāli, 65

Malāsar, 65
Māli, 19
Mālwani, 102
Mameluco, a class, 77
Mana, primitive idea of, 105
Mānbhāva, sectarian origin of, 55
  revolt against caste, 38
Mandalik, V. N., on internal economy of Shudra, 78
Māng, 21
Manu, 52
Manusmriti, 100
Maoris, social orders among, 78
Maratha, 20
Marital unions, geographical spread of, 114, 138
Marriage and 'gotra', 58, 113
Marriot, Mckim, 138–139
Martin, R. M., on the gradations of caste, 4
Marutta Avikshita, 27
Mass settling of marriages among Maithil Brahmins, 238
Mastan Brahmins, 65
Matanggali, groups among some Fijians, 78
Matrilineal descent, 68–69
Matrimonial advertisements, survey of, 238
Matthai, Dr. John, on the village panchayat, 13
Maudgala-Brahmins, mention in an inscription of, 57
Mayer, A. C., 97, 99
Mayers, J. L., 15
Megasthenes, 1, 15
Mehtar, 57
Meo, 57
Mestizos, 77
Metcalfe, Sir Charles, on solidarity of Indian village, 183
Mexico, classes in, 77
Meyer, Eduard, on Persian intolerance, 72
Middleton, on Government's responsibility for caste propagation, 148
Mina, 18, 57
Minākshi temple (Madura), 170
Missionaries, 154
Mixed unions, 56
Mlechha, 50
Mochi, Muchi, 19, 56
Modha, mention in Jain inscription of, 57
Moger, three sub-divisions of, 21
Monglo-Dravidian type, 70
Mongoloid, people, 71
Mongoloid type, 66, 70
Monolithic nationalistic societies, 186
Moreland, on castes in Akbar's time, 57
Morgan, Lewis, 182
Mudhokar (Justice), J. R., 234
Mulatto, 78
Muller, Max, on the initiation of Shudras, 32
Mundā, culture, 69
Mundā language, 59
Mundā people, 53, 57
Mundā type, 52, 55
Myra, 4
Musāhār, 4, 50–55
Mysore Government, classification of backward classes by, 220–225

Nabasākh, 4
Nagaland, 187
Nāgar Brahmins, 57, 107
Nāi, Nhāvi, 3
Naikda, nickname, origin of, 15–17
Nāmadev (Maratha Saint), 52
"Namah" (Obeisance), formula, 49
Nāmashudra, 154, 166
Nambudiri Brahmins, 4–6
Nanda, G. L., 175
Nasal index, 64–70
Nāyaka kings, 50–55
Nayakar, Naicker, 232, 239
Nāyar, 4–6, 224
Negritos, 72
Negroes, 77
Nehru, Jawaharlal, attitude towards caste, 209–212
Nemakavanika, 56
Nesfield, J. C., 20
Nhāvi, *see* Nāi
Nishada: partiality of Aryans for, 27–30
  degradation of, 40
Non-Brahmins: two divisions of, in Madras, 5–7
  movement, 113
  Saints, 55–58
  support to Buddha, 44

Occupational choice, freedom in, 156–160
Occupations, hereditary, 220
  urban, 168
Oil-pressers, 14
Oldenberg, 124
Oldham, C. E. A. W., 111
Oppert, Gustav, 189, 199, 206
Oraon, tribe, ethnic origin of, 13
  prevalence of marriage of grandfather with granddaughter, 58
Oswāla, 57
Out-castes, 35, 42, 44, 53, 95
  in Japan, 76

Paes Domingos, on Brahmin traders and cultivators, 57
Pakhah Rājputs, caste council of, 106
Pakka, food, 4
Pallan, 169–170
Palli, 6
Pan, 65
Panchagavya, 54
Panchajanah, 28
Panchmas, 6; *see* Untouchables
Panchavimsa Brahmana, 25–27
Panchāyat, governing body of a caste, 2, 11
  offences tried by, 2, 3
  punishments awarded by, 2; *see also* Standing Councils of castes
Panda Brahmin, 65
Pāndavas, 46
Pāndharpeshe,11
Pānini, 164
Pānini's grammar, 7, 42, 164
Paniyan, 67
Panka, caste, 18, 21
Pant, G. B., on Parliament's decision not to recognise caste for official purposes, 223, 225
  authorizing the states to recognize castes, 203

Paraiyan, 14
Parāshara, 53
Pārashava brothers, 53
Parashurama, destruction of Kshatriyas by, 33, 36
Pardhan, 22
Pārdhi, 22, 175
Pariāh, 13, 18, 65, 76
Pārvati temple, 205
Pāsi, 63–64
Patanjali, 166
  on physical characteristics of Brahmin, 66–68
Pataskar, H. V., opposing bill to abolish caste distinctions, 219
Pate, H. R., 197
Patel, Vallabhbhai, 175, 219
Patel, Vithalbhai, 144
Patricians, 75, 78–79
Pattanulkaran, 17
Pattasalin, 56
Patwa, 17
Paulkasa, origin of, 28
Peake, H. J. E., on appearance of Nordics in Asia Minor, 71
Peel, Lord, 149
Persians, 86–87
Peshwās, diaries of, 7
  rule of, 5, 7, 87
Petrie, Sir, W. M. Flinders, on social situation in Egypt, 74
Phooley, Jotiba, revolt against caste, 117, 179
Pillay, K. K., 13
Plato, on caste, 87
Pluralist national society, 186
Plural society, 185–187
Plural society, emergence of, in India, 185
  as resulting from 'reservation' policy, 215–216
Pocock, D. F., 118, 237
Pod, 65, 70
Political sociology, 177, 180
Politics, impact of, on social institutions, 184
Pollution, 5–6, 43, 51
Pope Gregory XV, 150
Potashākhas, 99, 103
Potter, 14, 17
Prabhu, Kāyastha Prabhu: prohibition of drinks, 4
  protest against certain caste restrictions, 179
  right of vedic rituals, 7
Prathamasāki Brahmins, 103
Prarthana Samaj, contrast with Arya Samaj, 150
Pratiloma castes, 29
Pratt, F. G., 17
Pravahana Jaivali, philosopher-king, 26
Pre–Dravidian type, 67, 69–70
Preferential mating, 120, 135–136
  recent data on, 137
Priests, replacement of Brahmin priests, 143
Ptolemies, 74
Pulayan, 5
Purānic ritual, 7, 55, 103
Purity, ideas of, 112, 161
  ceremonial, 112
'Purohita Maruppa Sangham' or Anti-Purohit Association, 240
Purusha-sukta, hymn, four orders of society in, 23

Rādhiya Brahmins, mention in Orissa inscription, 57
Raghubansi, sub-division of Rajputs, 57
Raja of Satara, diaries of, 13
Rajabansi, Kochh, 65
Rajashekhara, Brahmin, marriage with a Chamār lady, 53
Rājatarangini, 165, 168
Rājput, 3, 184
Ramachandran, Nirmala, 190
Ramdas, 8
Rāmānujachāryas, 191
Ram Mohan Roy, movement to liberalise religion and caste, 150
Ramāi, 55
Rāmanuja, 55
  efforts for betterment of untouchables, 191
Ramananda, establishment of a new sect by, 54
Ramaswami Naicker, E. V. (Periyar), 239
  starting 'Suyamariyathai Sangham' or 'Self-Respect Group', 239
Rāmāyana, 31, 46, 188
Ramoshi, 18
Ranade, M. G., 155, 179
Rao, M. S. A., 5, 178, 232
Rathakara, high status of, 37
  degradation of, 27, 43
Recruitment to public services, and caste, 161
"Reservation", evil effects of the prolongation of, 228; *see also* Plural Society
Reserved vacancies, Supreme Court on, 230
Richards, F. J., on sub-caste as unit of Hindu society, 11
'Right-hand' castes, 7
Rising of 1857, 149
Risley, Sir Herbert, 96, 111, 146
Roman Church, accommodation of caste in, 150
Rome, social history of, 88
Roy, S. C. Rai Bahadur, on Oraons, 163, 69
Rudolph, Lloyd L. and Sussanne Hoeber, 236
Russell, R. V., on traditional occupations of castes, 105
  on sub-castes as basis of Indian society, 9, 113

Sadgop, 65, 70
Sahjiya, sect, 55
Shagirdapeshā, 18
Saints, of Maharashtra, 55
Sakas, 69
Sakais, 69
Sale, Sali, 19, 56
Saliyan, 56
Samoans, six classes of, 78
Samurai, privileges of, 76–77
Samvarta Smriti, on pollution of water, 51
Sanadhya Brahmins, 9
Sangam literature, 190
Sangave, Vilas A., 235
Santāl tribe, 18, 67

Shantanu, marriage with fisherman's daughter, 46
Sassanian period, 75, 86
Sastri, Nilakantha, 56
Sat-Shudra, 4
Satyakāma, Jābāla, 25
Satyashodhaka Samaj, aims of, 286, 287
Satyavati, low family of, 46
Saurashtras, corporation of warriors, occupations of, 43
Savara, Mongoloid origin of, 67
Savarna, 44–45
Scandinavia, social classes in, 81
Scheduled Castes, national endeavour to uplift, 172–173
  as a separate caste entity, 214
  and reserved seats, 216
  security of adequate representation, 215–216
  and continuation of reservation of posts, 151, 153, 216, 220
Scheduled Castes and Scheduled Tribes order (Amendment) Act, 1956, 168
Schoebel, 189
Schoff, 71
Scytho-Dravidian type, 66, 70–71
Segregation of castes, 6
Self-Respect Group, 239
  advocacy of inter-caste marriage, 10, 240
Self-respect marriage, 240–241
  Madras High Court on, 240
Semangs, 69
Senart, E., 112
Shah, B. V., 238
Shānārs, 7, 109, 170
Shashan Brahmins, 65
Shenvi Brahmins: prohibitions of drinks, 63
  physical affinities, 62
Sherring, M. A., 11
Shinde, V. R., efforts to uplift depressed classes, 154, 171
Shiva Rao, B., on rooting out casteism, 223
Shrikant, L. M., 172
Siddiah, S. M., introducing Bill to appoint a Commission to report on welfare of Scheduled castes, 227
Silappadikaram, 190
Simon Commission, 161, 170
Sircar, D. C., 119
Skanda worship, decline, 194
Smārta Brahmins, 19
Social differentiation, 85
  stratification, 113
Social distinction, Harijan leaders interested in the perpetuation of, 231
Social horizon of the Congress Party, 218
Social Justice, securing of, 215
  inharmonious nature of the various articles on behalf of, 219
  and social atomization, 220
  cavalier-fashion implementation by Central Government of inharmonious provisions, for securing, 223
Solaga, 65
Soliya Vellālas, 109
Sonār, Soni, 17; *see also* goldsmith
Son Koli, physical affinity of, 92
Spaniards, in Mexico, 77
Special Marriage Act of 1872, 144
Shrāddha-dinner, 43, 52, 54
Sreshthis, their quarter, 6
Srinivas, M. N., 97, 135–136, 181
Standing Caste Councils: offences tried by, 142
  punishments awarded by, 75
  loss of importance of, 143
Steele, Arthur, 3
Stevenson, H. N., 97
Subba Rao (Justice), K., 230
Subbaroyan, P., ex-minister of Madras State supporting abolition of caste name, 219
Sub-castes, 10, 18, 95, 97, 101–102, 106, 107
Sub-caste, essential characteristics of, 89–90; Iravati Karve's view of, 95
Sub-sub-caste, 108
Subrahmanya, the deity, 194
Subramanian, N., 124
Shudra, 4–6, 9, 11
  sub-castes in Bengal, 11
  disqualification for sacrifice and sacraments, 48–49
  duties and occupations, 8, 25, 26, 29, 46, 48, 49
  origin, 34
  debarred from initiation, 32
    degradation of, 29
  adultery of Shudra male with Arya female, 33
Saints, 55
Sat, 53, 174
Shukraniti: non-availability of "namas" formula for Shudras, 50
  on issue of mixed marriages, 55
Sumerians, 75
Supreme Court, The, going by the directive principle of the constitution, 225, 230–231
Sutār, 2, 13, 17, 19
Sutradhār, 56
Suyamariyathai marriage (self-respect marriage), 239–241
  Madras High Court on, 240–241

Tachchan, occupational origin of, 17
Tagore, Devendranath, movement to liberalise religion and caste, 150
Tahitian Society, divisions of, 78
Taittiriya Aranyaka, 162
Tāmbat, 17
Tāmboli, 17
Tāmbulika, 56
Tamil Brahmins, 135
Tamilian allergy to Brahmins, 189
Tamilian opposition to north orientation, 206–207
Tamilnad Congress Committee, and Caste, 152
Tamil Nadu,
  caste system of, 126
  castes of: Agamudaiyans, 203–204
  Ambalakkaran (fisherman of Tanjore), 206–208
  Brahmins, 208
  Idaiyans (or Konans), 208

Kaikolans (weavers), 204–205
Kallans, 204
Anti-Kallar movement, 204
Kammalan (an artisan caste), 205
Maravans, 201–204
Pallans, 199, 209
Pallis, 198
Pandarams, 109, 195–196
Paraiyans, 209
Shānāns (Nādars), 200
conversion of, into Christianity, 202
conflict with Maravans, 204
political turn in Maravar-Shānār feud, 203
Valaiyans, 206–208
Vellālas, 9, 11, 14, 55, 136, 180, 190
Comparison of Tamil Nadu caste system with that of Uttar Pradesh, 126
destruction of national motto in, 187
disturbing patterns of public activity in, 187
faction fight in 19th century Tamil Nadu, 199
'Right hand' and 'Left hand' castes in, 189
events in, in regard to marriage, 239
self-respect marriage in, 241
Nelson's account of a Vellāla marriage, 240

Tamil proverb, ascetics and caste on, 198
Tamil, upsurge of, 192
Tanjore, 209
Tanti, occupational origin of, 17, 170
Tarkhan, occupational origin of, 17
Tawney, R. H., on class, 35
Teli-Baniā, 20
Teli-Kalar, 20
Teli (oil-presser), 14, 17, 51, 183
Teutonic peoples, class structure among, 79
Thakkar, A. V., 154
Thathera, occupational origin of, 17
Theodosian code, compulsion to follow hereditary occupation, 79
Thiruvalluvar, 136
Thurston, E., 61, 65
Tilak, B. G., 99
Tiyan, 5, 7–8, 18, 57, 65
Todā, tribe, 72
Togata, 65
Toreya, 65
Toynbee, A. J., 179
Trichinopoly, 206
Trusts & trust-units, registered with the Charity Commissioner, 234
1700 units in Maharashtra caste-based, 234
indicative of extreme atomization and upward-looking tendency of castes, 235
Tukārām, Maratha saint, 54
Turko-Iranian, type, 66
Twice-born, 4, 41, 49

Untouchability, 6, 28, 52, 94
efforts to eradicate, 171
Untouchability (Offences) Act (1955), 173
offences under the Act, 173
Untouchables, 171, 173, 183–184, 190, 199, 214
and entry on Vaikam roads, 154; and orthodox
Hindus, 212
militant solidarity of, 184; *see also* Depressed Classes
Upajātis, 99, 103

Vaidya, 19
Vaikam (Travancore) movement, 65
Vaina, mixed caste, 34
Vaishnavism: spiritual betterment of Shudra in, 48, 50, 54
Vaishya, duties and occupations, 33
marriage among, 26
Vakkaliga, 17
Vākātaka dynasty, 53, 129
Vallave (herdsmen), 56
Vāni, 2, 17, 19
Vaniās, 108
Vanika, 56
Vanamali, 179
Varna, 40, 92, 118
Varna organization, 98
Varna-dharma, 29
Varna-Sankara (mixture of castes), prevention of, 29
Vasistha, sage, rivalry with Visvamitra, 132
Vedic ritual, great sanctity of, 7
Vellāla, 9, 11, 14, 17, 55
Vellāla Chetty, 109
Venkayya, on names of individuals in South Indian inscription, 56
Village-Councils, inclusion of II castes in, 13
Vishvakarmans, 206
Vishvamitra, rivalry with Vasistha, 26, 35
Vriddhaharita Smriti, on pollution by contant, 52
Vyas, Narendra, 104
Vyādha, episode of, 35

Washermen, 6, 46, 154, 164;
importance of, at Kunbi-wedding, 14
Weaker section of the people, ameliorative activities by Govt. for, 218
Weber, Max, views on caste, 212
Widow remarriage Act, 143
Widow remarriage, 143
Woolley, C. L., on Sumerian class system, 75

Yadavs, Swaran Singh inaugurating all-India Yadav meeting, 232
demand for a separate Yadav regiment in the Army, 232, 237
Ahirs proclaiming as Yadav, 210
Yāska, 26
Yavanas, 46

Zarathushtra, 75
Zweig, Stephan, on Brazilian class structure, 78